NUMBER 4

CHEMICAL CORPS
HISTORICAL STUDIES

PORTABLE FLAME THROWER OPERATIONS IN WORLD WAR II

HISTORICAL OFFICE
OFFICE OF THE CHIEF OF THE CHEMICAL CORPS

PORTABLE FLAME THROWER OPERATIONS

IN WORLD WAR II

By

LT COL LEONARD L. McKINNEY, CML C-RES.

Historical Office
Office of the Chief, Chemical Corps

1 December 1949

NOTE TO THE READER

This is the <u>first</u> draft of "Portable Flame Thrower <u>Operations</u> <u>in</u> World War II." This study is <u>not</u> presented as a definitive and official <u>history</u>, but is reproduced for current reference use within the Military Establishment pending the publication of a definitive history.

Comments and suggestions relative to accuracy and adequacy of treatment are invited. At the close of the study, the reader will find forms for use in transmitting such comments to the Chief, Historical Office, Office of the Chief, Chemical Corps.

CONTENTS

Preface		xii
Table of Abbreviations		xiv
Chapter		Page

I   THE WEAPONS, DEVELOPMENT AND PROCUREMENT 1

     A. Flame Warfare Prior to World War II. 1

     B. Portable Flame Throwers. 12
         1. Requirement Established and Development
            of the Mark I Portable Flame Thrower 12
         2. The M1A1 Portable Flame Thrower. 13
         3. The M2-2 Portable Flame Thrower. 15

     C. Mechanized Flame Throwers. 17
         1. The Question of a Requirement. 17
         2. Auxiliary Type Mechanized Flame Throwers 19
            a. The E4-5 (Standardized as M3-4-3
               in 1945) 19
            b. The Periscope Model. 20
         3. Main Armament Types. 21
            a. Light Flame Tanks. 22
            b. Medium Flame Tanks 22
            c. The Navy Mark I Flame Thrower
               (E14-7R2). 23
            d. Main Armament Flame Tanks
               Produced in Hawaii 24
            e. Emplaced Flame Throwers. 25

     D. Allied Flame Throwers. 26
         1. Canadian 26
         2. British. 27
         3. Australian 28
         4. Russian. 29

     E. Enemy Flame Throwers 30
         1. German 30
         2. Japanese 32
         3. Italian. 33

     F. Flame Thrower Fuels. 34

II   SOUTH PACIFIC AREA (SOLOMON ISLANDS CAMPAIGN). 38

     A. Guadalcanal. 38
         1. Problems Encountered and Lessons Learned
            from the Guadalcanal Operation 40

Chapter			Page
	B.	New Georgia.	40
		1. Problems Encountered and Lessons Learned from the New Georgia Operation	43
	C.	Bougainville	44
	D.	Fuels Developed.	46
	E.	Tactical Doctrine Developed and Training Conducted.	48
		1. Flame Thrower Platoons	49
		2. Further Flame Thrower Training	52
	F.	Comparison of M1A1 and E-3 Models.	53
III	SOUTHWEST PACIFIC AREA (SWPA).		55
	A.	Early Employment in Papuan Campaign.	55
		1. Situation.	55
		2. Attempt to Employ Flame Throwers at Buna	56
		3. Corrective Action Taken.	58
	B.	Preparation for Further Operations	60
		1. Tactical Doctrine Established.	60
		2. Supply Situation	63
		3. Training Conducted and Fuel Developed.	63
	C.	Employment in the Bismark Archipelago Campaign	65
		1. New Britain.	65
		2. Admiralty Islands.	66
	D.	Employment in New Guinea Campaign.	68
		1. Hollandia, Netherlands New Guinea.	68
		2. Wakde Island - Maffin Bay Operation.	69
		3. Noemfoor Island.	72
		4. Biak Island.	73
	E.	Preparations for the Philippine Operations	90
		1. Critique on Previous Operations.	90
		2. New Training and Tactical Doctrine Established.	94
		3. Training Conducted for the Philippine Operations	98
		4. Supply Situation	101

Chapter		Page
	F. Employment in the Philippines.	104
	1. Leyte.	104
	2. Luzon.	114
	3. Corregidor	132
	4. Caballo Island	133
	5. Fort Drum.	134
	6. Panay and Negros	134
	7. Cebu and Bohol	135
	8. Problems Encountered and Lessons Learned	137
IV	CENTRAL PACIFIC AREA	141
	A. Training Conducted	141
	B. Gilbert Islands.	142
	1. Planning	142
	2. Employment	143
	C. Marshall Islands	143
	1. Planning and Training.	143
	2. Employment	146
	3. Comments	149
	D. Marianas Islands	150
	1. Planning	150
	2. The Operation.	150
	3. Comments	152
	E. Caroline Islands	154
	1. Planning	154
	2. The Operation.	154
	3. Comments	157
	F. Iwo Jima	157
	1. Planning	157
	2. The Operation.	158
	3. Comments	161
	G. Ryukyus Islands.	162
	1. Planning	162
	2. The Operation.	163
	3. Comments	167
	H. Defective Flame Throwers in CPA.	167

Chapter		Page
V	CHINA-BURMA-INDIA	169
	A. Employment by the Chinese at Tengchung	169
	1. Situation	169
	2. Employment of Flame Throwers	169
	3. Supply for the Tengchung Operation	172
	4. Comments on Employment at Tengchung	172
	B. Plans for 1945	174
VI	PLANS FOR EMPLOYMENT IN THE KYUSHU OPERATION	176
	A. Situation	176
	B. Training and Preparation	176
	C. Supply and Maintenance	179
VII	NORTH AFRICAN AND MEDITERRANEAN THEATERS	181
	A. North African Operations	181
	B. Sicily (10 July - 18 August 1943)	182
	C. Operations in Italy (9 September 1943 - 2 May 1945)	183
	1. To the Fall of Rome (Salerno, Anzio and Cassino)	183
	2. Pursuit to the North	187
	D. Critique	190
VIII	EUROPEAN THEATER OF OPERATIONS	192
	A. Preoperational Training and Plans	192
	1. Training Conducted	192
	2. Plans for Employment	193
	B. The Normandy and Northern France Campaigns	195
	1. Landing and Early Operations	195
	2. Brittany	197

Chapter			Page
	C.	Southern France.	200
		1. Preparation.	200
		2. The Operation.	201
	D.	Siegfried Line	202
	E.	Comments and Critique.	206
IX	EMPLOYMENT OF THE PORTABLE FLAME THROWER BY THE ENEMY.		209
	A.	Japanese	209
	B.	German	212
		1. The Fougasse Type.	212
		2. The German Portable Flame Thrower.	214
	C.	Italian.	216
X	SUMMARY AND EVALUATION		218
	A.	Tactical Doctrine.	218
	B.	Training Problems in the Theaters.	224
	C.	Employment	225
	D.	Maintenance and Servicing.	226
	E.	Supply and Logistics	227
	F.	Fuels.	228
	G.	Evaluation	228

APPENDICES

		Page
Appendix 1	Hqs., 25th Infantry Division, Training Memorandum Number 6, 27 March 1943, sub:	230
Appendix 2	Historical Statement on the Flamethrower Platoon of the 132d Infantry Regiment, April 1944.	233
Appendix 3	Hqs., XIV Corps, Annex Number 3 to Training Memorandum Number 8, 29 April 1944, sub: Training in the Use of Flame Throwers	248
Appendix 4	Hqs., 37th Infantry Division, Inclosure Number 2 to Training Memorandum Number 7, 26 September 1944, sub: Training in the Use of Flame Throwers.	253
Appendix 5	Hqs., Sixth Army, Training Memorandum Number 8, 1 October 1943, sub: Training in the Use of Flame Throwers.	258
Appendix 6	Hqs., 24th Infantry Division, Training Memorandum Number 54, 5 November 1943, sub: Training in the Use of Flame Throwers	261
Appendix 7	Hqs., I Corps, Training Memorandum Number 17, 10 December 1943, sub: Training in the Use of Flame Throwers.	265
Appendix 8	Hqs., 41st Infantry Division, Training Memorandum Number 19, 31 December 1943, sub: Use of Flame Throwers.	268
Appendix 9	Hqs., Sixth Army, Training Memorandum Number 18, 22 June 1944.	273
Appendix 10	Hqs., 33d Infantry Division, Training Memorandum Number 15, 15 July 1944, sub: Battalion Assault Team.	276

		Page
Appendix 11	Hqs., Eighth Army, Inclosure Number 7 to Training Directive Number 1, 1 October 1944, sub: Operations Against Japanese Fortifications.	278
Appendix 12	Hqs., Sixth Army, Training Memorandum Number 30, 6 August 1945	281
Appendix 13	Hqs., V Amphibious Corps, Corps Training Memorandum Number 13-43, 21 December 1943, sub: Demolition and Flame Thrower Training	284
Appendix 14	Hqs., V Amphibious Corps, Corps Training Order Number 17-43, 21 December 1943, sub: Flame Throwers.	286
Appendix 15	Hqs., U.S. Marine Corps, Pamphlet, April 1944, sub: Basic Tactics for the Portable Flame Thrower, Prepared by CWSTC, Camp Elliott, San Diego 44, California.	293
Appendix 16	Hqs., 3d Marine Division, Fleet Marine Force, in the Field, Training Order Number 45-44, 16 December 1944, sub: Organization for Employment of Flame Thrower, Rocket Launchers, and Demolition in the Infantry Battalion.	304
Appendix 17	Hqs., 3d Marine Division, Fleet Marine Force, in the Field, Training Order Number 50-44, 19 December 1944, sub: Tactical Employment of Flame Throwers.	307
Appendix 18	Hqs., Fifth Army, Training Memorandum Number 8, 5 April 1944, sub: Technique and Tactical Use of Flame Throwers	312
Appendix 19	Hqs., ETOUSA, Training Memorandum Number 33, 6 October 1943, Section II, sub: Portable Flame Thrower	317
Appendix 20	Hqs., ETOUSA, Training Memorandum Number 10, 5 April 1944, Section I, sub: Portable Flame Thrower	323
Appendix 21	Hqs., ETOUSA, Training Memorandum Number 4, 3 February 1945, sub: Training in the Use of Flame Throwers.	329
BIBLIOGRAPHIC NOTE		332

ILLUSTRATIONS

No.		Following Page
1	The M1 Portable Flame Thrower	14
2	Firing the M1 Portable Flame Thrower	14
3	The M1A1 Portable Flame Thrower	14
4	The M2-2 Portable Flame Thrower	16
5	Firing the M2-2 Portable Flame Thrower	16
6	The M3-4-3 Mechanized Flame Thrower—an Auxiliary Type	20
7	Main Armament Flame Thrower Tank (POA-CWS-H1)	24
8	German Model 42 Portable Flame Throwers	30
8a	German Model 41 Portable Flame Thrower, Including Gun Assembly	30
8b	German Model 41 Portable Flame Thrower, Including Gun Assembly	30
9	A Marine Demonstrates a Japanese Flame Thrower Captured at the Battle of Tenaru River, Guadalcanal	32
10	Italian Model 41 Portable Flame Thrower	34
11	New Georgia: An Infantryman Sprays a Japanese Pillbox During Mopping-up Operations	44
12	Bougainville: A Flame Thrower Assault Party Advances to Position	44
13	Bougainville: A Flame Thrower Operator Moving Up	44
14	An Assault Party of the Americal Division Attacking a Series of Jap Pillboxes Near Torokina River, Bougainville	44
15	Flame Thrower Assault Party Attacking a Jap Pillbox While Mopping Up on Bougainville in March 1944	44
16	The Flame Thrower Neutralizes a Japanese Bunker on Bougainville, March 1944	44
17	Burning Out Japanese Bunkers	44

No.		Following Page
18	Bougainville: Flame Thrower Operator of 129th Infantry Inspects Japanese Bunker After Flame Attack	44
19	Bougainville: A Dead Jap at the Entrance of His Pillbox	44
20	Buna, New Guinea: Front View of a Japanese Bunker (Pillbox)	58
21	The Author Inspecting a Japanese Bunker at Arawe, New Britain	66
22	Clarke Field Near Manila: A Flame Thrower Operator Advances. February 1945	114
23	The Entrance to Melinta Tunnel on Corregidor	132
24	Tarawa: Marines Force Japs Back Into Bunker While Assault Troops Close In	144
25	Flame Operator Attacks a Japanese Pillbox on Saipan, 17 June 1944.	150
26	Assault Squad During Flaming Operation	150
27	Marine Flame Operators of the 5th Division Move Toward a Concentration of Japanese Pillboxes on Iwo Jima, February 1945	160
28	An Infantryman Burns Out a Cave in the Clean Up on Iwo Jima, February 1945	160
29	An Example of What Happened to Thousands of Japanese Who Refused to Surrender	166
30	American Infantrymen of the 28th Infantry Division Employ Flame Throwers To Mop Up Enemy Resistance in Siegfried Line Defenses Near Elsemboen, Germany, 9 October 1944	202
31	A Japanese Flame Thrower in Action	210
32	Jap Use of Portable Flame Throwers, a Rehearsed Action, After the Fall of Corregidor, for Use as Propaganda	210

PREFACE

This History of Portable Flame Thrower Operations in World War II was prepared by Lieutenant Colonel Leonard L. McKinney, Chemical Corps (Res.), formerly Assistant Chemical Officer, Sixth U. S. Army. Lieutenant Colonel McKinney prepared the manuscript, including a comparable manuscript on the History of Mechanized Flame Throwers, during two six-week periods of duty in the Office of the Chief, Chemical Corps. Dr. Alfred J. Bingham prepared the section on "Flame Warfare Prior to World War II." The editorial work and a considerable amount of rewriting was done by the undersigned.

The reader will observe that the manuscript is not in the exact form of what might be termed a strictly narrative historical record but is rather a combination of a narrative history and a staff study. The preparation of the volume along these lines was dictated by several factors. The training and research and development agencies of the Chemical Corps required the earliest possible publication of data on the employment of flame throwers in World War II, such data to be in the form most readily adaptable to their immediate needs. These demands account for the inclusion verbatim of numerous detailed operational reports. Also, the fact that the author could be away from his regular position with the Department of Agriculture for only a limited time prevented his putting the manuscript in the most complete form. At the same time, the priority placed by Historical Division, SS USA, on the preparation of volumes for the official Department of the Army history has prevented personnel of the Historical Office from doing extensive editorial work on the manuscript.

Within the limitations imposed by the factors indicated above, an attempt has been made to prepare an accurate account of flame thrower employment and the numerous problems involved. It is not a definitive history but is considered a reliable analysis prepared by a person well-qualified on the basis of both sound research techniques and theater experience, especially in the Pacific areas where the weapon was employed most extensively.

The volume purports to present: a survey of flame warfare prior to World War II; a brief account of the flame weapons developed by both allied and enemy powers before and during World War II; the characteristics of the various types which were developed; what types were available to both allied and enemy powers; when and in what quantities the various models arrived in the theaters; the development of fuels; an account of the combat employment of the weapon in the theaters and areas where American troops were involved; and the problems of training, tactics, logistics, maintenance, fuels and propellants. Enough of the ground combat situation is included to indicate whether flame targets were encountered and, if so, the nature of the targets and how they affected the use of the weapon. An account of enemy employment of flame throwers is also included. It will be noted that the appendices include selected documents on flame thrower training directives and tactical doctrine.

A supplementary or continuation volume on the "History of Mechanized Flame Thrower Operations in World War II" is nearing completion and will be published soon. The manuscript on portable and mechanized flame throwers was prepared as a single study but, due to the size of the volume, publication as two studies was deemed advisable.

                                                Ben R. Baldwin
                                                Chief, Historical Office
                                                Office of the Chief, Chemical Corps

TABLE OF ABBREVIATIONS

AB	Airborne
AC CWS	Assistant Chief, Chemical Warfare Service
ACofS	Assistant Chief of Staff
AFHQ	Allied Force Headquarters
AFMIDPAC	Army Forces, Middle Pacific (See MIDPAC)
AFPAC	Army Forces, Pacific
AFWESPAC	Army Forces, Western Pacific
AGF	Army Ground Forces
AGO-HRS-CWS	Chemical Warfare Service files in Historical Records Section, AGO
APC	Shot, armor-piercing capped
ASF	Army Service Forces (War Department)
BAR	Browning automatic rifle
CBI	China-Burma-India theater
C Cml O	Chief Chemical Officer
CM-IN	Incoming classified message
CM-OUT	Outgoing classified message
Cml O	Chemical Officer
Cml Sec	Chemical section or office which is part of the special staff of a division, corps or high echelon organization
CMLWG	Historical Office, OC Cml C
CP	Command post

CPA	Central Pacific Area (See POA and MIDPAC)
CW	Chemical Warfare
EDC	Eastern Defense Command
ETO	European Theater of Operations
ETOUSA	European Theater of Operations, U.S. Army
FTF	Flame thrower fuel
FUSAG	First U.S. Army Group
LCI	Landing craft, infantry
LCM	Landing craft, mechanized
LCVP	Landing craft, vehicle-personnel
LSM	Landing ship, medium
LST	Landing ship, tank
LVT	Landing vessel, tank
MA Rpt	Military Attache Report
MEF	Middle East Forces (British)
MFT	Mechanized flame thrower
MID	Military Intelligence Division, G-2, War Department General Staff
MIDPAC	Middle Pacific Theater (Pacific Ocean Areas was redesignated Middle Pacific in June 1945. See also CPA.)
MTO	Mediterranean Theater of Operations (See NATO.)
MTOUSA	Mediterranean Theater of Operations, U.S. Army
NATO	North African Theater of Operations (The North African Theater of Operations was redesignated the Mediterranean Theater of Operations on 1 November 1944.)

NATOUSA	North African Theater of Operations, U.S. Army
OC Cml C	Office of the Chief, Chemical Corps (The Chemical Warfare Service was redesignated the Chemical Corps on 2 August 1946.)
ORB	Organizational Records Branch of Adjutant General's Records Administration Center, St. Louis, Missouri
PFT	Portable flame thrower
POA	Pacific Ocean Areas (Prior to 1 August 1944 this theater was known as CPA or Central Pacific Area.)
P.S.I.	Pounds per square inch
RCT(Sep)	Regimental Combat Team, Separate
SOS	Service of Supply, War Department (changed to ASF on 9 March 1942)
SPA	South Pacific Area
SPCWN	Intelligence Branch, OC CWS
SWPA	Southwest Pacific Area
TM	"Technical Manual," when referring to War Department publications. "Training Memorandum," when referring to theater of operations publications or directives.
USAFFE	U.S. Army Forces in the Far East
USAFISPA	U.S. Army Forces in the South Pacific Area
USAFPOA	U.S. Army Forces in Pacific Ocean Areas
USASOS	U.S. Army, Service of Supply (in SWPA)
WDGS	War Department General Staff
WP	White phosphorous

CHAPTER I

THE WEAPONS, DEVELOPMENT AND PROCUREMENT

A. Flame Warfare Prior to World War II.

The use of flame in warfare would appear to be as old as warfare itself.[1] Among primitive or rudimentary conceptions of warfare historical accounts mention three principal means of using fire on enemy personnel and property: animals carrying fire directly to enemy objectives, fire arrows, and fire ships. Contemporaneous with these early methods, however, various devices were developed for the specific purpose of projecting flame and other incendiary substances in the direction of the enemy and his installations.

It appears that the earliest record of the employment of flame as a weapon of war is contained in the Biblical account of the exploits of Samson which took place before the year 1000 B.C. The Book of Judges states:

> And Samson went and caught three hundred foxes and took fire brands and turned tail to tail and put a fire brand in the midst between two tails. And when he had set the brands of fire, he let them go into the standing corn of the Philistines and burnt both the stocks and also the standing corn with the vineyards and olives.

---

[1] The following account of the use of flame in warfare before World War II, unless otherwise indicated, is based on an article entitled "The History of Flame Warfare," Canadian Army Journal, Vol. 2, Nos. 4-8, July-November 1948, by Captain Henry Sorensen, Canadian Army Technical Liaison Officer at the Experimental Station, Suffield, Alberta, and formerly with the Directorate of Weapons and Development, Army Headquarters, Ottawa. Supporting and supplementary data were obtained in the articles entitled "Fireship," "Greece," "Greek Fire," "Roman Empire, Later" of the Encyclopedia Britannica (11th edition), from the article entitled "Flamethrowers" in Encyclopedia Britannica (11th edition), New Volume XXXI, and from the following books: G. T. Date, The Art of War in Ancient India; T. A. Dodge, Great Captains: Alexander; L. Montross, War Through the Ages (revised edition); C. W. C. Oman, A History of the Art of War in the Middle Ages, 2 volumes (2d edition); and J. T. Reinaud et I. Fave, Histoire de l'artillerie, du feu gegeois.

The Philistines took revenge by burning Samson's wife and father-in-law. In 200 B.C., Hannibal succeeded in routing the Romans at Casilinum by sending against them a herd of oxen with lighted faggots between their horns. The Mongol cavalry was thrown back in 1256 A.D. by the Egyptians by sending in advance of the main army a horse and rider equipped with a non-inflammable covering to which were attached small ignited torches. According to Prince Rupert's Journal, during the siege of Bristol by the partisans of Charles I of England in 1643, a mounted Royalist officer cleared a sector of the operation of its defenders with a torch known as a fire pike.

The employment of fire arrows was first described about 500 B.C. by the Chinese writer Sun Tzu Wu in The Art of War, the world's earliest known military treatise. The author explains that in order "to hurl dropping fire amongst the enemy," it was necessary to dip the tips of the arrows into a brazier in order to ignite them before shooting them at the enemy from powerful bows. A little later, in 480 B.C., during the capture of Athens, the Persians under Xerxes I first contaminated their arrows with an incendiary substance before directing them ignited at the enemy. In more recent times, fire arrows have been used by the Indians of both North and South America and, projected through blowpipes, by the Maoris in New Zealand.

Other primitive methods of throwing ignited projectiles or containers were known to ancient peoples. According to Amiot's Memoirs, the Chinese, in addition to fire arrows, used fire mines with an incendiary rather than an explosive charge, and fire sprinklers on the tip of a mace or war club.[2] The Indian writer Kautilya mentions the employment in India of pitch, burning oil, and baskets filled with glowing coals which were thrown upon the enemy by foot soldiers and from the backs of elephants.[3] Many centuries later, the Arabs employed inflammable substances in their weapons and engines of war. They threw flame pots by hand, wielded fire sprinklers on maces, hurled flame lances, shot fire arrows from bows and fire bolts from cross-bows or arbalests. In fact, fire became for them an important agent of attack and their flame weapons were feared and respected because of their incendiary and casualty effects.[4]

---

[2] J. T. Reinaud et I. Fave, Histoire de l'artillerie, pp. 182-85.

[3] G. T. Date, The Art of War in Ancient India, p. 23.

[4] Reinaud et Fave, op.cit., p. 51.

The only recorded mechanical method of throwing an ignited projectile or container was the catapult, a highly-developed siege engine employed during the Middle Ages. Its employment with incendiary missiles, however, was confined mostly to use by the Arabs against the Crusaders and against the Spaniards. In 1190, during the Third Crusade, according to the Norman chronicler Ambrose, the Saracens temporarily drove the Christian besiegers of Acre in Northern Palestine from this fortified town with catapulted flame pots which broke on impact, setting fire to wooden towers and siege engines erected outside the stone walls.[5] The French soldier and chronicler Joinville, present at the sieges of El Mansura and Damietta in Northern Egypt during the Seventh Crusade in 1249, tells how the besieging Saracens successfully used a type of catapult, called a petrary or perriere, to hurl barrels of a mixture similar to "Greek fire" at French towers and war engines. These wooden constructions were also effectively attacked by fire bolts shot from cross-bows into the wood which they ignited.[6] Catapulted flame pots were also used by the Moors against the Spaniards in defending Niebla in 1257, Algeciras in 1342, as well as in besieging Baza in 1326 and Tarifa in 1340.[7]

Fire ships are first mentioned by Thucydides as having been used in 413 B.C. by the defenders of Syracuse in their unsuccessful efforts to prevent capture of the town by the Athenian Greeks. In this action, the Syracusans filled an old merchant ship with faggots and pinewood, ignited its contents, and set it adrift to be blown by the wind toward the Greek ships. The Athenians, however, managed to check both the fire and the progress of the ship before it could do any damage. The Greek historian Diodorus of Sicily describes at some length the use of a single fire ship by the defenders of Tyre in Syria which was besieged and eventually captured by Alexander the Great in 332 B.C. While building a mole to approach the town, Alexander had to set up two towers, manned by bowmen at the end of the mole, to defend the workmen against enemy harassment. T. A. Dodge's account taken from Diodorus is as follows:

> The Tyrians saw that they must destroy these towers. From an old horse-transport...they constructed a fire-ship and loaded it with a quantity of bitumen, dry twigs, and other inflammable material. From the yard arms or booms, which stood out like antennae, they

---

[5] Ibid., pp. 62-64.

[6] C. W. C. Oman, *A History of the Art of War in the Middle Ages*, p. 48.

[7] Reinaud et Favé, op. cit., pp. 68-72.

hung cauldrons filled with sulphur, naphtha, chemical oils and similar substances. They towed this fire-ship between two triremes, one blustering day when the wind set well inland, towards the end of the mole and left the men who were put aboard to kindle the fires and to swim back to the city as best they might...The headway it acquired carried the fire-ship towards the mole in a few minutes. The poop was ballasted so as to throw the bows out of water and allow it to run up on the mole where it could be anchored firmly in place. The towers, breastworks and engines of war caught fire, the yard arm cauldrons emptied their inflammables; the wind lent its aid; despite manful fighting of the flames, all were destroyed...The missiles from the soldiers on the Tyrian vessels and from the garrison on the town walls made it all but impossible for the Macedonians to work at extinguishing the flames which were blown directly in their faces...Not only were the towers lost, but the end of the mole was cracked and weakened so as later to be washed away by the waves. The work of months and multitudes had been destroyed in a short hour.8/

Judging from its frequent employment thereafter, the fire ship was, until the nineteenth century, considered a dangerous and effective weapon. At the battle of Actium in 31 B.C., Augustus, using fire ships, routed 200 ships of Anthony and Cleopatra. They were also used in the assault on Rome in 455 A.D. by the vandal chieftain Genseric, during the siege of Paris in 885 by the Norsemen, and in the capture of Constantinople by the French in 1204 during the Fourth Crusade. Fire ships were successfully employed by the defenders of Antwerp during its siege in 1585 by Alexander Farnese, the Duke of Parma. In 1588, British fire ships drove the Spanish Armada from its anchorage at Gravelines off the northern French coast. Fire ships were a regular component of Louis XIV's navy after 1660. Lynn Montross also mentions their use by the Dutch against the British in the seventeenth century. The Dutch admiral, Martin Tromp, used fire ships in his engagements with the British naval units, commanded by Sir Robert Blake, in the English Channel during the years 1652 and 1653. Twenty years later, Admiral Michael De Ruyter employed them to

---

8/ T. A. Dodge, Great Captains: Alexander, pp. 331-32.

defeat a combined British and French fleet during two engagements in the Schoonveldt Channel on June 7 and 14, 1673.[9]

More recently, during their war of Independence in 1822, the Greeks under Constantine Kanaris burned the Turkish fleet with a single fire ship, thus securing command of the sea. The most spectacular modern example of the fire ship's demoralizing effect occurred at Basque Roads in 1809 when British fire ships repeated their feats against the Spanish Armada. The British vessels made up for the slight damage which they produced directly by the havoc which they wreaked among French warships. Excited French officers ordered cables cut, thus setting the vessels adrift on strong tides which caused them to collide with each other or run aground.

None of the preceding methods, largely improvised from existing weapons and engines, survived the nineteenth century. Since World War I, the employment of flame has been exclusively by means of special devices designed to project it free from any form of container. The antecedents of these devices, however, are over two thousand years old.

In 424 B.C. the Spartans fashioned and used successfully such an instrument against the defenders of a fort at Delium in Greece. According to Thucydides, it consisted of a tree trunk sawed in two from end to end, with the two halves scooped out, plated with iron and fitted together again like a pipe. This pipe was joined by an iron tube to the lower part of a cauldron filled with glowing coals, pitch, sulphur, and naphtha which was found in surface oil deposits. When the cauldron was placed next to a wooden section of the fort's wall, a large bellows was inserted into the pipe's open end. The blast of air rushing into the cauldron resulted in the projection of a fierce blaze which set fire to the wall and routed the defenders of the fort -- which was taken. The Romans successfully used a similar contrivance in 107 against the Dacians. However, powdered charcoal instead of coal was used in the cauldron and it was reported to be effective even against stone walls.

A notable improvement in the composition of the incendiary substance was made in Constantinople during the seventh century, with the invention of "Greek Fire" by the Syrian architect Callinicus.

---

[9] L. Montross, War Through the Ages, p. 334.

The formula and manufacture of this fuel, which was ignited on contact with water, remained state secrets and are not completely known even today. Sir Charles Oman believed that Greek fire was a semi-liquid substance composed of sulphur, pitch, dissolved nitre, and petroleum boiled together.10/ Colonel Heine, in his Gunpowder and Ammunition, concludes that quick-lime was the ingredient distinguishing Greek fire from all other preceding incendiary substances.11/ After disastrous experience, the Saracens learned that it could be extinguished only by sand, urine, wine or vinegar.

Hydraulic pressure was created by means of water pumps to force the flaming liquid through nozzles, probably fixed on swivels, and installed on the prows and sides of ships and on the walls of Constantinople. The Byzantines, using this weapon as well as divers who affixed containers of Greek fire on ships' keels, decisively defeated the Saracens at Cycicus in 673. Early in the eighth century, according to Lynn Montross:

> The final effort of Islam in 717 brought to Constantinople the most formidable armada of the Dark Ages...a fleet of 1,800 vessels supporting an army of 80,000...During the following spring the invaders were reinforced by a reserve fleet and another army. Nevertheless, the East-Roman forces seized the initiative as their fire ships [spouting Greek fire from bronze tubes] destroyed an enemy squadron while it lay at anchor. This success paved the way for another victory gained by troops which landed on the Bithynian Coast and surprised the Saracen army watching on the other side of the strait. After a year of reverses, the enemy withdrew, having suffered losses of 70,000.12/

10/ C.W.C. Oman, op. cit., Vol. II, p. 46.

11/ L. Montross, op. cit., p. 123.

12/ Ibid., pp. 124-25.

The Byzantines also used Greek fire ejected from ships to defeat the Russian fleet seeking a warm-water outlet to the sea in 941. The Byzantine historian and empress, Anna Comnena, in her *Alexiad* states that Greek fire used in this manner near Rhodes in about 1100 put to flight a naval squadron from the city-state of Pisa in Italy. The same authority, as well as Leo the Wise in his *Tactica*, refers to portable hand tubes for discharging Greek fire against enemy personnel by means of a strong, continuous blast blown down the tube. This flame weapon, like the Chinese and Arabian fire sprinklers on the tips of maces, an ancestor of the modern portable flame thrower, was used against the Normans by the Byzantine garrison at Dyrrhachium (modern Durazzo in Albania) in 1108.[13]

Although the Byzantines continued to use Greek fire in one form or another until the fall of Constantinople to the Turks in 1453, it was employed with diminishing success. The eventual discovery that Greek fire was more demoralizing than destructive decreased its effectiveness. Nevertheless, experiments with mechanically-projected incendiary liquids were carried on, though with no appreciable military success.

In 1702, the Prussian Army tested P. Lange's "serpent-fire-spray (Schlangen-Brand-Spritze)" designed to eject a sheet of flame twelve feet wide and 120 feet long. Two years later this contrivance was discarded as ineffective. Over fifty years later, an inflammable liquid invented by a French engineer, Dupre, when tested, set fire to a sloop in the port of LeHavre. During the British shelling of LeHavre in 1759, the French War Minister tried in vain to obtain royal authority to use this fuel. Liquid fire, employed during the American Civil War, consisted of phosphorus, sulphur and carbon which, at the siege of Charleston in 1863, was projected through tin pipes and hoses. The French chemist, Marcellin Berthelot, wanted to pump blazing petroleum at the Prussian besiegers of Paris in 1871. Berthelot noted that it was used by the Commune militia to burn a number of public buildings.

With the invention and adoption in the twentieth century of the flame thrower, both portable and carrier-borne or mechanized, the doctrine and employment of projected flame eventually became an integral part of military training and tactics. During World War I,

---

[13]/ C. W. C. Oman, op. cit., Vol. II, pp. 47-48.

most of the major belligerents planned to use portable flame throwers, but they were actually employed only by the Germans, the British and the French.

An incident, reported as occurring during German maneuvers sometime prior to World War I, may have accounted for the decision to develop the Flammenwerfer for tactical employment. During maneuvers a German major was told to hold a fortification at all costs. When the attackers reached the strong point, the Major, in desperation, turned a fire hose on them. He explained later, in the critique, that he was playing burning oil on his enemies. The idea was exploited and the "Flammenwerfer" used during World War I was the result. The weapon was first used in warfare by the Germans in an attack on French positions in the Bois d'Avocourt on the Verdun sector near the village of Melancourt on 26 February 1915. According to the German war correspondent, Hausenstein, the French fled in headlong panic towards the rear. The Flammenwerfer was again used against the French on 25 June 1915, near Verdun. The attack was made by a battalion of infantry, reinforced by special engineers, and was successful because of the psychological effect of the flame. The weapon was filled with mixtures of light and heavy oils, propelled by nitrogen at 25 atmospheres pressure. The Germans also used compressed air and even compressed oxygen as propellants, while the British and French used nitrogen. The fuel used in the Flammenwerfer was ignited by a mixture of chemicals -- barium nitrate, potassium nitrate, metallic magnesium, charcoal and a resinous binder. The chemical mixture (match head) was started by friction, and the weapon gave a horrific burst of flame at the short range of 17 to 20 yards.[14]

The German engineer, Richard Fiedler, the "rediscoverer of Greek Fire," in 1906 invented not only a suitable fuel but also a flame thrower to project it.

On 30 July 1915, the Germans drove back a British rifle brigade from trenches near Ypres by the use of flame throwers supported by small arms, machine gun, and mortar fire. When these trenches were re-occupied by the British ten days later, they captured two German flame throwers. According to the official British History of the Great War:

> These were found to consist of a cylindrical steel

---

[14] (1) Lt. C.E. Leone and Capt. F. L. Schaf, Jr., "A Study of Portable Flame Throwers", p. 2. In Cml C Sch Lib. (2) Maj. C. F. Atkinson, "Flamethrowers," Encyclopedia Britannica (11th ed.), New Vol. XXXI.

vessel about two feet in height, and fifteen inches in diameter, fitted with straps for carrying, and divided internally into a compression chamber and oil reservoir. The propellant was nitrogen at 23 atmospheres contained in the upper chamber. A short length of flexible hose ended in a nozzle in which was fitted the ignition device. As the oil emerged under pressure, it forced up the plunger of a friction lighter and ignited a core of fuse mixture surrounding the nozzle which remained alight long enough to enable a number of shots to be fired.

Subsequent use of the Flammenwerfer proved unsuccessful because of its short range. Operators had to move in so closely to pour flame into Allied trenches that it was considered a suicide mission. It is reported that the Germans resorted to using condemned criminals as operators. Such operators were not given close support by the infantry and when far enough away from their own lines, they threw away their flame throwers and surrendered.15/

Following the initial flame thrower attack by the Germans, portable flame throwers, which were either one- or two-man loads, were developed by all of the belligerents and used intermittently throughout the war, but with little success owing to their short range and the lack of adequate tactical doctrine designed to protect the operator in approaching the target.16/

The British did not put a flame thrower into the field until 1 July 1916, during the Battle of the Somme. Company personnel of a special brigade brought to the British sector of the Allied line sixteen small flame throwers and four large ones, the latter requiring a ton of oil for each shot.17/ It was possible to set up

---

15/ CWS, Chemical Warfare Magazine, Vol. 8, No. 7, 15 Jul 22, p. 13.

16/ Historical Monograph (British), Part III, Flame Warfare, p. 2. In CMLWG.

17/ Capt. Sorensen states that these large projectors were designed by a Mr. Livens and by his father F. H. Livens. According to Maj. Charles F. Atkinson, T.D. (British), formerly Staff Officer for Trench Warfare Research during World War I, the large projectors used by the British at the Battle of the Somme in 1916 were modified versions of a heavier experimental model submitted to the War Office in March 1915 by the American inventor, Joseph Menchen. After describing this modified Menchen flame thrower, Maj. Atkinson goes on to describe "a heavy flamethrower of an entirely different type...the Livens, designed by Capt. Livens, R.E." No mention is made of actual employment of the Livens flame thrower. See Maj. C. F. Atkinson, "Flamethrowers," Encyclopedia Britannica (11th ed.), New Vol. XXXI.

only two of these large machines in existing underground mine galleries in such a way that their location would remain undetected until the moment of actual employment. Captain Sorensen describes the effect of their large flame throwers as follows:

> At zero hour on July 1st two jets appeared out of the ground to a height of two or three feet above the surface; the ignition functioned perfectly and the two streams of oil were projected into the enemy trench, being traversed slowly from side to side. The flames were accompanied by dense clouds of black smoke, heavy machine gun fire was opened, and the British infantry occupied the trench without opposition. The ranges obtained by the projectors, as measured along the burnt ground, were 94 and 97 yards, respectively. The small portable machines intended for this operation were not used, as no opportunity presented itself.
>
> The large machines were fired on one or two occasions within the next few weeks but it had become evident that their local effect did not justify the great labour and difficulty of bringing them within range of their objectives.
>
> Only on one future occasion at Dixmude on October 27, 1917, was one of the large machines fired, and then only as a supplement to every other form of weapon. Indeed, it was learned subsequently from prisoners that the flame-thrower had caused no casualties, the garrison of the "Minotorie" against which it had been directed having already fled in terror.

In the British, French and German armies, during World War I, flame throwers were used by engineer units.[18] In the British army the weapon was employed by the Special Brigade, R.E. In the French army, seven units were activated and designated Compagnies Schilt, after Captain Schilt of the Paris sapeurs-pompiers, who designed the French flame throwers. The Germans organized a Guard Reserve Pioneer

---

[18] In his article entitled "Flamethrowers," Encyclopedia Britannica (11th ed.), New Vol. XXXI, Maj. Atkinson describes in detail several types of flamethrowers developed and/or employed during World War I. Among the heavy types described are the Menchen, invented by an American and adapted by the British; the French Hersent and the German Gros flamethrowers. Among the portable types described are the French Schilt, the German Klief and Wex, and the British Norris-Menchen and Laurence flamethrowers.

regiment which furnished personnel and both light and heavy flame throwers to "assault battalions" as required.

The flame thrower made available to American troops during World War I was called the "Boyd No. 3" and was also known as the "Knapsack (Overseas) Model." Due largely to changes in requirements by the American Expeditionary Forces, flame throwers were not manufactured on a large scale during the war.[19]

According to Major Atkinson, the bulk and weight of both the heavy flame thrower and of its fuels were such as to confine its use to static situations such as siege warfare, and then only in the absence of a handier and more economical weapon. Therefore, its future, as seen by this World War I observer, depended on its being mounted on a tank.

On the other hand, the lightweight or portable flame thrower, despite the difficulties of resupply in extreme forward positions, was found to be a useful, though not indispensable, support weapon for the infantry. It was used, among other purposes, to create panic just prior to an infantry attack; to clear trenches and dugouts and to block exits from captured positions, especially in mopping up isolated enemy concentrations; to engage a strong point frontally while infantry worked around the flanks; and to cover the retreat of raiding parties and other small infantry units.[20]

The lack of development of flame throwers in the United States during the interim between the two world wars is readily understood when one considers the opinion expressed by General Fries, then Chief of the Chemical Warfare Service, in the following statement made in 1921:

> Of the incendiary materials the least valuable is the flame thrower. In the Chemical Warfare Service it has been the habit for a long time not to mention the flame thrower at all, unless questions were asked about it. It is mentioned here to forestall the questions. Even the German, who invented it and who, during the two years of trench warfare, had full opportunity for developing its use, finally came to using it largely as a means of executing people that he did not want to shoot himself. Men falling

---

[19] Benedict Crowell, *America's Munitions, 1917-18*, (Washington, D.C., 1919), p. 220.

[20] Maj. C. F. Atkinson, "Flamethrowers," *Encyclopedia Britannica* (11th ed.), New Vol. XXXI.

in that class were equipped with flame throwers and sent over the top. The German knew, as did the Allies, that each man with a flame thrower became a target for every rifle and machine gun nearby. The flame thrower is very quickly exhausted and then the one equipped with it has no means of offensive action, and in addition, is saddled with a heavy load, hampering all movements, whether to escape or to advance.[21]

The Italian Army created somewhat of a sensation in March 1937, when they demonstrated flame throwers mounted in combat cars and other armed vehicles. Newsreels of the demonstration were widely shown in the United States and elsewhere with the result that tactical speculation about flame warfare came to center on the mechanized type of flame thrower even before a satisfactory portable weapon had been developed.

B. Portable Flame Throwers.

1. Requirement Established and Development of the Mark I Portable Flame Thrower. By 1940 intelligence reports revealed that both Italian and German flame throwers had been used on the Western Front and Italian portable models had been found and described. These reports were isolated enough to effect reasonable uncertainty about the extent to which enemy troops were prepared to commit flame throwers to combat.[22] Nevertheless, it was indicated that these weapons had been used with considerable success in attacks upon mechanized vehicles, and fortifications, such as Eben-Emael.

On 24 July 1940, the Chief of Engineers wrote to the War Department, requesting that the Chief of Chemical Warfare Service (now the Chemical Corps) be directed to develop, as soon as practicable, a suitable flame thrower for one-man employment.[23] Pursuant to this request the Chemical Warfare Service was charged, in September 1940,

---

[21] Brig. Gen. Amos A. Fries and Maj. Clarence J. West, Chemical Warfare (1st ed. N.Y. 1921), p. 401.

[22] Tech Intell Summary No. 12, 27 Dec 40, p. 3. AGF G-2 DD.

[23] Ltr, Chief of Eng to AG, 24 Jul 40, sub: Flame Thrower for Individual Use.

with the development, manufacture, storage and issue of the portable flame thrower.[24]/ During the next year an experimental model was developed. This model was known as the E1R1 ("E" for Experimental) and several were issued to troops and later, in the absence of an adequate supply of the standardized model, were taken overseas. During the summer of 1941, the latest design of the E1R1 was demonstrated at Edgewood Arsenal and in August was standardized as the Mark 1 (M1). This flame thrower consisted of: two fuel tanks, connected by a manifold, of approximately five gallons total capacity; a small steel pressure cylinder placed over and between them and filled with nitrogen to provide the projecting pressure; a reducing valve to reduce the 2000 p.s.i. to a working pressure of approximately 225 p.s.i.; together with a shut-off valve which released the pressure from the cylinder to the fuel containers. A hose then led to the gun, which had a Y-type valve, lever operated, and a long bent nozzle. Ignition was obtained by a compact electrical control system consisting of dry-cell batteries, interrupter, high tension coil, spark plug, and a small hydrogen bottle attached to the gun to provide fuel for the igniting flame. A button on the side served the dual purpose of releasing hydrogen and turning on the electric spark.

Shortly before Pearl Harbor a procurement program for 1000 of these M1's got under way. Early in 1942 it became apparent that the ignition was inadequate. Tests showed that the batteries had short lives and the system was put out of commission by the smallest amount of moisture. However, no substantial improvement was made during the next six months[25]/ and in the meantime troops were being equipped with what was known to be an unsatisfactory weapon.

2. *The M1A1 Portable Flame Thrower.* During 1942 research on thickened gasoline as a flame thrower fuel was intensified. By November 1942 the project had progressed to the point that specifications were drafted for napalm as a gasoline thickener. During this period it had become evident that the use of thickened fuel offered a practicable means of increasing the range of the portable flame thrower. Accordingly, the Chemical Warfare Service in cooperation with the National Defense Research Committee instituted an investigation to de-

---

[24]/ CWTC, Item 222, 10 Sep 40.

[25]/ "Report of Activities of the Technical Division During World War II," OC CWS, Wash. D.C., 1 Jan 46, p. 136. (Hereafter referred to as "Tech. Div. Rpt of Act.")

termine what changes were necessary to permit the use of thickened fuel in the M1 model. By August 1942 it had become apparent that slight changes only were necessary in the basic weapon, such as straightening the gun nozzle (the M1 model had a 10 degree bend), and redesigning the discharge valves. These modifications were agreed upon and, after further tests, the resulting model was standardized as the M1A1 portable flame thrower in December 1942.26/ With thickened fuel this model had an effective range of thirty-five to fifty yards. Its duration of fire remained the same as the M1 model, that is, from eight to ten seconds. The complete apparatus weighed thirty-two pounds while empty and sixty-eight pounds when filled. The fuel tanks were built to operate at 375 p.s.i., the hydrogen cylinder at 1,500 to 2,100 p.s.i., and the nitrogen cylinder at 1,800 to 2,000 p.s.i.27/ The fundamental defects of inadequate waterproofing and unreliability of ignition remained.

A total of 12,886 of this model was produced between December 1942 and July 1944. The troops were supplied with a service kit, a fuel-filling kit, and a fuel-mixing kit of which 1,729, 2,015 and 604 were produced, respectively.28/

The M1A1 flame throwers reached troops in the Southwest Pacific Area in August 1943.29/ In the Mediterranean Theater of Operations the M1 model was exchanged for the M1A1 in December 1943.30/ The history of the employment of portable flame throwers in the Asiatic-Pacific Theater of Operations is largely the record of the problems

---

26/ Ibid., p. 137.

27/ TM 3-375, Portable Flame Throwers, M1 and M1A1, May 43.

28/ Production Br, Procurement Div, OC CWS, "Report of Production, 1 Jan 40 through 31 Dec 45," pp. 18, 19. (Hereafter referred to as "Rpt of Production.")

29/ Ltr, Hqs USAFFE to CG Sixth Army, 21 Aug 43, sub: Flame Throwers, Portable, M1A1. In Sixth A Cml Sec records, 470.71, ORB.

30/ Ltr, AG NATOUSA to All Concerned, sub: Flame Throwers, 19 Dec 43. In NATOUSA Cml Records, 470.71, ORB.

Figure 1. The M1 Portable Flame Thrower.

Figure 2. Firing the M1 Portable Flame Thrower.

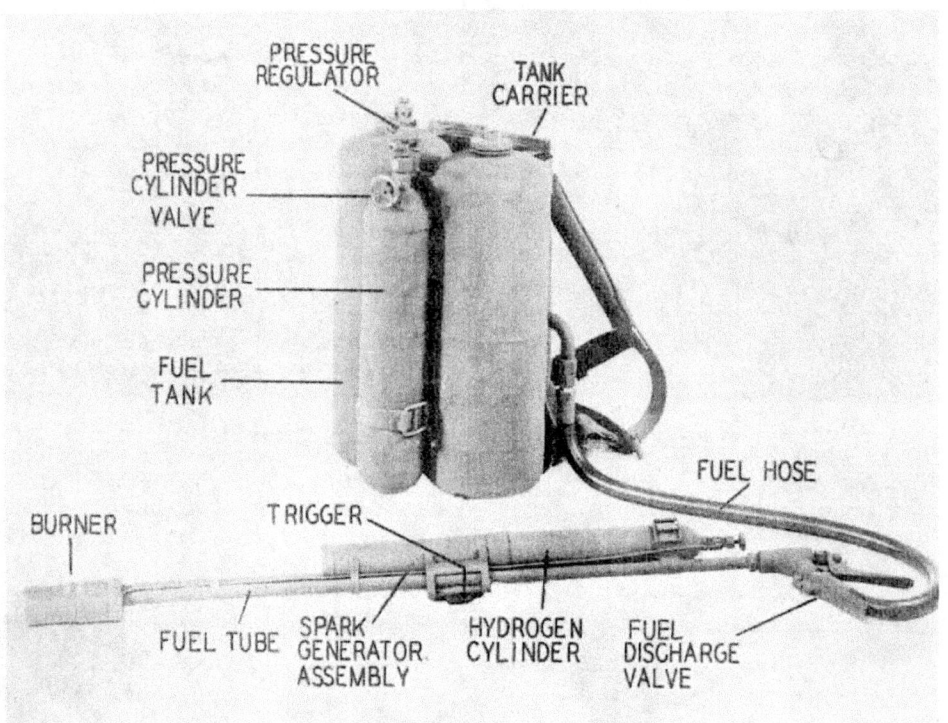

Figure 3. The M1A1 Portable Flame Thrower.

encountered with the defective and malfunctioning M1A1 model which required continuous surveillance and repeated training of operators in the care and maintenance of the weapon. Although the vastly improved M2-2 model began to trickle into theaters during the latter part of 1944, several infantry divisions were still equipped with the M1A1 model when the war ended. The measure of success achieved with the M1A1 flame thrower in the Southwest Pacific Area is attributable in no small part to the stringent policy of training, maintenance and servicing established after the fiasco at Buna when the E1R1 model failed to function. Following this experience every M1A1 flame thrower shipped to the area was taken apart and completely remodeled, and waterproofed to the extent that no malfunctioning occurred after eight hours under a shower or even after being immersed in water.[31] This remodeling did not, however, alleviate such basic weaknesses as fragility, inadequate electrical system and poor design in general.

3. <u>The M2-2 Portable Flame Thrower</u>. The Japanese entered the war with a cartridge ignition type portable flame thrower[32] and the Germans adopted such an ignition system in 1942.[33] Insistent demands from the theaters of operations for an improved flame thrower with a positive cartridge ignition system resulted in the initiation of such a development by the Chemical Warfare Service as early as 1942. The first experimental models, designated E3, were completed during the first part of 1943. This E3 model was demonstrated to the using arms in the Southwest Pacific Area by the Borden Mission[34] in October 1943, after which a requisition was submitted for 240, with the understanding that 100 would be made available by December 1943. This schedule was not met; the first shipment of 170 did not arrive in New Guinea until June 1944. Ignition cartridges did not accompany this shipment and twenty per cent of the weapons were found defective in one way or another.[35] The Central Pacific Area fared better as

---

[31] Ltr, Cml O USASOS to Cml O's Base Sections 2, 3, 4 and 7 and 10th Cml Maint Co, 16 May 43, sub: Flame Throwers. In Sixth A Cml Sect Records, 470.71, ORB.

[32] Ltr, CWS Laboratory, Fort Mills, P.I. to Cml O USAFFE, 19 Feb 42, sub: Japanese Flame Thrower Physical Examination, In CMLWG.

[33] Intell Div, CWS, ETOUSA, <u>German Chemical Warfare - World War II</u> p. 141. (2) Historical <u>Monograph (British), Part III, Flame Warfare</u>, p. 106. In CMLWG.

[34] Group of officers headed by General Borden to demonstrate jungle weapons.

[35] Memo, Hq Alamo Force, Cml Sec, for Cml O 6th Inf Div, 27 Jun 44. In Sixth A Cml Sec Records 470.71 F.T, ORB.

only twenty-seven of 494 in the early shipments were found defective.36/
The first units of this experimental model were actually issued to
troops in the Pacific during the latter part of 1944. The availability
of the new model was announced to the Mediterranean Theater in the spring
of 1944 and requisitions were placed at that time.37/ However, the
first shipment arrived without ignition cartridges in February 1945.38/

In October 1943, the Chief of Chemical Warfare Service announced
that development work on the new model had been completed and a limited
procurement program approved for service testing by the using arms.39/
The first 200 E3's were completed in early 1944 and submitted to the
Engineer Board and Infantry Board for approval. The model was standardized as the M2-2 Portable Flame Thrower in February 1944 and production commenced immediately. A total of 24,601 was manufactured by V-J
Day40/ and sufficient quantities were in the theaters to replace all
M1A1's.

The M2-2 portable flame thrower weighed forty-three pounds empty
and seventy pounds when filled. The fuel tanks had a capacity of four
gallons and differed little from the M1A1 fuel assembly. A larger
pressure cylinder which permitted operation up to 350 p.s.i. was used.
The gun assembly was $2\frac{1}{2}$ feet long, the barrel of which consisted of
a 7/8-inch diameter tube with a revolver-type ignition mechanism mounted
on the front end and a pistol type fuel valve mounted on the rear end.
The ignition cartridge consisted of a plastic cylinder with five cavi-
ties which were filled with an incendiary composition. A trigger on
the front handle pushed forward a pin, coated with match mixture, igniting the incendiary composition. The resulting flame, projecting approximately six inches, burned for eight seconds. A cone-shaped shield on
the nozzle served to concentrate the heat around the rod of fuel. The
plastic ignition cylinders were completely waterproofed, resulting in
reliable ignition.

36/ Ltr, Cml O CP Base Comm to OC CWS, 24 Jul 44, sub: Defects of E-3
Flame Throwers and Service Kits. In CMLWG.

37/ IOM, Cml O AFHQ to G-4 AFHQ, 19 Nov 44.

38/ Cml Sec, Fifth Army Hist Rpt, 1 Feb - 26 Feb 45. In Cml C Sch Lib.

39/ CWS Theater of Operations Letter No. 6, p. 34.

40/ Rpt of Production, p. 13.

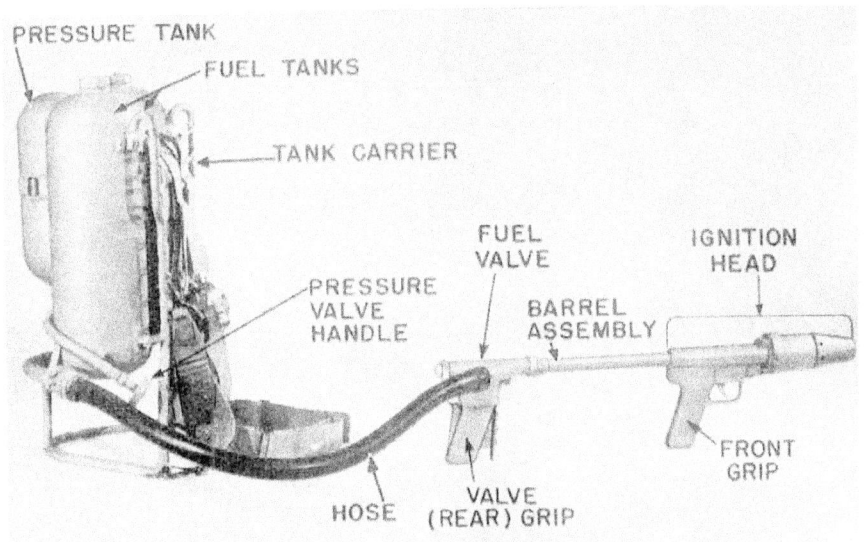

Figure 4. The M2-2 Portable Flame Thrower.

Figure 5. Firing the M2-2 Portable Flame Thrower.

C. Mechanized Flame Throwers.40a/

1. *The Question of a Requirement*. Although the enemy entered the war with mechanized flame throwers none was available to the Allies, with the possible exception of Russia.41/ Following the Battle of Guadalcanal, both the marines and army in that area experimented with improvising a mechanized flame thrower by mounting the portable model on tanks.42/ Experience had already shown that Japanese defense tactics employed well-camouflaged positions, protected by a lethal blaze of machine-gun fire. Against such defense, attacks by dismounted troops equipped only with light arms, obviously would involve extreme hazards as compared with the use of tanks. However, even though tanks could approach such defenses, they were not equipped with a suitable weapon for neutralizing dug-in positions. Nevertheless, the delay in furnishing mechanized flame throwers to troops was caused primarily by slowness in establishing a requirement. In 1941 it was the opinion that the inclusion of mechanized flame throwers in the armored forces was not warranted.43/

No change in policy is noted prior to a Canadian demonstration, in 1943, of the Ronson flame gun mounted on a tracked vehicle. Following this demonstration there developed a growing belief that the tank appeared to be the most logical vehicle for the employment of flame throwers.44/ In 1944 the Armored Force requested that the Chemical Warfare Service concentrate on developing and procuring an auxiliary type mechanized flame thrower.45/ Owing to the shortage of tanks in all theaters there was great hesitancy toward removing armament from the tanks, and the only proposal entertained by the Armored Force Board was that of including a flame thrower without sacrificing any of the tank armament. Consequently, a requirement for a main armament type flame thrower was not established until the spring of 1945.46/

40a/ The development of mechanized flame throwers is included here, along with other type flame throwers. Mechanized flame thrower operations, however, are treated in Cml C Historical Study No. 5.

41/ P. M. Sidorski, "Flame Projectors and How to Combat Them" (Moscow, 1941).

42/ See Cml C Historical Study No. 5 on "Mechanized Flame Thrower Operations."

43/ Armored Force Bd Rpt, P-58/2, 13 Sep 41, p. 2.

44/ Armored Force Bd Rpt, Project No. 460, 29 Oct 43, Appendix D, p. 5.

45/ Ltr, GNOFB P/508 Armd Force Bd to CG Armd Force, 3 Feb 44.

46/ Tech Div Rpt of Act., p. 144.

Although requests were made by the theaters of operations for mechanized flame throwers, field commanders were reluctant to recommend changes whereby flame throwers would become the main armament of tanks. At the same time it was the concensus that the auxiliary type weapon did not fulfill the requirements for mechanized flame throwers. In October 1943, the Southwest Pacific Area requested twelve flame throwers mounted in light tanks for combat tests. In March 1944 Sixth Army submitted a requisition for fifty auxiliary type flame throwers in the hope that they would be available for the Philippine operation.47/ In the Central Pacific Area (later Pacific Ocean Area) demands for mechanized flame throwers were more insistent, due primarily to requests from the Marines and Navy.48/ Although firm requirements were not established through command channels, developmental progress in the United States was watched closely, and in December 1943 a requisition was submitted for fifty auxiliary type weapons. Owing to high priority established by the Navy, the Marines actually received several of these weapons in time for use in the Marianas Operation during the late summer of 1944. Actually, when it became apparent to the commanding general, Pacific Ocean Areas, that mechanized flame throwers would not be forthcoming from the United States in sufficient quantities and types to meet requirements, positive action was taken to effect procurement and manufacture of the required weapons in Hawaii.

The European theaters were slower than those in the Pacific to establish requirements for mechanized flame throwers. In September 1944, the Twelfth Army Group urgently requested nine auxiliary type (E4-5) flame throwers per tank battalion.49/ However, a requirement for main armament type flame throwers was never established by the Twelfth Army Group. In January 1945, the commanding general, U.S. Ninth Army stated that there was no requirement for a special flame throwing tank that sacrificed its cannon armament.50/ However, in February 1945, the commanding general, Twelfth Army Group, requested

---

47/ 2d Ind, Cml O Sixth Army to C Cml O USASOS, 9 Oct 44, on Ltr, AC CWS for Fld Opns to C Cml O USASOS, 9 Aug 44, sub: Flame Thrower Tank Development by NDRC. In Sixth A Cml Sect Records, 470.71 FT-Tank Mounted, ORB.

48/ See Cml C Historical Study No. 5 on "Mechanized Flame Thrower Operations."

49/ TWX, Com Z, ETOUSA to Pembark, N.Y., 25 Sep 44, sub: Flame Thrower, in 12th Army Gp Records, 470.71, AGO.

50/ 1st Ind on Ltr, Hq 12th Army Gp to CG Ninth A, 13 Jan 45, sub: Mechanized Flame Throwers. In 12th Army Gp Records, 470.71, AGO.

ten main armament flame throwers for operational tests.51/

2. <u>Auxiliary Type Mechanized Flame Throwers.</u>

a. <u>The E4-5 (Standardized as M3-4-3 in 1945).</u> As the result of a conference held on 11 October 1943, the Army Ground Forces requested development of a medium sized flame thrower that could be installed in existing tanks in the field without replacing the main armament.52/ On 20 October 1943 the Army Service Forces firmed the requirement by suggesting that the gun from the E-3 portable model be provided with fuel tanks of ten to thirty gallons capacity for installation in the M5A1 light tank and M4A1 medium tank, with minimum alterations to the vehicles. Within a month a pilot model had been produced. This model consisted of two separate fuel tank installations, one for the light tank and one for the medium tank, the former having a capacity of ten gallons and the latter of twenty-five gallons. These were mounted on the right sponson of the tank and connected directly to the gun. The gun utilized gasoline-electrical ignition and was designed to be interchangeable with the bow machine gun. The change-over could be effected in a matter of one minute under combat conditions. These units were known as the E4 fuel tank and E5 gun when installed in medium tanks, hence the designation E4-5. After demonstration of the model, it was decided to begin production in order to take care of immediate demands from the theaters of operations. On 16 December an order was placed with a manufacturer for eighty-two units, including service kits at the ratio of one kit for each ten units.53/ On 6 January 1944 the quantity was increased to 100 units, and on 8 January the order was again increased to 150. On 22 February 1944, three units were shipped to the Armored Force Board, Fort Knox, Kentucky, for service testing. On 8 March 1944 ten units and one service kit were shipped to the Pacific for service tests. An additional fuel tank of twenty-five gallons capacity was designed and manufactured for installation over the transmission to increase the carrying capacity for the medium tank to fifty gallons. The first shipment of fifty E4-5 flame throwers, equipped with the twenty-five gallon sponson fuel tank only, arrived in the European Theater of Operations in November 1944.53a/ The transmission fuel

---

51/ TWX, Hq Com Z, ETOUSA to CG 12th Army Gp., Ref NR: E-11,734, 22 Feb 45, sub: Flame Throwers, Mechanized, E12-7R1. In 12th Army Grp Records, 470.71, AGO.

52/ IOM (Comment No. 4) SPCVE 470.71, C Tech Div to AC CWS for Materiel, 3 Aug 44, sub: Report of Development of Mechanized Flame Throwers. In AGO-HRS-CWS 470.71, 1943-44.

53/ Ibid.

53a/ Pers ltr, Cml O 12th Army Gp to Deputy C CWS, 7 Nov 44, No sub. In CMLWG.

units were not yet off the production line and were shipped a month later.54/ From time to time, during the course of production, certain design changes for improved functioning were found necessary. With revisions in design, the designation for the sponson fuel unit evolved through E4, E4R2 and E4R4 to be standardized as the M3. Meanwhile the designation for the transmission fuel unit was successively E4R1, E4R3 and E4R5. It was standardized as the M4 assembly. The flame gun to replace the bow machine gun was known as the E5 and E5R1 before being standardized as the M3. Hence the designation of the standardized unit for medium tanks became M-3-4-3.55/ A total of 1,784 units of this model was manufactured during the war 56/ and a sufficient number received combat tests for adequate tactical evaluation.

   o. The Periscope Model. The fuel system for the periscope model flame thrower was identical with that used with the gun which was interchangeable with the bow machine gun (E4-5 described above). The only difference was in the flame gun. There were two periscope flame guns developed during the war, one in the United States and one in Hawaii. The United States development will be described first.

   After the E4-5 flame throwers were placed in limited production in the spring of 1944, the Armored Force indicated that the gun should be considered an interim model only, since it replaced the bow machine gun. On 2 March 1944, the Army Ground Forces requested that a periscope-mounted gun be developed.57/ A contract for this experimental type gun was placed with an industrial concern and the first model was demonstrated at Edgewood Arsenal on 10 October 1944. Following the demonstration, the Army Service Forces directed the Chemical Warfare Service to procure 500 units.58/ The periscope gun was designated as the E6R1 with a subsequent revision as E6R3. The gun was mounted in a specially designed periscope holder, which could be installed in either the assistant driver's hatch door or in the turret periscope mount. The fuel was ignited by a small flame of atomized gasoline,

---

54/ TWX, First Army to 12th Army Gp, 5 Nov 44, sub: Transmission Tanks for E4-5 Flame Throwers. In 12th Army Gp Records, 470.71, AGO.

55/ (1) IOM (Comment No. 4) SPCVE 470.71, C Tech Div to AC CWS for Materiel, 3 Aug 44, sub: Report of Development of Mechanized Flame Throwers. In AGO-HRS-CWS 470.71, 1943-44. (2) TM 3-363, 1 Jun 45. (3) TM 3-364, 6 Jun 45.

56/ Rpt of Production, p. 13.

57/ Ltr, AGF to ASF, 2 Mar 44, sub: (?), 470.71 (c) GNRQT-6-74149.

58/ Ltr, Hq ASF to C CWS, 13 Oct 44, sub: Limited Procurement of Periscope Mounted FT's. In AGO-HRS CWS 470.71, 1943-44.

Figure 6. The M3-4-3 Mechanized Flame Thrower—an Auxiliary Type.

ignited by a spark plug. With thickened fuel, the maximum range was forty to sixty yards.59/ A total of 192 units had been completed by the end of the war 60/ but none were actually used in combat.

The Chemical Warfare Service in Hawaii was called on to design a periscope mounted flame gun that could be manufactured locally in order to meet the requirement of the Tenth Army for the Ryukyus Operation. On 12 September 1944, the Tenth Army established a requirement for a minimum of one and a maximum of two periscope-mounted auxiliary type flame throwers per medium tank platoon. The flame thrower was to be an added weapon, utilizing a fuel tank not to exceed twenty-five gallons capacity.61/ It was decided that this demand could not be filled by production in the United States and steps were taken to manufacture the units at Pearl Harbor. A "Seabee" group constructed a demonstration model, using the sponson fuel tank E4R2 of the E4-5 for a model and constructed a flame gun from a piece of metal tubing to which electrodes were attached to ignite the fuel. The simple high tension spark electrode was connected to the storage battery in the tank. Switches and valves were attached to the bent tube in order to complete the gun assembly. The range of this gun was approximately the same as that of the portable flame thrower with thickened fuel.62/ A total of 176 units were produced and employed in the Ryukyus campaign.63/

3. <u>Main Armament Types</u>. Due to the shortage of tanks throughout the war, commanders in the field were reluctant to recommend the development of main armament flame throwers. It was felt that, with only a limited number of tanks available, the cannon offered greater tactical value than a flame thrower. This attitude existed in all of the theaters of operations even though it was felt that the auxiliary type was inadequate.64/ As a result, as late as VE Day, no military requirement had been established for a main armament flame thrower. The

---

59/ TM 3-364, 6 Jun 45.

60/ Rpt of Production, p. 13.

61/ 1st Ind, Tenth Army, 12 Sep 44, on Ltr, CG POA, 470.71/3, 23 Aug 44, sub: Requirements for Vehicular Mounted Flame Throwers. In Hist CWS Mid Pac, Vol. III, Annex II C1, Ref. 25, 26.

62/ Hist CWS Mid Pac, Vol. II, Annex II C1, p. 39.

63/ Tenth Army AA Rpt Ryukyus 26 Mar - 30 Jun 1945, p. 4.

64/ (1) 1st Ind, 13 Jan 45 on Ltr, Hq 12th Army Grp to CG Ninth Army, 13 Jan 45, sub: Mechanized Flame Throwers. In CMLWG. (2) TWX, CG USAF South Pac to WD, 2 Jun 44, CM-IN-1140, 2 Jun 44.

Army Ground Forces had, however, backed up the development program in spite of recommendations from the theaters. This policy resulted in a main armament model having been developed when the requirement arose.65/ With the close of the war in Europe, tanks became available and General MacArthur established immediate requirements for main armament flame throwers for employment in the invasion of Japan. These requirements were far in excess of the weapons that could have been made available. For the Kyushu operation, Sixth Army requested that each tank battalion be augmented by a company of seventeen main armament flame throwing tanks.66/

      a. Light Flame Tanks. In the summer of 1943 the development of main armament flame throwers had progressed to the point where the National Defense Research Committee was directed to mount several units of what was called the "Q" model ("Q" for "Quickie") in M5A1 light tanks. These were available for tests by the Armored Force during the winter of 1943-44. Certain modifications were required to make the tanks battle-worthy. Four of these flame tanks were finally completed in early 1945 and shipped to Luzon, P.I., where they were combat tested during the latter stages of the Luzon Operation, April - June 1945. This model was designated E7-7 (Q model). The gun was inclosed in a simulated howitzer turret shield and replaced the conventional 37mm. gun.67/ The E-7 fuel unit consisted of six fuel tanks, piped in series, with a capacity of 120 gallons. This was the only main armament flame thrower manufactured and mounted in the United States that was actually employed in combat.

      b. Medium Flame Tanks. As a result of a conference between Army Ground Forces, representatives of the Army Service Forces, and the National Defense Research Committee early in the summer of 1944, it was decided to procure twenty main armament flame throwers for mounting in medium tanks (M4A1) without waiting for further refinement of models then under development. The flame thrower used was along the line of that developed for the light tank (Q model). The greatest

---

65/ Pers ltr, Deputy Chief CWS to Cml O US Group Control Council, Armd Forces Div, ETO, 29 Dec 44. In CMLWG.

66/ (1) Ltr, AG 470.71, CG AFPAC to CG AFWESPAC, et al, 31 July 45, sub: Main Armament Flame Throwers, E12-7R1 and Service Units, E-8. In Sixth Army Cml Sec Records, 470.71 PFT's, ORB (2) Ltr, 400-C, Hq Sixth Army to C-in-C, USAFPAC, 10 Jul 45, sub: Plan for Employment of the Tank, M4 series with Flame Thrower (Main Armament). In Sixth Army Cml Sec Records, 320.3, T of O, ORB.

67/ Tech Div Rpt of Act, p. 141.

difficulty encountered in this project was that of obtaining the medium tanks in which to mount the flame throwers.68/ These flame tanks were completed in March 1945 and twelve were requisitioned by the European Theater of Operations. However, they did not arrive in time for combat tests. This model was designated as E12-7R1. It was estimated that 115 of these weapons would have been available to Sixth Army for the projected Kyushu landing.69/ This flame thrower had a fuel capacity of 290 gallons and a range of 100-150 yards, depending upon wind and type of fuel.

    c. The Navy Mark I Flame Thrower (E14-7R2). Based on experience at Tarawa, 21 November 1943, the Navy Bureau of Ordnance initiated a request for the development and manufacture of some twenty ruggedly constructed flame throwers with a range greater than 100 yards to be mounted in an LCVP or similar assault craft. The intended employment of this weapon was to cover the beachhead with flame during the initial assault phase. The flame thrower was to be demountable so that, after flaming the beach, it could be removed and the LCVP used for landing troops and equipment.70/ These flame throwers were completed in a very expeditious fashion and delivered to the Navy Department by the National Defense Research Committee. This model was based on the "Q" design and consisted of a similar gun, mounted over a 200 gallon fuel tank, and cylinders of compressed air for propulsion. A shield of armor plate, providing some protection, was placed in front of the unit. Filled, the unit weighed 6,400 pounds.71/ On 29 April 1944, the commanding general, Fleet Marine Forces in the Pacific, reported that these units were too heavy for mounting on LCVP's. Five units were then turned over to the commanding general, Central Pacific Area for experimental use. On 3 June 1944, a Navy Flame Thrower Detachment with three Navy Mark I flame throwers and accessories joined the 1st Marine Division at Guadalcanal for the purpose of mounting the flame throwers on amphibian tractors for use in the approaching Pelelieu operation.

68/ Ibid.

69/ TWX, ASF to CG WESPAC, 10 Jul 45.

70/ Ltr, C-in-C USF to C-in-C USPF, 19 Apr 44, sub: Flame Throwers. In Hist CWS Mid Pac, Vol. III, Annex II C1, Ref. 9.

71/ Tech Div Rpt of Act, p. 142.

d. **Main Armament Flame Tanks Produced in Hawaii.** On 21 January 1944, at the request of the Fifth Amphibious Corps, a Canadian officer and two enlisted men visited Oahu and on 3 February demonstrated the Ronson flame thrower to interested groups. A considerable amount of interest was aroused in large flame throwers of the Ronson type and it was decided that an experimental installation should be made in an M3A1 light tank with the flame thrower replacing the 37-mm. gun. This job was assigned to the 43d Chemical Laboratory Company on 4 February and the model was demonstrated on 15 April 1944. The fuel capacity was approximately 170 gallons. Carbon dioxide was used as a propelling gas at pressures ranging from 180 to 250 p.s.i. As a result of the demonstration, a number of improvements were incorporated into the original design and the Marine Corps requested that the weapon be installed in twenty-four of their M3 light tanks which were being replaced by the new M5 light tanks. These flame tanks were completed and used by the 2d and 4th Marine Divisions in the Marianas Operation from 17 June through July 1944. Late in August 1944, the XXIV Corps requested nine of these light tank flame throwers. These nine units, with still more improvements over the earlier models, were constructed by Chemical Warfare Service personnel of the Central Pacific Base Command and by Navy Seabees. The flame tanks were taken to Leyte, P.I. by XXIV Corps but received little use because of the immobility of the light tank. 72/

At the request of the XXIV Corps, a Ronson flame thrower gun was mounted in an LVT-A1 amphibious tractor and demonstrated on 5 August 1944. This installation was made by the Chemical Warfare Service, POA. At that time XXIV Corps was scheduled to make a landing on Yap Island where terrain studies indicated the need for such a weapon. This operation was subsequently cancelled and the amphibious flame thrower was taken to Leyte, P.I., by the 7th Infantry Division but was not employed.

On 12 September 1944, the Tenth Army established its requirement for main armament flame throwers as one tank battalion of three companies, utilizing Ronson type flame throwers mounted on 54 medium tanks. The primary weapon was to be the flame gun and the fuel capacity was to be the maximum of attainment. 73/ At this time two battalions of new medium tanks were enroute to Hawaii to replace the older M4 tanks

---

72/ Ltr, Hq USAF, POA, Op. Res. Sec., to Office Fld Serv, OC CWS (thru WD), 13 Dec 44, sub: Interim Report on the Development and Construction of Flame Throwers in POA. In CMLWG.

73/ Ltr, AG 470.71/3, CG POA to CG Tenth Army, 23 Aug 44, and 1st Ind, 12 Sep 44. In Hist CWS Mid Pac, Vol III, Annex II C1, Ref. 26.

Figure 7. Main Armament Flame Thrower Tank (POA-CWS-H1).

which would then become available for modification. This program was carried out under the supervision of the chemical officer, Central Pacific Base Command, and was implemented by Army and Navy Seabee personnel. On 11 October the first model was ready for demonstration. In this vehicle the flame gun was enclosed in a shroud which simulated a 105-mm. howitzer. The profile of this vehicle was not approved by Tenth Army, which requested that the gun be contained in a 75-mm. gun barrel, actually or simulated. This request necessitated redesign of the flame gun to permit placing it in the gun barrel. The fuel unit for this flame thrower was carried in four cylindrical fuel tanks, connected in series, with a total capacity of 290 gallons. These fuel tanks were located in the bottom of the vehicle on either side of the propeller shaft and the floor of the basket was raised fourteen inches to clear the top of the tanks. Carbon dioxide for propulsion was stored in three commercial cylinders, each containing about fifty pounds, which were stowed in the rear of the right sponson. A heat exchanger was provided for vaporizing the carbon dioxide. By using carbon dioxide one-half as many bottles were required as would have been needed if nitrogen or compressed air were used. The flame gun incorporated the Inglehart principle of valving the flow of fuel. By use of this principle good cut-off was obtained and very little drool was encountered. Ignition was obtained by means of a gasoline jet with a standard spark plug as the primary igniter. Elevation and depression of the flame gun were the same as the original 75-mm. cannon but traverse was limited to 260°.74/ This tank flame thrower was designated POA-CWS-H1 ("H" for Hawaii).75/ Eight of these units were supplied to the Fleet Marine Force, Pacific, for the Iwo Jima Operation (February 1945) and fifty-four were used to equip the 713th Provisional Flame Thrower Tank Battalion for the Ryukyus Operation (April 1945).

e. <u>Emplaced Flame Throwers</u>. The development and manufacture of emplaced flame throwers operated by remote control was under way in 1940.76/ It was believed in some quarters that this type of weapon

---

74/ Ltr, Hq USAF, POA, Op Res Sec to Off Fld Ser OC CWS (thru WD), 13 Dec 44, sub: Interim Report on the Development and Construction of Flame Throwers in POA. In CMLWG.

75/ See Tentative Instruction Book for POA-CWS-H1 Mechanized Flame Thrower. In CMLWG.

76/ IOM, C Intell Div OC CWS for C Tech Ser OC CWS, 12 Jan 42, sub: Emplaced Flame Thrower. In CMLWG.

would prove useful in the defense of narrow beachheads, bridgeheads, defiles and road blocks, as well as harbor defenses, airports, and gates of industrial plants.77/ The several army, base and air commands, however, indicated in May 1943 that they had no requirement for such a weapon.78/ The CWS, therefore, discontinued development and procurement of the item and it became limited standard in July 1942.79/

D. Allied Flame Throwers.

1. Canadian.

The Ronson flame thrower was actually developed by the British during 1941. It was designed for mounting on the Bren gun carrier and fitted with two 60-gallon (Imperial) fuel tanks located outside at the rear of the carrier. Carbon dioxide was used as a propellant, giving an effective range of sixty to seventy yards with thickened fuel and a sustained duration of fire of two minutes at 200 p.s.i. The British War Office rejected it because of its short range and low hitting power (amount of fuel discharged per shot). The Canadian Army, however, accepted it and arranged for its production in Canada. Although it was the first mechanized flame thrower in commercial production it was never used as such. Its production was discontinued in 1943 upon development of the "Wasp."

The "Wasp" Mark IIC. (Official nomenclature -- Flame Thrower Transportable No. 2 Mark IIC) ("C" for Canadian). The "Wasp" likewise was a British development. The Canadian modification consisted mainly of eliminating one fuel tank, leaving room on the left side well of the personnel carrier pit for a third member of the crew with a light machine gun or 2-inch mortar. The Mark IIC also had the advantage that

---

77/ (1) Ltr, CO 3d Bn, 13th Inf Regt to CO Carolina Sub-Sector, 17 Mar 42, Sub: Recommendations for Emplaced FT M1. (2) Ltr, CG N.Y.-Phila Sector to CG EDC, 26 Mar 42, sub: Emplaced Flame Throwers; Ltr, CG EDC to CG SOS, 10 May 42, sub: Emplaced Flame Throwers. (3) Memo, C Fld Ser Div OC CWS for AC/S, Opns Div WDGS, 19 May 42, no sub. In CMLWG.

78/ Memo, Req Div GSC for AC/S Opns Div WDGS, 14 May 42, sub: Emplaced Flame Throwers. In CMLWG.

79/ Ltr, C Tech Ser OC CWS to CG EA, 17 Jul 42, sub: Emplaced Flame Throwers. In CMLWG.

the carrier engine was accessible when the flame equipment was mounted, whereas, with the British model the fuel tanks had to be removed before engine maintenance could be carried out. Also, the carrier could be used in its normal role without removing the flame equipment while the British model could not. The Mark IIC had a fuel capacity of 75 Imperial gallons and an effective range of 100 yards with thickened fuel. Carbon dioxide or "Inert gas" was used as a propellant. Experience in France proved the Canadian model to be superior to that of the British model.[80]

2. **British.**

The "Lifebuoy". (Official nomenclature -- Flame Thrower, Portable, No. 2, Marks I and II). Development of this portable flame thrower commenced in 1941 and it was standardized as the Mark I in May 1942. The fuel system consisted of an annular fuel container of lifebuoy shape, with a spherical pressure container, holding hydrogen, in the central hole of the annular torus. The fuel and pressure assembly was connected to the flame pistol by means of a flexible hose. Hydrogen was used for pressure, and also for ignition in conjunction with a high tension spark and gasoline spray. The weight of the equipment when filled was sixty-four pounds. The fuel capacity was four gallons, which gave a duration of fire of ten seconds. The effective range was thirty to forty yards with thickened fuel. A total of 500 Mark I's were manufactured and used primarily for training purposes. In the autumn of 1943, the Mark II Model was introduced. Production of the Lifebuoy ceased in July 1944 after 7,500 had been made. Approximately 3,000 went to India and 3,000 to the 21st Army Group. The Lifebuoy did not function properly in combat, primarily because of defective workmanship in manufacture.

The "Ack-Pack." (Official nomenclature -- Flame Thrower, Portable No. 5, Mark I). This flame thrower was a redesign of the Lifebuoy, using lighter weight metals to reduce the weight to forty-eight pounds when loaded, employing nitrogen (or "Inert gas") as a propellant, and incorporating a cartridge ignition system. This model got little further than the experimental stage and only limited production was effected.

The "Wasp." (Official nomenclature -- Flame Thrower Transportable, No. 2, Marks I and II). The Mark I was standardized in the summer of 1942. It contained two fuel tanks with a total capacity of 100 Imperial gallons, was pressured by carbon dioxide, and the flame gun incorporated an electrical high tension spark to ignite a gasoline spray. The fuel assembly was stowed inside the Bren carrier while the

---

[80] Hist Monograph (British), part III, Flame Warfare, pp. 18-20. In CMLWG.

gun was mounted over the left front outside the vehicle armor. The range was 80 to 100 yards with thickened fuel. The Mark II was placed in production in November 1943 and differed from the Mark I in that the gun was redesigned so that it could be mounted in the Bren gun slit of the carrier. In June 1944 production was switched over to the Canadian Model IIC and by the end of the war the Mark IIC was accepted as the standard British carrier-borne flame thrower.

The Badger. This flame thrower was made by mounting the Wasp Mark II on the "Ram" personnel carrier. They became available in February 1945 and were used primarily by the Canadians.

The Churchill "Crocodile." (Also known as the "Cobra.") This consisted of a Churchill Mk. VII tank armed with a 75-mm. gun and a Besa machine gun mounted in the turret, and a Wasp Mark II flame gun mounted in the hull. Each tank towed a two-wheeled trailer containing 400 Imperial gallons of fuel which was sufficient to furnish approximately 100 shots of flame. Nitrogen pressure bottles were also located in the trailer. It took thirty minutes to raise the pressure in the system and once the pressure was raised it could not be sustained for long periods. The trailer, which weighed 12,600 pounds when filled, could be jettisoned by a quick release gear and was armored to protect against small arms fire. The range of this weapon was 110 to 120 yards. A total of 800 were manufactured and were employed considerably both in the Mediterranean and European Theaters of Operations.

The Sherman Crocodile (also known as the "Adder") differed from the Churchill Crocodile in that the flame thrower was hooked up to American Sherman medium tanks (M4 series) instead of to the British Churchill. Only six of these were made during the war and four of these were issued to the 2d U.S. Armored Division after crossing the Rhine. 81/

3. Australian.

The "Frog" was developed independently by the Australians for the "Matilda" tank. The main armament was sacrificed but the secondary armament was retained. The fuel was carried in light tanks: 80 gallons in the turret; four small tanks with a combined capacity of 32 gallons, in the ammunition lockers adjacent to the turret; two chain locker tanks of 15 gallons; and a 100-gallon jettisonable tank carried on the outside. Actually, the chain locker and jettisonable tanks were not

---

81/ For comprehensive treatment of British flame thrower developments, see Historical Monograph (British), part III, Flame Warfare. In CMLWG.

used owing principally to vulnerability and weight. The "Frog" therefore went into action with 112 gallons of fuel. Ignition was by means of an electric spark and gasoline jet. The novel feature of this flame thrower was the absence of a high pressure gas propellant system. The pressure was provided by a pump which was operated by a generator fed from special batteries. The flame thrower could be fired in 10 gallon shots with a range of 80 to 100 yards. The fuel was fed to an air loaded hydraulic accumulator with a capacity of 10 gallons which required about thirty-five seconds to recuperate, thereby causing a delay between shots. These tank flame throwers were first employed at Balik Papan in the Southwest Pacific in 1945.[82]

4. **Russian.** The Russian Army was equipped with flame throwers, which they used effectively. Well before the other Allied Nations, the Russians had set up directives for the organization of flame-throwing troops.[83] The Russians possessed three types of flame throwers: a static type, the Fougasse, which the Germans copied; a manpack type; and an armored vehicle type. Their manpack type was so constructed as to resemble closely the appearance of the normal pack and rifle of the infantryman. They developed thickened fuels, which gave their flame throwers a performance similar to our own.

There is no record of exchange of information with the Russians on flame throwers. In one instance the Russian representatives in Great Britain were queried as to the type of thickened fuel used by the Russian Army and their method of supply, i.e., whether factory or field mixed. The Russians replied that they had no thickened fuel. About two weeks later detailed directions for the use of such fuel were found in a Russian pamphlet which was captured by the Germans and in turn captured by the British. When confronted with the pamphlet, the Russians laughed, shrugged and said, "Well, why worry? You've got it now!" In February 1945 the British released three Wasps and three Crocodiles to the Russians, together with handbooks and a quantity of

---

[82] Ibid.

[83] (1) Translation of Russian Handbook on the Training of Flame Thrower Operators for Rifle Units, 1941. File of AGF, G-2 Div. (2) P.M. Sidorski, Flame Projectors and How to Combat Them, (Moscow), 1941. In CWS C Intell files.

Heavy No. 1 flame thrower fuel.[84]

E. Enemy Flame Throwers.

   1. <u>German</u>.

      <u>Portable Flame Throwers</u>. The German "Model 35" portable flame thrower was developed in 1937. Its greatest drawback was its weight, which was eighty pounds when loaded. Development was directed toward reducing this overload on the operator and the first step in this direction was the ring type flame thrower, "Model 40," comprising fuel and pressure containers in concentric rings, similar in appearance to the British "Lifebuoy." Although the design apparently was satisfactory, many difficulties arose in manufacturing the pilot models and the project was abandoned in 1940. The next development was a reversion to a simpler manufacturing form consisting of two cylindrical containers each with a horizontal axis of rotation, the lower one for fuel and the upper one for nitrogen. A small hydrogen cylinder for ignition was mounted on the flame gun itself. This was known as "Model 41." This model weighed only forty-seven pounds when loaded but this reduction in weight was at the expense of fuel capacity, which was only one and one-half gallons. Later, in 1942, it was found that the ignition system, under the conditions of extreme cold during the Russian campaign, was unreliable and a new flame gun was developed with a cartridge ignition system. This "Model 42" remained the standard German manpack flame thrower until the end of the war. Further developments continued with the view of increasing both the range and fuel capacity without increasing the weight. To meet the latter requirement, the scaling up of the "Model 42" was attempted but without success. A new design, "Model 43," weighing about fifty-three pounds when filled with two gallons of fuel, emerged, but only a few samples were made. To meet the demand for greater range, work was begun on "Model 44" and "Model 44A," the latter of which utilized cordite as a propellant, whereas other models had utilized nitrogen. Models 44 and 44A did not fulfill the requirement underlying their design and their fuel capacity was small, one gallon and one and one-half gallons, respectively. Samples became available and it was reported that the Army had accepted "Model 44A" as the future manpack flame thrower. The range of all German portable flame throwers was about twenty-five yards. The Germans were aware, as early as 1941, of the increased range obtained with thickened gasoline, and they also captured Russian fuels of this type.

---

[84] Hist Monograph (British), part III, Flame Warfare, Ch XXIII. In CMLWG.

Figure 8. German Model 42 Portable Flame Thrower.

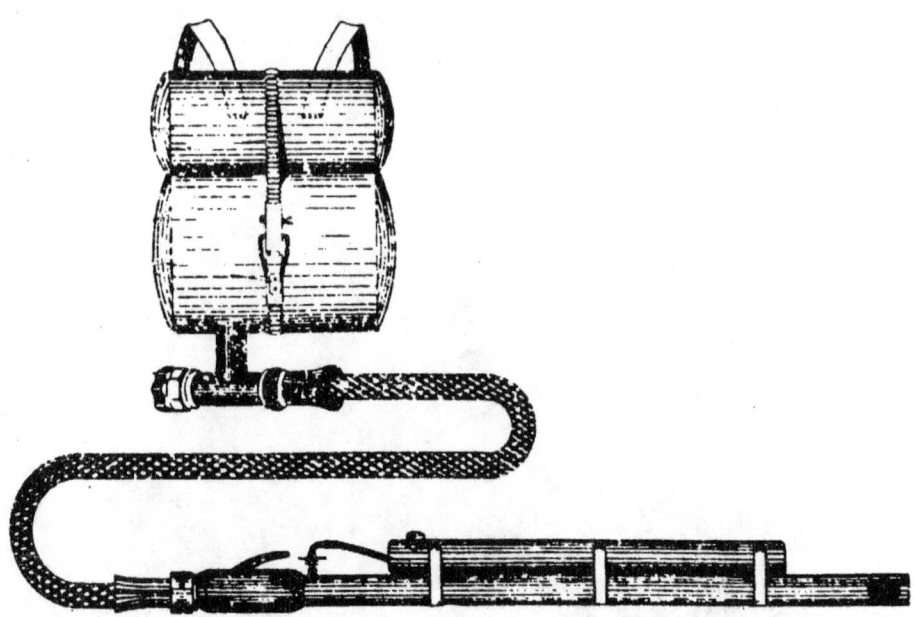

Figure 8a. German Model 41 Portable Flame Thrower, including gun assembly.

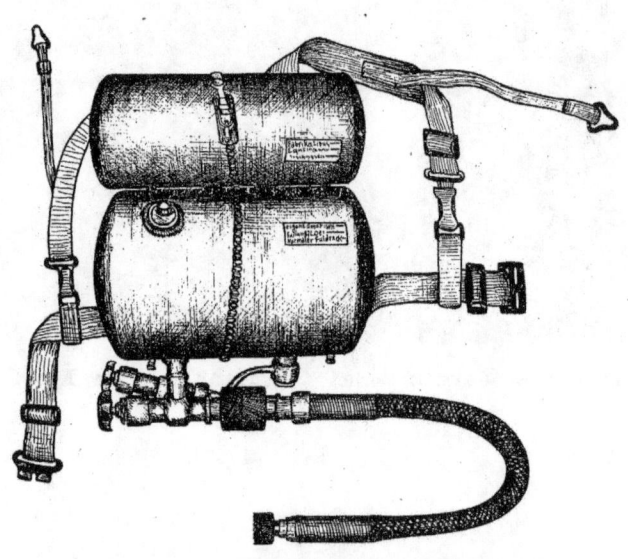

Figure 8b. German Model 41 Portable Flame Thrower, including gun assembly.

They were, however, short of stearate, and their synthetic gasoline did not lend itself to the production of a suitable thickened fuel.

The Germans are also reported to have developed and put into production by the end of 1944 a one-shot portable flame thrower for use by assault troops in close combat. This type, "Model 46" consisted of a cylindrical tube equipped with a pistol grip and trigger mechanism, was 23½ inches long, 2-3/4 inches in diameter, had a range of about thirty yards and gave a burst of a half-second duration. It appears, however, that this weapon never reached the troops.[85]

Mechanized Flame Throwers. Two models of tank flame throwers were developed by the Germans. The first of these, Pz. Kpfw. II tank mounting the Sd. Kfz. 122 flame thrower, consisted of two nitrogen operated flame projectors mounted in two small turrets set forward on the two track guards, each with 180° traverse. Each flame thrower was provided with thirty-five gallons of fuel, which was stored in externally fitted fuel tanks provided with armored shields. Ignition was by means of an acetylene flame. This model is reported to have been used "on a small scale" in the Spanish Civil War.[86]

The flame thrower for Pz. Kpfw II tank was superseded by a model for the Pz. Kpfw III tank. This was a pump operated type in which the flame gun replaced the normal tank gun in the turret and which it was disguised to represent. A total of 225 gallons of fuel was stored internally. Ignition was by means of gasoline and high tension spark. The effective range of German tank models was only about forty yards.

The Sd. Kfz. 25111 model flame thrower was mounted in an armored track vehicle. This unit had two large pump operated flame throwers mounted at the side of the vehicle and a small one at the rear. The fuel tanks were fitted against the inside wall on either side of the vehicle. The large flame throwers had a range of forty yards and were electrically ignited, while the small gun at the rear utilized cartridge ignition.

The Fougasse Flame Thrower. The Germans also developed a static type flame thrower which was copied from a Russian design. These

---

[85] Hist Monograph (British), part III, Flame Warfare, p. 107. In CMLWG.

[86] Capt. Henry Sorensen, "The History of Flame Warfare," Canadian Army Journal, Oct - Nov 1948, p. 18.

weapons were for employment in batteries against advancing troops at road blocks or on beaches, and were intended to form a flame barrage which was fired by remote control. It was a single-shot weapon with a fuel capacity of about five gallons. It had a range of forty to fifty yards and the fuel was expelled through a projector tube by pressure generated by a slow burning explosive.87/

2. Japanese.

Portable Flame Throwers. The Japanese entered the war with two models of portable flame throwers: Type 93 and Type 100. The fuel systems of these two models were identical. The guns differed only in that the Type 100 had been refined and the weight reduced from 10 to $8\frac{1}{2}$ pounds.88/ In principle, the ignition was superior in that it employed an incendiary cartridge to ignite the fuel. In practice, however, misfires were frequent because the incendiary mixture was contained in a paper cartridge which deteriorated on exposure to moisture. The firing mechanism was contained in the nozzle which incorporated a cylinder with ten holes for the ignition cartridges. The cylinder revolved on a cam operated by each stroke of the firing handle which also turned on the fuel. The fuel unit consisted of two tanks, connected by a manifold, with a fuel capacity of about $3\frac{1}{2}$ gallons. The pressure for propulsion was obtained from a relatively large pressure tank designed for only 250 p.s.i. The whole assembly was of light construction because high pressures were not employed. The low pressure system, however, resulted in short range.89/

Mechanized Flame Throwers. There is no record of the Japanese having employed flame tanks during the war. That they were equipped with such weapons is evidenced by the fact that eight were captured during the fighting on Luzon in 1945. The vehicles resembled somewhat the U.S. amphibious tractor or DUKW ("Duck"). These Japanese vehicles were equipped with three different arrangements of the flame thrower armament: one arrangement consisted of two flame guns, one forward and one aft, with a fuel tank located on the outside rear; another arrangement consisted of one flame gun mounted in the bow and two on each sponson; and a third consisted of one flame gun in the bow and three on each sponson. The ignition system was of the carbon arc type with

---

87/ (1) Hist Monograph (British), part III, Flame Warfare, p. 108.
(2) MID, Enemy Tactics in Chemical Warfare (Special Series No. 24), 1 Sep 44, p. 56. In CMLWG.

88/ Off C Cml O Hq USASOS, SWPA, CWS Tech Intell Summary No. 7, 1 Feb 44. In CMLWG.

89/ Ltr, 1st Lt Frank L. Schaf, Jr., C CWS Lab, Fort Mills, P.I., to Cml O USAFFE, 19 Feb 42, sub: Japanese Flame Thrower--Physical Examination. In CMLWG.

Figure 9. A Marine Demonstrates a Japanese Flame Thrower Captured at the Battle of Tenaru River, Guadalcanal.

current take-off from the engine generator.90/

3. **Italian.**

The Portable Type. The Italians may be considered pioneers in the endeavor to make flame throwers an important weapon of modern warfare.91/ Both portable and mechanized types had been developed before World War II, and the British encountered a number of the portable type during the siege of Tobruk in Libya.92/ It was known that in both North Africa and Sicily, the tables of organization of the Italian Army provided for flame thrower companies composed of 150 men, equipped with at least forty-five portable flame throwers.93/ However, no report has come to hand indicating that these companies were established. Likewise, there is no report of the Italians having ever made use of their equipment in combat. Two models of portable flame throwers were captured from the Italians, "Model 35" and "Model 41." The "Model 41" (Lanciafiamme 41) was a modification of the earlier model. It had a fuel capacity of 1.8 gallons. There were two fuel tanks, between which was located the pressure cylinder, in much the same manner as with the United States models. The assembly was made of aluminum alloy with brass fittings. The flame gun was of tubular aluminum alloy fastened to the tanks by a ball and socket joint for maneuverability. The gun was fifty inches long and had a control handle at the rear, very similar to a motorcycle handle bar grip. This handle was pulled rearward to operate the gun. The nozzle was fitted with a tapered head about six inches long, into one side of which was fitted a spark plug. This head also provided for mounting a pull-type Roman candle igniter as an auxiliary igniter. The spark plug was connected to a small generator mounted below the pressure tank under a false front. The generator was operated by a small fly-wheel which rotated the generator shaft by action of air pressure when the control handle was opened. The current generated was sufficient to throw an adequate spark for ignition. The weight of the weapon when filled was forty pounds. It had a range of seventeen to twenty-two yards with Italian

---

90/ I Corps, Cml Intell Periodic Rpt No. 9, 13 Jun 45, Incl. No. 2. In Sixth Army Cml Sec Records, 319.1, ORB.

91/ MEF "Technical Intelligence Summary," No. 12, 27 Dec 40, p. 3. AGF, G-2 Div.

92/ Capt. Henry Sorensen, "The History of Flame Warfare" in Canadian Army Journal, Oct - Nov 1948, p. 18.

93/ (1) MA Rpt, Egypt, No. 947-43, 16 Jan 43. (2) MA Rpt, Italy, No. 160, 30 Aug 43.

fuel, and the duration of fire was five to six seconds.[94]

Mechanized Type. The Italians developed a pump operated tank flame thrower for which the fuel was carried in a trailer. This model was known as the "C.V. 33." A captured unit was tested in the Middle East where its possibilities were reported to be in the defense of vital points and permanent fortifications, or against low-flying aircraft. The following account describes this weapon and what appears to have been its first employment:[95]

> The re-appearance of the flame-thrower as a weapon of war occurred during the Italian-Abyssinian War, 1935-36, when the Italians employed the first tank-borne flame thrower against the Abyssinians with reputed success. The tank employed, the CV 33, was very light (approximately five tons), with a machine gun and flame gun mounted co-axially in the fore hull. It was of the trailer type, having a fuel capacity of 100 gallons and a range of approximately 30-40 metres. One of these was captured during the Second World War at Tobruk, but there is no official report of its use in action.

F. Flame Thrower Fuels.

One of the most important factors in the successful operation of flame throwers is that of providing fuel with optimum properties. Until the first part of World War II, flame thrower fuel consisted of crude oil or other heavy oil to which sufficient gasoline or volatile fraction had been added for the purpose of lowering the flash point to a temperature where ignition was insured. Neither the Germans nor the Japanese developed thickened gasoline suitable for flame thrower fuels. The enemy was, however, aware of the value of high viscosity fuels and usually added as much asphalt or pitch as could be tolerated for ignition. Low viscosity fuels gave a horrific blast of flame of short range and duration. Furthermore, with a 12 o'clock wind, the operator was in danger of being smothered.

---

[94] (1) Report of Cml O, Seventh Army, 24 Jul 43, SPCWN 470.71.
(2) MA Rpt, London 47581, 7 Jun 43. In CMLWG.

[95] MEF, Tech Intell Sum No. 36, 18 Aug 41.

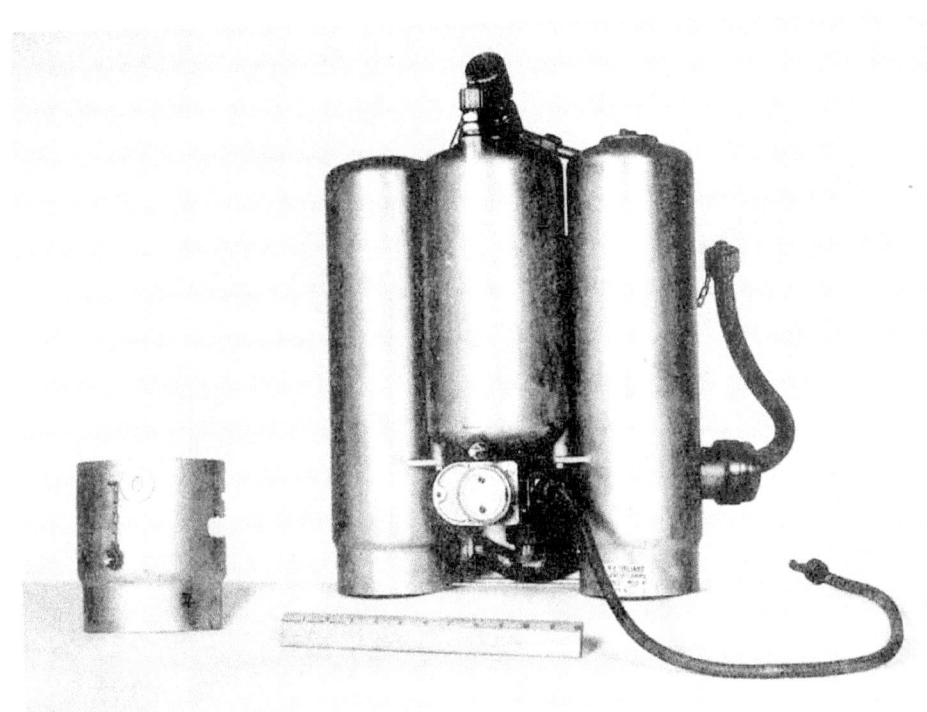

Figure 10. Italian Model 41 Portable Flame Thrower.

Late in World War I, the American University research group recognized the importance of increasing the viscosity of flame thrower fuels without increasing vapor pressure. That is, if gasoline could be thickened by the addition of a small amount of high viscosity material, the vapor pressure would not be affected materially. The practice of making lubricating greases by heating petroleum oils with sodium, calcium or aluminum soaps is an old art. Sodium stearate (soap) was investigated but proved to be a poor choice because it failed to increase viscosity, giving instead a material with the appearance of applesauce. However, this basic research laid the ground work for the successful developments carried out during World War II.

As the war clouds gathered, interest was revived in thickened fuel for various types of incendiaries, including flame throwers. During 1941 and 1942 the Chemical Warfare Service and the National Defense Research Committee conducted studies on such thickeners as rubber, copolymers of butadiene-styrene and butadiene-acrylonitrile, polyisobutylene, polymethylmethacrylate, polyisobutyl-methacrylate, stearates of sodium, calcium and aluminum, and aluminum naphthenate. These agents were studied alone and in various mixtures with such hydrocarbons as terpentine, benzene, divinylacetylene and gasoline. A mixture containing about 75 percent of the aluminum soap of coconut fatty acids and 25 percent aluminum naphthenate proved to be the most practicable. This product was called "napalm" ("na" from naphthenate and "palm" from the coconut fatty acids). In November 1942 specifications for napalm were drafted and full-scale production by one manufacturer started in January 1943. By the end of 1943 ten manufacturers were producing napalm.[96]

The first shipments of napalm arrived in the theaters during the summer of 1943.[97] The early lots were packed in cardboard cartons and the napalm, being hygroscopic, soon picked up moisture and became unserviceable.[98] These early shipments had to be discarded and it was not until late 1943 that shipments of dependable quality became avail-

---

[96] Tech Div Rpt of Act, pp. 43-45.

[97] (1) 1st Ind WD ASF to OC CWS, 2 Jun 43, on ltr, Hq USAFFE, Off Cml O, 11 May 43, sub: Flame Thrower Fuel (Gasoline Thickener). (2) Ltr, Hq USAFFE, Off Cml O, to 2d Engr Sp Brig, 1 Jul 43, sub: Fuel, Napalm, Thickener. In CMLWG.

[98] Ltr, Hq USASOS, Off Cml O to Adv Hq USASOS, 10 Jan 44, sub: Unserviceable Type A Napalm. In Sixth A Cml Sec Records, 470.71, ORB.

able to troops in the field.99/ Napalm, therefore, became the standard gasoline thickener used by American forces throughout the war, although its properties were far from ideal. The viscosity obtained depended somewhat on the type of gasoline used and no standard grade for use as flame thrower fuel was ever made available. The stability of thickened gasoline was not dependable. In many cases where fuel was pre-mixed before an operation, the using troops later found a product with a viscosity little greater than that of raw gasoline.100/ The amount of moisture present affected the viscosity, and apparently the stability, obtained. Dry gasoline was never available in the field because of the presence of moisture in the container.

Beginning in 1944, research groups of the Chemical Warfare Service and National Defense Research Committee conducted intensive studies to establish the optimum percentages of napalm to be used in flame thrower fuel, but the field accepted the results of these studies hesitantly, and the percentages to be used remained an open question throughout the war. A mixture of 8 percent napalm was recommended by the Chemical Warfare Service in 1942. In August 1943, the Corps of Engineers recommended 4.5 percent, whereas the Infantry Board favored a "bushy" flame and recommended a 3 percent mixture. In October 1944 the Infantry Board approved the use of 4.2 percent napalm to which sufficient water had been added to give a viscosity equivalent to a 3 percent fuel. The psychological effect of flame warfare still had its supporters at the end of the war and the hot blast of flame with its short range was still being recommended in certain quarters. As a result of scientific investigations by the United States, Canada, and Great Britain, it was definitely established that a roaring blaze outside of a pillbox did little harm to the occupants and that only fuel burning inside was effective. These results emphasized the necessity of a fuel that could penetrate an embrazure at an appreciable range. Unthickened fuel was proven to be almost worthless at ranges in excess of ten yards. One difficulty observed with napalm was that the burning rate slowed down considerably when gasoline was thickened sufficiently to give maximum range. This weakness had not been overcome at the end of the war.101/ In this

---

99/ Ltr, Cml O Americal Div to CG Americal Div, 27 Nov 43, sub: Flame Thrower Fuel. In CMLWG.

100/ Pers ltr, Cml O USAFPOA to AC CWS, 16 May 45. In CMLWG.

101/ Ibid.

connection, the Canadians actually developed highly compounded fuels that gave ranges up to 300 yards with mechanized flame throwers.

Owing to the scarcity of good quality napalm in the South Pacific Area during the early part of 1944, steps were taken to procure locally a gasoline thickener. Through the efforts of the chemical officer, 25th Infantry Division, then stationed at Aukland, New Zealand, a gasoline thickener, composed of the aluminum salts of naphthenic and stearic acids, was obtained in quantity. This thickening agent became known as "Metalex." Cresylic acid was used as a peptizing agent and when mixed with gasoline a fuel of honey-like consistency was obtained. This thickener was used successfully by the 25th Infantry Division throughout the war, first for training and later in combat during the Luzon campaign.[102]

The British thickener was known as FRAS (Fuel Research Aluminum Stearate). The fuel was supplied to troops pre-mixed and ready for use. It consisted of gasoline thickened with aluminum stearate and stabilized with xylenols (or cresols). The British fuel was widely used by American forces in the European Theater and some units employed it in preference to napalm.[103] FRAS had to be machine mixed in a special plant, whereas napalm could be either pre-mixed or issued as a powder and mixed in the field by the using troops. Napalm thickened fuel was stiffer than FRAS fuel and gave greater range. FRAS fuel, on the other hand, was pourable and burned with greater vigor on the target. Furthermore, there was a tendency for napalm gel to channel in the fuel tanks, resulting in incomplete exhaustion of the fuel.

---

[102] Cml O 25th Inf Div, Rpt on "Metalex" Flame Thrower Fuel Thickener, 30 Nov 44. In Tab B to USAFFE Bd Rpt No. 191, 27 Jan 45.

[103] CWS Sec ETOUSA, "Activities of Technical Division," 8 Aug 45.

CHAPTER II

SOUTH PACIFIC AREA (SOLOMON ISLANDS CAMPAIGN)

A. Guadalcanal.

The landing of the 1st Marine Division on Guadalcanal and Tulagi on 7 August 1942 marked the beginning of an island hopping campaign that was to culminate three years later when the last of the outlying islands that protected the Japanese homeland had been taken. Initially, the primary mission of the Marines was to secure Henderson Field and keep it in operation. This mission was accomplished without a great deal of opposition from Japanese defenses. For the first three months opposition consisted mainly of air and naval attacks and determined attacks by Japanese ground troops. During October and November the Marines were reinforced by the Americal Division which had been activated in New Caledonia for that purpose. The 2d Marine Division arrived 4 November and the 25th Infantry Division landed in December to relieve the 1st Marine Division early in 1943. The 25th was committed to action on 5 January 1943 and attacked on 10 January. After reinforcements arrived, offensive action destined to clear the Japanese troops from the island was stepped up.1/

It was at this time (November, December and January) that American forces first encountered a type of defense, manned by an enemy who was willing to fight until he was killed, which proved to be such a lucrative target for flame throwers throughout the war. On Guadalcanal these defenses consisted of bunkers constructed of coconut logs in such a manner as to provide a port about four to six inches high on a level with the top of the ground. The top of the bunker was covered with alternate layers of logs and coral and thoroughly camouflaged. These bunkers proved to be impervious to artillery and mortar fire. They were generally located on steep inclines with a field of fire down the deep valleys or slopes which they defended. In general the bunkers were manned by from five to ten Japanese with one or two machine guns. Also, one bunker usually constituted the position's main defense and was not mutually supported by nearby bunkers. Because of their location on the terrain, it was usually possible to approach them from behind through defilade.2/ Even though these positions could be reached by the soldier, they were not easily taken with ordinary infantry weapons such as hand grenades and sub-machine guns. The only opening on the

---

1/(1) OPD Pacific Diary. (2) MID World War II Chronology, Aug-Dec 1942.

2/ Extract of Ltr, Cml O XIV Corps to Cml O USAFFE, 11 Aug 43. Sixth Ar Cml Sect Records, 470.71 PFT, ORB.

- 38 -

back side of the bunker was a tunnel which the occupants used for an entrance. It was possible to close the tunnel with explosives but this did not kill the defenders who continued to fire through the ports at the front and sides. To instantly neutralize such positions, a weapon that would fire around corners was needed. The portable flame thrower offered such possibilities.

The Table of Equipment for the Marine Division authorized seventy-two (72) M1 portable flame throwers for the engineer combat battalion while in the infantry divisions twenty-four were authorized for the engineer combat battlion. At this time the status of training of engineer troops in the employment of flame throwers was not satisfactory and in December 1942 a CWS officer from the Army conducted a short school for the Marine engineers in order to test the weapon against some Japanese bunkers which were holding up the advance. The first employment of the M1 portable flame thrower by U. S. troops in World War II took place simultaneously on 15 January 1943 in two different places on Guadalcanal. Personnel participating in the weapon's inauguration was drawn from the combat engineers of the 8th Marines, 2d Marine Division, operating near the beach, and from the combat engineers of the 35th Infantry, 25th Infantry Division, attacking in the Mt. Austin sector. As used by the Marines, the flame thrower proved effective against enemy beach installations. Under cover of rifle and automatic rifle fire, two Marine engineers crawled into position and fired the flame thrower into a bunker (twenty-five yards away) which had proved troublesome. Two of the enemy managed to escape, but five bodies were found in the bunker. Of the two that escaped, one lay three feet from the escape hatch and the other had gone fifteen feet before he succumbed from the effects of the flame. These Marines destroyed two more bunkers the same day. 3/

On 15 January 1943, the Assistant Chief of Staff, D-3, 2d Marine Division, conferred with the Chemical Officer, Americal Division, regarding a school for training flame thrower operators for the Marines. The school was started immediately and troops from the 2d Marine Division and later from the 25th Infantry Division were given sufficient technical instruction in the flame thrower to enable them to operate, service and maintain the weapon. Upon completion of the training a situation soon arose requiring the use of a flame thrower. A large bunker situated near the top of a slope had held up the advance of a battalion for several days. Small arms fire was placed on the bunker while a team of two men spent four hours crawling around to the rear

---

3/
On 15 Jan, FT's were employed near the beach by the 8th Marines (2d Div) and on Mt. Austin by the 35th Inf (25th Div). See 35th Inf Jrnl 15 Jan 43 and Opn Rpt 8th Marine Regt for 15 Jan.

of it. The flame thrower was fired at a range of twenty-five yards and ten Japanese were killed. The flame thrower had established itself as a formidable weapon to those troops who had used it and it continued to be used, as a last resort, throughout the mopping-up stage which lasted until the middle of February 1943.

1. **Problems Encountered and Lessons Learned from the Guadalcanal Operation**. No engineer personnel were available due to road building and construction activities. Therefore, flame throwers were issued on the basis of two per infantry battalion pioneer platoon. Owing to the lack of spare parts, maintenance activities were limited mostly to the interchange of serviceable parts on flame throwers which had become partially defective because of improper storage. By such cannibalization the 1st Marine Division was able to salvage and use forty-eight of their authorized supply of seventy-two flame throwers. Likewise, in the 25th Infantry Division, twenty-one out of thirty-five flame throwers authorized for the entire division were put into operating condition. Among defects noted, the most important one was the loss of over one-half of the original 2,000 pounds pressure in most of the nitrogen and hydrogen cylinders. This was the result of: (1) pin holes in spongy metal cylinder walls; (2) malfunctioning of valves due to improper seating or excessive tightness; (3) stripped or off-size threads at gas line connection; (4) absence of nozzle caps. Ignition failures were caused by the spark generator unit short circuiting either through metallic contact or through moisture, as well as by fouling of spark plugs by the fuel. Poorly adjusted pressure regulating valves caused range variations of as much as fifteen yards. Gas lines were often twisted, broken or plugged up. Essential parts and tools were missing from both the accessories kits and the service kits.4/

B. New Georgia.

Beginning on 15 July 1943, the operation to capture Munda airfield in New Georgia was placed under the command of XIV Corps. The initial landing had been made on 18 June at Segi Point on Rendova Island which is located five miles south of Munda. On 1 July, Munda airfield was brought under fire by 155-mm. guns located on Rendova six miles away. Immediately following the landing on Rendova, elements of the 37th and 43d Infantry Divisions began landing in the Rice Anchorage and Zanana Beach areas respectively on New Georgia, enveloping the west end of

---

4/
(1) Rpt, Cml O Americal Div, n.d., sub: Hist of Amer Div Cml Sec from Org on Jan 23, 42 to Sep 30, 43, Sect 15. In CMLWG. (2) Ltr, Cml O 25th Inf Div to OC CWS, 25 Apr 43, sub: Rpt of CW Activities on Guadalcanal Island, pp. 3-7. In CMLWG.

the island.5/ The 161st RCT, 25th Inf Div, was sent in to reinforce the two divisions after determined opposition had slowed down the attack. It was soon learned that Munda airfield was protected by a series of mutually supporting bunkers organized in depth. The whole area was covered with jungle. Lambetti Plantation, which was adjacent to the airfield, had not been kept up and was covered with jungle growth. Defense positions had been organized on both the high ground and the low ground. These emplacements had been prepared for a considerable length of time and were usually covered with logs upon which coral had been placed to form a mound. Jungle vegetation had had time to grow and form a natural camouflage making the positions extremely difficult to locate. Each bunker or emplacement usually contained a machine gun and one or two men. The ports were located at ground level and were five or six inches high and twelve or fourteen inches long. Usually there were ports on at least two sides for mutual support. Narrow lanes of fire of only a few yards in length had been provided by removing the least possible amount of vegetation. The enemy would sight his machine gun along this very narrow path and squeeze the trigger when he observed the ankles or legs of our soldiers. As usual, snipers were liberally located throughout the defensive sector. These snipers would often fire and quickly move to a nearby position.6/

The XIV Corps had assumed command of the forces in the South Pacific area on 21 January 1943 and, after noting the successful employment of the portable flame thrower during the Guadalcanal operation, had conducted CWS schools in the technical aspects of the flame throwers in preparation for the New Georgia operation. Steps had been taken to train operators in the pioneer and ammunition platoons and each infantry battalion was issued as many as two of the twenty-four (24) flame throwers authorized for the engineer battalion. However, neither the 37th nor the 43d Division had seen action on Guadalcanal and the defenses encountered on New Georgia did not lend themselves to envelopment as readily as those found at Guadalcanal. As a result, no attempt had been made to employ flame throwers during the early part of the operation.

On the morning of 25 July, all units of the 37th and 43d Infantry Divisions on the line were ordered to attack and break through the defenses that were holding up the advance. The main effort was placed on the right of the line in the zones of the 148th and 169th Infantry

---

5/
  Biennial Rpt, CofS USA, 1 Jul 43 to 30 Jun 45, p. 67.

6/
  Extract of ltr Cml O XIV Corps to Cml O USAFFE, 15 Sep 43. In 6th Ar Cml Sect Records, 470.71 PFT, ORB.

across a 300-yard ridge extending inland from the Lambetti Plantation. The main effort succeeded in breaking through the enemy's outer defenses but the two regiments broke contact with the 103d Infantry on the left, which had been unable to advance since 18 July. The 169th Regiment was facing a strong point in the middle of the Lambetti Plantation. This strongpoint was about 800 yards from the Jap-held Munda airfield and consisted of three coconut log bunkers built at ten yard intervals. Their machine gun fire interlocked in a lethal blaze of cross-fire. The three bunkers were so well camouflaged in the thick, waist-high grass which covered the coral island that infantry patrols had moved to within three yards of the positions without spotting them. In the tropical climate piles of coconuts sprout into small mounds of vegetation within a few weeks. Taking advantage of this fact, the Japanese had built their bunkers to resemble coconut piles and it was almost impossible to distinguish the bunkers from the innocent mounds which dotted the plantation. It was imperative that the strong point be neutralized immediately because the main effort could not advance further without exposing the flank to enfilade fire. The corps commander dispatched a CWS officer to confer with the regimental commander relative to the use of flame throwers on this position. The conference took place at 0800 26 July and a plan was approved. Six volunteers were obtained from Company C, 118th Engineer Combat Battalion, only one of which knew anything about flame thrower tactics. The six men were instructed for one hour in the operation of the M1A1 flame thrower and how to approach the positions. A team of seven flame throwers with operators manned by engineers reported to the battalion commander to carry out the attack. The jump-off took place at 1225 on 26 July. The operators crawled seventy-five (75) yards to the company CP and from that point the men spread out so that there were two flame throwers on each flank and three on the center bunker. Each operator carried a thermite grenade for use in case of a mis-fire. At 1154 the artillery laid down a thirty-minute preparation. As the barrage lifted, the infantry moved up ten yards and stopped twenty (20) yards short of the bunkers, covering them with small arms fire. A couple of bursts were received from the bunker on the left but the other two remained silent. At 1305 the center flame thrower operator had reached a point fifteen yards from the approximate location of the center bunker. Two of the operators opened fire, criss-crossing the stream of flame in order to burn off the grass. The bunkers became visible and the other flame throwers opened fire. The whole action of the flame thrower firing lasted less than a minute. Upon examination two bodies were found in the center bunker and one in each of the end bunkers. These bunkers were thirteen feet square inside and four feet deep. The news of the successful employment of the flame thrower on this strong point passed up and down the line and all units began to bring up their flame throwers. During the next five days thirty more bunkers were neutralized with flame. Munda airfield was captured on 5 August 1943. The flame thrower continued to be employed during the mopping-up stage and accounted for a total of seventy-four bunkers.7/

One instance was reported in which the Japanese attempted to use a flame thrower against our troops. One of our tanks was thoroughly covered with flame thrower fuel which failed to ignite. Five or six Japanese flame throwers, filled and ready for use, were captured. These flame throwers were of the same type as those captured at Guadalcanal and were equipped with a cartridge ignition system, the principle of which was superior to the electrical ignition system employed on the M1A1 model, with which our troops were equipped. However, the ignition cartridge employed by the Japanese flame thrower was not waterproof, which appeared to account for the ignition failure.

1. **Problems Encountered and Lessons Learned from the New Georgia Operation.** Flame thrower operators had not been trained in such a way that the use of ignition switch prior to the operation of the fuel valve was automatic. Adequate infantry support was not forthcoming and about six operators were killed or wounded. In some instances not one rifleman was furnished as protection, and in all cases there was practically no reconnaissance. Flame thrower operators were frequently sent into action informed that there was only one enemy machine gun position to be cleared, but when the operator arrived he was confronted by a dozen bunkers instead of one. Consequently, the flame thrower proved powerless to cope with such situations. Guides were frequently lacking and the operators were merely given the general direction of a bunker or other enemy position. Proper reconnaissance would have indicated a demand for intense artillery and mortar fire on a position before attempting to employ flame throwers.

Company and battalion commanders were familiar with neither the technical limitations of the flame thrower nor the correct principles for its tactical employment. In addition to a flame thrower school for operators, a tactical school, at which the attendance of every company commander should be mandatory, should have been conducted. Although a number of men from each unit were trained as operators prior to the operation, these men were given other duties, such as water and ammunition details, and were not available as flame thrower operators when needed. There were cases of company commanders, ignorant of flame thrower tactics, selecting untrained men and ordering them forward to "burn out the Japs." In such instances, and with inadequate reconnaissance, neither the company commander nor the untrained operator knew the strength of the position to be attacked. Application of the age old principle of envelopment would have been possible more often

---

7/ Capt. James F. Olds, Jr., CWS, "Flamethrowers Front and Center," CW Bull, Vol 30, No. 3, Jun-Jul 44, pp. 6-8.

if a proper reconnaissance had been made and if artillery and mortar fire had eliminated most of the supporting fire from snipers and open positions before attempting to employ flame throwers.8/

Due to an improper functioning ignition system, a number of operators were obliged to light the hydrogen at the nozzle with a match. Thermite grenades were also used for emergency ignition of fuel which had been projected on targets but had not been ignited upon projection. However, because of duds, the M14 thermite grenade was not altogether satisfactory. The operator usually strapped the fuel tanks to his back and carried the flame thrower as it was designed to be carried. However, experience showed that this method offered a substantial target to the enemy. Many operators dragged the flame thrower along with them as they crawled forward through the jungle undergrowth, thereby presenting a smaller target.9/

At the completion of the New Georgia operation the chemical officer, 37th Infantry Division, recommended that the plan of training operators in infantry and combat engineer companies be continued and that the flame throwers be held in battalion supply to be furnished on call.10/

C. Bougainville.

In preparation for the Bougainville Operation, the CWS officers conducted flame thrower schools to train operators in infantry and engineer units in the South Pacific Area. A small amount of napalm had been received and experiments were conducted to determine a suitable mixture for use in the jungle. It was found that the 8 percent mixture prescribed by the War Department in TM 3-375, May 1943, was unsuitable for use in the presence of heavy vegetation because the gelled gasoline clung to the heavy undergrowth and burned without

---

8/ Ltr, Cml O Interm Sec USASOS to Cml O Adv Sec, 9 Jun 44. In Sixth A Cml Sect Records, 353 FT Tng, ORB.

9/ Extracts Ltr, Cml O XIV Corps to C Cml O USAFFE, 15 Sep 43, no sub. In Sixth A Cml Sect Records, 470.71 PFT, ORB.

10/ Rpt, Hq 37th Inf Div, O of Cml O, 21 Aug 43, sub: Chemical Operations during Munda Campaign. In Hist Records Sect, AGO.

Figure 11. New Georgia: An Infantryman Sprays a Japanese Pillbox During Mopping-up Operations.

Figure 12. Bougainville: A Flame Thrower Assault Party Advances to Position.

Figure 13. Bougainville: A Flame Thrower Operator Moving Up.

Figure 14. An Assault Party of the Americal Division Attacking a Series of Jap Pillboxes Near Torokina River, Bougainville.

Figure 15. Flame Thrower Assault Party Attacking a Jap Pillbox While Mopping Up on Bougainville in March 1944.

Figure 16. The Flame Thrower Neutralizes a Japanese Bunker on Bougainville, March 1944.

Figure 17. Burning Out Japanese Bunkers.

Figure 18. Bougainville: Flame Thrower Operator of 129th Infantry Inspects Japanese Bunker After Flame Attack.

Figure 19. Bougainville: A Dead Jap at the Entrance of His Pillbox.

reaching the target.11/

At 0645 hours on 1 November 1943, the Third Marine Division, under I Amphibious Corps, began the assault to secure a beachhead at Empress Augusta Bay, with the primary mission of seizing ground to establish an airbase. Only light opposition was encountered during the first few hours, but as the beachhead was extended the enemy counter-attacked and losses began to mount. On 8 November, the 37th Infantry Division began landing. The command passed to XIV Corps on 15 December 1943, and the Americal Division was brought up two weeks later. The attack was resumed early in December, but the Marines were stopped at Hill 1000,12/ where the Japs had dug into the side of a cliff and had emplaced four heavy and five light machine guns. The hill held up the advance for more than a week, during which time it was dive-bombed and pounded relentlessly by artillery and 4.2-inch chemical mortars. Finally, after the 21st Marines had been repulsed in one of their many attempts to take the hill, the regimental commander, at a chemical officer's suggestion, ordered six M1A1 flame throwers to take position with the infantry. One-half hour later the artillery laid down a barrage and as it lifted the flame thrower operators, supported by the infantry, moved in. These operators, trained during September and October, were familiar with the job to be done. Within a few minutes the flame throwers had neutralized the position, killing thirty-one Japs and permitting the infantry to secure the hill.13/

The flame thrower was reported to have been employed successfully many other times by both army and marines during the latter stages of the operation. Also, many inherent weaknesses of the M1A1 flame thrower were reported to have caused considerable trouble to troops during employment. Failure of the diaphragm in the pressure regulator was probably the most common cause of trouble and the shortage of spare regulators and diaphragms caused many flame throwers to be deadlined. Ignition failures due to dead batteries were also encountered; hydrogen lines were too fragile and broke frequently; hydrogen cylinder

---

11/
Extracts from ltr, Cml O XIV Corps to C Cml O USAFFE, 11 Aug 43, sub:(?)

In Sixth A Cml Sect Records, 470.71 PFT, ORB.

12/
Hill 1000 on Marine maps is the same as Hill 608 on Army maps.

13/
Capt. James F. Olds, Jr., "Early Bougainville Experiments" **CW Bull**, Vol. 30, No. 4, Aug-Sep-Oct 44, p. 7.

valves were difficult to keep tight and, once tight, pliers were required to open them. During the latter part of the operation M2-2 flame throwers were employed. They were equipped with Hoke pressure regulators which proved entirely unsatisfactory. Two of these regulators failed in actual combat. The operators had worked their way laboriously up to the objective, opened the pressure cylinder valve and the safety discs blew out. They were able to retire without casualty but they had failed to accomplish their mission. This incident temporarily destroyed the confidence of 37th Infantry Division operators in the fuel unit of the M2-2 flame thrower which was subsequently adapted to the fuel unit of the old M1A1 model.[14]

D. Fuels Developed.

Prior to the receipt of napalm in the South Pacific Area during the second quarter of 1943, liquid fuels were used in the flame thrower. These fuels consisted of various mixtures of gasoline with Diesel oil, motor oil and navy bunker oil. The large volume of flame and heavy black smoke produced was considered advantageous in areas where heavy vegetation covered the ground, since the large burst of flame was effective in burning off vegetation around a bunker. Both the smoke and the flame produced some screening effect and the large volume of flame covered a large target, making it unnecessary to score a direct hit on the ports of a bunker. However, the range obtained with liquid fuels was limited to approximately twenty yards, and it was felt that this range could be increased considerably with the use of napalm. Early reports on the use of napalm in the jungle were adverse, principally because Section VII, TM 3-375, May 1943, prescribed a mixture of 8 percent by weight of napalm which gave a gelatinized fuel instead of a viscous, thixotropic liquid. In November 1943, the chemical officer, 25th Infantry Division, reported that liquid flame thrower fuels were highly effective in the Solomon Islands against enemy pillboxes which were not easily reduced by other weapons. The comparatively short range of the liquid fuels made such operations hazardous for the flame thrower operator and the longer range of the standard gelatinized fuel (5.25 pounds per ten gallons of gasoline) tended to reduce this hazard. Combat experience, however, revealed the following deficiencies in the newer fuel: (1) it tended to stick to vegetation without penetrating the thick jungle growth; (2) it did not readily penetrate dugouts except from a position perpendicular to the entrance; (3) it required accurate aiming at well camouflaged and frequently invisible targets concealed behind dense undergrowth; (4) its

---

[14] Rpt of Activities of Flamethrower Team, SWPA and SPA, 22 Nov 44, Incl 3, pp. 16-17. In CMLWG.

incendiary and psychological effects were inferior to those of liquid fuels; (5) its preparation was complicated by the rapid setting at tropical temperatures; and (6) extra units of this gelatinized fuel could not be issued to front line troops because allowances of filling kits were inadequate to permit refilling of fuel tanks.15/ Also, early shipments of napalm were made in cardboard cartons and deteriorated in the tropics to such an extent that it was not dependable. One such shipment was received by a marine organization in the South Pacific and failed to thicken gasoline. A sample was forwarded to the Office of the Chief of Chemical Warfare Service which reported in a letter dated 14 July 1943 that the defects of early shipments had been recognized and that it would probably be six months before the defects could be overcome and shipments to the theaters resumed.16/

During the last quarter of 1943, experiments were conducted on Guadalcanal to find a fuel that would combine the features of both gelatinized and liquid fuels. A study was made of various mixtures of gasoline, Diesel oil and crankcase oil, ungelatinized or gelatinized in varying degrees, by use of various ratios of thickening agent. It was concluded that a mixture consisting of equal parts of gasoline and Diesel oil gelatinized with 2.4 pounds of napalm per ten gallons gave the most desirable results. This mixture produced a hot, smoky, bushy flame which was favored in jungle operations for screening, clearing vegetation, and for psychological effect. This mixture gave a range of thirty to thirty-five yards which was considerable improvement over the range obtained with liquid fuels not containing napalm. Also, the fuel was sufficiently fluid to permit filling of flame throwers in the field without using a filling pump.17/ In November 1943 the Americal Division, after extensive tests, reported a mixture of fifteen gallons of gasoline, five gallons of Diesel oil and 5.3 pounds of napalm as being the best fuel found. This fuel gave a range of forty yards with a good volume of flame and smoke. These results were published by the Chief of CWS in January 1944 and constituted the first information made available to the theaters on increasing the range of liquid

---

15/
  Ltr Cml O 25th Inf Div to C CWS, 3 Nov 43, sub: Test of Flamethrower Fuel Mixtures. In CMLWG.

16/
  Ltr ACCWS Fld Opns to Cml O SPA, 14 Jul 43, sub: Defective Napalm. 470.6. In CMLWG.

17/
  Ltr Cml O 25th Inf Div to C CWS, 3 Nov 43, sub: Test of Flamethrower Fuel Mixtures. In CMLWG.

fuels by the addition of less than 8 percent napalm. 18/

Owing to the scarcity of napalm in the South Pacific Area during the early part of 1944, steps were taken to procure a gasoline thickener locally. At this time the 25th Infantry Division was sent to New Zealand for rest and recuperation and the division chemical officer arranged for the purchase of a thickener from Morcom-Greene, Ltd., Auckland, New Zealand. The telegraphic code name of Morcom-Greene, Ltd. was "Metalex" and the thickener accordingly became known as "Metalex." It was composed primarily of the aluminum salts of naphthenic and stearic acid and could be peptized with cresylic acid when used to thicken gasoline. Substantial quantities of Metalex and cresylic acid were obtained and thoroughly tested. The 25th Infantry Division used it in training and later used it in combat during the Luzon campaign. Tests were conducted on thickened flame thrower fuels made of both napalm and Metalex. Opinions were obtained from personnel of all ranks of interested organizations in the 25th Infantry Division and the fuel adopted as the most desirable was one prepared by dissolving the contents of one 5-pound can of Metalex and two pounds of cresylic acid in eight to ten gallons of gasoline. The range of this fuel was approximately thirty-five yards. The flame at the impact area was intensely hot and of short duration. When fired into the jungle it destroyed green leaves, charred twigs, and burned a trajectory area, forming a crude tunnel approximately four yards high, two to three yards wide and thirty to thirty-five yards long. Only leaves and twigs hit with the fuel were burned. 19/

E. Tactical Doctrine Developed and Training Conducted.

Early flame thrower tactical doctrine is indicated by a training memorandum issued by the 25th Infantry Division in March 1943. 20/ This directive reflected the policy of the XIV Corps, to which the division was assigned, in regard to training infantrymen as well as engineers in the operation of the flame thrower. It directed that eight men from the pioneer platoon of each battalion attend a one-day school conducted by the division chemical officer, for training

---

18/ CWS Theater of Opns Ltr No. 10, 31 Jan 44, p. 21.

19/ Cml O 25th Inf Div, Report on Metalex Flame Thrower Thickener, 30 Nov 44. In Sixth A Cml Sec Records, 470.6 FT Fuels, ORB.

20/ See Appendix 1.

flame thrower operators and assistant operators. The division was equipped with the M1 flame thrower at the time and provisions were made to issue two portable flame throwers complete with accessories to each battalion. It is presumed that the eighteen flame throwers required to equip the infantry were to be taken from the twenty-four authorized the division engineers, since there was no mention of an increased allowance and since the supply of flame throwers in the area was critical at that time. Servicing was to be done by men from the battalion's pioneer platoon at the battalion supply dump. After firing six charges the complete assembly was to be exchanged with the Division Chemical Section for a newly reconditioned assembly. This precaution was taken in order to insure against misfires that might occur after prolonged use. It was stated that the tactical use of the flame thrower was in the development or experimental stage and that plans for its use must take into consideration the factors of weight (portability), range, limited time of fire, availability of fillings, security, and whether or not it was the best weapon to accomplish a given mission.

In approaching the enemy position, security was to be obtained by use of cover or smoke or by supporting fire from the infantry which would force the enemy to take cover. The directive also stated that limited experience in offensive jungle operations indicated that the flame thrower was most useful in mopping-up operations, against tanks, and especially against well prepared dugouts in rocky hillsides or under large trees. The following operational procedure was prescribed: The weapon was to be kept in readiness at a convenient point in the battalion area until an obstacle was encountered which could not be reduced by ordinary weapons. The obstacle was to be by-passed by the advancing forces and enemy resistance in the area eliminated by flame. A flame thrower operator and a security detachment consisting of possibly two automatic riflemen and two riflemen were to approach the target, taking maximum advantage of cover. Upon approaching the target, two riflemen were to form a fixing or holding force to keep the enemy under cover; the nitrogen, fuel-line, and hydrogen valves and the ignition system of the flame thrower were to be given a final test by the operator as he crawled forward, holding the gun in one hand and dragging the fuel assembly behind him. Upon reaching a position approximately twenty yards from the target, a few bursts of flame were to be fired in the openings of the obstacle.

It should be noted that the above policy provided for employment of flame throwers by infantry troops instead of making them dependent on the engineers for this type of support. This policy was adopted, it appears, because the engineers were usually engaged in construction and were not available to furnish flame thrower operators.

1. **Flame Thrower Platoons.** At the close of the Bougainville operation infantry units of the South Pacific Area embarked upon a

training program to train replacements and to correct all types of deficiencies observed in past operations. One of the deficiencies noted was that of the employment of the portable flame thrower. It had been found that the flame thrower was often placed in the hands of a soldier who was hastily trained when the immediate occasion for its use arose. Under such circumstances, the soldier had no confidence in the weapon because he neither knew how to operate it effectively nor had any desire to learn. Commanders were not familiar with the characteristics of the weapon and rifle units were not cognizant of the support to be given the operator. Also, maintenance of the weapon in combat was not satisfactory.

An exception to the general lack of training and a well-formulated tactical doctrine is found in the flame thrower activities of the 132d Infantry, Americal Division. During the early part of the campaign the 132d had experienced the same difficulties with flame thrower operations as had the other units. On 18 February 1944, however, a provisional flame thrower platoon was organized and assigned to the Regimental Headquarters Company. This unit was organized for the specific purpose of effecting an efficient and mobile flame thrower-rifle unit for quickly reducing enemy strong points which could not be effectively reduced by other weapons.

The platoon consisted of a headquarters, with a personnel strength of one officer and four enlisted men, and six squads of six men each, or a total strength of 41. Platoon headquarters consisted of the platoon leader (1st or 2d Lt), a platoon sergeant, two messengers and a driver. The personnel of each squad consisted of the squad leader, an assistant squad leader, two automatic riflemen and two shotgunners. It was general policy to man the platoon entirely with volunteers because of the relative hazardous nature of flame thrower operations. Unwilling operators could not be relied on to carry out a perfectly coordinated attack.

The principal items of equipment of the platoon were:

Rifle, cal. .30, M1	9
Carbine, cal. .30	2
Pistol, cal. .45	6
Rifle, BAR, cal. .30	12
Shotgun, model 97 riot type	12
Flamethrower, M1A1	12
Truck, $\frac{1}{4}$-T, 4x4, C&R	1
Truck, $\frac{1}{4}$-T, 2-wheel	1
Knife, trench, M3	32
Mask, gas, service	41

In addition to the above organizational equipment, fragmentation, smoke and thermite grenades were issued for use in each operation. Fragmentation grenades were employed for anti-personnel purposes; smoke grenades were used by each man for his personal protection and to screen the advancing squad from aimed enemy fire; and thermite grenades were carried as a precautionary measure, for use in the event the ignition system of the flame gun failed.

The platoon leader served as Regimental Flame Thrower Officer, was a member of the Regimental Special Staff and divided his time with the platoon and the commander of the unit being supported. The platoon sergeant was second in command and directed most of his responsibilities from the refueling point. Each squad leader, in addition to commanding his squad, was the flame thrower operator. Other members of the squad acted as target designators, protected the flame thrower operator with small arms fire and smoke, and one member was responsible for maintenance and refueling of the flame weapon.

Tactical doctrine governing the employment of the weapon was fully developed, including the coordination to be effected between the platoon, the unit being supported and CWS personnel and units. In order to assure the effective execution of this doctrine, a very thorough training program of three weeks duration was provided.

The effectiveness and potentialities of this platoon are indicated by the fact that, with only partial or sketchy training prior to its first operation, it reduced eight pillboxes in 100 seconds "of actual firing." For a full report on the organization, tactical doctrine and training of this platoon see Appendix No. 2. Because of the effectiveness of the provisional flame thrower platoon in the 132d Infantry, the Americal Division formed similar platoons in each of the other two regiments.[21]

The platoons were given intensive training which included weapons, practice and combat firing, servicing and maintenance of weapons, and tactical problems in approach and assault of Japanese type fortifications.

Later when the Americal Division was committed in the Southern Philippines Campaign the flame thrower platoon proved to be an effective organization for reducing bunkers and dug-in positions, but it was too large an organization for a regiment to hold in reserve when casualties began to mount and every man was required to carry out the

---

[21] 2d Lt Thomas B. Allen, FT Plt Ldr, 132d Inf Americal Div, sub: Flame Thrower Platoon, Inclosure to ltr, Capt. Lloyd D. Sand to Lt Col Orbie Bostick, 17 Apr 44. In Sixth A Cml Sect Records 319.1 Overseas Inspection, ORB.

normal infantry functions of a regiment. As a result, the platoons were broken up and the men reverted to the rifle companies.

2. **Further Flame Thrower Training.** In order to prepare units for future operations, XIV Corps, on 29 April 1944, issued Annex Number 3 to Training Memorandum No. 8, establishing minimum requirements for training in the employment of the portable flame thrower.22/ This directive indicated the basic principles governing the employment of flame throwers. Their essential mission was the destruction and neutralization of enemy strong points during attacks and in mopping-up operations, and also their possible use in breaking up enemy attacks. The weapon was to be used only when the location and construction of the obstacle precluded the effective use of other weapons. Its principal advantages over other types of weapons were its incendiary and demoralizing effects. Tactics governing its employment were to conform to the basic infantry principles of fire and movement. The fullest exploitation of the capabilities of the weapon depended upon the using elements being familiar with its limitations with respect to range, mobility, security, limited time of fire and the availability of extra pressure tank charges. Instructions relative to training, the selection of targets and preparations for the attack were included.

This directive also stated that the tactical capabilities of the weapon had not yet been fully developed and that its use must be considered as being in the experimental stage. It prescribed that provisions must be made for servicing and maintenance by the "flame thrower teams." These teams actually varied in organization from the "provisional flame thrower platoon" of forty-one men in the Americal Division to a team or squad of twelve men in the 37th Infantry Division. It was stated that a suitable security detachment consisted of two BAR's and two riflemen for flanking attacks but that it should be increased for a frontal attack.

In accordance with the XIV Corps directive, referred to above, the 37th Infantry Division issued a training memorandum which prescribed a minimum of one "flame thrower team" for each infantry rifle company, each infantry battalion ammunition and pioneer platoon and each engineer company. A suggested "flame thrower team" was to consist of:

        Team leader   1 man
        Assistant team leader   1 man
        2 BAR groups   4 men

22/
   See Appendix 3.

```
              2 Flame Thrower groups    4 men
              1 Smoke group             2 men
                                       12 men
```

It was also prescribed that each operator be qualified in maintenance as well as operation, functioning, and tactical employment.23/

While the 25th Infantry Division was in New Zealand, the assistant division chemical officer and the operations sergeant were detailed as flame thrower instructors to the division weapon school which began on 9 January 1944. Instruction was conducted mostly with the M1A1 flame thrower but, on special request to USAFISPA, one E-3 model was made available for trial and demonstration. When the division was moved to New Caledonia to prepare for the Luzon Operation, extensive flame thrower training was conducted. Flame thrower platoons under the command of the regimental gas officers were planned for each regiment; instead of platoons, however, a "flame thrower squad" for each infantry battalion and one for each regimental headquarters company was finally adopted. This personnel was thoroughly instructed in the care, operation, and tactical use of the weapon. Field problems included reconnaissance of targets, use of supporting fire by the infantry and the employment of smoke grenades. Selected personnel of the 65th Combat Engineer Battalion (division engineers) received similar training.24/

F. Comparison of M1A1 and E-3 Models.

The first shipment of E-3 flame throwers arrived in the South Pacific Area during the second quarter of 1944. The XIV Corps conducted extensive tests before a representative group of flame thrower officers and operators, with combat experience, in order to compare it with the M1A1. The following is a summary of the comparison resulting from these tests. The M1A1 was not well adapted for thickened fuel and therefore obtained a shorter range than the E-3; ignition was not positive; and its construction did not result in a comfortable man-pack. It had the advantage, however, of being more readily serviced near the front lines. The E-3, with its fuel gun adapted to both thickened and unthickened fuel, attained maximum range with all types of fuel used; had positive ignition; and had a more conveniently handled gun group. The ignition cartridge, however, while being more reliable, was of a

---

23/ For a complete copy of this training memorandum see Appendix 4.

24/ Cml Sec 25th Inf Div, Historical Report for 1944, 9 Apr 45, pp. 1-2.

special type and could be depended on for only one ignition and, therefore, increased the problems of procurement and supply. A further test was made in which the E-3 gun assembly was attached to the fuel and pressure assembly of the M1A1. Results obtained with this combination were comparable to those obtained with the E-3. It was therefore considered advantageous to equip the existing M1A1's with the E-3 gun group.

From the above tests it was concluded that the E-3 was the better of the two models, and had fewer operational disadvantages. It was better designed from the standpoint of the operator; the gun was more easily handled; longer range was obtained; and the ignition cartridge never failed, though after the initial ignition the cartridge was generally useless for additional firing. This deficiency apparently resulted from inadequate insulation between the cartridge chambers. The following specific suggestions for improving the E-3 were made in the theater: better construction of the ignition cartridge to provide better insulation between the rounds; an improved design of the fittings including large wing-nuts on the pressure tank to facilitate changes in the field; the addition of a shut-off valve in the fuel discharge line; and improvement in design of the carrier pack for greater comfort of the operator.25/

In connection with the report on these tests, it should be noted that no reference was made to the waterproof characteristics of the E-3. This was an exceedingly important factor in the Pacific where humidity and precipitation were very high.

On 15 June 1944, the South Pacific Area was disbanded as a separate command, the greater part of which was turned over to General MacArthur and merged with the Southwest Pacific Area. Thousands of Japanese still remained in the Solomon Islands, cut off from all source of supply and doomed to starvation. In November 1944, New Zealand, and Australian forces relieved American forces of police and mopping-up duties and American forces were withdrawn to prepare for future operations.

25/
(1) Ltr Cml O XIV Corps to CG SPA (Attn Cml O), 4 May 44, sub: Results of Tests of Relative Merits of Flame Throwers: Models M1A1, E2, E3; (2) 1st Ind Cml O SPA to C CWS, no date, on basic ltr above. In pers files of Col. Harold Riegelman, formerly Cml O I Corps.

CHAPTER III

SOUTHWEST PACIFIC AREA (SWPA)

A. Early Employment in Papuan Campaign.

1. **Situation.** Japanese forces landed at Lae and Salamaua, Papua, New Guinea on 8 March 1942. Throughout the second and third quarter of the year reinforcements were landed and a base was built up at Buna Mission for an overland push over the Owen Stanley Mountains, by way of the Kokoda Trail, to Port Moresby, which was the Allied advance base on the south coast of New Guinea. By 14 September 1942, the Japanese, in an advance which demonstrated great skill in mountain and jungle fighting, had crossed the Owen Stanleys and had succeeded in pushing Allied ground forces to within twenty air miles of Port Moresby.[1]

Elements of the Australian Sixth and Seventh Divisions were committed to stem the Japanese advance on Port Moresby. By 28 September the Australians were reinforced by the 126th and 128th RCT's of the 32nd Infantry Division, which was transported by air from Brisbane, Australia. These troops annihilated most of the enemy forces that had crossed the mountains and forced the remainder back along the Kokoda Trail to the Northeast coast of Papua. This advance was made under extremely adverse conditions and over some of the most rugged country in the world. The Kokoda Trail winds its way up from the hot, sun-baked area of Port Moresby, where the average annual rainfall is less than thirty inches, through the cold, wet, windswept pass at 10,000 feet, up and down steep canyon walls, where it sometimes required a whole day to march an air-line distance of 500 yards. The trip from Moresby to Dobodura required 45 minutes by air but it required six weeks for troops moving on foot. Early in November the Australians secured Dobodura Airstrip. Meanwhile, the remainder of the 32nd Division was moved by water to Port Moresby and the Allied Air Forces transported it across the mountains to Dobodura. By the end of November the enemy had been confined to pockets along the coast near Buna, Gona and Sanananda Point. The division's equipment was limited to what was carried in on the person and all supplies came by air. The division's artillery consisted of one 105-mm howitzer and a few Australian field pieces which had been flown over the mountains.

---

[1] CofS USA Report on the Army, Jul 1, 1939 to Jun 30, 1943, p. 112.

I Corps, under the command of Lieutenant General Robert Lee Eichelberger, assumed command of the Buna operations on 1 December 1942. The offensive was resumed immediately afterwards on a battlefield that was covered with dense jungle growth and kunai grass flats. The foliage was wet and the ground was muddy from the continuous heavy rains.[2]

The enemy (Japanese Marines) had prepared defenses consisting of dug-in bunkers, covered with coconut logs and earth in such a manner as to render them impervious to mortar fire. These bunkers were thoroughly camouflaged, being located in the dense jungle and kunai grass without cleared fields of fire. They were protected by numerous snipers located in trees. The low flat ground was traversed by muddy streams that had to be crossed by infantry in the face of murderous fire emitting from machine guns located in bunkers which were situated on the edge of the jungle on the opposite bank. At high tide these streams were too deep to wade and at low tide the banks were either muddy and steep or flooded. Upon encountering enemy bunkers, the infantry was forced to attack with small arms and grenades after a mortar barrage had been laid down on positions, because they had no suitable weapon for reducing such positions. The losses suffered by such tactics were heavy.

2. **Attempt to Employ Flame Throwers at Buna.** On 6 December 1942, the commanding officer, 126th Infantry Regiment requested the 114th Engineer Battalion to send forward two flame throwers and operators to assist in reducing enemy machine gun emplacements in the vicinity of Buna. This battalion was equipped with the E1R1 type flame thrower, later standardized as the M1, which had been used many times in training exercises and demonstrations. On the afternoon of 6 December the battalion serviced and tested the equipment and it was discovered that some of the gas cylinders had developed leaks, apparently by rusting through from the inside. Number 6 Diesel oil was used with a nitrogen pressure of 2200 pounds per square inch and a hydrogen pressure of 2000 pounds per square inch. In these tests the flame throwers functioned reasonably well, giving a maximum range of twenty yards.[3] On 7 December the two flame throwers, twenty-five gallons of fuel, two refill tanks and four engineer operators arrived at the regimental area. The regimental commander personally required a representative of the Division Chemical Section to look over the situation and check the flame throwers prior to their being used in combat.

---

[2]
  Memo, Hq, Advance Base, APO 929, Office of the Cml O for C Cml O USASOS, 12 Jan 43. In CMLWG.

[3]
  Ltr, CO 114th Engr Bn(C) to Cml O, Adv B S, 19 Dec 42, sub: Malfunctioning of Flame Throwers. In CMLWG.

On 8 December the regimental S-3 called for the flame throwers to be used against a strongly constructed enemy machine gun nest, which was located on the left flank at the edge of Buna village. This position had been holding up the advance for several days and had taken a heavy toll in killed and wounded. While the flame throwers were being brought up to the zone of action of Company E, 126th Infantry, an infantry lieutenant accompanied by a sergeant from the Division Chemical Section went forward to make a personal reconnaissance. The bunker was located and fire was deliberately drawn from it to locate the port holes. This bunker was typical of those encountered during the Buna Operation. As was learned later, when it was finally charged by doughboys and taken, that it was a four-man structure containing two machine guns. A trench connected it with well dug-in living quarters fifteen yards away. The reconnaissance revealed that it was ingeniously concealed and was located on the left edge of the kunai grass flat, an area of about 100 by 200 yards. A dense jungle and a swamp were located at its rear.

For several days the infantry company had been pinned down in the kunai grass by the automatic fire coming from the bunker. One sniper armed with an automatic weapon covered the area about the position. He was fifty to seventy-five yards away but was never located. At least two other snipers covered the position from trees located 150 to 200 yards away on the opposite side of the kunai flat. The bunker could be approached by cover which consisted of a partially demolished breastworks, located about thirty-five yards from the bunker. From one end of the breastworks, a shallow trench went forward another five yards which placed the observer within thirty yards of the objective and in comparative safety except for sniper fire from above. The snipers seemed to prefer holding their fire except on those occasions when someone attempted to advance closer to the bunker than the end of the shallow trench. The position could not be outflanked because of the dense jungle and swamp on the left, as well as another bunker covering that area.

After the reconnaissance, a report was made to the regimental commander who concurred in the plan to employ flame throwers against the position. The infantry lieutenant then took the operator (an engineer corporal) forward to the breastworks and again drew fire from the bunker to point out the exact location of the portholes. Upon returning he presented his plan of attack: the operator, with his flame thrower well camouflaged in a burlap sack, was to advance as far forward as possible in the shallow trench. This would put the operator within thirty yards of the objective. An alternate operator was to cover his advance and take over should he become a casualty. Three men with automatic weapons were to crawl around as far as they could to the left flank and open fire at the rear of the bunker to cover the operator's advance and furnish a diversion. The lieutenant, the CWS sergeant and four riflemen were to take positions at the breastworks and rush the bunker with grenades in the wake of the flame thrower operator. The operator was to advance at least five yards before releasing the flame and keep advancing until the fuel was exhausted. The flame thrower was checked at this time to insure ignition.

Under cover of the diverting fire from the men on the left flank, the operator advanced seven or eight yards from his position at the end of the shallow trench without being fired upon. At this point he released the initial burst of the flame thrower, which turned out to be a mere ten to fifteen yards in length. Those who were to rush the objective immediately advanced from behind the breastworks. One rifleman from this group was instantly hit and returned to cover. The operator continued to advance in a crouching position, trying time and again to get the weapon to function properly, but without success. When less than fifteen yards from the bunker, a bullet struck the front of his helmet and he was knocked unconscious. The lieutenant was killed and the others withdrew under very heavy enemy fire. That night the operator regained consciousness and crawled back to safety. The next day a rifleman was killed in an attempt to recover the flame thrower. It was finally recovered two days later after the infantry had rushed the position and taken it.

The Division Chemical Section was instructed to make one more effort to get flame throwers in condition for operation. New flame throwers were flown in from Port Moresby and were tested but were in an unserviceable condition and failed to function. They were cannabilized and parts interchanged in an attempt to get one that would function properly but they were in such bad condition that all efforts were unsuccessful.4/

3. <u>Corrective Action Taken</u>. In January 1943, the Chief Chemical Officer, USAFFE, made the following report to the Chief, Chemical Warfare Service:

> The condition of flame throwers needs but little comment, in view of the reports which I have been sending through in the past two weeks. The way the flame throwers let the infantry down at a critical point brought them into such ill-repute that I am afraid they may never want to use them again. Our reserve of ten flame throwers were [Sic] sent to New Guinea before the report of their failure was received. The maintenance company reconditioned them before they were sent, to make sure that they were in

---

4/
  Rpt, Act of 32d Inf Div Cml Sect During Papuan Campaign, dated 18 Feb 43, pp. 5-8, 18. In Hist Records Sect, AGO.

Figure 20. Buna, New Guinea: Front View of a Japanese Bunker (Pillbox).

working condition. The deficiencies needing
correction were rather astounding and are being
reported separately.5/

During the first half of 1943, the 10th Chemical Maintenance Company, which was located at Brisbane, Australia, conducted extensive tests with the objective of correcting as many of the deficiencies of the M1 flame thrower as possible. All flame throwers in the hands of units in the SWPA were withdrawn and thoroughly tested. It was determined that none of them could be expected to function properly under the combat conditions found in the jungle where all equipment was continuously subjected to moisture and tropical temperatures. Among the common causes for failure was low pressure in the nitrogen, hydrogen and fuel cylinders. Approximately sixty percent of the pressure cylinders were found to have pin holes. Batteries were found to deteriorate under conditions of high temperatures and high humidity. Also, owing to the way the flame thrower was constructed, moisture penetrated all parts of the gun, rendering the ignition system unserviceable by corrosion.

In order to correct these deficiencies a method was developed for waterproofing the flame gun by rebuilding it and sealing all openings in such a manner that it could be fired after being immersed in water for twenty-four hours.6/ Pin holes in pressure tanks were welded and fittings were repaired. Gauges for testing pressures in the field and adapters to fit all types of commercial pressure cylinders were added to the service kits.7/ Tests were also conducted with an eighty foot extension hose inserted between the fuel unit and the flame gun. The addition of the hose decreased the range to about fifteen yards and it was concluded that there was not sufficient fuel capacity to justify such a modification on the portable flame thrower. It was made standard operating procedure to thoroughly test, repair, and waterproof all flame throwers shipped to the SWPA or brought in with units as organic equipment.8/

5/
  Ltr, C Cml O USAFFE to C CWS, 6 Jan 43, no sub. In CWS file
    319.1/101.

6/
  10th Cml Maint Co, "Instructions for changing the battery in
    the waterproofing," 28 May 43. Sixth A Cml Sect Records
    470.71 FT, ORB.

7/.
  Memo, Hq Advance Base, Office of the Cml O to C Cml O, USASOS,
    12 Jan 43. In CMLWG.

8/
  Ltr, Cml O USASOS to Cml O's, BS #2, 3, 4, 7, and CO 10th Cml
    Maint Co, 16 May 43, sub: Flamethrowers, Sixth A Cml Sect
    Records, 470.71 FT, ORB.

Since units in this area were not to be completely equipped with the M2-2 flame thrower before the war ended, it was necessary to prescribe strict maintenance and servicing procedures throughout the war to keep the M1A1 flame throwers in half-way serviceable condition. Its inherent weaknesses had been fully realized after the catastrophy at Buna Village and every precaution was taken to prevent a recurrence.9/ By October 1943, rigorous tests conducted on waterproofed flame throwers satisfied Sixth Army that these weapons, if properly handled and serviced, were dependable and effective.10/

B. Preparation for Further Operations.

1. <u>Tactical Doctrine Established</u>. The Sixth Army Headquarters under command of General Walter Krueger, who also commanded Alamo Force, was established in SWPA on 16 February 1943. Originally stationed at Camp Columbia near Brisbane, Australia, this headquarters operated directly under General Headquarters, Southwest Pacific Area throughout the war. Immediately after its activation, the Sixth Army initiated extensive studies to analyze the operations of the Papuan Campaign, conducted by the 32d and 41st Infantry Divisions, and to mount out two task forces of regimental combat team size for occupation of the Trobriand Islands. A forward echelon for Army headquarters was established at Milne Bay, New Guinea, on 10 June 1943 (effected on 30 June 1943), to conduct the operation, and to maintain liaison with other Allied forces scheduled to attack up the coast of New Guinea to seize Salamaua, Lae and Finschhafen.

Meanwhile, studies were being made at the rear echelon to find a suitable method for reducing Japanese bunkers of the type that had caused so much difficulty during the Papuan Campaign. Many instances had been reported where the infantry had been able to approach to within twenty yards of a bunker, or a line of bunkers, and then had to withdraw in order that the enemy positions could be softened up with mortar and artillery before being charged by doughboys. It had been found, however, that neither artillery nor mortars had been able to reduce such positions.

During the battle for Sanananda Point, the 41st Infantry Division had developed a method of attack which proved quite profitable against targets located on kunai grass flats. Upon encountering a line of bunkers

---

9/
  Ltr, Hq USAFFE, Office of the Cml O, 12 Apr 43, sub: Auxiliary Equipment for Flame Throwers. FECW 470.71/6. In CMLWG.

10/
  Memo, Actg Cml O Sixth Army for Cml O Alamo Task Force, 24 Oct 43, no sub. Sixth Army Memos from forward echelons. In Sixth A Cml Sect Records, ORB.

the infantry would withdraw to a distance of fifty yards from the objective and a mortar artillery barrage was laid down. The instant the barrage lifted, the infantry would rush the position, spraying the inside of each bunker with sub-machine guns and following this with grenades. During such attacks it was necessary for the men to keep moving until they located cover, because once they stopped they were picked off by snipers located in nearby trees. In one such attack 240 Japanese were killed with a loss in American troops of only six killed and nineteen wounded. This method required perfect timing and was not always possible because of the swampy terrain. An example of the swampy terrain which the Japanese chose to defend during this campaign is illustrated by the fact that a complete enemy hospital built up on stilts was captured.

Investigations revealed that engineer combat troops would be overworked on construction during operations conducted in primitive jungle country and would not always be able to furnish flame thrower and demolition parties to the infantry without handicapping their all important construction efforts. Accordingly, Sixth Army requested GHQ to authorize the issue of portable flame throwers to infantry and dismounted cavalry on the basis of twelve per infantry regiment and eight per cavalry regiment. These were to be in addition to the twenty-four currently authorized each combat engineer battalion by WD tables of equipment. 11/

The request was approved in October 1943, after Sixth Army had issued its first training directive, Training Memorandum Number 8, dated 1 October 1943, on the use of the portable flame thrower. 12/ This directive prescribed the training of "flame thrower teams" for use in assault parties, as described in War Department Training Circular No. 33, dated 11 March 1943. A "flame thrower team" was defined as an operator and an assistant operator. It was not intended that the flame thrower team be the principal team of assault parties, but that such teams be trained in sufficient numbers as to be available for use in both infantry and engineer assault parties when required for the reduction of fortified positions as described in War Department Training Circular No. 33. The minimum number of flame thrower teams to be trained for specific type units was as follows: two teams for each authorized flame thrower in parachute infantry regiments, and separate combat engineer companies and battalions; two teams each in

---

11/
(1) Ltr, CG 6th Army to CG USAFFE, 4 Oct 43, sub: Portable Flame Throwers; (2) Ltr, 6th Army to Distribution, 24 Oct 43, sub: Portable Flame Throwers. 6th A Cml Sect Records, 470.71 FT, ORB.

12/ For this TM see Appendix No. 5.

infantry battalions, ammunition and pioneer platoons, and rifle company or troop; and four teams in each pioneer and demolition section of the service troop in cavalry regiments.

The Sixth Army directive provided that each individual of the teams receive technical training to include: (1) disassembly and assembly; (2) care and cleaning; (3) maintenance and repair; (4) functioning; (5) mechanical operation and adjustment; (6) preparation of fuels; (7) servicing and filling fuel tanks in preparation for firing; (8) charging pressure and hydrogen cylinders; and (9) technique of firing flame throwers. It should be noted that such a program should have resulted in each operator and assistant operator being qualified as a flame thrower technician. It was felt that this extensive training was necessary to insure operation of such a delicate weapon in combat. It was also directed that, at the completion of technical training, which was made a CWS responsibility, flame thrower teams were to be included with specially organized assault parties for tactical training. Field exercises involving the coordinated attack of Japanese type fortified positions by assault parties were to be conducted along with other combined training, which had been prescribed for all combat units arriving in SWPA. The following type assault party was listed as a guide:

Personnel	Number
Detachment leader	1
Assistant leader	1
Rocket launcher personnel	2
Flame thrower party	6
Demolition party	2
Automatic riflemen	2
Riflemen with bayonets & grenades	4

The following was listed as a guide for arms and equipment used by assault parties: submachine guns, automatic rifles, rifles and bayonets, carbines, demolition charges, bangalore torpedoes, rocket launchers, flame throwers, smoke grenades, hand grenades, rifle grenades, wire cutters, and signal projectors.

It was felt that the doctrine established by the above directive would overcome many of the deficiencies in the employment of flame throwers as reported from the Papuan Campaign, and the New Georgia Operation which had been completed in the South Pacific Area. For example, three flame throwers were recommended for each assault party in order to allow for misfires and to insure sufficient flame; a high standard of proficiency of technical training for operation was prescribed; and the principles of tactical employment required that "flame thrower teams" be included in "assault parties" instead of being employed alone.13/

2. **Supply Situation.** The increased allowance of portable flame throwers which became effective in October 1943 increased the theater requirement from 184 to 344, not including maintenance stocks. Anticipating this increased requirement for Sixth Army, USASOS had initiated action to procure additional flame throwers and accessory kits as early as June 1943.14/ A shipment of M1A1 flame throwers, to replace the obsolete M1 type, arrived in August. These flame throwers were turned over to the 10th Chemical Maintenance Company for remodeling, waterproofing and testing in accordance with theater policy.15/ A great many of these flame throwers were found to be unserviceable at the time of arrival due to missing parts, improper adjustment and defective parts. During this period Sixth Army was preparing five divisions and two separate regimental combat teams for future operations, and supply agencies experienced a great deal of difficulty in making available sufficient flame throwers and accessories to carry out the training program. The supply of spare parts and accessory kits was especially critical and continued to be so throughout the war. Another problem was that of furnishing hydrogen and nitrogen or compressed air for use in the pressure cylinders. It was impossible to obtain either cylinders or gas from the U.S. in sufficient quantities to meet the training requirements. Cylinders were purchased in Australia, necessitating the addition of numerous adapters to the filling kits, because Australian cylinders were equipped with several types of fittings. The only source of hydrogen was Sidney, Australia, which presented a shipping problem, especially to New Guinea. It was necessary to obtain high priorities and make numerous shipments by air in order to meet requirements. Leaky cylinders also presented a problem and often cylinders would arrive with 600-1400 p.s.i. instead of 2200.

3. **Training Conducted and Fuel Developed.** During the period of October, November and December 1943 all divisions and separate regimental combat teams in SWPA conducted intensive training for assault

---

13/
  Ibid.

14/
  Ltr, Cml O USASOS to Supply O, Cml Br, SFPOE, 7 Jun 43, sub: Portable Flame Throwers, New, M1A1, and Accessories. GSCW 470.7. In CMLWG.

15/
  Ltr, Cml O Sixth Army to Cml O, I Corps, 18 Aug 43. In pers files of Col Harold Riegelman, formerly Cml O, I Corps.

parties. The training of flame thrower operators presented a major problem for CWS officers. A minimum of 240 operators and assistants per division was required by the Sixth Army directive, and division commanders usually required the training of additional teams.16/ At that time, the 1st Cavalry Division, 24th Infantry Division and 41st Infantry Division, were in Australia.17/ In order to train instructors and assist these divisions in training operators, the 10th Chemical Maintenance Company, under supervision of the Chemical Warfare Training Center, conducted a series of five-day classes. The 24th and 41st Divisions were under I Corps,18/ which established an assault school near Rockhamton, Queensland, for conducting tactical training for operations in jungle terrain. The 1st Marine Division, 32d Infantry Division, 112th Cavalry RCT (Sep) and 158th Infantry RCT (Sep) were stationed in New Guinea and the Trobriand Islands where an intensive training program was being carried out. In order to assist these units in the technical training, the Sixth Army Chemical Section formed a traveling training team, consisting of a CWS officer and three CWS non-commissioned officers, which conducted three-day schools for all units in the forward area.19/

One of the problems that arose at this time was that of the most effective fuel for flame throwers. The only information available was that contained in Section VII, TM 3-375, May 1943, and it was the concensus that this fuel was not suitable except in special situations. After considerable testing in the field, it was concluded that both a liquid and a thickened fuel were necessary to meet requirements. For liquid fuels, the standardized filling was established as three and a half gallons of SAE 50 motor oil and one gallon of gasoline. An effective range of twenty-five to thirty yards, accompanied by intense heat and quantities of black smoke, was obtained from this fuel. It was found that heavier weight motor oil was more effective from the standpoint of heat and range but such oil was not readily available. The

---

16/
    Ltr, Cml O Alamo Force to G-3, 9 Feb 44, sub: Trained Flame Thrower Personnel. Sixth A Cml Sect Records, 353 FT Tng, ORB.

17/
    See Appendices 6 and 8 for TM's issued by the 24th and 41st Inf Divs at this time.

18/
    See Appendix 7 for I Corps TM.

19/
    Sixth A Cml Sect Records, 353 Tng (FT), Sep - Dec 1943.

Marines were able to obtain SAE 90 oil and standardized its use in the preparation of unthickened fuel. For thickened fuel it was found that one can (5.3 pounds) of napalm to thirteen-twenty gallons of gasoline was desirable. For a gelatinized fuel suitable for elevated firing, giving a parabolic trajectory, thirteen or fourteen gallons of gasoline per can of napalm was found most effective. When fifteen or more gallons of gasoline were used to a can of napalm, a viscous and relatively fast-burning liquid, giving a range of thirty-forty yards, was obtained.

C. Employment in the Bismark Archipelago Campaign

1. <u>New Britain</u>. On 15 December 1943, the 112th Cavalry RCT (Sep) landed on Arawe Peninsula on the south coast of New Britain for the purpose of diverting the enemy forces from Cape Gloucester where the 1st Marine Division was to land eleven days later. Troop B, 112th Cavalry landed at Wabmete Village, Pilelo Island (south of Arawe Peninsula) at 0530 and proceeded to Winguru Village. At 0615 the leading platoon reached the village and the advance was stopped as one trooper was killed by frontal fire from caves. Reconnaissance disclosed that the enemy was resisting from two caves. Bazooka fire was employed and closed the entrance to one cave, but the other cave was protected by log pilings in such a manner that bazooka and machine guns did no apparent damage. The troop had landed with two filled flame throwers carried by trained operators. These were called forward. Tests revealed that one flame thrower was not functioning properly. The troop's assault party was formed, including one flame thrower team augmented by a machine gun. Fire was placed on the entrance to the cave while the flame thrower operator crawled up to within fifteen yards and fired the entire charge. The assault platoon then advanced to the cave entrance and threw in hand grenades. Seven enemy dead were found in the cave. All of them were badly burned and their clothes were still ablaze. The operation was completed at 1130 without further loss to the cavalry.

Arawe Peninsula is shaped like a boot and its seizure was bitterly contested by the Japanese, who counter-attacked after the first day and dug in across the coral peninsula near the "top of the boot." Although the advance of the cavalry was held up by these positions until tanks were sent in as reinforcements, no further attempt was made to employ the portable flame thrower during the operation.[20]

---

[20] 112th Cav RCT, Hist Rpt, 10 Feb 44.

The 1st Marine Division landed at Cape Gloucester on the northern coast of New Britain at dawn on 26 December 1943. Because of the northwest monsoons at this time of the year, it was the dry season on the south coast and the wet season on the north coast. The marines operated under most adverse weather conditions. The incessant downpours converted the alluvial soil into a morass. It was not unusual for ten to twenty inches of rain to fall during a twenty-four hour period; streams were swollen and equipment was soaked. In spite of the waterproofing given to the M1A1 flame thrower, its electrical ignition system became damp and undependable. Several instances of misfires were reported and the weapon was not used extensively during the operation.21/ The commander of one marine unit which finally used the flame thrower was reluctant to employ the weapon because his men had had little experience in its operation. When it was used, at the order of this unit commander's superior officer, dense foliage and heavy fire greatly increased the difficulty of locating the openings of enemy positions.

2. *Admiralty Islands.* The initial landing was made on the Island of Los Negros on 29 February 1944 by a squadron from the 1st Cavalry Division. The primary mission of this squadron was to make a reconnaissance and flame throwers were not carried. The landing was made near Momote airstrip with little opposition and the squadron dug in to await reinforcements. On the first night the Japanese made a series of fanatical counterattacks which resulted in killing over 800 of the enemy with slight losses to the cavalry.22/

The 2d Brigade combat team which included the 7th and 8th Cavalry Regiments landed on Manus Island at Lugos Mission Plantation on 15 March 1944. Each regiment carried eight flame throwers filled and ready to be put into instant action. However, opposition to the landing was negligible and no suitable targets for these weapons were found until 19 March. On this date a lone Jap was discovered occupying a bunker which the assault troops had bypassed. Flame thrower fire was desired to eliminate the Jap because of the characteristics of the position. Investigation revealed that flame throwers were not available. Because of their

---

21/ Ltr, Det 93d Cml Comp Co to Cml O Sixth Army, 30 Dec 1943, sub: Official Rpt on Tactical Use of FT. In Sixth A Cml Sect Records, 470.71 PFT, ORB.

22/ Memo, Cml O Alamo Force for C Cml O USASOS, 31 Jan 44, sub: CW Intelligence. Sixth A Cml Sect Records, 386.3 Captured Enemy Equipment, ORB.

Figure 21. The Author Inspecting a Japanese Bunker at Arawe, New Britain.

weight and lack of targets, they had been discarded along the route of advance from Lugos Mission to Lorengau airstrip. The commercial cylinders of hydrogen and nitrogen were in forward positions on "Machine Gun Ridge" behind the airstrip while the service kits were 800 yards to the rear. The brigade commander ordered his chemical officer to collect all flame throwers and equipment and take charge of all flame thrower operations. The 2d Brigade chemical officer operated directly under the brigade commander for the remainder of the operation. The flame throwers were just behind the attacking troops at all times ready for use on call from unit commanders. The chemical officer went with the attacking troops, seeking suitable targets and ready to organize and direct a flame thrower assault group when needed.

The use of tanks precluded the use of flame throwers for neutralizing bunkers and they were not employed until "Hill No. 1" was reached. The Japs had been pulling the trick of letting the first assault troops go past the bunkers in order to create the impression that they had retreated or had been killed. Immediately after the first wave passed, the Japs would open fire from the rear. This procedure, even though being performed by only a few of the enemy and sometimes even by wounded enemy personnel, was causing some casualties among our troops. In order to avoid this nuisance, the command instituted a mopping-up procedure. Flame thrower teams followed the assault troops, shooting fire into every bunker. Demolition teams followed the flame throwers and blew up each bunker in order to prevent the Japs from infiltrating back at night and reoccupying positions. Fifteen bunkers were treated in this manner on "Hill No. 1" alone.[23]

In clearing the enemy from the small islands, the 1st Squadron, 7th Cavalry Regiment, landed on Pityilu Island on 30 March. Toward one end of the island, Troop A encountered resistance from a position located in a dense jungle on the edge of a small clearing which was about seventy-five yards across. The troops' assault party, consisting of a flame thrower team and a demolition team, with a submachine gun as one of their weapons, was following the troop. When resistance was encountered, the assault party took cover in a bomb crater which was located on the opposite side of the clearing. The assault party leader, a sergeant, and an air liaison officer took cover behind a tree stump located forward of

---

[23]
   Ltr to Cml O USASOS, 14 May 44, sub: Report on Use of CW Weapons. Extracts in CMLWG.

the bomb crater. Troop A withdrew about 100 yards from the enemy position to the jungle on the opposite side of the clearing. Nineteen Japs counterattacked across the clearing, apparently thinking that Troop A was retreating. These were mowed down by the assault party but the air corps officer was killed by a Jap who had sneaked up from behind. This Jap was in turn killed by the sergeant who was with the officer. Fire continued to be received from the enemy position and the troop commander ordered the sergeant to make a reconnaissance for the purpose of employing the assault group. The bunker was located and the sergeant led the assault party to it, taking advantage of cover offered by the dense undergrowth. When the flame thrower operator reached the firing position, he discovered two bunkers instead of one. He immediately started firing short bursts, alternating between the two locations until his fuel was exhausted. The demolition team followed immediately and closed the entrances to what was found to be a coral cave with two openings.24/

D. Employment in New Guinea Campaign.

1. Hollandia, Netherlands New Guinea. I Corps, consisting of the 24th Infantry Division and the 41st Infantry Division (less 163d RCT), landed respectively at Tanahmerah and Humboldt Bays on the morning of 22 April 1944. Regiments of the 24th Division brought in their flame throwers as organization equipment and, since the landing was not contested, they left them on the beach at Tanahmerah Bay. The 34th Infantry was moved to the Hollandia area to reinforce the 41st Division. In the 41st Division, the 162d Infantry (beachhead troops) had landed with twelve flame throwers filled and ready for instant use, while the 186th Infantry (enveloping or driving force) was similarly equipped with six flame throwers when it came ashore.

Little opposition was encountered on the landing at Hollandia Bay and troops immediately proceeded inland to secure Sentani airstrip some fifteen miles away. The 186th Infantry continued to carry its six flame throwers inland for use in case of emergency. On the afternoon of 29 April, the 34th Infantry encountered resistance from an enemy bunker that could not be reduced with available weapons. Since the regiment had left its flame throwers on the beach, a detail was dispatched to the nearby 186th Infantry to borrow two flame throwers. Three hours after the bunker was encountered, the flame thrower arrived and the attack was resumed. When the position was occupied, it was discovered that the enemy

---

24/
 Lt Col Kenneth W. Hass, "The Pacific is Another War,"
  CW Bull, Vol. 30, No. 5, Nov-Dec 44, pp. 17-18;
  ltr, GSCW 319.1, Hq USASOS, 14 May 44, sub: Report on Use of CW Weapons.

had evacuated the bunker during the time that had elapsed while the flame throwers were being brought forward. Flame throwers were not used at any other time during the operation, but thirty-four were lost in a fire caused by an enemy bombing raid on 23 April.25/

2. Wakde Island - Maffin Bay Operation. On 17 May 1944, the 163d Infantry RCT, including the 27th Engineer Combat Battalion, landed at Arara on the mainland of New Guinea, opposite the Wakde Island Group, with only slight opposition. The mission of this task force was to occupy the Wakde Island Group and the mainland opposite as far east as the Tementoe River and as far west as Sarmi Village. Action was immediately initiated against Insoemoar Island, Wakde Island Group, supported by artillery located on the mainland and 4.2-inch mortars firing from nearby Insoemanai Island. Insoemoar was the main island of the Wakde Group and was defended by a battalion of Japanese marines who fought to the last man. During the three days of ground fighting on this island approximately 500 Japanese were killed and eight captured. The employment of tanks precluded extensive use of flame throwers in this bloody battle. Company A, 27th Engineer Combat Battalion, was assigned the mission of clearing the caves on the northeast shoreline comprised of coral shelving extending from the ocean up a steep slope. This slope was honey-combed with connecting tunnels and caves, in which the last remnants of the enemy forces entrenched themselves and resisted to the last. Air, naval and artillery bombardments had failed to neutralize these caves. Dynamite, bazookas, flame throwers, fragmentation grenades and M-15 WP grenades were used at different times by the engineers. The fragmentation grenades proved useless against the curved tunnels. WP grenades achieved some success in driving the Japanese from the caves but proved ineffective against the tunnels, except to indicate alternate entrances. The flame thrower proved to be the most effective weapon for this type combat and was employed on approximately eight different occasions, either killing the Japanese outright or driving them from the tunnels, where they became easy rifle targets. The following account gives an example of how the flame thrower was used in mopping up these caves.

25/
   Memo, Cml O Alamo Force for ACofS G-3 Sixth Army, 4 May 44, sub: Report on Chemical Support during Aitape-Humboldt Bay-Tanahmerah Bay Operations. In Sixth A Cml Sect Records, 314.7 Hist Rpts, ORB.

Five or six Japs held a tunnel approximately thirty feet deep. One soldier climbed up the side of the parapet built around the entrance of the tunnel and was shot. He fell inside the parapet and all efforts to get him out under cover of rifle fire failed. A flame thrower was brought up and the company commander directed the operation from a position at the side of the parapet. The operator approached from the front while the enemy was held back from the tunnel by rifle fire from above. The operator placed his flame gun over the parapet and fired at the roof of the entrance so that the flame would billow out and downwards. One Jap who was not burned to death came out and was killed with the last burst of flame. The body of the soldier who had fallen inside was recovered but it was discovered that he had been shot through the heart.[26]

The 158th Infantry RCT (Sep) relieved the 163d Infantry during the latter part of May in order that the 163d might rejoin the 41st Division at Biak early in June. The 27th Engineer Battalion remained with the task force in support of the 158th Infantry which continued to employ the flame thrower in subsequent operations.

The following is an example of the use of the flame thrower during the fighting on the mainland. Company B, 27th Engineer Battalion, was attached to the 3d Battalion, 158th Infantry, for operations on the west side of the Tor River. An infantry company was held up for over three hours by a strong point on high ground covering the main trail. The terrain would not permit the use of tanks so the engineers were called upon to employ their flame throwers. The Japanese, entrenched in a dugout under the floor at one corner of a native hut, were armed with one heavy and several light machine guns. Under cover of friendly machine gun and rifle fire, one flame thrower operator was able to advance to a position behind a tree twenty-five feet from the dugout. The full charge of the flame thrower was fired, enveloping the entire hut in flames. The Japs who were not killed instantly by the flame were shot by the infantry when they tried to escape.[27]

The 6th Infantry Division relieved the 158th Infantry RCT about the middle of June in order that the 158th might prepare for the Noemfoor operation. When the 6th Infantry Division resumed the offensive to secure Maffin Bay, it encountered determined resistance from numerous coral caves, both natural and

---

[26]
   Ltr, CW Intell Team No. 4, Hq US Forces APO 704, to C Cml O HQ USASOS, 24 Jun 44, sub: Report on the Use of CW Weapons and Munitions. In Sixth A Cml Sect Records, 350.05 Wakde, ORB.

[27]
   Ibid.

artificial. The following account is illustrative of the employment of the portable flame thrower, M1A1, by the 6th Division at Maffin Bay.

On 19 June 1944, a platoon on patrol east of the Tirfoam River encountered three bunkers supported by sniper fire. When all efforts to destroy the strong point had failed and the platoon was pinned down, a second patrol, with three tanks and one flame thrower was assigned the mission of relieving the original patrol and to knock out the pillboxes. The tanks sprayed the pillboxes and trees with machine gun fire and fired several 75-mm. shells at the largest bunker which was located at the base of a large tree. At this point the tank commander, standing uncovered in the turret hatch, was killed by a sniper and the tanks immediately withdrew. Fire continued to come from the pillboxes and the use of the flame thrower was ordered. Under cover of thick undergrowth and automatic fire, the operator managed to crawl within fifteen yards of the target, the location of which was indicated by tracer bullets. Following verbal instructions for fire direction, given by the assistant operator, the operator placed a two-second burst in the frontal port and, by crawling to the left, fired another short burst at the other port. A third burst caused cries of agony and silenced the bunker. Later, the charred bodies of four Japs were found inside. A four-second burst was fired at one port of the second bunker which had been previously vacated. The third pillbox, in which there was only one Jap, was then pointed out to the flame thrower operator. Knowing his fuel was practically exhausted, he nevertheless thought the target could be reached at the short range of ten yards. The Jap evidently came to the same conclusion, for when the flame thrower was fired he blew himself up with a grenade. The flame had fallen short of the target. The flame thrower in this action was credited with five Japs killed and an unknown number of probables.[28]

The strongly coordinated and mutually supporting enemy positions at Rocky Point had been established both at the edges of two superimposed cliffs and on nearby hills. These positions consisted of natural interconnected caves and of bunkers and dugouts commanding all lanes of approach. The flame thrower, in conjunction with AT-rifle grenades, machine guns, M1 rifle fire, and demolition charges, was used on numerous occasions in attacking these positions. From twenty to twenty-four flame throwers were used with excellent

---

[28] Pers ltr, Cml O Alamo Force to Cml O Sixth Army, 21 Jun 44, no sub. Sixth A Cml Sect Records, 470.71 FT, ORB.

results in these operations. On 23 June, troops of the 1st Infantry Regiment discovered a pillbox within a cave manned by a single Jap. Covered by submachine gun and rifle fire, the flame thrower operator fired several short bursts into the opening and an engineer officer then demolished the pillbox with a large charge of TNT. The following day, an enemy 70-mm. gun sank an LVT Buffalo while it was landing troops on the west side of Rocky Point. At the regimental commander's orders, an assault team was formed and equipped with one flame thrower, two submachine guns, some M1 rifles and AT-rifle grenades, and a sixty-one pound TNT demolition charge. The flame thrower operator and the grenade launcher crawled into a shell hole about fifteen or twenty yards to the left of the cave containing the enemy 70-mm. gun. Supported by rifle and submachine gun fire, the flame thrower operator fired short bursts, then the grenadier fired all his grenades, and finally the engineers placed the charge. The enemy gun was knocked out and the Japs were buried under the debris. During the next few days, the flame throwers of the 1st Infantry, used in assault teams, helped clean out the ravine at Rocky Point. Altogether, thirteen of the enemy, four pillboxes, and ten caves or tunnels were eliminated in this fashion. The excellent fire cover afforded the flame thrower assault teams is evidenced by the fact that only one operator was slightly wounded in the action. No misfires were recorded, indicating thorough preliminary maintenance.29/

3. <u>Noemfoor Island</u>. The 158th Infantry RCT (Sep) reinforced by the 27th Engineer Combat Battalion made the initial landing on Noemfoor Island on 2 July 1944. A total of twenty-four flame throwers was available to these two units and the assault wave carried one flame thrower in each Buffalo. Each flame thrower was filled and ready for instant use should fortifications be encountered on the beaches. The resistance encountered on the beaches was easily overcome without use of the flame thrower. However, five of them received considerable use during the first day in mopping up the numerous caves dug into the coral bluff bounding the east side of Kamiri airdrome. Upon later inspection, seventeen

---

29/
(1) Ltr, CG Sixth Army to Dist., 6 Sep 44, sub: CW Activities during the Wakde Island-Maffin Bay Opns. (2) Rpt, 2d Lt Theodore Frankel, AT Plt Ldr and 2d Lt J. J. Harnes, 2d Bn Gas O, 13 Jul 44, sub: Rpt on Use of FT in Maffin Bay Area, Dutch New Guinea. In Sixth A Cml Sect Records, 319.1 and 350.05 Wakde, ORB.

enemy dead were found in these caves.30/

The 503d Parachute Regiment (Sep) used eleven of their twelve flame throwers on the outer perimeter around Kamiri Airfield during the latter half of July. All using units were favorably impressed both with the weapon and with napalm as a fuel. Maintenance and repair were carried on by a four-man flame thrower servicing shop under direct command of the Task Force chemical officer. Early in July, the using units ran out of many spare parts and also lost some repair kit parts. It was necessary in August to call in all flame throwers for complete overhaul and to pool all spare and repair kit parts for checking and redistribution.31/

4. <u>Biak Island</u>. Following a thorough naval and air bombardment of the beaches, elements of the 41st Infantry Division went ashore in the vicinity of Bosnek on the morning of 27 May 1944. The 186th Infantry (initial beachhead and east force) landed in the assault with eighteen portable flame throwers fully serviced and ready for action, while the 162d Infantry, which landed from LST's after the beachhead was secured, brought in twelve. These flame throwers were carried by operators within the company and battalion assault teams. The remaining twenty-two flame throwers of the other division elements were carried in the Task Force bulk-loaded CWS supplies to be landed on Z-Day and Z+1.

Based on lessons learned during the Hollandia operation, two mobile charging sets had been provided. Each set consisted of a $\frac{1}{4}$-ton truck and a $\frac{1}{4}$-ton trailer. Two commercial hydrogen cylinders, five commercial nitrogen cylinders and a fuel-mixing kit were carried in each trailer. A service kit and a fuel-filling kit were carried in each truck. A notched rack had been mounted on the trailer for use when the servicing unit was to be placed in operation. The commercial cylinders could be placed on the racks and the manifolds attached. Upon arrival in a regimental or battalion service area, the trailer could be detached, the truck unloaded and returned to the CWS dump to pick up five-gallon beadons previously filled with blended and thickened fuel mixtures. Four

---

30/
(1) Sixth Army, Report of the Tabletennis Operation, 7 Dec 44. In Hist Records Sect, AGO. (2) Cyclone Task Force, Rpt of CW Fld Intell Team No. 4, Appendix B, "Use of CW Equipment by Cyclone Task Force," 22 Jul 44. InSixth A Cml Sect Records, 350.05 Noemfoor, ORB.

31/
(1) Ltr, Cml O Tabletennis Task Force to Cml O Sixth Army, 16 Jul 44. (2) Ltr, Cml Supply O Sixth Army to Cml O Tabletennis Task Force, 12 Oct 44. (3) Ltr, Cml O Tabletennis Task Force to Cml O Sixth Army, 11 Jul 44. (4) Memo, CO Cml Unit 1 for Cml O Sixth Army, 16 Jul 44. In Sixth A Cml Sect Records, AG 300.6 Memos US Forces APO 704, ORB.

flame thrower repair men from the chemical composite platoon, attached to the division, were to accompany each portable charging unit.32/

Because of the intense shore bombardment, there was little opposition to the landing. Nevertheless, the regiments continued to carry the flame throwers because it was soon learned that the coral island abounded with a network of caves to which the defending Japanese had fled. These caves ranged in size from shallow ones large enough to accommodate two or three men, to underground networks large enough to accommodate 800 to 900 men. For example, the Ibdi pocket, situated on the coral ridge north of Ibdi, was about 400 yards long by 250 yards wide, and was covered with thick jungle brush and dense rain forest. All approaches to the crest of the higher ridges were commanded by numerous natural pinnacles of coral and brush. The intervening cuts and depressions were honeycombed with caves conveniently incorporated into a system which air, naval and artillery bombardments had been unable to neutralize.

Pillboxes of coral and log construction, and other hasty emplacements built of the same materials, were numerous. These were mutually supporting and arranged in depth. These positions were mainly situated on the pinnacles, at the bases of large trees and in defiles. The enemy had developed this pocket extensively and had converted it into a formidable defensive position. From it, he repulsed concentrated infantry attacks, supported by artillery, mortar and tank barrages, to the east, south, and west of the pocket. During the attacks, rocket launchers, flame throwers and rifle grenades were extensively used, but the targets were too numerous to be reduced one by one, and our troops sustained casualties out of proportion to the results obtained. Owing to the nature of the terrain and the proximity of our advance troops to the enemy positions, it was necessary to withdraw them during artillery concentrations. This action, although highly imperative, retarded progress. The enemy was so well dug in that artillery and air strikes produced only negligible results.33/

32/
    Ltr, Cml O 41st Inf Div to Cml O Alamo Force, 30 Jun 44,
       sub: Preliminary Technical Report - Letter Report No.
       2. In CMLWG.

33/
    41st Inf Div G-2 Rpt of Opns - Biak. In Hist Records
       Sect, AGO.

I Corps, General Eichelberger commanding, took over the operation, arriving early in June with the 163d Infantry RCT (41st Div) and the 34th Infantry (24th Div) as reinforcements, and the offensive was stepped up for the purpose of securing the island at the earliest practicable date. The following detailed accounts of the employment of portable flame throwers during the Biak Operation is reproduced verbatim from a technical report prepared by the chemical officer, 41st Infantry Division.

> 28 May - the 186th Infantry, reported that a flame thrower was employed against a cave occupied by two Japs. The cave was so deep and extensive that the flame thrower fire was ineffective.
>
> 29 May - 2d Battalion, 186th Infantry's operation against a Jap occupied cave north of Bosnek:
>
> Detailed Account. One of several caves along the shore line was occupied by an unknown number of the enemy. Headquarters Company, 186th Infantry met heavy resistance from this cave. A flame thrower team accompanied by a rifle squad was assigned the mission of clearing this cave. On approaching this particular cave, the flame thrower team moved close under cover of the embankment to within twenty feet of the cave. Several members of the rifle squad deployed across the beach and covered the approach of the flame team. The flame thrower operator fired one burst into the cave. He then moved into a better position and emptied the contents of his flame thrower into the cave. Just after completion of the fire delivery, a Jap appeared at the entrance and fired at the operator. The bullet penetrated the nitrogen cylinder of the flame thrower without injury to the operator. Three other Japs rushed out of the cave and were killed by our supporting riflemen.
>
> Effectiveness. The exact effect of the flame thrower's fire other than causing the four Japs to emerge into the open is unknown, since no attempt was made to enter the cave. However, no further enemy activity was observed from this cave.

Critique. This is an unusual incident. The tactics employed were satisfactory. The composition of the assault group was sufficient to permit it to close on the enemy position and accomplish its fire mission. There is some disagreement by the participants as to just what actually happened. Some claim the Japs emerged from the objective cave, while others insist that they appeared from an adjacent cave which had not been subjected to fire. Perhaps the exact details may never be known, but apparently the flame thrower's employment flushed the cave garrison so that they were killed by rifle fire and the position finally reduced.

30 May - 2d Battalion, 186 Infantry's operation against an enemy occupied cave north of Bosnek:

Detailed Account. A flame thrower team accompanied by six riflemen from Company E were in the process of clearing out caves along the shore line. At this particular cave, containing an unknown number of enemy, the operator moved along the embankment until he was approximately 30 feet from the cave. The six riflemen covered the operator's approach to the firing position. The operator fired, discharging approximately half the contents of the flame thrower. This engagement was preparatory to the destruction of the cave by explosive charges.

Effectiveness. No examination was made of the cave following the flame thrower's fire and prior to its destruction by dynamite, however, no enemy action resulted after the employment of the flame thrower. It is probable that the flame thrower was responsible for the temporary neutralization of the installation and thus permitted the emplacement of the explosive charges and in this manner assisted in the complete reduction of the cave.

Critique. This is another example of specialized flame thrower employment. The party composition and tactics employed permitted satisfactory fire delivery upon the target. The use of demolition in conjunction with flame techniques is recommended where complete destruction of the objective target is desired. The use of the flame thrower as a means of temporary neutralization of an enemy fortification to permit the safe emplacement of high explosive charges is a recommended procedure.

31 May - 1st Battalion, 162d Infantry's operation against a Japanese held position in the cliffs northwest of Ibdi:

Detailed Account. At 1400 hours, 31 May 1944, an attempt was made to neutralize the Japanese positions on the ledge. Two flame throwers were employed, supported by one platoon of riflemen who were to cover the top of the ridge with rifle fire while the flame throwers worked forward through secondary growth to the base of the steep slope. The rifle platoon attempted to go up the trail over the ridge. On reaching the top of the ridge, the leading man was wounded by rifle fire delivered from the Jap position on the ledge. When the platoon attempted an assault with several men, the Japs used knee mortars and hand grenades which immobilized the platoon's forward progress. The flame thrower operators, under cover of the rifle support, crowded up the ledge to within a few yards of the Jap position where the flame thrower fire was directed toward the general vicinity of the enemy installations.

Effectiveness of the Assault. Operators could not direct the flames into the Jap fortifications because of the height of the intervening ledge. Effect of the flame throwers' fires are unknown, but subsequent Jap action in the objective area indicated it to be ineffective.

Critique. This combat example provides considerable material for academic discussion. The particular situation encountered is an example where the principle of mass is particularly applicable. The employment of four or six flame throwers in an attack on a target of this type is clearly indicated. It must be emphasized that a thorough reconnaissance is an absolute requisite prior to the commitment of an assault party. Such reconnaissance is necessary in order to plan the attack, i.e., to determine the strength of the assault group, the exact composition of the party, the support to be rendered, the type fuel to employ and the tactics involved. The assault party leader and the flame thrower operators must have all available information affecting the mission prior to launching the attack in order to insure the maximum success. All commanders and leaders in the chain of command must understand the capabilities and limitations of the flame thrower before the effects of this weapon can be satisfactorily exploited. It must be emphasized that the flame thrower is not a weapon of opportunity but that it is a weapon to be employed when normal attack techniques utilizing organic weapons, have failed. When employed, the flame thrower party must be supported in a carefully coordinated overall attack pattern, employing rifle, automatic weapons and mortar fixing fires which neutralize the fires of the enemy objective position and its supporting installations during the approach of the flame thrower group. In this situation, mortar fires should have been employed. Such supplementary support would materially assist each flame thrower party to advance to a predetermined firing position within the range capabilities of the flame throwers from which the objective target could be engaged. In the absence of natural cover, smoke must be employed to conceal the approach and intent of the assault force. Further, smoke may be profitably employed in any situation to reduce the effectiveness of the enemy's fire. All personnel should be thoroughly versed in smoke technique and tactics in order that this munition may be employed to overcome the disadvantage of terrain and fire power. In the case being reviewed, the employment of thickened fuel is indicated rather than the blended gasoline and oil mix which was used. Definite targets must be assigned to the flame thrower party instead of employing the weapon for the delivery of area fire. Flank attacks are usually preferable to the frontal assault. When frontal attacks must be employed, it is usually necessary to increase the complement of flame throwers in the assault party, as well as provide greater supporting fires. While the terrain features encountered may have precluded the adherence to many of the fundmentals outlined in this discussion and the ledge may have materially impaired effective fire delivery, it is felt that considerable time must be spent in the indoctrination of all officers and non-commissioned officers in sound principles of flame thrower tactics. This training is necessary in order that this weapon may be successfully exploited to the maximum in furnishing assistance to infantry elements.

1 June - 2d Battalion, 186th Infantry's operation against an enemy occupied cave north of Bosnek:

Situation. The cave entrance was situated in a depression approximately fifty feet in diameter. A tunnel about 20 feet long descended from the cave mouth on a slope of about 15 degrees and terminated into a large chamber. This chamber had accommodated an estimated 150 Jap occupants. There was a small second opening leading into the chamber from just above the depression. The cave had been attacked and 7 Japs killed around the cave entrance. It was thought that the cave had been cleared of Japs and a party started down the incline tunnel, whereupon they drew fire from the large chamber.

Detailed Account. The Battalion Commander ordered up the flame thrower in order to neutralize this cave. At this time only one serviced flame thrower was available to the battalion. The operator was provided with rifle support. From a distance of less than twenty feet, he first fired three short bursts down the small secondary opening; then quickly moved to the mouth of the incline tunnel and fired several long bursts down the aditway and into the large chamber. These fires filled the whole chamber with flame and smoke. There was a fifteen minute lapse before the smoke had sufficiently cleared out of the large chamber to permit our troops to enter and appraise the situation.

Effectiveness. The garrison of the cave was found to consist of one Jap who had been killed as a result of the flame thrower operation. His clothes were still burning as well as some Jap stores within the cave.

Critique. The above example clearly demonstrates the value of flame thrower technique. The approach to firing positions in this case presented no special problems. The operator and commander showed decided initiative and foresight in this operation. Lacking additional flame throwers to embody the principle of mass, the flame thrower operator covered two firing positions, the first being delivered for temporary neutralization to facilitate movement to a more exposed position for delivery of the destructive fire. Operators must be trained to respond to the situation as in this case. They must be prepared to accomplish a mission with any portion of the flame throwers present by taking over the assignment of supporting elements in the event such elements become unable to complete their functions. The above example shows that an estimate of the situation was made and a decision was reached and executed which permitted the exploitation of the means available.

<u>7 June</u> - 1st Battalion, 162d Infantry's operation on the ridge north of Ibdi:

<u>Detailed Account</u>. The battalion was moving east to clear the Jap occupied ridges. Two companies were abreast with one platoon on each large ridge. Company A's Third Platoon was held up by the Jap pill boxes on Ridge No. 7. At 1330 hours, two flame throwers were employed to neutralize the position. Five riflemen, acting as a security detachment, advanced along the sides of the ridge and ahead of the flame throwers. The operators had to crawl along the knife-like ridge in order to move forward to the firing position. Little natural cover was afforded by the coral formation and tree trunks. From the vicinity of the last available sparse cover, flame thrower fire was directed at the position from which the enemy's fire had been received.

<u>Effectiveness</u>. The operation was ineffective. The vegetation adjacent to the enemy pill boxes precluded locating the exact position of the target. The range at which the flame throwers were employed was beyond the capability of the weapon.

<u>Critique</u>. Had the flame throwers in this situation been able to fire from a position within their range capabilities, it is probable that they would have been able to neutralize the objective. It must be brought to the attention of all commanders, from the infantry squad up, that the flame thrower is a special weapon whose effectiveness can only be exploited when it is employed in a coordinated attack pattern. Smoke laid by grenades or from mortars would have permitted closing

in to an effective range from which the fire could have been delivered. Thorough reconnaissance and planning must precede a flame thrower assault. Definite targets must be assigned. The flame thrower is not a weapon for area fire, and to employ them as such only results in exposing the team to enemy fire. Fuel is an all important consideration. All personnel concerned with flame thrower planning and use should be conversant with the types of fuel, their use and effectiveness. In this situation a thickened fuel is indicated. Flame throwers can only be successfully employed when all personnel in the chain of command have a thorough knowledge of the tactics and techniques concerned. Additional training of all personnel in the use of this weapon is indicated.

7 June -- 3d Battalion, 186th Infantry's operation against a series of caves in the vicinity of Sboeria:

Detailed Account. Headquarters Company, 3d Battalion, 186th Infantry, employed four flame throwers to mop-up a number of caves. These caves were situated along the bank adjacent to the sea and were within the battalion perimeter. Riflemen were employed to provide the necessary security to the flame thrower operators. One flame thrower was employed at a time. The operator moved as close to the bank as possible to reach a suitable firing position. Firing one burst from this flanking position to temporarily blind the entrance to the cave, the operator moved into a position directly in front of the cave opening where the remainder of the fire was delivered directly into the cave.

Effectiveness. The heat from the burning fuel appeared to be very intense for some distance within the caves. The fires within the caves continued to burn for some time, apparently having set fire to combustible material stored within the caves. No attempt was made to enter the caves to assess the damage.

Critique. This is another very effective use of the flame thrower. The normal blended oil and gasoline blended fuel produces a flame which rolls and billows into all cracks and corners. It is superior to hand grenades in this respect for this type operation. The flame thrower's use for this purpose is not confined to caves but it may be satisfactorily employed against emplacements, dugouts, buildings and other structures.

12 June - 3d Battalion, 162d Infantry's operation against pill boxes north of Mokmer Village:

Detailed Account. The enemy position had delivered automatic fire on the assault echelon of Company I, 162d Infantry. The position could not be directly observed and its exact nature was not determined, but the location was believed to be at the base of a large tree on the north slope of the ridge, with fairly heavy scrub and vine growth surrounding it. The installation had a field of fire covering a slight pimple from which the assault company was attacking. At 1100 hours, a flame party was organized from the Pioneer and Ammunition Platoon, 3d Battalion, Headquarters Company, 162d Infantry. This party consisted of the platoon leader, platoon sergeant and two flame thrower operators. It was discovered that only one of the flame throwers was in working order. The mission of this party was to support Company I, 162d Infantry, by neutralizing the suspected enemy pill boxes which were holding up the company's advance along the crest of the ridge immediately north of Mokmer Village. Initially, a 30-round 60-mm mortar barrage was laid in the enemy area. Following the barrage one squad of riflemen with one BAR moved along the steep south slope of the ridge to prepare the way and allow safe approach of the flame thrower group. During the movement the BAR fired several bursts to draw fire from the position, but this BAR was not answered by the enemy. A covered route to a good firing point was found. The flame thrower party, following the security squad, gained a suitable position on the ridge at a distance of 15 yards from the objective. The position of the flame thrower operator was such that he could lay the tank element of the flame thrower on the ground and operate the gun unit without encumbrance. Following his preparations, he fired three bursts. This fire was followed by an envelopment of the position by the riflemen who reached the installation and found it untenanted. The installation had been a temporary LMG position, cover being obtained by deep interstices between the roots of the tree. This position had been vacated prior to the delivery of the flame attack.

<u>Effectiveness</u>. Examination of the target showed good coverage by the flame thrower's fire, and it would undoubtedly have been very effective against any enemy personnel occupying the position. It is possible that the occupants had observed the party, detected the presence of the flame thrower and evacuated immediately. The flame thrower operated normally, no malfunctioning or stoppage being noted.

<u>Critique</u>. In this employment, adequate support was provided, consisting of covering rifle and automatic weapons fire and a preparatory mortar barrage. A single flame thrower was used from necessity, the second weapon being defective. The execution and tactics employed were excellent. The group accomplished their mission, employing the principles of fire and maneuver.

<u>21 June</u> - 1st Battalion, 162d Infantry's operation against the West Caves:

<u>Detailed Account</u>. The battalion, attacking the West Caves, had neutralized the east depression with grenades and rifle fire supported by tank-mounted machine guns and 75-mm cannon and 37-mm HE and canister shot. One platoon of Company B, supported by a tank, was trying to neutralize the fire coming from the cavern mouth of the middle depression. The fires of this unit were unable to neutralize the enemy machine gun and mortar fire. At 1400 hours two flame throwers were employed to burn out the mouth of the cave and neutralize Jap fire; and also to drive the enemy out of a log position near the edge of the depression.

The flame thrower operators first moved forward from the Battalion CP to the 1st Platoon of Company B, in order to reconnoiter the enemy position and secure information for planning the methods to be employed in delivering the flame attack. Upon completion of this reconnaissance the operators returned to the Battalion OP where the flame thrower had been left. Equipped with the flame throwers, they then crawled forward to the right of the platoon, which supported them with rifle fire. One squad of riflemen moved forward with the flame throwers and protected their right flank. The flame teams were able to get into a position at the edge of the depression from where they could shoot the flame into the mouth of the cave. Only a little vegetation was available for cover and concealment.

Effectiveness. The flame throwers silenced the fire from the mouth of the cavern, but failed to drive the Japs out of the large cave net. The effectiveness would have been greater, had the operators been able to advance to the mouth of the cave itself. The cave net was too large for the flame throwers to completely neutralize the installation.

Critique. In this execution we find that necessary steps had been taken to insure the success of the operation which were lacking in previous flame thrower employments by this battalion. Reconnaissance was made by the operators and stronger supporting fires were given to assist the assault group in advancing to its firing position. Normally, for engaging a target such as this, several flame throwers should have been employed in a mutually supporting pattern. The magnitude of the cave net would preclude complete neutralization by portable flame throwers; however, the temporary overcoming of enemy resistance at the portals could be effectively accomplished for a short period, as was done in this operation.

21 June - 1st Battalion, 162d Infantry's operation against Jap log and coral fortification:

Detailed Account. The situation followed that which was described above. Several Japs were in a fortification covered by logs and coral. This position could not be taken by rifle and grenade fire. Likewise, the tank could not fire into the position because of its location just over the crest of the depression. At 1430 hours one flame thrower was employed to neutralize the position. The second flame thrower of the flame thrower party had developed a pressure leak while being brought forward. Two riflemen accompanied the flame thrower operator over an open approach to within 20 feet of the Jap installation. The only cover available was that afforded by a large stump. When the operator reached the stump, the riflemen fired at the position. The flame thrower operator then fired a burst at the target. After appraising the result of the first burst, he fired a second. One of the Japs jumped out of the position just as the third and final burst was fired.

Effectiveness. The Jap position was neutralized. Four Japs occupying the fortification were killed as a result of the flame attack. The clothing was completely burned from the Jap who had attempted to evacuate the position.

Critique. While only a single flame thrower was employed, terrain conditions permitted the occupation of a firing position well within the range capabilities of the weapon. The operator showed good judgment in appraising his burst before proceeding with additional fires. The support given the flame thrower in this situation accomplished the mission; however, the support normally should be greater. Use of smoke munitions by the assault detachment and supporting elements must be stressed. The employment of smoke against the objective will conceal the advance of the flame group and may also draw the positions' fixed defensive fires, thus definitely locating the target. The target was within the capabilities of the weapons employed hence the principles of mass and economy of force were observed. [34]

---

[34] Ltr, Hq US Forces, APO 920, Office of the Cml O (Cml O 41st Inf Div) to Cml O Alamo Force, 11 Aug 44, sub: Preliminary Technical Report No. 9. In Sixth A Cml Sect Redords, 350.05 Biak, ORB

21 June - During the action against the West Caves or Sumps large drums of gasoline were poured into the cave through seepage points that had been found on top by observing emission of smoke from the smoke munitions that had been used against the cave. The gasoline was ignited and a series of explosions were heard lasting on to the following day. Information obtained from a prisoner of war revealed that at 0300, 22 June, Colonel Kuzume, Commanding Officer of the Japanese 222d Infantry, held a ceremony in the cave. The Colonel was reported to have stated that all able bodied soldiers should attempt to withdraw to the north in any way they might find possible. Documents were then destroyed and the regimental colors burned. When the colors had been burned, the troops yelled the traditional "Banzai!" The cave was not completely neutralized until the engineers had lowered 850 pounds of dynamite into the entrance, which was shaped like a well, and set it off. Only a few Japs survived the explosion; most of whom came running out; one at least was insane. 35/

The 163d Infantry reported that on 4 July 1944 Company "K", while in the Ibdi area, heard a movement in the undergrowth on their flank. A burst from the flame thrower was fired into this area. Five Japs immediately jumped up and commenced to run. They were fired on with our rifle fire and another burst from the flame thrower. When the smoke of the flame thrower's fire had cleared, three dead Japs were seen. The infantry was unable to determine what had become of the other two Japs. Another burst of the flame thrower was directed into the area from where the five Japs had been initially found. Three additional Japs, all aflame, jumped up from this same area. Two were killed by rifle fire and the other disappeared over the cliff. This procedure may be exploited in the future in

---

35/ I Corps, Biak Operation, 15 - 27 Jun 44.

developing a defensive use for the flame thrower against personnel. Area fire by the flame thrower against a fortified position is non-productive in results, but it appeared to be quite efficient against personnel.

10 July - 3d Battalion, 163d Infantry's operation against a Jap fortification in the Ibdi pocket:

Detailed Account. On 10 July 1944, efforts of the 3d Battalion to reduce an enemy pill box were unsuccessful. Three unsuccessful attempts were made to reduce the Jap installation by a flame thrower attack. Due to the terrain features and the natural cover available to the installation, it was impossible to close to a point where effective flame thrower fire could be delivered on the target. On the morning of 11 July 1944, infantry elements succeeded in moving under cover on the south side of the ridge and in overcoming the fortification from the rear. This cleared the way for the attack of the key bunker installation. The pill box at this point was reinforced with coral and was emplaced on the side of the ridge. A small ridge in front of this position protected it from small arms fire as well as from bazooka and rifle grenades; therefore, in order to reduce the position it was necessary to use a flame thrower. Due to the active and heavy enemy sniper fire in this area, a BAR was included in the flame thrower detail in these two employments. Movement of the team was considerably hindered by the rough terrain and sniper fire. These factors made it necessary for the flame thrower detail to crawl most of the way to the firing position. The movement to the firing position from the captured strong point No. 1 required thirty minutes. The firing distance was set at approximately twenty yards.

Effectiveness. Immediately following the flame thrower burst, three Japanese, all of whom were on fire, ran out of the pill box. A second burst was fired and four of the enemy, three of whom were on fire, evacuated the pill box. The third burst flushed the final Jap occupant who was apparently unharmed by the fire effect. The neutralization of the position was complete. Comment by the infantry:

>'In this particular instance the flame thrower proved to be a valuable weapon in the neutralization of the enemy position which could not be brought under fire by other organic weapons.'

Critique. In the 10 July 1944 attack which was unsuccessful, we find several basic principles violated. The employment of smoke would have permitted closing to a point where the target could have been brought under effective fire. The support given this attack was inadequate. The inclusion of a BAR with the flame thrower detail was a necessary security measure as a protection against snipers. Flame throwers are very vulnerable and must be protected. The use of only one flame thrower in each instance violates the fundamental principle of mass. The terrain in this area was very difficult and the infantry may have been justified in incorporating only one weapon into these assault parties. In the employment of 11 July 1944, using the natural route of approach and covered by supporting fires placed on adjacent enemy installations, the flame thrower detail was able to proceed to the firing position. The difficulty can be imagined when the thirty minute approach is considered. The employment of only one flame thrower precludes the fire and movement obtainable when these weapons are used in pairs. In both cases, preparatory supporting fires were not in evidence. In the second attack, the flame thrower accomplished the mission of reducing the pill box. 36/

During the Biak operation, 27 May to 19 August 1944, fifty-nine fuel fillings were expended in combat by the infantry. Types and amounts of fuel employed were as follows:

36/
Ltr, Hq US Forces, APO 920, Office of the Cml O (Cml O 41st Inf Div) to Cml O Alamo Force, 11 Aug 44, sub: Preliminary Technical Report.- Report No. 9. In Sixth A Cml Sect Records, 350.05, Biak, ORB.

15 gals. gasoline to 1 can napalm - 8 fillings or 32 gals.
13 gals. gasoline to 1 can napalm - 31 fillings or 124 gals.
    Blended gasoline and SAE 30   - 20 fillings or 80 gals.

Also expended were twelve hydrogen and thirty-nine nitrogen cylinders as well as 225 pounds of napalm.37/

The infantry reported that, on several occasions, flame throwers failed to function when the operator arrived at firing positions, although tests made immediately before going into position indicated a properly functioning weapon. Malfunctioning was mostly attributed to damp ignition systems, leakage of gas in hydrogen or nitrogen pressure system, dead batteries, and fouled spark plugs. It was found that dampness alone could produce a "short" in spark plugs. A tested plug could be placed in a perfectly operating flame thrower and after a lapse of eight to twelve hours during rainy weather would be "shorted" out.

Seventy-two flame throwers were available to the task force and a total of 3,344 man-hours were consumed by the 273d Chemical Composite Platoon on flame thrower service and maintenance during the eighty-six days of the operation. This time included the erection of a base shop, the operation of forward service points, as well as mixing fuels and making repairs at the task force CWS dump, and was indicative of the amount of work required to keep the M1A1 flame throwers in operation.38/ The value of chemical service troops in a division had been thoroughly demonstrated in performing these duties as well as other essential Chemical Warfare Service functions.39/

37/
    (1) Ltr, Asst AG Sixth Army to Dist, 3 Sep 44, sub: Chemical Warfare Activities during the Biak Operation, p. 11. In Sixth A Cml Sect Records, 350.05, Biak, ORB. (2) Rpt, Cml O 41st Inf Div, n.d., sub: Chemical Phase and Section Historical Record of HORLICK Operation. In CMLWG.

38/
    Ltr, Hq US Forces APO 920, Office of the Cml O (Cml O 41st Inf Div) to Cml O Alamo Force, 11 Aug 44, sub: Preliminary Technical Report - Report No. 9. In Sixth A Cml Sect Records, 350.05, Biak, ORB.

39/
    Cml Sect 41st Inf Div, Chemical Phase and Section Historical Record of Horlick Operation. In Hist Records Sect, AGO.

A base repair establishment was maintained at the Task Force CW Service Area for the performance of third and fourth echelon flame thrower repair and maintenance beyond the scope of the mobile detachments. Functions such as spark plug, spark coil assembly and trigger assembly repair, quantity fuel mixing, and salvage were conducted at this installation.

The mobile flamethrower service units proved to be a necessity during the operation. Both units were landed on Z-Day with the Chemical Composite Platoon and held by this unit for dispatch on call. The first call was received from the munitions officer of the 162d Infantry on Z-plus-2.

During the early part of the operation these units operated on call from the Task Force CW Service Center. However, as the beachhead was extended, the mobile units established permanent forward service positions for servicing infantry units in the area. Even with the mobile unit, it was often necessary for the operators to carry the flame thrower as far as a mile to reach the "Jeephead." A study of the operation disclosed that more extensive chemical warfare assistance was required. Complete service by technical CWS personnel should have been provided to the lowest echelon rather than just to regimental service areas as was practiced. The technical nature of such service required constant surveillance by technically trained CWS personnel to insure mechanical functioning and employment of the proper fuel. 40/

E. Preparations for the Philippine Operations

1. <u>Critique on Previous Operations</u>. In May 1944, General

---

40/
    Ltr, Cml O 41st Inf Div to Cml O Alamo Force, 30 Jun 44, sub: Preliminary Technical Report - Letter Report No. 2. In Sixth A Cml Sect Records, 350.05, Biak, ORB.

Krueger, Commanding General, Sixth Army, informed his chemical officer that he was disappointed in the employment of flame throwers in past operations.41/ Accordingly, a study was made by the Army G-3 for the purpose of revising the current policy, embodied in TM 8, dated 1 October 1943. A review of past operations revealed several outstanding deficiencies which needed correction. For example, during the Arawe Operation the portable flame thrower was successfully employed during the first day by Troop A, 112th Cavalry, and was not used again during the operation, although the advance had been held up for two weeks by defenses suitable for flame thrower targets. The advance had not been resumed until reinforcements, consisting of the 158th Infantry RCT (Sep) and Company B, 1st Marine Tank Battalion, 1st Marine Division, arrived.42/ At Cape Gloucester the marines had reported the flame thrower as being unreliable because of the heavy rains experienced during the operation. Six months prior to the Admiralties Operation, the 1st Cavalry Division had trained over 300 flame thrower operators, but when the time came to use the flame throwers it was found that the weapons had been abandoned and were found scattered all over the battlefield. In fact, the initial landing force, consisting of the 2d Squadron, 5th Cavalry Regiment, came ashore at Los Negros without flame throwers. At the conclusion of the Admiralties Operation, it was found that six flame throwers had been completely lost. During the Hollandia Operation, an observer reported three flame throwers abandoned in a ditch along the side of the road.43/

Many reports had been received of a flame thrower operator

41/
    Ltr, Cml O Alamo Force to Cml O I Corps, 17 May 44, no sub. In pers file of Col Harold Riegelman, former Cml O, I Corps.

42/
    112th Cav RCT, Hist Rpt, 10 Feb 44.

43/
    Ltr, Cml O Alamo Force to Cml O I Corps, 17 May 44.

having been sent forward without sufficient fire support and it was felt that the flame thrower was being employed as a primary assault weapon instead of being used as "another weapon" in the assault party, as originally intended. In other instances, a hastily formed security detachment had been used to assist flame thrower operators. This arrangement had not afforded the most efficient means of attacking fortified positions because such detachments had never been trained as a team. In many cases, infantry officers had not demonstrated proper knowledge of the employment of assault parties, indicating a requirement for further training. Instances had been reported where one flame thrower had been used when three or four would have been required to reduce the objective. Other deficiencies noted were: lack of adequate reconnaissance; insufficient knowledge of the limitations and capabilities of the weapon; definite targets not assigned; insufficient use of smoke; and use of the improper fuel. 44/

Recommendations from Sixth Army units revealed that one of the greatest causes of deficiencies could be traced to the fact that the flame throwers were employed as a secondary weapon. It was noted that during training periods units would attain a high standard of proficiency in training assault parties, but when committed to combat several months later the trained assault parties would no longer be intact when a requirement arose for their employment. This condition was attributable in part to the fact that upon completion of the training period secondary assault weapons such as flame throwers and rocket launchers had been returned to unit supply and had not been issued again until required for combat. At such time, operators had to return to regimental supply in order to service and fill the weapons, duties in which operators had little or no training. In the meantime, transfers, promotions, and casualties had disintegrated the assault parties to such an extent that it was no longer feasible to keep them together on the battlefield. Also, the fact that flame throwers had not been issued to individuals as a primary weapon presented a problem of maintenance which had not been solved. Instances

---

44/ Ltr, Hq US Forces APO 920, Cml O 41st Inf Div to Cml O Alamo Force, 11 Aug 44, sub: Preliminary Technical Report - Report No. 9. In Sixth A Cml Sect Records, 350.05, Biak, ORB.

were noted, both in training and on the battlefield, where flame throwers, supposedly serviced and ready to fire, had misfired after being issued to operators in an unserviceable condition.45/

In order to correct this basic deficiency a great deal of thought was given to the idea of establishing a permanent organization to which assault weapons were assigned as primary weapons and whose primary mission would include the assault of fortifications. The Assistant Chief of Staff, G-3, I Corps, favored the employment of CWS troops to operate the flame thrower. Accordingly, I Corps recommended converting a chemical mortar company to a "flame thrower company." This company was to be assigned on the basis of one per division and would have assigned to it the division's sixty flame throwers together with fuels and accessories. Normal attachment would be one platoon of the converted company per infantry regiment. Each platoon would consist of two flame thrower assault parties to be further attached by regimental headquarters to battalions or companies as required. As a temporary solution, I Corps suggested the establishment at headquarters, out of regimental strength, of a provisional flame thrower platoon of thirty men.46/

The 41st Infantry Division favored organizing the antitank company of each infantry regiment into a "flame thrower company" or, as an alternative, to organize a "flame thrower platoon" from each antitank company, similar to the "provisional flame thrower platoons" that had been organized by the Americal Division in the

---

45/
(1) Cml O Sixth Army, Inspection Rpt, 19 May 44, sub: Inspection of Chemical Activities in the 1st Cavalry Division, p. 5. In Sixth A Cml Sect Records, 333 Inspection Rpts, ORB. (2) Memo, Cml O Sixth Army for G-3 Sixth Army, 21 May 44, no sub. In CMLWG.

46/
Pers Ltr, Cml O I Corps to Cml O Alamo Force, 13 Jun 44, no sub. In Sixth A Cml Sect Records, AG 300.6 Memos I Corps, ORB.

South Pacific Area.47/ The chemical officer, I Corps, looked with favor upon any plan by which trained personnel and flame throwers would always be available whenever needed. In addition to concurrence with suggestions outlined above, he was also interested at this time in converting one or more chemical processing companies into flame thrower companies. Assault parties of squad dimensions would be attached to infantry units as the situation demanded.48/ Other units recommended that the assault parties be organized from engineer units. Technically, the engineers appeared to be the best qualified to operate and maintain assault weapons. However, to assign engineers to the assault of fortified positions was contrary to War Department policy as contained in Engineer Field Manual, FM 5-6, 23 April 1943, which stated in paragraph 59: "Assault of permanent fortifications is normally an infantry mission and an infantry platoon is the basic tactical unit used." It should be noted that the idea of providing a separate organization for the employment of flame throwers is not new. The need for such organizations had already been recognized by Germany, Italy, and Japan, who had separate Tables of Organization for flame companies.49/

2. **New Training and Tactical Doctrine Established.** After extensive studies, Sixth Army published a new training memorandum,

---

47/
  Ltr, Cml O 41st Inf Div to Cml O Alamo Force, 30 Jun 44, sub: Preliminary Technical Report - Letter Report No. 2. In Sixth A Cml Sect Records, 350.05, Biak, ORB.

48/
  Pers ltr, "Bob" (Col Robert N. Gay, Cml O XIV Corps) to Cml O Sixth Army, 9 Jun 44, no sub. In Sixth A Cml Sect Records, 353 FT Tng, ORB.

49/
  CW Intell Bull No. 50, OC CWS, 15 Feb 45, Part I, Sect V; and No. 34, 1 Jun 44, par. 3f, and No. 16, 1 Jul 43, Sect IV, 2d.

TM 18, dated 22 June 1944 (See Appendix No. 9) which rescinded the previous training memorandum (See Appendix No. 5). Instead of emphasizing training in the use of the flame throwers, the new directive prescribed a program for the technical and tactical training of an assault party. It directed that each infantry battalion and each cavalry squadron (dismounted) would form and maintain one assault party, permanently organized and equipped in accordance with the following table:

Personnel	Arms and Equipment
1 party leader	Carbine or M1 rifle, hand grenades
1 assistant leader	M1 rifle, hand grenades
2 flame thrower operators	2 flame throwers, 2 pistols
2 assistant flame thrower operators	2 M1 rifles, WP and hand grenades
4 rocket launcher men	2 rocket launchers, 2 pistols
2 demolition men	2 M1 rifles, demolition charges, wire cutters, WP grenades
1 BAR operator	1 BAR
1 assistant BAR operator	1 M1 rifle
4 riflemen	4 M1 rifles, grenade discharger and rifle grenades, WP and hand grenades

It was also directed that all rifle battalion or squadron commanders, executive officers, S-3 and rifle company commanders would familiarize themselves with the capabilities, limitations and tactical employment of an assault party, and that the assault party would be initially held in reserve during combat in order to be immediately available upon demand.

The tactical doctrine established at this time was discussed in detail in a publication issued by the commanding general, Sixth Army, in mid-August 1944, which read as follows:

The necessity for perfecting the assault of permanent fortifications becomes more evident as operations proceed forward. Although the basic principles of tactics and techniques in assaulting fortifications are the same in all theaters, there are methods of applying these principles which are peculiar and applicable to each area or operation. In the operations in this theater to date the landings have not been made against fortifications such as those existing on the coast of France or on the atolls in the Central Pacific. Log type pill boxes and other lightly constructed fortifications have normally been encountered after the initial landing and during the advance from the established beachhead to the objective.

Based on past operations and anticipating the type of opposition which may be encountered in future operations the following principles are set forth as a guide in training divisions under this command in their preparation for assaulting fortified positions:

Assault of fortifications is normally an infantry mission with the infantry platoon as the basic tactical unit used. The infantry battalion used in the assault is provided with weapons adapted for use against fortifications. These include flame throwers, smoke, hand grenades, rifle grenades, demolition equipment and rocket launchers. Direct fire artillery weapons are normally attached. When necessary, engineers may be used for breaching obstacles. Chemical troops may be included. A company of an assault battalion may reorganize one or more platoons for assault missions to best utilize the special weapons issued. A platoon may be formed into an assault party. Because, in the majority of past operations in this theater, a properly trained assault party has not been available when needed by the battalion (squadron) commander, this headquarters issued Training Memorandum No. 18. This training memorandum prescribes the minimum requirements for a battalion (squadron), insures the presence of at least one assault party per battalion (squadron) and is designed to add emphasis to assault party training.

The question often arises as to what part the combat engineers will take in the assault of fortified positions. It must be remembered that the primary mission of divisional engineer troops in the type of operations common to the theater has, by necessity, been construction and maintenance of communications, particularly roads, docks, bridges and dump areas. In this theater the division of engineers from their basic mission is particularly undesirable due to the great volume of engineer work and the difficulty of providing and maintaining routes of communication. The primary responsibility of the infantry must therefore be stressed. Consequently, upon encountering fortifications the infantry units rather than the engineers should locate and attack the positions utilizing assault parties, reinforced, if necessary with additional demolition men, automatic weapons, mortars and supported by elements of the cannon company, organic anti-tank guns, artillery, 4.2" chemical mortars, tanks, airplanes or any other means available at the time. If the situation demands, these assault parties can further be reinforced by detachments of combat engineers who are more highly trained in the use of demolitions and who have larger quantities of supplies. However, this use should be exceptional and the principal engineer effort concentrated on the primary engineer mission.

If, in an operation, an amphibious landing is to be undertaken on a beach where previous reconnaissance and intelligence indicates the existence of extensive heavy steel and concrete fortifications or underwater obstacles, then engineer units should be in the initial assault waves to assist in breaching these specific fortifications and obstacles. Prior to an operation of this nature the assault battalion and attached engineer units should have adequate and realistic training along the lines of that given to the troops that participated in the Marshalls operation.

This headquarters considers the infantry as the basic arm responsible for assaulting fortified positions. When the situation so requires, the maximum use of all available supporting arms may have to be employed to support and reinforce the infantry in accomplishing its mission. Moreover, the battlefield is not the place to employ the various combat echelons together as a team for the first time. This must be accomplished in previous realistic combined training of all units available to a division commander, thus having teams composed of many combinations, all members of which have confidence in each other.[50]

3. **Training Conducted for the Philippine Operations.** The original plans for the invasion of the Philippines called for the initial landing to be made by the Sixth Army at Sarangani Bay on the southern coast of Mindanao, to be followed by the Leyte landing at a later date. The Third Fleet began probing operations in the Philippines during the latter part of August 1944. After striking the central Philippines on 12 September, Admiral Halsey recommended that intermediate operations be cancelled and that our forces attack Leyte as soon as possible. Admiral Nimitz offered to place the 3d Amphibious Force which included the XXIV Corps, then loading in Hawaii for the Yap Operation, at General MacArthur's disposal for an attack on Leyte. The plan was referred to General MacArthur who advised that he was prepared to shift his plans to land on Leyte on 20 October instead of 20 December as previously

---

[50] Sixth Army, Combat Notes, No. 2, 15 Aug 44, In Hist Records Sect, AGO.

planned. The plan was approved by the Joint Chiefs of Staff on 13 September and the XXIV Corps was placed under the operational control of Sixth Army.51/

This change in plans required a change in training schedules. In addition to the XXIV Corps, it was decided to employ the X Corps, consisting of the 1st Cavalry Division and 24th Infantry Division, for the assault against Leyte and to bring in the 32d Infantry Division as reinforcements or as garrison troops. Since the termination of the Admiralties Operation on 18 May, the 1st Cavalry Division had been training for further combat, 52/ while the 24th Infantry Division had been on a training and garrison status since the end of the Hollandia Operation on 6 June 1944. Both of these divisions had carried out considerable flame thrower and assault party training. However, as late as mid-August, the 32d Division had been withdrawn from a hard-fought battle at Aitape, New Guinea. This division conducted flame thrower schools and assault training during August and September.53/ The 112th Cavalry RCT (Sep) was also pulled out of the line at Aitape during August and immediately began to prepare for the Leyte Operation. The 11th Airborne Division which had been stationed at Oro Bay since April had completed an extensive assault training program by September and was designated as Army reserve.

Early in October, the newly arrived Eighth Army assumed command of the remaining troops in New Guinea. It was charged with mounting out troops for Sixth Army's Luzon operation as well as troops to be employed by the Eighth Army itself during the Visayan operations. Among divisions preparing for the Luzon Campaign under I Corps were the 6th Division at Sansapor, the 25th at New Caledonia and the 43d at Aitape. XI Corps units committed

---

51/
CofS USA, Biennial Rpt, 1 Jul 43 to 30 Jun 45, p. 71

52/
1st Cav Div, TM-5, 20 Jun 44. Sixth A Cml Sect Records, 353 CW Tng, ORB.

53/
Ltr, Hq Unit 4, 94th Cml Comp Co to CG XI Corps, APO 471, 1 Sep 44, sub: Historical Report. In Hist Records Sect, AGO.

for the Luzon Operation included the 33d 54/ at Finschafen and the 38th at Oro Bay. In addition, at Cairns, Australia, the 158th Infantry Regiment (Sep) and the 503d Parachute Regiment (Sep) were training for the Luzon Campaign. The 31st and 41st Divisions, slated to participate in the Visayan Campaign, were training at Aitape and Biak respectively. 55/ Eighth Army accepted the doctrine established by Sixth Army for the employment of the flame thrower and carried on with the training program where it was left off by Sixth Army. 56/

During August 1944, the Chemical Warfare Training Center, located at Oro Bay, New Guinea, trained two assault parties and offered their services as a demonstration team to assist in training assault parties in infantry battalions. Eighth Army and I Corps, which was under Eighth Army, employed these teams throughout October and November for demonstration purposes. It was felt that the teams were especially valuable in training commanders in the employment of assault weapons. Smoke, demolitions, and live ammunition were used in these demonstrations which were conducted on previous combat terrain. Demonstrations were conducted for the 6th, 24th, 32d, 33d, 38th, 41st, and 43d Infantry Divisions, as well as for the 112th Cavalry RCT. 57/

In general, the minimum training requirements for assault parties as prescribed by Sixth and Eighth Armies were exceeded by the units. I Corps added a communications detail to the group and recommended a mobile service unit per regiment, similar to

---

54/
   See Appendix 10 for 33d Div TM.

55/
   (1) Cml O 25th Inf Div, Hist Rpt, 9 Apr 45, sub: CW Section 1944. (2) Cml O I Corps, Hist Rpt, Period 2 Oct - 20 Nov 44. (3) Memo, CG 38th Inf Div, 10 Sep 44, no sub. In Sixth A Cml Sect Records, 353 FT Tng, ORB. (4) Ltr, Cml O Task Force Hq APO 704 to Asst Cml O Sixth Army, 23 Sep 44. In Sixth A Cml Sect Records, 470.71 FT, ORB.

56/
   See Appendix 11 for directive issued by Eighth Army.

57/
   (1) Cml O I Corps, Hist Rpt Period 2 Oct - 20 Nov 44, n.d., no sub. In pers files of Col Harold Riegelman (former Cml O I Corps.) (2) Memo, Cml O I Corps for Actg Cml O Sixth Army, 11 Nov 44. In Sixth A Cml Sect Records, 300.6 - Memos Sixth Army, ORB.

the one employed by the 41st Division at Biak.58/ The 41st
Infantry Division attempted to train an assault party for each
rifle platoon, while other divisions trained as many as one
assault party per company.59/

  4. <u>Supply Situation</u>. While units prepared for the
Philippines operation, the supply of flame throwers, accessory
kits and spare parts became extremely critical. The Borden
Mission had demonstrated E-3 flame throwers to SWPA units in
October 1943 and at that time Sixth Army sent in a requisition
for 240 of them on highest priority. The E-3 had been standardized as the M2-2 on 4 March 1944, 60/ and on 1 April the
theater listed its total requirements for this model through
December 1944 as 702. During the first week in April the
theater was informed of shipment of the 240 M2-2's requested
the previous October. The weapons arrived at Finschafen in
June and July 1944. 61/ It was planned to make immediate issue to units scheduled for the Philippines Operation. Investigation revealed, however, that ignition cartridges had not
accompanied the shipment and were not enroute to the theater.
They arrived a month after initiation of the Leyte operation.62/

58/
 I Corps, TM 13, 20 Jul 44. In CMLWG.

59/
 Ltr, Cml O 41st Inf Div to Cml O I Corps, 15 Aug 44, no
  sub. In pers files of Col Harold Riegelman.

60/
 Ltr, TAG to CINC SWPA, 22 Mar 44, sub: Transmittal of
  Manuals on Flame Throwers to the Commander-in-Chief
  SWPA. In Sixth A Cml Sect Records, 470.71 FT, ORB.

61/
 (1) Rad, CM-IN 671, 1 Apr 44; and CM-OUT 19798, 7 Apr
  44. (2) Memo, Cml O Alamo Force for Cml O 6th Inf
  Div, 27 Jun 44, sub: Your Letter on E-3 Flame Throwers.
  (3) Ltr, CG Sixth Army to CG USAFFE, 25 Jul 44, sub:
  Extra Pressure Cylinders for M2-2 Flame Throwers. In
  Sixth A Cml Sect Records, 470.71 FT, ORB.

62/
 (1) Report of Activities of Flame Thrower Team, SWPA and
  SPA, 22 Nov 44. (2) Ltr from Fld Opns Div, OC CWS to
  Cml O I Corps, 17 Oct 44. In CMLWG. (3) Pers ltr,
  Asst Cml O Sixth Army to Cml O 41st Div, 24 Nov 44.
  In Sixth A Cml Sect Records, 300.6 Misc. Memos, ORB.

It was also found that all flame throwers had to be equipped with safety heads, adjusted and thoroughly checked before issue because a number of leaky pressure cylinders and bad connections were found. Also, it was found that the Hoke regulator, with which the M2-2's were equipped, was not dependable.63/ Six ignition cartridges had been included in the box with each flame thrower. The 11th Airborne Division was equipped with E-3 flame throwers prior to the Leyte operation and was furnished ignition cartridges taken from the boxes. The decision to give priority to the airborne division was based on the fact that the 75-mm. artillery with which it was equipped was light and greater use of assault parties might be expected. Also, the problem of dropping the flame thrower by parachute was simplified with the new flame thrower. Ignition cartridges finally became available during November, and in December the M2-2 flame throwers were shipped to Leyte for issue to the infantry.

It was felt that the supply of M1A1 flame throwers would be somewhat improved upon the arrival of 400 at Finschafen in July and of 500 at Oro Bay in September. However, when the latter shipment arrived it was found that all of the pressure bottles were one and a half inches too long. All of these had to be modified by lengthening the pressure tubing connection at the top in order that the full weight of the loaded flame thrower would not rest on the protruding pressure cylinder and break or loosen the connections at the top.64/

63/
   Ltr, Cml O Base F to Cml O USASOS, 14 Sep 44, sub: Technical Report of Malfunctioning of an E-3 Flame Thrower at CWS Center, Base F, on 11 Sep 44. BFCW 470.71. In CMLWG.

64/
   (1) 1st Ind, Cml O Interm Sect to Cml O Sixth Army, 30 Jul 44, on basic ltr, 25 Jul 44, sub: Shipments of Flame Throwers. In Sixth A Cml Sect Records, 470.71 FT, ORB. (2) Rpt, Lt Col W. A. Johnston, et al to OC CWS, 22 Nov 44, sub: Report on Activities of Flame Thrower Team. In CMLWG.

Spare parts were obtained by cannibalizing both old and new flame throwers. However, there still existed a critical shortage of batteries and pressure regulators.65/ In November, while preparing for the Luzon operation, the chemical officer, 6th Division, made the following report:

> Regarding flame throwers, we have at present 40 serviceable M1A1's on hand and parts enroute to make 54 in serviceable condition. The remaining six which we have are beyond repair. Actually, the so-called "serviceable" M1A1's are in a pretty "dead tired" condition and I frankly dislike to see the Division use them in the coming operation.66/

Base section chemical officers drew the attention of the chemical officer, Sixth Army to the high rate of loss of the flame thrower due to the failure of combat troops to take care of their equipment and the failure of combat commanders to understand the capabilities and limitations of the flame thrower. Examination of flame throwers used in combat revealed the following main defects, due exclusively to mishandling and faulty maintenance: (1) dirt in burner heads, spark plugs, fuel discharge valves, and in service and fuel kits; (2) waterproofing removed, paint worn off, and consequent rust on the entire weapon; (3) loose connections of ignition cables and between spark-coil and push-button assemblies; (4) threads stripped or otherwise damaged on hydrogen and pressure cylinders, manifolds, and other connections; (5) insufficient cleaning and fuel-draining after firing; and (6) improper wrapping and packing.67/

65/
 Ibid.

66/
 Ltr, Cml O 6th Inf Div to Cml O I Corps, 10 Nov 44, no sub. In pers files of Col Harold Reigelman.

67/
 (1) Memo, Cml O Interm Sect USASOS for Cml O Sixth Army, 8 Jun 44, sub: Flame Throwers. (2) Ltr, Cml O USASOS to Cml O Sixth Army, 24 Oct 44, sub: Use of the M1A1 Flamethrowers. In Sixth A Cml Sect Records, 470.71 FT, ORB.

Past experience had demonstrated that CWS personnel were required in divisions and separate regimental combat teams in order to maintain the M1A1 flame thrower and to prepare the proper fuel for use in each specific flame thrower operation. Among the duties of chemical service units was the local procurement of all possible flame thrower parts in Australia, cannibalization of obsolete M-1 flame throwers for spare parts, and the manufacture and adaptation of parts not otherwise available locally.68/ By early September M1A1 parts became plentiful in the theater.69/ In August 1944, Sixth Army initiated action to disband the chemical composite companies assigned to the Army and activate separate chemical service platoons therefrom. Further command action had been initiated to obtain sufficient service platoons to provide for the attachment of a platoon to each division. For the Leyte operation, a provisional platoon was attached to each of the divisions in X Corps. The request for reorganization was approved in November and immediate steps were taken to attach a chemical service platoon to each division to be employed in the Luzon Operation. The presence of these troops in divisions enabled the CWS to carry out its responsibility for maintenance of CWS equipment.70/ Besides the sixty flame throwers authorized each infantry division, six were authorized for maintenance and were carried by the chemical service platoon.

F. Employment in the Philippines.

1. Leyte. On the 17th and 18th of October 1944 the 6th

68/
(1) Ltr, Cml O Alamo Force to Cml O Base A, 28 Jan 44, sub: Flame Thrower Parts. (2) 1st Ind, Cml O Interm Sect to Cml O Sixth Army, n.d., no sub, on unlocated basic ltr. (3) Ltr, Cml O USASOS to Cml O Base 7, 18 Apr 44, sub: Local Procurement of Flame Thrower Parts. In Sixth A Cml Sect Records, 470.71 FT. ORB.

69/
Ltr, Cml O Interm Sect USASOS to Cml O Sixth Army, 6 Sep 44, sub: Availability of Spare Parts. In Sixth A Cml Sect Records, 470.71 FT, ORB.

70/
Ltr, CG X Corps to CG Sixth Army, 13 Jan 45, sub: Report of CW Activities, pp. 12, 16. In Sixth A Cml Sect Records, 319.1 Leyte Opn Rpts, ORB.

Ranger Infantry Battalion was landed on Dinagat, Suluan and Homonhon Islands, to secure the entrance to Leyte Gulf; and minesweepers immediately went to work to clear the gulf of mines. Meanwhile a vast armada composed of the 3d and 7th Fleets approached the east coast of Leyte with the Sixth Army. This array of vessels included six heavy battleships with "their screen of cruisers and destroyers, 18 escort aircraft carriers, 53 assault transports, 54 assault cargo ships, 151 LST's, 72 LCI's, 16 rocket ships and over 400 other assorted amphibious craft".71/ At dawn on 20 October 1944, the Army went ashore with the X Corps on the north flank and the XXIV Corps on the south flank. The shore bombardment laid down by the Navy previous to the landing had been so devastating that the Japanese 16th Division, which garrisoned the island, had abandoned the thirty miles of beach defense which they had so diligently prepared and fled inland a short distance. As a result, there was only sporadic opposition to the landing. Also, the enemy had expected a landing in Mindanao instead of Leyte and the 16th Division was completely unprepared to meet the assault. In fact, the division was conducting maneuvers in the Leyte Valley at the time of the landing and was cut off from the bulk of its supplies which were located north of Tacloban.

The portable flame thrower was first employed by the 6th Rangers against a fortified lighthouse on Dinagat Island and continued to be used by the infantry throughout the operation, which terminated 25 December. A total of 583 portable flame throwers were brought in by the seven divisions, one separate regimental combat team and the ranger battalion. The 7th, 77th, and 96th Infantry Divisions, which came from the Central Pacific Area, were equipped with the new cartridge ignition, M2-2 flame throwers. The 1st Cavalry Division, 24th and 32d Infantry Divisions, 112th Cavalry RCT (Sep) and 6th Ranger Battalion were equipped with the old M1A1 type, while the 11th Airborne Division carried the M2-2 and E-3 models which, however, were not used.72/

71/
 CofS USA, Biennial Report, 1 Jul 43 to 30 Jun 45, p. 73.

72/
 Ltr, CG XXIV Corps to CG Sixth Army, 20 Dec 44, sub: Report of CW Activities. In Sixth A Cml Sect Records, 319.1 Leyte Opn Rpts, ORB.

An indication of the number of times the flame thrower was employed in combat is obtained from the Sixth Army chemical ammunition expenditure report for the operation. A total of 2,025 cartridge ignition cylinders (M2-2), 430 commercial nitrogen cylinders (220 cubic feet), and 60 commercial hydrogen cylinders (1800 fillings for M1A1) were reported as expended in combat, as well as 5,240 pounds of napalm. [73]

The following is a report submitted by the commanding general, 24th Infantry Division, at the close of the Leyte operation:

> Employment of Portable Flame Throwers. The portable flame thrower, M1A1, was used by the 24th Division in the current operation and was employed with some measure of success. The two regiments of the Division that landed on Leyte Island placed flame throwers only with the assault battalions. The procedure of servicing the flame throwers was handled differently by the regiments.
>
> The 34th Infantry. Mixed liquid fuel, filled all flame throwers and filled 'blitz' cans with extra fuel before debarkation. Hydrogen and nitrogen cylinders were filled and checked over a period of several days for leaks and placed on the gun units and fuel tanks before debarkation. Spare cylinders in the fuel filling kit were filled and carried by the regiment. Despite the fact that the cylinders were thoroughly checked and recharged every day until a constant pressure was obtained, the Regimental Gas Officer was compelled to recharge cylinders that had lost pressure on A-Day and A plus 1.
>
> The 19th Infantry equipped a $2\frac{1}{2}$ ton truck with spare 'blitz' cans of fuel and carried hydrogen, nitrogen, and all kits on the truck. Early on the morning of A-Day, the Regimental Gas Officer and the

---

[73] Sixth Army, Report of the Leyte Operation, 20 Oct - 25 Dec 44, p. 237.

flame thrower or maintenance men charged all cylinders and checked the guns. This Regiment reported no trouble with cylinders that had lost pressure.

Examples of Employment. Approximately 400 yards off the beach strong fire was received from a large Japanese bunker. Machine gun, rifle, and direct fire from light tanks failed to silence the position. Flame throwers were called for and were used several times with no success. After several hours the position was covered with a dozer and it was later determined the ineffectiveness of the flame throwers was due to the tremendous size of the position and the presence of large connecting trenches. The 603d Tank Company had one medium tank equipped with an auxiliary type tank flame thrower of 25 gallon capacity but this was not available because the LST had not yet beached.

After arriving on Leyte Island, the 21st Infantry was in action at Pinamopoan. During the heavy fighting there in the vicinity of 'Breakneck Ridge', flame throwers were used extensively by all three battalions. The actual number of times the flame throwers were employed is unknown but they were used over a two week period. The following is a brief account of the employment of flame throwers by the 21st Infantry: All three battalions of the 21st Infantry used flame throwers on 'Breakneck Ridge'. The Japanese were in caves (natural and hand made) situated at the bottom of hills and ravines. Our men were unable to see the Japanese and our rifle fire was ineffective against the positions. Flame throwers were used against these positions with great success. The 3d Battalion had received more training with assault teams than the 1st and 2d Battalions, and as a result their attacks on the Japanese were with the assault teams that had been previously trained. The 1st and 2d Battalions had only two or three assault teams trained as such, and with attacks on many positions going on at the same time additional assault parties had to be organized 'on the spot.' At one time flame throwers and operators were borrowed from the 3d Battalion to operate with the other two battalions.

Maintenance. Flame throwers were kept in operating condition by a great amount of substitution, repair, and 'cannibalism' of other flame throwers. The division was unable to obtain batteries and spark plugs before debarkation and those items proved to be critical throughout the operation. Permatex was again proven to be of no value in waterproofing of the spark plug. The tendency to absorb oil and swell far overshadows its dubious waterproofing qualities. The availability of maintenance parts and waterproofing materials continues to be critical items.

Fuel. Napalm thickened fuel was not mixed or carried by units of the division because they like the effectiveness of the liquid fuel (SAE 30-40, $3\frac{1}{2}$ gallons; gasoline, 1 gal) much better. In the field where fighting is heavy and transportation is a problem, Napalm is of little value because the filling kit is not always available.[74]

The following instance was reported by the 1st Cavalry Division: A heavy artillery concentration was placed on the strongly defended enemy position to the north near Sinayawan. An attack by the 2d Squadron of the 7th Cavalry followed closely. Heavy enemy fire from machine guns, rifles and grenades from well-concealed positions prevented any advance. On 12 November, the 2d Squadron fought within fifty yards of the enemy's perimeter on the ridge and dug in for the night. Observers for the

---

[74] 24th Inf Div, Report of CW Activities, 18 Dec 44. Extract in CMLWG.

2d Squadron were able to pinpoint and call artillery down on fifteen Japanese bunkers including four machine guns which were definitely located. The enemy position was subjected to artillery, 81-mm., and 4.2 mortar fire; while G Troop made the frontal attack, F Troop moved in from the rear. Every type of weapon, including flame throwers, was used in the attack which annihilated the enemy and secured the position at 0835. Over thirty bunkers were found, ten of them in the rear, dug into the base of trees, with openings in all directions and with interconnecting tunnels.[75]

The 7th Infantry Division reported the following unusual employment of flame throwers in the Battle for Dagami on 29 October. The 3d Battalion, 17th RCT on the right (east) of the road advanced without resistance to the cemetery south of Dagami. Weeds seven to ten feet high filled the cemetery which contained old-fashioned, Spanish-type stone crypts built off the ground. As Company L entered the cemetery, Company I came into position for the night to the right (east) of the cemetery. Elements of Company L passed through the cemetery and Company I also moved into position without incident. The 1st Platoon, Company L, in company support behind the lead elements of the company, beat the brush without encountering the enemy. Just as this platoon crossed the east-west path dividing the cemetery in half, a headstone tilted back revealing four Japanese in the grave with rifles and an American BAR. Small-arms fire was instantly placed on the enemy, who could not be dislodged until a flame thrower was brought forward to burn them out. The platoon received enemy fire from all directions simultaneously and, in a matter of seconds, several casualties were suffered. Small "killing details" were then organized which pushed through the cemetery and destroyed the enemy as they were located.

Company K, following Company I, deployed the platoons abreast behind Company L. It too reached the center path without incident, but upon pushing through the weeds, drew heavy fire from the stone crypts. The enemy had removed the bodies from the crypts, punched small holes through the stone and were using the crypts as individual pillboxes. The commander of Company K withdrew his company to the cemetery path, reorganized,

---

[75]
History of the 1st Cavalry Division, Leyte, P.I., 20 Oct - 25 Dec 44, dated 4 Mar 45.

and then advanced through the cemetery with his men shoulder-to-shoulder, preceded by a battery of six flame throwers burning and smoking out the enemy. 76/

The 7th Division found the flame thrower to be very effective during the relatively static operations carried out on the flat terrain of eastern Leyte. Supported closely by small arms and automatic fire and supplemented at times by explosive charges, the flame thrower was successfully employed to reduce enemy pillboxes, concrete bunkers, reinforced shelters, trenches and emplacements within bamboo thickets. Tactical and transportation difficulties precluded use of the weapon during the mobile operations in the rough, precipitous terrain of western Leyte. 77/

Early in November, Yamashita began sending reinforcements to Leyte in such numbers that the greater part of five Japanese divisions was annihilated. Although the period was accompanied by incessant rains, including violent typhoons, creating extremely adverse flying conditions, a large number of these enemy casualties were inflicted by Army and Navy bombers. Many enemy ships and small boats were sunk while unloading, which resulted in many troops getting ashore with little equipment. The original Leyte garrison numbered approximately 20,000. The number of reinforcements that got ashore is indicated by the fact that a total of more than 82,000 Japanese were killed on Leyte. Among the reinforcements to arrive was the Japanese Imperial 1st Division, Japan's finest. Japanese soldiers of the 1st Division did not make foolish "banzai" charges and did not retreat. They were crafty and disciplined soldiers who took advantage of every defensive position, fighting until they were annihilated. When one position was destroyed with flame nearby positions were not abandoned by the enemy as had been done so often in the past. It was not until 21 December, after the remnants of 500 exhausted soldiers made their last stand at Kilometer 79 on the Ormoc

---

76/
  RCT 17, Hq 7th Inf Div (29 Oct 44) AGRO-H 307-70.2, Log-in 3488.

77/
  (1) Ltr, S-3 17th Inf Regt to CG 7th Inf Div, 15 Dec 44, sub: CW Activities. In Sixth A Cml Sect Records, 319.1 Leyte Opn Rpt, ORB. (2) Ltr, Exec O 32d Inf Regt to Cml O 7th Inf Div, 16 Dec 44, sub: Report of CW Activities. In Sixth A Cml Sect Records, 319.1 Leyte Opn Rpt, ORB.

highway, that General Kataoka, with a little band of the once proud division, fled to the south and west.78/

The veteran United States 32d Infantry Division arrived at Leyte on 14 November and two days later was thrown into the line opposite these crack Japanese troops, with the mission of clearing the enemy from the Limon zone and advancing to the south to capture Ormoc. The 32d was not combat loaded and initially only a minimum of equipment accompanied the troops into the line. However, it soon became evident that assault parties in hand-to-hand fighting would be required to clear the determined enemy from the dug-in positions in the zone of action that led through rugged, muddy, mountainous terrain. The M1A1 flame throwers were sent from the ships directly to the front line and were employed immediately without being checked by technicians. This resulted in misfires and completely unsatisfactory results. They were then turned over to the trained technicians, properly serviced and were subsequently employed successfully. During the next month this division used the flame thrower continuously to reduce dug-in positions along the line of advance.79/

Employment of flame throwers by the 32d Division is illustrated by the following account of operations in the Ormoc Corridor from 15 to 19 December 1944. In this area of steep mountains, narrow ravines and jungle growth, the enemy was well entrenched in caves, dugouts and pillboxes. These positions were mutually supporting, well-defiladed to artillery and mortar fire and proved ideal for enemy delaying tactics. The situation called for the maximum use of assault teams, including flame throwers. In the late afternoon of 15 December, troops of the 126th Infantry met strong resistance (in the vicinity of 05.9-62.9) and, after other assault methods had failed to overcome the resistance, flame throwers were called for and an attack was planned for the next morning at 1000. The strong point consisted of well dug-in rifle positions and a pillbox located about twenty yards from the crest of a steep hill. The flame thrower assault party, consisting of two operators, fifteen riflemen and a bazooka team,

---

78/
   CofS USA, Biennial Rpt, 1 Jul 43 to 30 Jun 45, p. 75.

79/
   Ltr, CG 32d Inf Div to CG X Corps, 19 Dec 44, sub: Report of CW Activities in the Leyte Operation. In Sixth A Cml Sect Records, 319.1 Leyte Opn Rpts, ORB.

advanced to within twenty yards of the rear of the enemy positions before launching the attack, which consisted of the simultaneous use of fragmentation grenades, bazooka fire and the flame throwers. One flame thrower operator fired on the pillbox while the other fired on the enemy rifle positions. After the flame throwers were fired the operators withdrew and the riflemen moved in on the positions where they killed twelve of the enemy. While the flame throwers were not credited with killing any of the enemy riflemen, the latter were badly burned, demoralized and were easily overcome. When the pillbox was occupied it was found to contain two heavy machine guns and three dead and badly burned Japanese.

On the following day, 16 December, a similar type strong point (in the vicinity of 05.6-62.7) was encountered on the narrow crest of a hill that was covered with dense wood and undergrowth. Several casualties had been suffered in attempts to dislodge the enemy with grenades and rifle fire and at 1530 hours flame throwers were ordered up. One operator, supported by fifteen riflemen and faced with machine gun fire, advanced to within ten yards of the target. At this point, and under the protection of WP grenade smoke, the operator opened fire. Troops of the 126th then advanced and occupied the positions without further casualties. The flame had caused the Japs to leave eight rifle positions, leaving their arms and other equipment behind. The machine gun position contained a dead Japanese, who was badly burned and one heavy machine gun.

Three days later, on 19 December, troops of the 3d Battalion of the 126th were receiving heavy grenade fire from an enemy position atop a steep bank (in the vicinity of 05.9-61.9). After suffering casualties in attempts to neutralize the position with other weapons, flame throwers were ordered up. The flame thrower operator was unable to get closer than twenty yards and fired at that range. When the infantry closed in they found a cave-type fox hole with a trap door and two Japs inside; one was badly burned and both were easily overcome. Eight additional supporting positions were found, but the occupying enemy was so demoralized that they were killed without further casualties to our troops. Twenty-two of the enemy were killed in this area. Later in the day, strong opposition was encountered from a hill which was heavily wooded and covered with dense undergrowth. In this instance, flame thrower operators fired two area missions (firing in the general direction of the enemy) which, while not killing any of the enemy, caused him to evacuate the positions and enabled our troops to occupy the strong point with only slight opposition the next morning. Twenty-five Japs were killed during this action.

Flame throwers were employed on several occasions on or about 15 December by the 127th Infantry. In one instance, three companies were pinned down by machine gun fire from the crest of a brush covered hill about forty-five yards beyond our front line (in the vicinity of 05.0-65.2). Flame throwers were called for and an operator, with supporting fire from his assault party, advanced to within thirty yards of the enemy and fired on the position. The infantry then advanced and found a light machine gun and two dead Japs, both badly burned. Several of the enemy discovered later who were killed by rifle fire were also burned about the face and hands. An attack on a nearby target (vicinity of 04.9-65.2) forced the enemy to evacuate the position, in which scorched weapons (two mountain guns and one light machine gun) were found.

One section of "Bloody Ridge" consisted of a deep gully or "dry wash," along the sides of which there were about thirty fox holes. The key to this strong point was a large tree at the end of the wash with three openings leading to positions among its roots. A volunteer flame thrower operator, with the protection of supporting fire and WP grenade smoke, maneuvered to within ten yards of the enemy and fired successive bursts into the three openings, went back and refilled the weapon, returned and repeated the flaming of two of the openings. The report of this action is not perfectly clear, but it appears that nine Japanese were killed ("very badly burned") by flame and others were less seriously burned. In another instance, a flame thrower operator discovered something wrong with the gun, withdrew to the rear for another, and was killed by an enemy mortar shell.

The report, on which the above account of flame thrower operations in the 32d Division is based, indicates only a limited amount of successful use of the weapon by the 128th Infantry. In fact, it appears that both the 127th and 128th failed, in the operations reported above, to employ flame thrower assault teams in the manner prescribed by Sixth Army. This departure from established doctrine is especially noticeable in the inclusion of only one operator in an assault team. This same deficiency is also noted in one or two instances in the 127th. 80/

2. <u>Luzon</u>. On 9 January 1945, the US Sixth Army, composed of I and XIV Corps hit the beaches in Lingayen Gulf. Each of the four assault divisions, the one division in floating reserve, and one separate regimental combat team carried flame throwers filled and ready for immediate use. However, the enemy was either surprised or chose not to defend the beaches and by nightfall, 68,000 troops were ashore and in control of a beachhead fifteen miles long and three miles deep. The landing had caught every major enemy unit on the move with the exception of the 23d Infantry Division, which was caught in the onslaught of I Corps (the 6th, 25th and 43d Divisions, and the 158th RCT (Sep)) which was located twenty-five miles north of Lingayen Gulf. XIV Corps (37th and 40th Divisions) pushed rapidly down the Lingayen Valley to Clarke Field where they met stiff enemy resistance for the first time. 81/ However, these enemy troops, consisting in the great part of air corps personnel, were soon pushed back into the Zambales Mountains where they dug in in typical Japanese fashion, presenting suitable flame thrower targets for the 40th Division and later for the 43d Division which replaced the 40th.

Meanwhile, in I Corps zone of operation, flame thrower targets began to develop during the latter part of January as the Japanese fought a stubborn withdrawal action toward Baguio and Balete Pass (later renamed Dalton Pass in honor of General Dalton who was killed there).

On 29 January, XI Corps with the 38th Infantry Division, reinforced, landed at Subic Bay and drove eastward into Zig-Zig Pass which was well fortified with typical Japanese bunkers and cave defenses protected by snipers. Flame throwers were used extensively during the reduction of these defenses. Losses were heavy during this action and several flame thrower operators were killed.

On 31 January, the 11th Airborne Division, under XI Corps, made an amphibious landing at Nasugbu in Batangas Province (south of Manila Bay) with two glider infantry regiments, followed three

---

80/
  Rpt, Cml O 32d Inf Div to CG X Corps, 15 Jan 45, sub: Supplementary Report of CW Activities in the Leyte Operation. In Sixth A Cml Sect Records, 319.1 Leyte Opn Rpts, ORB.

81/
  Sixth Army, Report of the Luzon Campaign, Vol. I, p. 24.

Figure 22. Clarke Field Near Manila: A Flame Thrower Operator Advances, February 1945.

days later by the division's parachute regiment being dropped at Tagaytay. Flame throwers accompanied all three regiments and were employed some 200 times during the division's operations around Laguna de Bay.

The 1st Cavalry Division, also assigned to XI Corps, arrived on the first of February, followed by the 32d and 33d Infantry Divisions. The 1st Cavalry Division proceeded to Manila upon arrival and later conducted operations in the mountains east and south of Manila, where flame throwers were employed in the reduction of caves. The 32d and 33d Divisions were assigned to I Corps and committed to action against the Japanese who had fled to the mountains and were defending the Villa Verde trail and Baguio area. These divisions found the enemy well dug-in and the flame thrower came into play quite extensively. The 32d Division employed the flame thrower more than 200 times while fighting along the Villa Verde trail.[82]

In general, employment of the portable flame thrower during the Luzon Campaign followed the same principles as in previous operations. However, the extensive use made of it indicated a better understanding of the limitations and capabilities of the weapon by infantry commanders than ever before. Expenditures included 3,319 ignition cylinders, 666 nitrogen cylinders (200 cubic feet), 145 hydrogen cylinders, and 9,526 pounds of napalm, not including that expended by air units in support of ground operations.[83]

The following flame thrower operations for January and February are reported by units under I Corps:

During the week of January 21 through 28, a group of seven caves dug into the base of hills above Damartis in northwest Luzon were holding up the advance of the 3d Battalion, 158th RCT. Incendiary grenades thrown into the cave area burned off the waist-high grass on the slopes and in the valleys covering the interconnecting trenches. Flame throwers were then employed successfully

---

[82]
Interv, Hist O with Lt Col James P. Sutton, former Cml O, 32d Inf Div.

[83]
Sixth Army, Rpt of the Luzon Campaign, Vol. III, p. 90.

at the entrances to the palm log reinforced cave openings.84/
On 26 January, Company K, 3d Battalion, 158th RCT, was attacking in the vicinity of Cataguintingan and encountered strongly held tunneled positions which resisted the combined use of rifles, machine guns, grenades and bazookas. The company ordered its assault team to employ flame throwers. Under the protection of WP grenade smoke, the operator, using unthickened fuel, fired a long burst into the opening of the first tunnel. After a number of burning Japs ran out of the entrance and were killed with small-arms fire, a series of similar emplacements were reduced in the same manner. When the attack had moved forward, the tunnels were examined and found to extend about thirty feet into the slope where they branched out in "T" formations. Bodies were found along the corridors and at the remotest points in the tunnels. Flame had shot "around corners" and had proved lethal by both burning and suffocation, due to carbon monoxide and the lack of oxygen resulting from the blast. Fifteen casualties were attributed directly to the flame thrower and a much larger number were killed as they fled from the tunnels.85/

An outstanding example of employment occurred during the occupation of Hill 2500 on Luzon 10,000 yards northwest of Kitakita on 24 February 1945. The flame thrower operator of the assault party fired twelve bursts into a deep cave protected by a large boulder near the crest of the hill. Twenty-six Japs were flushed, one of them afire. All were promptly killed by supporting riflemen. One Japanese attempted to escape by the rear exit. The operator's fuel was exhausted but, using the flame gun as a club, he broke the Jap's neck.

During the advance up the Arboredo Valley, infantry elements were held up by enemy machine-gun fire. These positions were in thick brush near an embankment and direct fire had little effect on the positions. A flame thrower was brought forward and fired from behind the embankment in an effort to silence the position

---

84/
  Ltr, CO 5250th Tech Intell Co to CG I Corps, Attn: Cml O, 28 Jan 45, sub: Jap CWS Materiel Found on Luzon during period of 21-28 Jan 45 (Wkly Rpt #3). In Sixth A Cml Sect Records, 350.05, Luzon Intell Rpts, ORB.

85/Rpt, Cml Sect Hq 158th RCT, Cml Intell Rpt, 28 Jan 45, sub: Use of M1A1 Flamethrowers, 3d Bn, 158th Inf Regt. In Sixth A Cml Sect Records, 350.05, Luzon Intell Rpts, ORB.

with side blast heat. The flame thrower set fire to the brush and the position was overrun and eleven bodies counted. It could not be determined how many were killed by the flame thrower since heavy small-arms fire was delivered on the position as soon as the enemy guns were silenced and the brush had been burned away.

The Cabaruan Hill defenses were dug deep and well camouflaged. They were reduced as of 27 January by 1st Infantry Regiment, 6th Division, supported by artillery and mortars, after ten days of assault. A battalion employed flame throwers here as single weapons, resulting in the killing of one operator and the wounding of another. Later they were employed with success as part of an assault party. Twenty positions were reduced and seventy Japanese killed when the battalion operated correctly with assault party support. Flame throwers were also used on bamboo clumps to burn out snipers.

At San Manuel, on 27 January, a single flame thrower, supported by 25th Division troops using BAR's and "tommy" guns, reduced a machine gun position at twenty-five yards range. Five Japanese were killed. At Lupao, on 9 February, a group of Japanese was located by the 35th Infantry, 25th Division, in an underground chamber at the base of an eight-foot vertical shaft. A single inexperienced operator, with rifle support, acted as flame thrower operator. Unable to secure ignition, he sprayed the position with the fuel which was ignited by tracer bullets. Seven Japanese were killed. The 3d Battalion, 35th Infantry, 25th Infantry Division, attempted to use a flame thrower during the mopping up of Lupao to destroy a Japanese tank, which had previously been knocked out, in order to prevent it from being used again by snipers. The flame thrower failed to fire because of a faulty pressure tank.[86]

Other instances of employment at Puncan, Putlan, and other contested areas were reported. One division chemical officer stated that, due to proper reconnaissance and fire support, no flame thrower operator was killed in his zone of action. "The flame throwers," he said, "have not been used as a weapon of opportunity, but only on selected targets, usually those which could not be reduced by other means." Usual ranges were up to twenty-five yards and untrained men were used occasionally as operators. This had been the case with the 43d Division in New Georgia when such men were killed. Fortunately, this consequence was not repeated here, due partly to adequate fire support and partly to Japanese

---

[86] Rpt, S-3 35th Inf Div to CG 25th Inf Div, 25 Mar 45, sub: Report on CW Weapons in Combat. In CMLWG.

panic in the face of the threat of flame. The same chemical officer also stated that, "Low gas pressure occasionally developed, despite precautions. Skilled operators sense by tension of the fuel hose whether pressure is adequate when the valves are opened. In open terrain as in jungle, a medium range flame (twenty to thirty yards), with great heat and rapid burning properties proved most effective. Thickened fuels were generally prepared by dissolving five pounds of New Zealand Metalex and two pounds of Peptizer in eight to ten gallons of gasoline." The weapon was not frequently employed in the more inaccessible mountainous areas by reason of the prohibitive weight of the assembly under extremely difficult march and transport conditions. There was no serious complaint concerning malfunctioning. The weather was dry and the weapons thoroughly serviced.87/

During street fighting in Manila for the possession of the Philippine General Hospital on 14 February, three missions were fired by personnel of the 2d Battalion, 148th Infantry Regiment, 37th Division. The first mission, fired by six flame throwers, permitted friendly troops to occupy the ground floor of the hospital. The other two missions, accomplished with two flame throwers each, achieved an undescribed success, in spite of malfunctioning of one of the weapons in each case. Flame throwers were also used by the 37th Division with outstanding success against enemy installations in and near the Intramuros Area of Manila, south of the Pang River.88/

During the fighting in the Zambales Mountains west of Clarke Field late in February, the 40th Infantry Division encountered resistance from numerous caves and dug-in positions. The following report was submitted regarding the reduction of these positions:

> With movement canalized by the steep slopes and with the enemy in excellent observation positions, the close approach to each position required careful reconnaissance, extreme

---

87/
(1) Cml O I Corps, Report of Chemical Warfare Phase of I Corps Luzon Operation, 9 Jan - 9 Mar 45. In Sixth A Cml Sect Records, 370.2 Luzon Opns Rpts, ORB. (2) CO 5250 Tech Intell Comp Co to ACofS G-2 USASOS, 19 Feb 45, sub: CWS Technical Intelligence Team 3 Activity Report, 5 Feb to 19 Feb 45. In Sixth A Cml Sect Records, 350.05 Luzon Intell Rpts. ORB

88/
Rpt, CG XIV Corps to CG Sixth Army, 19 Jun 45, sub: Chemical Warfare Activities in the Luzon Campaign. In Sixth A Cml Sect Records, 370.2 Luzon Opn Rpts, ORB.

caution in movement making full use of available cover and concealment, and well coordinated supporting fires. A base of automatic fire was first established on commanding terrain held by friendly troops. Under this fire the assault team made its approach toward the enemy position. When the assault team came into the danger area of the long range supporting fires, a red panel was displayed as a signal to cease fire. At this time the covering group of the assault team took the enemy positions under fire as the assault group continued to advance and maneuvered to a position from which to attack the target enemy cave. When the assault group was in range, WP grenades were thrown inside. Then covered by the resulting smoke and the close support team, armed with Thompson sub-machine guns, the flame thrower team advanced directly to the entrance of the cave and expended its entire load into the cave. Simultaneously, the demolition team approached the position from above; a trench was dug approximately 18 inches deep and wide enough to allow the insertion of a crater charge as near the center of the position as possible; the charge was then lowered into the trench. After being securely stamped and packed, W-110 wire was strung back to a covered position preparatory to detonating the charge. On a prearranged signal all members of the team within the danger area withdrew to a covered position and the charge was then detonated by the use of a Battery BA-38. In 90 percent of the cases the explosion successfully neutralized the position. Each adjacent cave position was approached one by one and neutralized in the above manner.[89/]

[89/] 40th Inf Div Combat Notes - Luzon.

On 14 January, a single flame thrower operator, supported by troops of the 169th Infantry Regiment, 43d Division, using fragmentation grenades and rifles, crawled along a communication trench to within fifty feet of a cave on the western slopes of Mt. Alava near Rabon. From this position the operator fired his entire load in one burst which inspection disclosed killed all eight occupants of the cave. During the next five days, the flame thrower was successfully employed over a score of times to blast paths through shrubs and grass eight feet high, revealing many enemy snipers who were disposed of by rifle fire.90/

Reports of flame thrower operations by XI Corps units included the following from the 1st Cavalry Division:

> Flame thrower tactics: effectiveness, and technical information:
>
> 1. Flame thrower used by 1st Squadron, 7th Cavalry; Location: "The Pimple;" Date-5 March 1945. Circumstances: TNT was first used on a small number of Japs in a tunnel, the explosive was ineffective. Next, five gallons of gasoline was poured into the tunnel from above and ignited, it was also ineffective. Finally, a flame thrower was tried. The flame went around a turn and forced six Japs to evacuate by another entrance. There was no further enemy resistance from the tunnel.
>
> 2. Flame thrower used by 2d Squadron, 7th Cavalry: Date: 1 March – 10 March 1945. Circumstances: An attempt was being made by Pioneer and Demolitions men to seal the entrance to a tunnel with explosives. A flame thrower was used to cover the tunnel entrance while the P and D men got into position to place their explosive charge. The flame thrower accomplished the mission assigned effectively

---

90/
 Ltr, Cml O 43d Div to Cml O I Corps, 2 Feb 45, sub: Miscellaneous Summary Report #2. Sixth A Cml Sect Records, 319.1 Weekly Act. Rpts, Divs, ORB.

in that the P and D section did not receive casualties in placing this charge and were not fired upon.

3. Flame thrower used by 2d Squadron, 7th Cavalry: Date: 1 March - 8 March 1945. Circumstances: A flame thrower was used to drive Japs from a tunnel from which they were firing on our troops. The flame was shot into the tunnel entrance and made 15 Japs evacuate by another entrance nearby. No further enemy resistance was received from the position.

4. Flame thrower used by 2d Squadron, 7th Cavalry: Date: 5 March - 10 March 1945. Circumstances: A flame thrower was committed against a machine gun position. The operator did not advance within range of the flame. The flame did not reach the machine gun or the gunner and its use was without effect.

5. Flame thrower used by 2d Squadron, 7th Cavalry: Location: Ravine 200 yds S of Taytay-Antipolo road. Date: 9 March 1945. Circumstances: Used 3 times in attempts to reduce caves but because of terrain features operators were not able to approach entrances close enough for best results.

6. Flame thrower used by 1st Squadron, 8th Cavalry: Location: Hill 500 and main objective just east of Hill 500. Date: 5 March 1945 to 10 March 1945. Circumstances: Used approximately 40 times during entire operation to burn enemy hiding in caves, dug into Hill 500.

7. Flame thrower used by B Troop, 8th Cavalry: Location: Ridge between Hill 500 and Antipolo. Date: 8 or 9 March 1945. Circumstances: Flame thrower used to mop up ridge already occupied by friendly troops. Operator fired first blast from about 20 yards and then moved up to 6 or 7 feet of the Jap position and fired directly into cave. 12-15 Japs came out the

other side of hill and were killed by MG's and 60-mm mortars. Operator was covered by 1 rifle squad. Immediately afterwards with same charge of fuel the operator fired at a Jap in a slit trench 20 yards to flank of cave entrance and the Jap flipped out burning and his body burned to a crisp.

8. Flame thrower used by 2d Squadron, 8th Cavalry: Location: Hill BM 11. Date: 7th, 8th, and 9th March 1945. Circumstances: Used approximately 12 times in reduction of caves with excellent results. Liquid fuel, only, used. Operator approached within about 20 yards of the caves, protected by a rifle squad. He shot flame in caves, after which P and D men ran up and threw in demolition charges with time fuze. There were no casualties among the P and D men. No Japs came out of the caves directly after firing flame in entrance and no fire was received from these caves.

9. Flame thrower used by 1st Squadron, 8th Cavalry: Location: Northern edge of Santo Tomas University. Date: 24 March 1945. Circumstances: Flame thrower used to wipe out two bunkers in culverts. Japs had blocked up ends of concrete culverts and turned them into pillboxes and bombproof shelters. When American troops were advancing the Japs would come out of the culvert, set up machine guns on the road and fire on our troops until their fire was returned, at which time they would withdraw with their weapons to the cover of the culvert. Flame was shot into the culverts from almost directly in front of the entrance. Operators were covered by a rifle squad. After burning out each culvert no further resistance was encountered from Japs therein. Flame was shot into manholes of the Santo Tomas sewer system to neutralize Japs hiding there; their use for that purpose was effective.

10. Flame thrower used by 1st Squadron, 8th Cavalvy: Location: Culvert by RR tracks SE of Santo Tomas University. Date: 24 March 1945.

Circumstances: Flame thrower used for mopping up. Results were not determined because at this point as at other places in Santo Tomas the flame thrower was used on many places suspected of harboring Japs. The combat troops did not search places where the flame thrower was used and did not determine how many casualties were caused by its use.

11. Flame thrower used by 1st Squadron, 8th Cavalry: Location: Malvar. Date: 27 March 1945. Circumstances: Flame thrower was used to mop up culverts similar to use in Santo Tomas.91/

After mid-April, the flame thrower was used effectively in mopping-up operations around New Bosoboso to force the few remaining Japs to emerge from shallow caves and fox holes. Troops of the 43d Division, carrying out these missions, used the weapon to cover demolition squads placing charges designed to seal the caves, and also to burn off brush obstructing observation of enemy cave and trench positions. A total of eighteen dead resulted from these missions.92/

In the fighting following capture of Ipo Dam, in the latter part of May, Company L, 169th Infantry (43d Division) burned out two caves in the Bigti area. Enemy fire was received from the first cave but the position was flanked by the use of WP grenades and the operator approached within twenty-five yards of the entrance. From this position he released a four-second burst from a 30° angle and then

---

91/
    Ltr, Cml O 1st Cav Div to Cml O Sixth Army, 14 May 45, sub: Report of Chemical Warfare Activities (Luzon Campaign). In Sixth A Cml Sect Records, 370.2 Luzon Opns Rpts, ORB.

92/
    (1) Rpt, Cml O 43d Div to Cml O XI Corps, 15 Apr 45, sub: Weekly Miscellaneous Report, 0724001 to 1424001 Apr 45. In Sixth A Cml Sect Records, 319.1 Wkly Act. Rpts. - Divs. (2) Rpt, Cml O 43d Div to Cml O XI Corps, 22 Apr 45, sub: Weekly Miscellaneous Report, 1424001 to 2124001 Apr 45. In Sixth A Cml Sect Records, 350.05 Luzon Intell Rpts, ORB.

released the remainder of the filling from the front. Inspection of the position disclosed a zigzag tunnel but the sole occupant, about twenty feet from the entrance, armed with a LMG was killed by the blast. The second cave was not actively defended but signs of Japs made it advisable to burn it out. The flame thrower started a fire which set off explosives and made any inspection inadvisable. Both firings by the 169th Infantry were filled with half Diesel, half gasoline, and 2.5 percent napalm. 93/

Scattered reports indicate that the portable flame thrower was used once on Carabao Island after mid-April by troops of the 1st Battalion, 151st Infantry Regiment, 38th Division. This regiment subsequently trained twenty operators per rifle and heavy weapons company and twelve operators per cannon and regimental headquarters in the use of the M2-2 flame thrower. During the first half of May, the 1st Battalion, 152d Infantry Regiment, 38th Division, burned out five caves with five fillings from the M2-2 at ranges between forty-five and fifty yards. The 2d Battalion used M1A1 flame throwers to burn out a bamboo draw and a thicket growth during the same period. The 1st Battalion, 145th Infantry Regiment, 37th Division, attached at this time to the 38th Division, used the weapon on a pillbox defended by three Japs and a machine gun. The 3d Battalion, 145th Infantry Regiment, successfully employed the flame thrower on caves on top of Mt. Binicayan. During the latter part of April, the 158th RCT (Sep), under XIV Corps, used both M1A1 and M2-2 flame throwers on Bicol Peninsula to route enemy troops from dug-in positions. 94/

The following actions which took place in April 1945 were reported by the chemical officer of I Corps early in May: 95/

93/
  Report of Chemical Officer, Sixth Army, Luzon Campaign, 9 Jan - 30 Jun 45, p. 13. In CMLWG.

94/
  (1) Ltr, Cml O 38th Div to ACofS G-3 38th Div, 21 Apr 45, sub: CW Act Rpt of Carabao Opn. In Sixth A Cml Sect Records, 319.1 Wkly Act. Rpts - Divs. (2) Rpt, Cml O XI Corps, 16 May 45, sub: Cml Act Rpt #1. (3) Rpt, Cml O XI Corps, 23 May 45, sub: Cml Act Rpt #2. In Sixth A Cml Sect Records, 319.1 XI Corps Cml Act. Rpts. (4) Cml O 158th RCT to Cml O Sixth Army, 6 May 45, sub: CW Intell Rpt for Period 2400I 29 Apr to 2400I 5 May 45. In CMLWG.

95/
  Rpt, Cml O, I Corps, 9 May 45, sub: Cml Opns and Tech Period Rpt No. 2, Annex B. Im CMLWG.

Elements of [the 128th Infantry Regiment, 32d Division] were halted by enemy machine gun and small arms fire from a highly organized position vicinity Hill 506a.... The position consisted of twelve or more caves, many of which were interconnecting. The infantry troops worked around to the flank of the position and located two positions; one, a single entrance cave and the other, three inter-connecting caves of which the former was selected as the first target for the flame thrower. The operator, covered by an infantry platoon advanced to a point 12 feet from the position and threw one blast into the cave. Four Japs were killed. A second flame thrower was brought up and the operator proceeded to the three inter-connecting caves. His first blast permitted him to rush the position and fire point blank from four feet. Heavy brush screened the entrances to the case. On the third entrance to the position, the tunnel made an angle turn very close to the entrance, and when the operator fired from four feet, he was burned from the back-blast. Unconfirmed reports list more than fifty dead Japs in the three caves. It is not known how many of these were killed by the flame thrower. It was noted that the eyeballs of four of the dead Japs protruded from 1 to 2 inches from the sockets. Another Jap was in a stunned condition only. Others were badly burned. The necessity for an alert support party was graphically illustrated in this assault. The operator turned and saw a Jap move from a cave and aim his rifle at him. The operator fumbled for his pistol but was unable to get it out of the holster. Just before the Jap completed his aim, one of our supporting riflemen shot him through the head. The flame thrower operator is now out of the hospital with no after effect of the back-blast. He is enthusiastic and is very anxious to get back to his flame thrower....

On [another] occasion, the advance was halted in a narrow defile by two enemy machine guns concealed in a cave located in the face of a sheer cliff.... The flame thrower operator and assistant climbed four hours to reach the top of the cliff. Then came the difficult part of the job - getting into a position from which to fire the weapon. The operator solved the problem by dangling over the cliff, with the aid of his assistant. The flame thrower was fired, the Japs cremated, and our advance continued....

/One/ target was a fortified enemy tunnel with /the/ entrance screened by heavy growth and supported by sniper fire....When the flame thrower was fired at the entrance of the tunnel, one enemy sniper was flushed and immediately killed by rifle fire. The flame was ineffective in the tunnel as it did not penetrate beyond the first bend. Due to high and shifting winds in this particular area, napalm was used; gasoline and oil would have been preferred....

/Another/ target was a fortified enemy tunnel.... The first firing was unsuccessful due to high wind and heavy brush around entrance. During the second attempt the wind momentarily calmed and the operator approached the tunnel from a different direction. This time excellent results were obtained. Fuzed TNT, which had been previously placed in the tunnel, was exploded by the flame and the tunnel sealed....

The target was a pillbox at /an/ unreported location. On this occasion, the only covered approach to the pillbox led into the face of a strong wind. The operator sprayed the position with unignited fuel mixture and then ignited it with a WP grenade. The pillbox was not reduced at this time, but a satisfactory harassing effect permitted close in use of grenades by members of the assault party....

/On another occasion/ the target was a log constructed pillbox with three exits, dug in to the side of Hill 504.... The flame thrower operator, supported by a rifle platoon, advanced and fired

from 20 feet of the main entrance. Japs
(number unreported) trying to escape by way
of alternate exits were killed by rifle fire.
The pillbox was then destroyed by demolitions....

[One] target was a cave on the side of Hill 504,
occupied by [two or] three Japs. The flame thrower operator approached the position from above and fired
at 15 feet. Results were undetermined as the
operator's precarious perch above the cave did not
permit him to look inside. However, the position
was silenced....

The targets were three well camouflaged, mutually
supporting pill boxes, each approximately 10 feet
square, and located on the south side of Hill 504.
Three flame thrower teams with a rifle platoon in
support, assaulted the positions frontally, using
the combined casualty and screening effect of M-15
grenades to cover the advance. The assault was
successful. The number 1 pillbox had three exits
and led to an underground room. A flame thrower
was fired from 30 feet, using 4.2 per cent Napalm.
Three Japanese were killed. The number 2 position
was also fired on from 30 feet. Two Japanese were
killed and one heavy machine gun captured in this
position. The number 3 position consisted primarily of a shaft 20 feet in depth, with no alternate entrances. Two Japanese were killed in this
position....

[In another instance,] the target was a dug-in
pillbox vicinity Hill 502....Two flame thrower
teams, supported by one platoon of infantry, approached to a point 30 feet from the enemy position, using a small draw for cover and concealment. The flame throwers were filled with gasoline and oil. After one of the flame throwers
was fired, both teams were forced to withdraw due
to an enemy attack on their flank. Results of the
fire were not ascertained prior to withdrawal; however, screams were heard from the pillbox....

Three instances were reported in which flame throwers were used to burn out brush and foliage screening
suspected enemy positions. Using gasoline and oil,

results were only moderately successful. In one of the instances, a cave position was uncovered vicinity Hill 507.... Bangalore torpedos were pushed inside and two Japs killed....

In the cliffs [overlooking the march of the 25th Infantry Division along] Highway No. 5 near Puncan, the Japs had dug deep caves and had emplaced field pieces of various calibers therein. One was a 47-mm field piece in a tunnel about fifteen feet above the level of the road. The gun was pointed diagonally across the road in a southeasterly direction. The tunnel could be approached from the north as a slight bulge in the cliff existed just north of the cave. One rifle company was in the woods east of Highway No. 5 and commanded the top of the bluff and both sides of the cave. The battalion commander called for a flame thrower. The operator and two other men took the flame thrower across Highway 5 well to the north of the cave and worked south along the face of the bluff. [While] hugging the cliff, the operator was within five yards of the cave, when he ignited one of the ignition squibs, leaped around in front of the cave's entrance, and fired a five or six second burst. He then quickly retired around the bulge to safety. Almost immediately the Jap gun fired again the crew was unhurt it seemed. However, a large explosion was heard shortly thereafter which was assumed to be ammunition set on fire by the flames. The cave was later sealed by a demolition charge....

Portable flame thrower operations during May were reported by I Corps as follows:96/

[One] target was an enemy cave position. The flame thrower operator fired four bursts of Napalm into the cave from 30 feet. A Japanese officer, with saber, ran out of the cave screaming. The flame thrower operator reported that

---

96/
Rpt, Cml O I Corps, 6 Jun 45, sub: Cml Opns and Tech Period Rpt No. 6, Annex I. In CMLWG.

he also yelled, and fired the remaining contents of the flame thrower, hitting the Jap full in the face. A second flame thrower was fired into the same cave, and two more Japs ran out. These were killed with rifle fire by members of the support party. Filipino carriers were employed to transport the flame throwers from service point to the objective area some 1200 yards distant over the difficult mountain terrain of the sector....

[Another] target was a group of caves on both slopes of a small draw. A flame thrower operator [from the 32d Infantry Division] fired into five caves with the 12 bursts he obtained from one filling. Two of the caves were fired on from four feet, and the remaining 3 from 15 - 20 feet. The position was not entirely reduced on this occasion and exact results were undetermined. When the position was later neutralized, four badly burned Japs were found. The operator was slightly burned from the backblast when he fired at the caves only four feet away. This same operator, who is one of the most enthusiastic operators in this division..., was hospitalized several weeks ago from backblast resulting from firing at too short ranges. Filipino carriers were employed to transport the flame throwers from the service point to the objective area some 1200 yards distant over the difficult mountain terrain of the sector....

[In another instance the] target was a deep enemy cave. One flame thrower fired into it from seven feet with no results. A second flame thrower fired, and after four bursts, exploding ammunition was heard inside the cave. Filipino carriers were employed to transport the flame throwers from the service point to the objective area some 1200 yards distant over the difficult mountain terrain of the sector....

Early in June, personnel of Company F, 129th Infantry Regiment, 32d Division, west of Highway 5 and north of Consuelo, overran an enemy machine gun nest, driving the gun crew into a cave which was then neutralized by a flame thrower. At the same time, Company L personnel reported killing three Japs with flame throwers.

An enemy cave was located in the vicinity of Hill 515....This position was approximately 100 yards ahead of the perimeter of the 127th Infantry Regiment, 32d Division. An assault party was ordered to reduce it. One Napalm filled flame thrower, two BAR men, demolition men and 17 riflemen moved into position, and while BARs and rifles covered the entrance to the cave, the flame thrower operator moved up and fired the contents of his weapon from 15 yards. During his fire, two Japs ran out of the cave and were killed by our riflemen. After the flame thrower had been fired, the operator withdrew, and demolitionsmen moved toward the cave to seal it. As they approached the cave, an enemy machine gun opened fire from a position just 15 yards from the cave entrance. Our casualties were 1 KIA and 5 WIA. Enemy casualties were 7 KIA. From the position of the machine gun, the Japs could have fired on the flame thrower, which was the obvious target. It is believed that the Japanese fear of fire kept them hidden until the flame thrower operator had left the area. Rather than reveal their position by opening fire, and possibly having flame directed at them, the enemy machine gunners elected to allow the flame thrower /to/ fire its entire contents into a cave containing at least two of their comrades and a position which they were apparently covering. 97/

Between Hills 515 and 516, two operators from the 32d Division supported by heavy fire were used to reduce one cave defended by two enemy soldiers and another containing five. All seven were killed either by the flame throwers or by pole charges used to seal the caves. Flame

---

97/
  Rpt, Cml O I Corps, 25 May 45, sub: Cml Opns and Tech Period Rpt No. 4, Annex I. In CMLWG.

throwers were also employed frequently to burn off brush and grass from enemy positions on reverse slopes of Hill 516. 98/

In the vicinity of Hill 508 /troops of the 32d Division/ received machine gun fire during the night from a large cave on the slope of the hill. The following morning a flame thrower party reduced the position. Reduction followed standard assault party techniques, with two flame throwers firing a gasoline and oil mixture into the cave. Demolition men then sealed the cave. Enemy were known to be in the cave, but a count was not made. 99/

On one of the ridges adjoining Hill 508, one flame thrower filled with Napalm fuel fired into two enemy occupied caves. In both cases demolition men immediately sealed the positions, and the actual results were unknown. 100/

A Japanese soldier was observed running into a cave in the vicinity of Mountain-Trail-Ambuclao Road Junction. Riflemen pinned the Jap in the cave while others moved forward to the entrance. A fragmentation grenade was thrown into the cave and the Jap threw it back. A WP grenade was thrown into the cave. The Jap came out with bayonet fixed, yelling "Banzai!" One short burst from the flame thrower silenced him. 101/

In April the chemical officer, 32d Division, made the following report:

> We are using the flame thrower increasingly on the Villa Verde Trail on the way to Balete Pass. The Japs continue to defend ridge after

---

98/
  Rpt, Cml O I Corps, 17 May 45, sub: Cml Opns and Tech Period Rpt No. 3, Annex A. In CMLWG.

99/
  Rpt, Cml O, I Corps, 25 May 45, sub: Cml Opns and Tech Period Rpt No. 4, Annex I. In CMLWG.

100/
  Ibid.

101/
  Rpt by Cml O I Corps, 1 Jul 45.

ridge and we have been forced to resort to
frontal attacks in many cases. In using the
flame thrower, we are hampered by lack of
covered approaches to the enemy defensive positions.
However, we have used about 150
gallons of Napalm fuel in the past two weeks.
The technique is faily standard. Firepower
is used to get the flame thrower in positions,
followed by detonating an explosive to seal
up the tunnel without any effort being made
to determine the actual number of casualties
within.102/

3. <u>Corregidor</u>. On 16 February 1945 the 503d Parachute Infantry made an airborne landing on "Topside" of Corregidor. At the same time the 34th Infantry RCT (24th Infantry Division) made an amphibious assault at San Jose near the South Docks on the lower end of the island. Both regiments brought in flame throwers and employed them frequently against the well dug-in positions on the island. During the period 16-28 February, the Demolitions Platoon, 503d Regiment, alone expended forty-three fillings.

During the systematic mopping up of "Topside" and the western portion of the "Rock," patrols operated against enemy pockets of resistance. Each patrol was closely supported by heavy weapons and artillery, as well as by teams of assault and demolition personnel armed with flame throwers and plentifully supplied with explosives and WP. While submachine gun men and riflemen covered other personnel advancing on cave entrances, WP and flame throwers were used to inflict casualties or drive the enemy further in. Those who tried to escape were cut down by automatic or rifle fire. Caves were then blown shut by high explosives. By 23 February, 164 caves had been sealed.

75-mm howitzer fire was laid directly on cave and tunnel entrances, using a high percentage of white phosphorus. In many

---

102/
    Ltr, Cml O 32d Div to OC CWS, 19 Apr 45.

Figure 23. The Entrance to Melinta Tunnel on Corregidor.

instances these weapons were broken down, hand-packed to new positions, and reassembled for this mission.103/

4. **Caballo Island.** This Island is situated off the tip of Corregidor Island in Manila Bay. A preliminary reconnaissance, made by elements of the 38th Infantry Division on 19 March, disclosed that it was held by a Japanese garrison. On 27 March, the 2d Battalion, 151st Infantry, landed on the island with the mission of securing it. It was soon learned that the enemy was defending from underground positions that had been constructed by the U. S. Coast Artillery prior to the Japanese occupation. Portable flame throwers were completely ineffective against these positions. At the request of the battalion commander, the division chemical officer prepared ten drums of 4 percent napalm fuel. On 31 March, elements of the 113th Engineer Battalion arrived and, by means of a pulley moored to a tunnel shaft and a cable attached to an LCM, poured thirteen drums of Diesel oil and two drums of napalm into the shaft before knee mortar and rifle fire stopped the operation. Efforts to ignite this thickened fuel with 81-mm. WP shells were ineffective. The engineers then installed a 1,000 gallons per minute, 280-foot head aviation gasoline pump on the LCM, connected it to two navy pontoons and laid a pipe line to the tunnel shaft. On 6 April, 2,255 gallons of fuel, consisting of two parts Diesel oil and one part gasoline, were pumped into the fortifications and ignited with 81-mm. WP shells. Upon ignition, the fuel burned rapidly, resulting in several explosions near the aperture opening of the pit. One thousand two hundred and sixty-five gallons were then pumped into the burning oil and additional explosions took place. On 7 April the procedure was repeated with similar results by pumping 2,310 gallons into the tunnel shaft of another pit. On 8 April, two captured Japs stated that conditions in the underground pits were almost unbearable, and that the officer in charge had given his men the choice of suicide or an attempt to escape. On 9 April, 2,500 gallons of fuel were pumped into another ventilator shaft and ignited. Terrific explosions resulted, with smoke and fumes emitting from all openings. On the morning of 10 April, one of the prisoners entered the cave and returned, reporting twenty Japs still alive. During the night of 12 April, muffled shots were heard from within. A patrol from the 2d Battalion, 151st Infantry, entered on 13 April, killed one Jap and counted fifty-nine badly burned and mangled bodies.104/

103/
USAFFE Board Report No. 308, Corregidor Island Operation (16 Feb - 8 Mar 45).

104/
Ltr, Cml O 38th Inf Div to Cml O Sixth Army, 25 Apr 45, sub: Operations on Caballo Island, pp. 2-4. In Sixth A Cml Sect Records, 319.1 Opn Rpts, ORB.

5. **Fort Drum.** This fortification is located on El Fraille Island. It is constructed like a battleship and covers the entire rock. Drawings of its construction were available and it was known to be impervious to naval and air bombardment. Reconnaissance elements of the 38th Infantry Division explored this fortress in March 1945 and discovered that it was occupied by a Japanese force of unknown strength. On 13 April 1945, elements of the 2d Battalion, 151st Infantry, and 113th Engineer Battalion successfully reduced the fortress without a casualty. The LCM used at Caballo Island was employed in this venture together with two navy pontoons, total capacity about 2,500 gallons. The landing was made by attaching a fifteen-foot ramp to the conning tower of an LSM. This ladder was lowered to the dock of the fort after the craft was securely moored, and infantrymen and engineers effected a landing. The oil-bearing LCM was moored to the fort and the oil discharge line, a four-inch water hose, was laid to one of the vents. Upon starting the pump, oil began draining into the sea through a hole that had been blasted into the casement by naval gun fire. The line was then laid to another vent and the remainder of the fuel, approximately 2,000 gallons, consisting of two parts Diesel oil and one part gasoline, was pumped into the fort. One hundred and twenty pounds of explosive was placed in one of the vents and 480 pounds in another. The explosives were equipped with thirty-minute fuzes. Troops were withdrawn and at the end of thirty minutes there was a terrific explosion. Smoke and fumes boiled out from all openings and crevices. A patrol endeavored to enter the fort two days later but were unable to do so because of the intensity of the heat still being radiated. The patrol entered seven days after the explosion and counted seventy dead Japs at the machine shop level. All had apparently died of suffocation. A large section of the top deck just over the kitchen had been blown away.[105]

6. **Panay and Negros.** Late in February 1945, the 40th Infantry Division was withdrawn from the line west of Clarke Field, Luzon, to prepare for operations in the Visayan Islands under Eighth Army. The 108th Infantry RCT was shipped immediately to Leyte for the purpose of garrisoning the island and, since it was not to be engaged in immediate combat on the far shore, flame throwers were carried in unit supply. The remainder of the division was given approximately two weeks to get ready for combat movement. During this time, the flame

---

[105] Ltr, Cml O 38th Inf Div to Cml O Sixth Army, 25 Apr 45, sub: Reduction of Ft. Drum on El Fraille Island. In Sixth A Cml Sect Records, 319.1 Opn Rpts, ORB.

throwers, consisting of only three of the M2-2 model and forty M1A1's, were repaired, tested, and serviced in order that they might be carried in on the assault ready for use. The M1A1 flame throwers with which this division was equipped had been through two campaigns and had been used considerably in training. As a result they were in poor condition. New M2-2 flame throwers for this division finally arrived in August, just at the end of the war.

On 18 March, the 40th Infantry Division (less 108th RCT), reinforced, landed fourteen miles west of Iloilo, Panay. Resistance to the landing was light and on 29 March elements of the division, assisted by the 503d Parachute RCT, executed an amphibious landing on Negros. The division reported that during these operations flame throwers were utilized, together with automatic weapons and demolitions, by eight-man assault groups who moved in to attack caves while a six-man covering group provided supporting fire. This system was the same as that employed in the Zambales Mountains, west of Clarke Field, Luzon. Flame throwers were not employed extensively because the constant rains caused continuous trouble with the functioning of the M1A1 model, in spite of all precautions having been taken to waterproof the weapon as well as possible.106/

7. **Cebu and Bohol.** The Americal Division moved from Bougainville to Leyte in January 1945. During January and February it was engaged in mopping up and garrisoning Leyte and Samar. It had not been employed in combat since the Bougainville operation, after which a flame thrower platoon was organized in each regiment and extensive training conducted in its employment. However, during the two months of mopping up on Leyte, evidence began to accumulate indicating the impracticability of maintaining a separate flame thrower platoon in each regiment. On Leyte, operations consisted almost entirely of patrol action in the mountains and flame throwers were not carried. The flame thrower platoon was employed as a normal rifle platoon and, as a result of casualties, sickness and transfers, the organization began to be depleted of trained operators. For example, the 182d Infantry had a total of forty well-trained operators when it arrived in the Philippines. However, when it embarked for Cebu,

---

106/
    Ltr, CG Eighth Army to CofS USA, 3 Jan 46, sub: Employment of Flame Throwers in the Visaya Operations, Incl. 1. AG 470.71 (FE). In CMLWG.

only twenty operators were available. These platoons were valuable assets to regiments when needed, but, in a normal situation where they were not required, they became a luxury which a regiment could not afford. Both the 132d and 182d Infantry were forced to conduct schools to train operators before the campaign was over, because operators had become casualties while acting as riflemen during periods when flame throwers were not needed.

On 26 March 1945, the Americal Division, less one RCT, initiated landings south of Cebu City on the Island of Cebu and proceeded on its mission of destroying the enemy in order to reestablish the civil government on the island. On 11 April, elements of the division made an amphibious landing on the island of Bohol.

For these operations the division was equipped with twenty-three M2-2 and fifty E-3 flame throwers. A total of seventy-two missions were reported as having been fired in the two operations. Two operators were slightly wounded, one by rifle fire and the other by a grenade. This low casualty rate indicated that the operators received proper support. The operator who was wounded by rifle fire was carrying a completely serviced flame thrower and before abandoning it, he fired his .45-caliber pistol into the fuel tanks. The fuel did not ignite or explode. In the case of the other casualty, the flame thrower hit by the grenade caught fire and burned.

The flame thrower was employed against the usual targets of improvised rock and coconut log bunkers, caves, and tunnels, and concrete pillboxes. The following are a few examples of employment. During the Villaba Campaign on Leyte, Company L, 3d Battalion, 164th Infantry, was held up by a series of spider-type dugouts. Two flame throwers were used in the early phase of the final attack on these positions. The flame throwers knocked out two of the front positions, one of which contained a machine gun, opening the way for the final elimination by the infantry.

In the 182d Infantry, Company E was the first to employ flame throwers. A pillbox of reinforced concrete construction was encountered on Watt Hill on Cebu. A flame thrower was brought up and the entire charge was fired at it, followed by demolitions. The position was not destroyed and fire was received from it several minutes later. The flame thrower was found to be ineffective in destroying, but successful in neutralizing it long enough for demolitions to be placed. A few days later, the 2d Battalion made extensive use of the flame thrower, both in the assault and in mopping-up operations, on Bolo Ridge. A total of twelve targets were engaged with good results. Two by-passed tunnels blew up when the flame hit them, indicating the presence of ammunition. An estimated twenty Japanese were in another tunnel when it was burned out. Most of these targets were engaged at ranges under twenty yards in order to allow the operator to put the flame into the opening. It was found that caves having more than one entrance usually caused a draft which sucked the flame into the mouth of the tunnel.

The 1st and 3d Battalions on Cebu used flame throwers to mop up four by-passed pillboxes on Horse Shoe Ridge. On Coconut Hill, the 1st Battalion burned out fourteen bunkers and caves, which were either holding up the advance or had been by-passed. On Hill 20 one operator, using thickened fuel, blew up an ammunition cave at a range of sixty yards.

Accessory kits were not available in sufficient quantity to allow the issue of a set to each battalion prior to the operation. Flame throwers in the 132d and 164th Infantry were serviced at regimental level, causing considerable inconvenience to battalions. Often battalions were operating too far from the regimental supply points to permit the ready servicing of flame throwers. In the 182d Infantry, each battalion was self-sufficient in filling and service kits and operated its own servicing point. As a result, filled flame throwers were always available to the front line companies. This system partly accounts for the fact that this regiment employed the flame thrower more than the other two regiments combined.107/

8. **Problems Encountered and Lessons Learned.** Sixth Army units were partially equipped with the M2-2 flame thrower at the beginning of the Luzon Campaign. During the campaign, the M1A1 models were replaced with the M2-2 as rapidly as the latter became available.108/ Units were not completely equipped with it until after the campaign closed. However, a sufficient number of the M2-2 models was in the hands of all units before the end of the campaign to demonstrate its superiority over the old M1A1. The policy adopted in the Southwest

---

107/
   Ibid. Incl No. 2.

108/
   Report of the Chemical Officer, Sixth Army, Luzon Campaign, 9 Jan - 30 Jun 1945.

Pacific of attaching a chemical service platoon to each division made flame thrower technicians available to the infantry and operational failures became rare. 109/ Cases occurred, however, where flame throwers misfired when the division's chemical service unit personnel were not being employed at flame thrower maintenance. 110/ It was also noted that full advantage was taken of the properties of thickened fuel when chemical service troops were available to furnish the proper mixture.

Complaints were received regarding the inability of the M2-2 flame thrower to maintain the necessary operating pressure in the pressure cylinder over a period of a week or longer. It is important that the pressure be maintained in charged flame throwers during amphibious operations when troops and equipment are enroute for several days. 111/ This deficiency was attributed to lack of proper training, poor maintenance, and inherent weakness of the portable flame thrower. In charging cylinders, it was not always realized that heat was generated and that a pressure drop of 200 pounds could be expected after the cylinder cooled off. 112/ Fittings often needed refacing or replacing and leaks had to be welded. The care and maintenance required to maintain 2,000 - 2,200 pressure p.s.i. was not generally realized by infantry troops. Operators complained that lack of a good seal in the filling plug seat on the M2-2 frequently caused pressure loss, which could not be detected until the valve was opened. 113/

The Philippine Operations were conducted at least partly during the rainy season and the usual malfunctioning of the M1A1 flame thrower due to faulty ignition was reported. 114/ Water-

---

109/
    32d Inf Div, GO 277, 27 Aug 45.

110/
    Hq 9th SvC Ft Douglas, Utah, Report No. 2928, 30 Jul 45.

111/
    Ltr, Cml O 41st Inf Div to Cml O Alamo Force, 30 Jun 44, sub: Preliminary Technical Report - Letter Report No. 2, p. 5. In Sixth A Cml Sect Records, 350.05 Biak, ORB.

112/
    Rpt, CG Sixth Army, 25 Nov 44, sub: Mistakes Made and Lessons Learned in K-2 Opn, p. 21. In Sixth A Cml Sect Records, AG 314.7 Hist Rpts, ORB.

113/
    Memo, Cml O Sixth Army for ACofS G-3, 10 Apr 45, sub: Summary of Lessons Learned in Luzon Campaign. In Sixth A Cml Sect Records, 370.2 Luzon Opns Rpt, ORB.

114/
    Ltr, CG Eighth Army to C/S WD, 3 Jan 46, sub: Employment of Flame Throwers in the Visaya Opns, Incl 1. AG 470.71 (FE).

proofing was only partially effective since water condensed on the spark plug gap and batteries deteriorated rapidly. Native porters, when not constantly watched, did not keep the flame throwers dry during transit.115/

Complaints regarding the excessive weight of the flame thrower were received during both the Leyte and Luzon operations. Reports cited instances in which a small single-shot flame thrower would be of value during operations in mountainous areas.116/

On Cebu, the Americal Division reported considerable difficulty with the pressure system on the M2-2 and E-3 models. Operators would often turn on the pressure release valve before going into action, thus allowing the pressure to go into the fuel tanks. Upon exposure to the direct rays of the sun, the safety disc blew out, apparently due to building up the pressure to more than 500 p.s.i. in the fuel tank. This division also reported that filling the pressure tanks to more than 1800 p.s.i. resulted in blowing out pressure regulators. This was the first time that such a report had been received by Sixth Army. It is not known whether the flame throwers concerned were equipped with the spring-type regulator which quickly established a reputation of being unsatisfactory. It was also reported that the fuel valve located in the gun group would often stick, and when the valve lever was released the flame gun would continue to operate until all fuel was expended.117/

During the Leyte operation and the early part of the Luzon Campaign, the supply of spare parts for the maintenance of flame throwers was entirely unsatisfactory. As soon as parts reached the theater, air priority was established to fly them to the battlefield where they were badly needed.118/ The Hoke pressure regulators

---

115/
    Ltr, CG 32d Inf Div to CG X Corps, 19 Dec 44, sub:
       Report of CW Activities in the Leyte Operation. In
       Sixth A Cml Sect Records, 219.1 Leyte Opn Rpts, ORB.

116/
    Report of the Chemical Officer, Sixth Army, Luzon
       Campaign, 9 Jan - 30 Jun 1945. In CMLWG.

117/
    Ltr, CG Eighth Army to CofS WD, 3 Jan 46, sub: Employment
       of Flame Throwers in the Visaya Operations, Incls. 1 or
       2. AG 470.71 (FE). InrCMLWG.

118/
    Hq USASOS, Chemical Section History, Jan 45.

with which the E-3 and M2-2 flame throwers were equipped when received were entirely unsatisfactory. Replacement by the new Dome or Grove type regulators had been completed by the end of the Luzon Campaign.

The assault parties prescribed by Sixth Army (See Appendix 9) proved successful until casualties began to mount and then it was found to be impracticable to hold such "permanently organized" detachments in reserve. As a result, the personnel from the separate assault parties in each battalion had to be returned to the line companies to fill the ranks. As the operation progressed it became necessary to organize assault parties within the companies as the need for them arose. With few exceptions, however, the basic principle of employing assault parties, instead of employing assault weapons separately, was followed even after the original permanently organized party had been disbanded.

CHAPTER IV

CENTRAL PACIFIC AREA 1/

A. Training Conducted.

Based on reports received from the South Pacific Area, the Hawaiian Department conducted a portable flame thrower demonstration on 28-31 July 1943 for the purpose of familiarizing organizations operating flame throwers in the Central Pacific Area with the employment of the weapon in the reduction of Japanese type defenses. These field exercises were attended by 620 students from all branches of the Army and Navy, and 756 guests from the Army, Army Air Forces, Navy, Marine Corps, and the British Navy. The demonstration was a reproduction of a combat operation reported from the South Pacific. A strongly protected bunker was constructed and the attack carried out by chemical troops acting as infantry and engineers. It covered all phases of the operation: approach by troops to limit of cover; placing of screening smoke to cover the approach of flame thrower operators to within firing distance; use of grenades and supporting fire power to keep the enemy under cover; neutralization of the fortification with flame throwers; placing of explosive charges and destruction by engineer troops; and the final mopping-up of the vicinity by attack troops. Excellent realism was obtained through simulated casualties and their removal under fire.

In order to assist units that were staging or mounting out of the Hawaiian area, the Hawaiian Department established a school for the purpose of conducting training in the maintenance, servicing and tactical employment of the portable flame thrower. Initially, the courses included eleven hours of instruction. However, in April 1944, the length of the course was increased to eighteen hours. The extent of this training is indicated by the following data: 2/

1/ South Pacific Area (SPA) was taken over by Southwest Pacific Area (SWPA) and Central Pacific Area (CPA) on 15 June 1944. On 1 August 1944, CPA was reorganized and redesignated as Pacific Ocean Area (POA). (See Biennial Report of C of S, USA, 1 Jul 43 to 30 Jun 45.)

2/ Hist CWS Mid Pac, Vol II, Annex IIb, pp. 1-2.

- 141 -

Date	Unit Attending	Number of Students
6-7 Sep 43	115th Engr Bn (40th Div)	51
4-6 Oct 43	13th Engr Bn (7th Div)	50
26-29 Oct 43	6th Inf Div	113
7-8 Feb 44	Army Defense Battalion	16
18-21 Apr 44	77th Inf Div	54
25-27 Apr 44	306th Inf (77th Div)	56
2-4 May 44	77th Inf Div	61
13-16 Jul 44	306th Engr Bn (81st Div)	45
7-10 Aug 44	96th Inf Div	56
14-16 Sep 44	98th Inf Div	51
28-30 Sep 44	391st RCT (98th Div)	50

The above courses were designed primarily to train instructor personnel for divisions. This personnel returned to divisions and in turn assisted in conducting divisional schools and training. In addition to the schools listed above, such training continued through the remainder of 1944 and 1945.[3]

B. Gilbert Islands.

1. **Planning.** During the planning phase of the Gilberts Operation, detailed studies, based on available intelligence information, were made of the Japanese defenses which it was expected would be encountered. As a result of these studies and past experience in the South Pacific, the employment of portable flame throwers was definitely indicated. The engineer battalion of the 27th Infantry Division was equipped with twenty-four flame throwers and sixty were issued to the 2d Marine Division upon the request of the division commander.[4] Flame thrower schools were conducted and tactical training was carried out. Personnel from the division engineer battalion were trained to employ the flame throwers even though there was some feeling that the weapon should have been included as equipment for each infantry

---

[3] Ibid., Annex IC, pp. 1-2. (See "Outline for 3-Day PFT Sch.")

[4] Ibid.

platoon.5/

2. <u>Employment</u>. On 20 November 1943, the 165th Infantry RCT landed at Makin Atoll and the 2d Marine Division assaulted Tarawa. The assault boats carrying the marines ashore stalled several hundred yards from the beach when they struck the coral bottom of the shallow water and the marines were forced to wade ashore through several feet of water and under a lethal blaze of cross-fire emitting from the highly concentrated beach defenses which had survived both the naval and air bombardment. Once ashore both the marines and army troops found strong, dug-in positions which had to be neutralized by fierce hand-to-hand fighting. Demolitions and the all too few flame throwers were put to effective use, saving many lives and much time.6/

As a result of experience gained in the operation, it was recommended that the allowance of flame throwers be increased to 192 per division, or 6 per rifle company plus 20 per engineer battalion, and that the infantry also be trained in the employment of the weapon.7/

C. Marshall Islands.

1. <u>Planning and Training</u>. The 7th Infantry Division and 4th Marine Division were each equipped with 192 M1A1 flame throwers and the necessary accessory kits for the Marshall Islands Operation.8/ Early in the planning stages of the operation, the 7th Infantry Division decided, after a study of aerial photos, military intelligence and reports from the Gilbert Islands Operation, that the formation and training of assault teams was imperative. An infantry regimental report called attention to the importance of further development of the assault team, especially for amphibious operations, and indicated the training required for the assault on Kwajalein by platoon teams.

> The mission of the assault team was to be the reduction of enemy strongpoints and obstacles such as pillboxes, wire entanglements, block houses and

---

5/ Hist CWS Mid Pac, Vol I, Sec 3, p. 18

6/ Ibid., Vol II, Annex IIb, p. 3.

7/ Ibid., Vol II, Annex Id, p. 30.

8/ Ibid., Vol II, Annex IIb, p. 5.

- 143 -

gun emplacements, which had withstood the naval and air bombardment and which, if not reduced rapidly, would delay or even prevent entirely the successful completion of the task force's assigned mission. The mission was accomplished by landing combat engineers in the assault waves with infantry rifle troops. After landing, the engineers were able to move forward, covered by the fire of infantry troops, and destroy the enemy installations.

[In training the assault teams,] it was recognized that the basis for teamwork could not be attained by lectures or even by dry-run rehearsals, but that realistic situations which could be met and overcome by infantry and engineers working together and developing joint procedure were required during the training period.

A combat firing range was constructed which included positions that were similar to Japanese strongpoints encountered at Makin and Tarawa. No effort was spared to create realism. Pillboxes were mutually supporting and protected by wire. The area between the beach and strongpoint was leveled, cleared and pitted with shell-holes. The fortified position was about 150 yards in depth and 100 yards wide.

Due to the unavailability of craft or amphibious vehicles for training, the landing was simulated. When the assault elements arrived at the simulated beach, the infantry took whatever cover was offered and delivered a heavy volume of fire on all apertures of the pillboxes. Through, under and between this fire the engineers crawled and ran to the barbed wire, placed their bangalore torpedoes and then withdrew to cover. The explosion of the bangalores was the signal for the infantry to advance by rushes, utilizing the smoke and dust from the explosion as a screen. One point stressed during this phase was that the infantry was to rush by small groups, while other groups maintained the fire, in other words fire and movement. The risk involved by having men moving rapidly through friendly fire was considered to be less than the risk of lifting all fire from the enemy positions thereby permitting return fire.

Figure 24. Tarawa: Marines Force Japs Back Into Bunker While Assault Troops Close In.

Once through the wire, a heavy volume of fire was again built up on the apertures of the pillboxes. The engineers went forward with satchel and shaped charges. While bullets were hitting the pillboxes barely inches from where they were working, the engineers placed their charges and withdrew to take cover from possible flying fragments. The explosion was the signal for a concerted rush to the pillboxes themselves. The infantry mopped up with bayonets and grenades and then moved on in the pursuit. Flame throwers were employed where necessary both in the assault and in the mopping up phases. In some instances smoke grenades were used to cover the advance of the engineers, but, in general, it was believed that the loss of control entailed by the use of smoke made this means of concealment somewhat of an emergency measure.

Inasmuch as there was a constant movement of troops during the "fire-fight" with both engineers and infantry running or crawling through and under friendly fire, the utmost control of fire was required. It was found that the problem developed superlative control in noncommissioned officers and officers. Despite the hazardous nature of the training, not a man was hurt.

All rifle platoons of the regiment, each with its complement of engineers attached, were run through this course several times. No attempt was made to control the problem from the standpoint of safety regulations. Ball ammunition, demolitions, including 25 pound satchel and 10 pound shaped charges, and loaded flame throwers were used. The engineers moved freely through friendly small arms fire and learned to depend on the infantryman's ability to deliver aimed fire accurately. The infantry gained confidence in the engineers' ability to place their demolitions rapidly and effectively.

/In forming the assault team,/ the engineer platoon which was assigned to each battalion landing team was broken down into three provisional squads, each consisting of a normal engineer squad plus additional personnel from platoon headquarters to furnish a strength of 14 per squad. One of these provisional squads was attached to each rifle company. Following is a list of the personnel in the provisional engineer squad showing each individual's weapon and load: 9/

1 – Squad Leader	'03 rifle	10# shaped charge
1 – Asst squad leader	M1 rifle	10# shaped charge
1 – Flame thrower operator	Pistol	Flame thrower
1 – Asst flame thrower operator	Carbine	Packboard with refill for flame thrower:
		5 gal Diesel fuel
		1 cyl hydrogen
		1 cyl nitrogen
4 – Wire cutter men	M-1 rifle	Searchnose wire cutters 2–5' bangalore torpedoes
6 – Demolition men	M-1 rifle	1 – 25# satchel charge of TNT

The tactical doctrine established by the Marines, based on experience in the Gilbert Islands Operation, is indicated by two directives issued by the Fifth Amphibious Corps in December 1943. 10/

2. <u>Employment</u>. On 1 February 1944, after two days of intense naval and air bombardment, personnel of the 7th Infantry Division, veterans of Attu, landed at Kwajalein, while the 4th Marine Division attacked the northern tip of Namur and Roi islands. It was a joint Army-Marine operation under the operational control of the V Amphibious Corps and the total forces involved, including both assault and garrison forces totaled 84,415. 11/ A Sixth Army report contained the following account of the effectiveness of assault teams whose weapons included portable flame throwers:

9/
   Sixth Army, Combat Notes No. 2, 15 Aug 44.

10/
   See Appendices 13 and 14.

11/
   Hist CWS Mid Pac, Vol. II, Annex I, d, pp. 32-33.

All initial landings in the Marshalls were made with the first four assault waves of battalion landing teams embarked in amphibious tractors (LVTs), with the remainder coming in on call in small boats of LVTs, depending on the reef conditions. Two reinforced rifle companies usually landed abreast in column of platoons. The two assault platoons, each with a provisional squad of engineers, were transported in the first wave of eight LVTs.

A resupply of explosives was taken to the beach on the LVTs of the first and fourth waves. These supplies were distributed as equally as possible among the LVTs of the wave and were unloaded on the beach by the crews of the LVTs. Additional supplies were loaded on Dukws (amphibious trucks) and were available on call.

The value of assault training was proved at Kwajalein where the assault teams moved rapidly and methodically through enemy defenses. As one of the soldiers remarked: "We hit the beach and there was a pillbox staring us right in the face. We hit the ground and put all the fire we could on it, just as we did in training. The engineers got right in there, and before we even had a chance to get scared, the pillbox blew sky-high and we moved through."

The fortifications encountered which necessitated the use of the assault team were many and varied. Air raid shelters made of coconut logs and sand construction or thick reinforced concrete were the most common. The Japanese fired from the doors and vents. Another type of fortification was the pillbox, constructed of either coconut logs or concrete. The concrete pillboxes were similar to our portable reinforced pillboxes except that they were usually hexagon shaped with ports to the front and both flanks. Few were found with all around firing ports. The concrete was of good quality and well reinforced and the thickness of the walls varied from approximately 18 inches in front to 12 inches in rear. The ports permitted fairly wide fields of fire. The Coconut log pillboxes were generally located on the perimeter of the islands, with small ports facing the ocean or lagoon. There were also many concrete cisterns and tanks in the building areas in which the Japanese took cover. As the concrete was usually thin, the reduction of these positions did not present much of a problem. 12/

Supplementing the above account is the following evaluation made by the 7th Infantry Division:

In the last analysis the campaign on Kwajalein was a battle of small units properly supervised by higher command and staff echelons, where the squad leader and platoon leader accepted responsibility and initiative with a superior type of leadership, employing in each case the agencies available such as tanks, mortars, machine guns, grenades, satchel charges, dynamite, and flame throwers, to overcome what appeared to be an almost impossible task of blasting the Japanese out of mutually supporting, reinforced concrete pillboxes and log bunkers. The technique developed for assaulting the positions during training in Oahu proved entirely satisfactory. Assault teams of the infantry or engineers reduced enemy defenses by covering the apertures with fire, breaching the walls of pillboxes with satchel charges or shaped charges and destroying the enemy with grenades or flame throwers. 13/

Flame throwers were reported as being especially valuable in neutralizing the underground positions which honeycombed the Engebi and Parry Islands. One marine operator was credited with killing fourteen Japs in one pillbox on Engebi Island. He stated that he was called upon to use a flame thrower on one position which riflemen couldn't reach and when the Jap saw the flame thrower, "he shot his brains out with his rifle by pulling the trigger with his big toe." Another marine who had never used a flame thrower before killed five or six Japs in an underground position after brief instruction from another operator. Another flame thrower operator killed twenty-four Japs in one underground position. The marines also used flame throwers against enemy tanks which had been placed in ditches to lower the silhouette. 14/

12/
Sixth Army, Combat Notes No. 2, 15 Aug 44.

13/
Rpt, 7th Inf Div, Kwajalein.

14/
T/Sgt William K. Terry, MC, "24 Japs in a Hole," CW Bull, Vol. 30, p. 19.

During the assault on Kwajalein, on 1 February, Company B, 184th Infantry, made contact with the main enemy defensive positions. The following is an account of the employment of flame throwers in these positions. Riflemen stood by to cover the advance of the flame thrower operator who usually got within five feet of pillboxes and bunkers before loosing the flame. He was conspicuous throughout the morning. He was a small soldier and his burden weighed seventy pounds. Each fuel load which gave about ten seconds of flame was usually exhausted in one burst. At the completion of each mission, this operator would go back to the dump 400 yards away and return with a refueled weapon. On two occasions the gun broke and he had to go back for a new one. Although he attacked about twelve bunkers, necessitating as many trips back and forth, he apparently did not tire. He stated that excitement kept him going. Once the hose sprang a leak while the operator was carrying the flame thrower up to a position but he closed one hand around the leak and carried on, shooting the flame into a large air raid shelter which lay in the path of the platoon he was supporting.[15]

Following the speedy and successful termination of the Kwajalein Operation on 15 February, a task force composed of the 106th Infantry RCT and the 22d Marine RCT sailed from Kwajalein Atoll and landed on Eniwetok Atoll on 18 February. The amount of bombing and naval preparation was considerably less than at Kwajalein and the defenses were of an entirely different type. Concrete fortifications and heavy log pillboxes were almost completely absent. The defenses were limited to field fortifications constructed from materials available on the site, and were completely underground. They were consequently weaker and more primitive than at Kwajalein. Flame throwers were used very successfully in mopping up these underground shelters and fortifications and numerous enemy dead were found burned to death in these bunkers.[16]

3. *Comments*. At the end of the Marshall Islands Operation it was found that 192 portable flame throwers per division were more than were needed and it was recommended that the allowance be reduced to 141.[17] The operation also confirmed the belief that the infantry should employ the portable flame throwers rather than assign the operation of them solely to engineer troops. The carrying of additional

---

[15] Lt Col S.L.A. Marshall, "One Day on Kwajalein," *Inf Jour*, Aug 44, pp. 20 ff.

[16] Maj Leonard D. Frescoln, "Post Mortem on the Marshalls," *CW Bull*, Vol 30, pp. 33-34.

[17] Hist CWS Mid Pac, Vol II, Annex Id, p. 40.

fuel in five gallon "blitz" cans with extra pressure cylinders tied to them was eminently successful and allowed servicing nearer the front lines than when fifty-five gallon drums were used as in the Makin Operation.18/ Stocks of spare parts proved to be entirely inadequate and flame throwers had to be deadlined instead of being repaired.19/

D. Marianas Islands.

1. <u>Planning</u>. In preparation for the Marianas Operation the inexperienced 77th Infantry Division conducted an intensive training program on the employment of flame throwers. One hundred seventy-one officers and enlisted men were trained in an 18-hour school conducted by the Hawaiian Department and this personnel in turn conducted further training within the division. After the Gilberts Operation, the 27th Infantry Division reorganized and retrained its assault parties in preparation for future combat. One hundred forty-one flame throwers were issued to each division. The 27th was equipped with the old M1A1 type while M2-2's were flown from the United States and issued to the 77th Division.20/

The tactical doctrine considered by the Marines at this time is indicated by a pamphlet issued by Headquarters U.S. Marine Corps in April 1944.21/

2. <u>The Operation</u>. The operations on Saipan and Tinian were under the control of the V Amphibious Corps, while the III Amphibious Corps was in command of operations on Guam. On 15 June 1944 the 2d and 4th Marine Divisions landed on Saipan, followed on 16 June by the 27th Infantry Division. On 9 July, after twenty-five days of extremely heavy fighting, the island was secured, though mopping-up operations continued for months.22/ The Japanese attempted to predict the landing points of the invaders and fortified those beaches strongly. For

---

18/ Ibid., Vol I, Sec 3, p. 22.

19/ Ibid., Vol II, Annex Id, p. 38.

20/ Ibid., pp. 40, 42.

21/ See Appendix 15.

22/ C of S USA, Biennial Rpt, 1 Jul 43 - 30 Jun 45, p. 71.

Figure 25. Flame Operator Attacks a Japanese Pillbox on Saipan, 17 June 1944.

Figure 26. Assault Squad During Flaming Operation.

example, the beaches of Magicienne Bay were strongly protected with trenches, wire entanglements, gun positions, blockhouses and beach mines. Fortunately, the landing was not made against these fortifications. Positions on the high ground inland and in caves in the cliff above the beaches covered all approaches and had to be reduced by assault parties.[23]

When the operation entered its final phase, the Japanese took refuge in natural caves which honeycombed the cliffs along the south shore. Frontal attack was frequently impossible, and overhanging ledges protected the caves from overhead approach. Many caves had several openings, and each one presented a different problem. It was found necessary in most situations to supplement standard procedure with new and experimental methods, but it was found that cave attack was like attacks against pillboxes, except that it required more ingenuity on the part of the attacker.[24] The 106th Infantry reported that one strong point, housing about twenty of the enemy, was reduced by an engineer assault party using flame throwers and demolitions.[25] After the operation the commanding general, 27th Infantry Division, made the following statement regarding the use of portable flame throwers:

> The standard Engineer portable flame thrower used during the Saipan campaigns definitely performed up to all expectations. It was very effective on the enemy; there were no operational faults and it could be used with a maximum of safety to the carrier.
>
> Prior to the Saipan assault the soldiers grumbled about the flame throwers. They felt the fire weapon was merely added weight for them to carry. After Saipan, the troops were enthusiastic about flame throwers.

---

[23] (1) "Japanese Minefields," MID, Tactical and Technical Trends, No. 54 (Jan 1945), pp. 1-11. (2) "Japanese Island Defense," MID, Tactical and Technical Trends, No. 59 (June 1945), pp. 40-45. In CMLWG.

[24] "Cave War," Special Technical Intelligence Bulletin No. 10, 24 Jun 45.

[25] 106th Inf (27th Div), Rpt Forager Opn, 19 Jun-5 Aug 44.

> There was a sufficient supply of flame throwers on hand. A flame thrower team was organized, usually two to a platoon. There was one flame thrower operator, a demolition man and a rifleman armed with a M1-or sub-machine gun to provide cover.
>
> The flame throwers were very effective against the Japanese spider type of underground installations.[26]

On 21 July, the 77th Infantry Division, 3d Marine Division and 1st Marine Provisional Brigade (later to be expanded into the 6th Marine Division) landed on Guam. The assault made steady progress and resistance ceased on 10 August. In the 77th Division, flame throwers were employed solely by the infantry throughout the operation and were not used by the engineers as in the 27th Division. The number of flame throwers available was sufficient although it was learned that transportation for moving flame throwers and servicing equipment forward with the infantry was essential. No provisions had been made for providing such transportation and on many occasions operations were slowed down while flame throwers were brought forward by hand carry.[27]

3. *Comments*. In the 77th Infantry Division, flame throwers were maintained and serviced by personnel from the ammunition and pioneer platoon of each battalion.[28] In the 27th Infantry Division, the 102d Engineer Combat Battalion serviced, maintained and supplied flame throwers for the division during the Saipan Operation. A total of thirty-six flame throwers was issued to each regimental combat team and nine to each engineer line company. The plan for the initial assault requirements of companies was as follows: Companies charged their nitrogen and hydrogen pressure cylinders and filled their fuel units on board ship on D-1. These supplies were furnished by the shore parties on board each ship. In addition, the companies filled 5-gallon cans with flame thrower fuel and carried them on their person or in 1/4-ton trucks. In order to support the

---

[26] Hist CWS Mid Pac, Vol II, Annex IIb, pp. 3, 4.

[27] 77th Inf Div Rpt Forager Opn.

[28] *Ibid.*

operations following the landing, the shore party landed their flame thrower supplies and set up refueling and servicing points on the beaches behind each battalion landing team. The shore party battalion carried the following:

- 97 flame thrower nitrogen pressure cylinders
- 30 commercial nitrogen cylinders
- 9 commercial hydrogen cylinders
- 3 fuel-filling kits
- 3 service kits
- 27 spare flame throwers
- 1500 gallons of fuel in 55-gallon drums

As the assault companies moved forward, it became necessary to draw equipment and supplies from the shore party and set up refueling and servicing points in each regimental area. These points were operated by the engineer combat company supporting the regiment. Each engineer company drew the following equipment from the shore party for this purpose:[29]

- 10 commercial nitrogen cylinders
- 3 commercial hydrogen cylinders
- 1 service kit
- 1 fuel-filling kit
- 1 mixing kit
- 54 5-gallon cans fuel

The marines employed flame thrower teams composed of the following:

- 1 Sgt. w/shotgun and demolitions pack
- 1 Cpl. w/flame thrower and pistol
- 1 Asst. flame thrower operator w/shotgun and extra charge
- 2 Pvts. w/M1 rifles and demolitions
- 1 Pvt. w/pistol and ammunition cart containing 2 fillings for flame thrower and 150 pounds of explosives

These teams were on call in each infantry battalion CP and were employed extensively. Some operators strapped or wired a carbine to

---

[29] AC of S G-4 27th Inf Div, Supply Phase of Forager Opns, 26 Jul 44.

the right side of the flame gun. For this purpose the stock of the carbine was cut off just back of the pistol grip and the arrangement enabled the operator to have fifteen shots immediately available for self-protection.30/

E. Caroline Islands.

1. _Planning_. In preparation for the Palau Operation the inexperienced 81st Infantry Division conducted intensive flame thrower training while stationed in Oahu. Forty-five men were trained by the Hawaiian Department and these, in turn, conducted schools within the division.31/ The 1st Marine Division had received experience in Guadalcanal and New Britain and had studied the employment of the flame thrower by the 2d and 4th Marine Divisions in the Marianas. The training which was conducted was based on these previous experiences.32/ Both divisions were equipped with the new M2-2 flame thrower.

2. _The Operation_. On 15 September 1944, the 1st Marine Division, with one RCT of the 81st Infantry Division in reserve, landed on Peleliu Island. Two days later the 81st Infantry Division (323d RCT) landed on Angaur Island south of Peleliu. The 323d RCT made an unopposed landing on Ulithi on 23 September. Heavy resistance was met by the marines and by 22 September they had been reinforced by two RCT's of the 81st Division.33/ Capture of Peleliu was complete by 30 September except for isolated enemy groups in caves that held out for another two months. It was against these caves that flame throwers found their greatest use during the campaign. The following is a description of the reduction of one of these caves:

> Large caves which were difficult to neutralize were encountered by U.S. Marines on Peleliu. Attacks with flame throwers, tanks, small arms, and demolitions over a period of five months killed all but six of more than 1,000 Japanese trapped in one extensive series of caves and tunnels on Peleliu Island. The

---

30/ 1st Marine Div D-2, Special Bulletin No. 2, 17 Jul 44.

31/ History of the CWS in the Middle Pacific, Vol II, Annex IIb, p. 2.

32/ 1st Marine Div D-2, Special Bulletin No. 2, 17 Jul 44.

33/ C of S USA, Biennial Rpt, 1 Jul 1943 to 30 Jun 1945, p. 73.

following story of what happened within the cave has been obtained from partially confirmed enemy sources.

A Japanese naval air force unit withdrew to the caves after their airport was knocked out by U.S. naval shelling and air bombardment. This withdrawal took place on 3 September 1944, nearly two weeks before D-day. The series of caves in which the unit sought shelter was a part of the cave system in which the Japanese made their last stubborn defensive stand on Peleliu.

These caves had been constructed primarily as air raid shelters and storage points. However, the Japanese had realized their defensive possibilities. The great majority of the caves had been formed by the dissolving of limestone by underground streams and seepage. The Japanese had improved on nature by cutting fire ports, secondary entrances, and escape routes and by enlarging the inside.

At first there were over 1,000 men in the series of caves, including many construction workers and other non-military personnel sent there for protection while awaiting evacuation. However, apparently no Japanese were evacuated until after the marines landed on 15 September, and then only some of the wounded were taken off the island by barges.

On 28 September all the military personnel were organized for an attack on the American forces holding the hill directly over the caves. The Japanese rushed out from all nine entrances and succeeded in driving the U.S. troops off the hill, but only at the expense of heavy casualties. When the Japanese reassembled in the caves, there were only about 50 military men left. The naval lieutenants who had been in command in the caves did not return and were presumed to have been killed in this Banzai charge.

The survivors moved their wounded into the three

largest tunnels in the rearmost section of the cave system. The construction workers occupied the central caves and tunnels, while the military personnel were established near the cave entrances at the brow of the hill.

The morning following the Japanese attack, U.S. forces assaulted the main entrance to the caves in which the Jap military personnel were located. The attack was carried out with a tank, machine guns, and flame throwers. The Japanese counter-attacked and all military personnel were killed except a few who remained behind a barricade in a branch tunnel or who were in the lower passages.

The flame penetrated into the caves and was reported to be the most effective weapon used, since in this first attack alone it reached points more than 100 yards from the cave entrance, killing some of the construction workers in the central tunnels.

Later the tank and flame throwers were used at most of the other entrances along both sides of the hill and when U.S. forces finally withdrew, only 30 Japanese were left alive. The marines had discovered the entrances to the tunnels where the Japanese wounded were located and flame thrower attacks had killed all the wounded. Most of the men who survived had taken refuge in a tunnel which branched off from the main entrance where the U.S. forces had first attacked. There was also a direct entrance at the side of the hill to this tunnel, but it was so well hidden that the marines did not discover it.

The U.S. forces at least partially blocked all entrances and the Japs remained holed up in their caves. Occasionally the Japs would fire upon soldiers who wandered inside the entrances not completely closed. These sniping activities brought renewed U.S. attacks with flame throwers and demolitions. However, the surviving Japs were safe in their undiscovered tunnel.

About 1 January 1945, very large explosive charges were set off in all the entrances except that for the tunnel in which the Japs were hiding. The force of these explosions killed 19 of the remaining 30 Japanese, and three more were badly injured. Near the last of January the hidden tunnel was discovered and the survivors moved into another section of the caves with the three wounded men, leaving behind two guards who were eventually killed when gasoline was poured into the cave and ignited.

On the night of 1 February the five Japs who were in good physical condition dug their way out of the entrances, intending to escape to the Jap-held islands to the north. They were armed with one American rifle, one Jap rifle, one Jap pistol, and hand grenades.[34]

3. <u>Comments</u>. In the 81st Division, the flame throwers were serviced, refueled and maintained by both engineers and infantry. It was believed that better results could be obtained if each infantry battalion organized its own facilities for servicing and maintenance.[35]

In the marine division it was necessary to assign two men to each flame thrower because of the rugged terrain and long distances over which the heavy weapon had to be carried. One instance was reported where a marine was burned by his own flame thrower when it sprang a leak and the fuel was ignited.[36] Insufficient information was given in the report to determine the cause of the leak.

F. Iwo Jima.

1. <u>Planning</u>. In preparation for the Iwo Jima Operation, the 3d Marine Division issued two training orders which reflected the tactical doctrine on the employment of the portable flame thrower at that time. The first of these orders, dated 16 December 1944, (See Appendices 16 and 17) prescribed the organization for the employment of flame throwers, rocket launchers, and demolitions in the in-

---

[34] "Japs Continue Extensive Use of Cave Fortifications," MID, <u>Tactical and Technical Trends</u>, No. 58 (May 1945), pp. 21-26.

[35] Hist CWS Mid Pac, Vol II, Annex IIb, p. 3.

[36] "Invasion of Palau Island," MID Rpt No. 919, 18 Dec 44.

fantry battalion. It directed the organization of an assault platoon in each infantry battalion. Personnel for these platoons were to be obtained by drawing six men from each of the three rifle companies and two from battalion headquarters company, making a platoon strength of twenty men. All men of this platoon were to be trained in the technique, operation and tactical employment of flame throwers, rocket launchers and demolitions. In addition, it prescribed that one man from each rifle squad be trained in the operation, servicing and maintenance of the flame thrower in order to provide a replacement for the regular operator if he became a casualty. This platoon was placed under the control of the battalion commander for attachment to the assault companies as the situation required. Normally six flame throwers were to be assigned to each assault company during landings. An allowance of twenty-seven flame throwers was prescribed for each battalion. For maximum support it was recommended that nine flame throwers be in operation, while nine were being serviced and the remaining nine were serviced weapons ready for use. The assault platoon (pioneer and ammunition platoon) was made responsible for servicing and maintenance. It was also prescribed that the battalion commander furnish transportation to keep the equipment as far forward as the tactical situation permitted.[37]

The second training order prescribed the tactical employment of flame throwers. It stressed the employment of the flame thrower as an assault weapon to be used on targets that could not be put out of action with other weapons. At least one BAR team should furnish direct support for the operator during his approach and withdrawal. In addition, there should be a holding force with automatic weapons to neutralize the enemy supporting weapons by pinning down occupants of the target position and supporting positions during the advance of the flame thrower operator. Cover and smoke should be used during the approach and withdrawal. The following type targets were listed as profitable: emplacements, tanks and armored vehicles, and positions concealed by growth and underbrush. Proper reconnaissance was considered essential. The use of thickened fuel was reported as being the most effective fuel for all purposes except as an incendiary.[38]

2. <u>The Operation</u>. On 19 February 1945, the V Amphibious Corps,

---

[37] 3d Marine Div Training Order No. 45-44, 16 Dec 44.

[38] 3d Marine Div Training Order No. 50-44, 19 Dec 44.

consisting of the 4th and 5th Marine Divisions in the assault and the 3d Marine Division in floating reserve, landed along the south coast of Iwo Jima, 775 miles from the main Japanese Island of Honshu. The fighting was extremely heavy and it was a month before the island was secured.

Work on strengthening the elaborate system of defenses on Iwo Jima was begun by the Japanese soon after the fall of Saipan. Fortification engineers, including cave specialists, came from Japan to Iwo Jima at about this time and drew up specifications for the construction of the caves which constituted the backbone of the defensive system. These caves were so planned that apertures could not be hit by direct shelling, and most of the construction work was done by hand, with some blasting. The caves varied in size from those with a capacity for only a few men, to some large enough to accommodate 300 to 400 persons. Most of the caves were built with multi-entrances to permit escape; almost all were stocked with food and water, while the most important had electric lights. 39/

The defenses of Iwo Jima represented Jap cave tactics brought to their peak. The enemy remained in their deep defenses during the heavy preliminary barrage, and pushed troops and weapons to the surface only when the ground assault jumped off. Prisoners reported that the preliminary bombardment was "terrifying," but it did not produce many casualties. Trenches, foxholes and pillboxes were tied into the cave network, and into the underground passageways wherever possible, so that destruction of an emplacement did not necessarily mean destruction of its defenders. Repeatedly, the Japs pinned down the attackers with heavy fire, only to withdraw into the ground when the attacking commander called down artillery and air support. When the position was overrun it was found to contain only a few dead Japs. Few of the enemy were seen in the open during the entire operation.

These tactics caused comparatively heavy casualties among the attackers, a terrific expenditure of ammunition, and slowed up the operation. The Japanese commander expressly forbade mass heroics such as a banzai charge and his troops clung to their positions to the end, to prolong the defense and to exact as heavy toll as possible. Once a position had been neutralized, it was by no means

---

39/
  Hq, Expeditionary Troops, TF 56, G-2 Report Iwo Jima.

safe. Japanese infiltrated at night, both on the surface and by underground passages, and reoccupied positions previously taken by American forces.40/

The following account, based on the records of the 3d Marine Division, is illustrative of the employment of flame throwers during the fighting on Iwo Jima. From the previous two days action the enemy's defense system in the pocket had been definitely established and on 22 March, Company I, 9th Marines, with a platoon of tanks plus one flame thrower tank attached, was ordered to attack and seize the enmy position. The attack was to be made from the west and south, with the assistance of protective fire from the high ground on the western side of the draw. The small Japanese force was entrenched along the base of the "sugar-loaf" hill from the southern end of the hill northwest to the head of the draw. A couple of machine gun bunkers were built into the trench parapet at key points and were still in operation. It was assumed, and later established, that caves extended from the bottom of the trench into a large main cavern under the hill, which enabled the Japanese to vacate the trench and return to it at will. Since the tanks which had been requested were late in arriving and because a passage through masking ground had to be bulldozed before the tanks could get in position to engage the main targets, Company I did not make the assault until about 1300.

At about 1220 regular tanks moved into position within fifty yards of the target and fired APC and HE for twenty minutes. The commander of Company I, assisted by a marine who knew the targets, directed the fire from the platoon leader's tank. The entire trench system was thoroughly and heavily worked over, all visible caves in the hill side fired into, and the last remaining MG bunkers completely destroyed. The flame thrower tank then moved into position and, at a range of about forty yards, sprayed its charge back and forth along the trench until its fuel was exhausted. Five or six Japanese were shot while attempting to escape from the trench as the flame diminished, and others were seen to blow themselves up with grenades. As the flame thrower tank ceased firing, the two assault platoons closed with the objective and, using their portable flame throwers on targets which the tank had missed, almost immediately

---

40/ "Cave War," Special Technical Intelligence Bulletin No. 10, 24 Jun 45.

Figure 27. Marine Flame Operators of the 5th Division Move Toward a Concentration of Japanese Pillboxes on Iwo Jima, February 1945.

Figure 28. An Infantryman Burns Out a Cave in the Clean Up on Iwo Jima, February 1945

occupied it. The platoon from the west, with the platoon which had enveloped and come up along the spur from the south covering the main length of the trench, moved into the trench and systematically closed each of the "communication" caves, which connected with the large chamber under the hill, with large demolition charges.

Two main entrances to the large caves were found; one lead from the south end of the trench and one was in the south side of the hill itself. Fragmentation and smoke grenades, flame and large TNT charges were thrown into these, resulting in a great amount of activity and commotion in the cave. Engineers were brought in to complete the job of sealing all the caves and, where they were too large to completely seal with charges, they were closed with bulldozers. Two 81-mm. mortars and a good supply of ammunition were removed from a section of the trench. An infantry platoon was then sent to the top of the hill and, by working from the top down on the reverse side with flame throwers and demolitions, destroyed the last two emplacements of the center of resistance.[41]

The portable flame thrower was used extensively throughout the operation. It proved to be an excellent weapon for use in assaulting emplacements, pillboxes, caves, and fortified positions when it could be moved up to within range. Due to the nature of the Japanese defensive positions, considerable difficulty was encountered in approaching positions and casualties among flame thrower operators were extremely high. In fact, during the latter stages of the operation, it was difficult to keep flame throwers manned with experienced personnel.[42]

3. Comments. The large number of flame throwers available (twenty-seven per battalion) permitted great elasticity in employment. In the assault landing, one flame thrower was carried by each rifle platoon, nine with each battalion supply section, and twenty-seven with each regimental service platoon. This insured rapid replacement of lost or damaged weapons and servicing and repair was accomplished by forwarding charged weapons to battalions and returning the emptied weapons to the regiment. This system operated with a high degree of efficiency and speed and insured elasticity of employment. It was found, however, that the number of flame throwers available exceeded

---

[41] 3d Marine Div, 9th Marines Action Rpt, Iwo Jima, Incl. C.

[42] Action Rpt, 3d Marine Div Action Rpt, Iwo Jima, 30 Oct 1944 - 16 Mar 1945, and Incl. D.

requirements and it was recommended that the allotted number be reduced by one-third. The system for servicing and resupply continued to function with an adequate margin against loss or destruction of weapons. It was felt, however, that the allotment should not be reduced below eighteen per battalion.43/

It was recommended that a 1- or a 1½-ton truck be added to the table of Equipment of each battalion for the purpose of transporting flame throwers instead of using the transportation of other units as was done during the operation.44/ Operators in the 4th Marine Division were not equipped with pistols, as was done in the 3d Marine Division, and it was recommended that in future operations pistols be issued to all flame thrower operators.45/ The 24th Marines (4th Division) used constantly the assault platoons organized in each battalion and recommended that the battalion Table of Organization be revised to include such an organization.46/ It was also reported that the rear safety grip on the M2-2 flame thrower was brittle and broke easily and that maintenance in general was unsatisfactory because of a lack of spare parts.47/ The extent of the resupply problem is indicated by the fact that the 24th Marines reported forty-five flame throwers lost in battle while the 25th Marines reported forty-six destroyed in combat.48/

G. Ryukyus Islands.

1. Planning. For the Ryukyus Campaign, the new Tenth Army was composed of four veteran army divisions under the XXIV Corps, which had been through the Leyte Operation, and three veteran marine divisions under the III Amphibious Corps. These divisions were all experienced in the employment of the portable flame thrower and made the necessary preparations prior to the operation. Schools were conducted in servicing and maintenance; assault teams were organized and

---

43/ 4th Marine Div (RCT 23) Opn Rpt, Iwo Jima, Annex Fox.

44/ 3d Marine Div Action Rpt, Iwo Jima, 31 Oct 1944 - 16 Mar 1945, Incl. D.

45/ 4th Marine Div Opn Rpt, Iwo Jima, Annexes Fox and How.

46/ 4th Marine Div (RCT 24) Opn Rpt, Iwo Jima, Annex George.

47/ 4th Marine Div (RCT 25) Opn Rpt, Iwo Jima, 15 Apr 45, Annex How.

48/ Ibid.

tactical training carried out.49/ All new flame throwers were thoroughly checked and adjusted. For example, the 27th Infantry Division received ninety-six new M2-2 flame throwers, forty of which had defective threads in the check valve connections. New parts for the connections were made in the navy machine shops before embarkation. Another deficiency, which indicated poor workmanship and inspection, was in the connection to the base of the Grove pressure regulator where insufficient space was provided for the washers necessary to make an air tight fit.50/

M2-2 flame throwers were authorized on the following basis:

Army:	1 per rifle platoon	81
	4 per bn. assault team	36
	24 per engr. combat bn.	24
		141 per division

6 per non-divisional engr. bn.51/

Marines: 243 per division

Each army infantry battalion organized and trained an assault party similar to the ones employed by the marines at Iwo Jima. In addition, each rifle platoon trained a team consisting of the following: one flame thrower operator, one assistant operator armed with a submachine gun, and one demolitions man equipped with satchel charges. The operators were made responsible for their own maintenance.52/

2. The Operation. On 26 March 1945, the 77th Division landed on the outlying islands of Kerama Retto to secure the approach to the key island of Okinawa. The Kerama chain was captured at the end of three days fighting and the XXIV Corps and III Amphibious Corps landed on the west coast of Okinawa on 1 April. Opposition on the beaches was light. The Marines turned north and secured the northern part of the island which was lightly held. The Army Corps turned south toward the principal city of Naha where it was confronted with the main Japanese force elaborately entrenched. It was here that flame throwers were used on a large scale. Elements of the 77th Division

---

49/ 7th Inf Div Opn Rpt, Ryukyus Campaign, 1 Apr - 21 Jun 1945.

50/ Rpt, Lt Col Wm R Maull to C CWS, 28 Sep 45, sub: Rpt of Official Travel, Sec III, p. 19. In CMLWG. (Lt Col Maull was the CWS representative on the Borden Mission.)

51/ Hist CWS Mid Pac, Vol II, Annex IIb, p. 5.

52/ Med Div, Rpt No. 17, Final Report of Duty in SWPA and POA.

landed on the lightly but tenaciously held island of Ie Shima on 16 April and after a week of bitter fighting overcame the enemy resistance there. By the end of April the 7th, 27th, 77th and 96th Infantry Divisions had been thrown into the line north of Naha. The marines soon completed the drive to the north of the island and were then thrown into the line north of Naha where bitter fighting continued until the middle of June when the Army and Marines broke through the heavily fortified Naha-Shuri defense lines. There were 65,000 to 70,000 fighting Japanese holed up in the south end of the island, supported by some 500 artillery pieces of 75-mm. size and larger. The terrain was decidedly rugged and cut up with many cliffs, natural and man-made limestone and coral caves, and thoroughly organized into an underground defense system. 53/

The following account, taken from a report submitted by the 96th Infantry Division, is typical of the employment of flame throwers for the reduction of caves:

> Numerous types of caves and underground emplacements were encountered at Okinawa and practically every one required a different method of reduction. Usually, however, direct fire weapons were first employed against the cave openings and embrasures to permit demolition units and flame throwers to work up to within close range of the cave. Machine guns and riflemen, from supporting positions near the cave being assaulted, were always employed to cover the operations of the demolition team. After the demolition crew had cautiously worked its way forward to the cave entrance or embrasure, a smoke grenade was thrown through the opening to blind the Japs while the satchel charges were being emplaced, and to permit the location of additional cleverly camouflaged embrasures or openings to the same cave. In many instances when smoke grenades were tossed into cave openings, smoke could be seen coming from several other openings along the hillside. Each of these openings was then spotted and additional demolition crews sent forward with

---

53/
  C of S USA, Biennial Rpt, 1 Jul 43 to 30 Jun 45, pp. 82, 83.

satchel charges to destroy the emplacement. It was usually found that a 20-pound satchel charge with 30 to 45 second fuse would effectively seal most caves and emplacements.

The incident of the 3d Platoon, Co. K, 381st Inf, in reducing an enormous cave in the YAEJU-DAKE hill area on 13-14 June is typical of much of the Inf combat engaged in during this operation. This cave was located along the cliff of the YAEJU-DAKE ESCARPMENT. At the base of the cliff were two entrances 50 feet apart and banked with coral to form a parapet. Ten feet above the two bottom entrances and further apart were two more holes, much smaller and about the size of firing ports, in the sheer wall of the cliff. On the top of the escarpment, about 100 feet from the bottom entrance, were two pillboxes and three holes of entrance or exit 20 to 60 feet from the edge of the cliff. The cave was extensive, being dug into the solid coral wall of the escarpment. To get to the different floors, of which there were three that were actually seen, the enemy used ladders and platforms of 20 foot intervals. The terrain in front of the cave was a mass of large coral knobs, and the left edge of the cave was covered with brush.

The cave was assaulted from below and from the right side without knowing its full size. Word was received from the Bn OP that there was an exit on top as they could see the Japs rushing out. By a physical count, 9 Japs were killed in the cave and 5 outside in their sniping positions on the coral knob. In the preparatory concentrations on the escarpment the high port on the right was hit either by a direct fire weapon or artillery and it was enlarged over eight feet in diameter, but it was still tenable and was occupied. The enemy employed continuous rifle fire and made extensive use of the hand grenade, throwing them out of the top entrance and off of the top of the escarpment. Supporting riflemen put covering fire on the top edge of the escarpment keeping the enemy back from the edge to limit their use of hand grenades. The BAR was used to neutralize the two high ports and grenades were used along the bottom entrances.

Nine AT rockets fired from the Bazooka were employed at 20 yards to blow out the parapets of the bottom entrances. Eight fragmentation grenades were then fired into the different ports from the rifle grenade launcher by using the adapter. This grenade firing was successful because the grenades went deep into caves. By using WP grenades it was determined there were no more entrances. Due to the draft in the cave, however, the smoke was drawn out the top and several of the enemy smoked out. One squad of 8 men was left to hold the ground taken and keep the Japs busy while the others went around to flank the cave from the left and eliminate a sniper firing from deep in the cave. Working a man in under cover of smoke, a satchel charge was placed in the bottom entrance. On detonation it did very little physical damage to the cave and raised a large cloud of dust. The charge didn't stop the sniping so the portable flame thrower was employed. Each entrance was given a two to three second burst and a heavy machine gun section 600 yards to the rear of Hill 99 had a field day shooting the Japs as they came out the top. The estimate was that more than 30 Japs ran out.

The 3d Platoon, consisting of one 8-man squad and one 7-man squad plus a runner, medical aid man and Lt platoon leader, worked on toward the cave. The 8-man squad was organized into two BAR teams of two men each, and the remaining four men carried a satchel charge per man. The 7-man squad was organized into one BAR team of two men, one rocket launcher team of two men carrying 9 rounds, one man carrying the flame thrower, and the two remaining men carrying satchel charges. Each man carried four fragmentation and one WP grenade and two bandoleers of ammunition. The squad leader carried the rifle grenade launcher and 8 adapters. Smoke was used very effectively to screen the enemy's vision so that the platoon could work right on the enemy position after it had been held up twice by enemy rifle fire.

Even after this through assault, the cave was not completely reduced. It was sufficiently

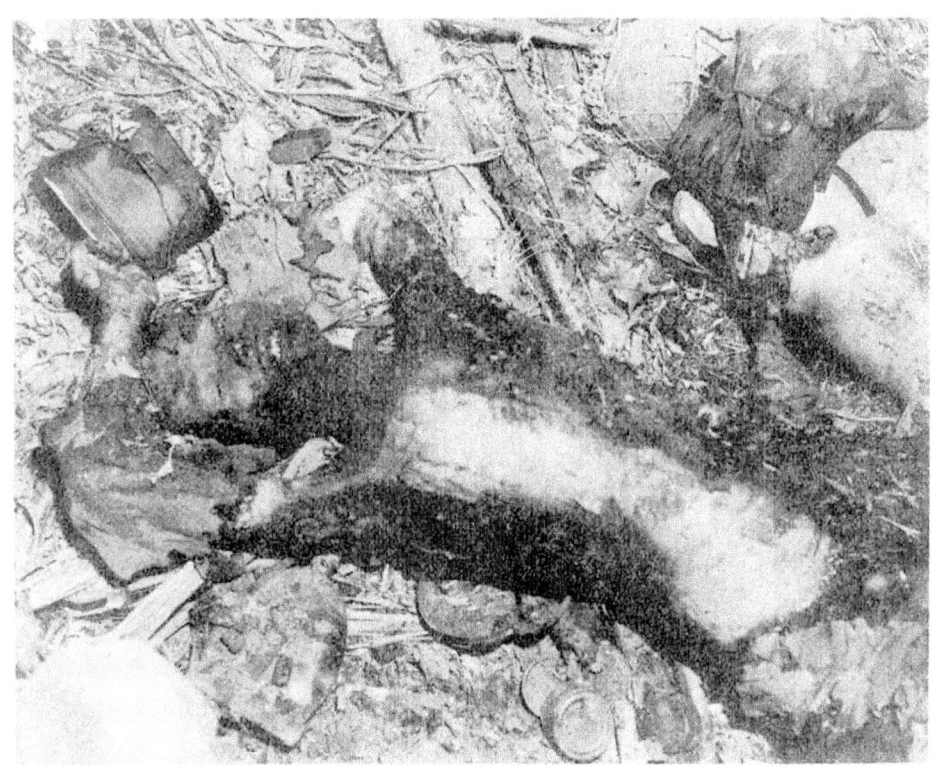
Figure 29. An Example of What Happened to Thousands of Japanese Who Refused to Surrender.

neutralized, however, so that further advances in this area were possible as long as the cave was offensively guarded. When the top of the escarpment had finally been secured, organic engineers were employed to finally and completely reduce this position.54/

Throughout the fighting on the southern part of the island, flame throwers were used extensively. An indication of the number of times the portable flame thrower was employed is reflected in XXIV Corps ammunition expenditures which reported the following number of portable flame thrower fillings expended in combat: 7th Division - 402; 77th Division - 2,336; 96th Division - 1,625.55/

3. Comments. Spare parts for M2-2 flame throwers were not available during the Okinawa Operation and cannibalization was necessary to keep them in operation.56/ Thickened fuel was prepared before embarkation for the operation. Upon arrival in Okinawa, however, 70 percent of this fuel was too thin for use. Much of this fuel had a consistency little better than that of raw gasoline. Because of this experience, thickened fuel was made up on the field only a few days before it was required for use.57/

H. Defective Flame Throwers in CPA.

Deficiencies in New Flame Throwers. It was originally assumed that new flame throwers received from the United States had been inspected and tested for serviceability and both flame throwers and kits were normally issued without being checked. After numerous complaints were received from using organizations concerning the unserviceability of new flame throwers, it became standard operating procedure to thoroughly test each flame thrower before it was issued from the depot. Out of a shipment of 106 M1A1 flame throwers and

---

54/
   96th Inf Div, Action Rpt, Ryukyus Campaign.

55/
   XXIV Corps, Action Rpt, Ryukyus Campaign, 1 Apr - 30 Jun 1945.

56/
   Rpt, Lt Col Wm. R. Maull to C CWS, 28 Sep 45, sub: Rpt of Official Travel, Sec III, p. 19. In CMLWG.

57/
   Ltr, Cml O POA to C CWS, 18 May 45, sub: Ltr 43d Lab Co, "A New Theory and Tactic of Flame Thrower Warfare." POCML 470.71/463. In CMLWG.

accessory kits received from the United States in September 1943, ten were found defective. Also two service kits and two fuel-filling kits were found to have shortages in tools. 58/ In another shipment of 146 M1A1 flame throwers, received in December 1944, 124 were unserviceable. Common defects in these weapons were found to be: gauge adapters did not fit fuel units; hydrogen lines leaked; batteries were dead; valves were not tightly fitted; spark generators were out of order; pressure regulators were unserviceable; and spark plugs were imperfect and would not function. The scope of these defects indicated improper inspection in the United States prior to shipment overseas. 59/ Deficiencies continued to be found when the new cartridge ignition type flame thrower was received in the theater, indicating that proper corrective action based on previous reports had not been taken. Out of a shipment of 494 E-3 flame throwers, which arrived in the theater in June 1944, twenty-seven were found to be defective when received. The following defects were noted: leaks in the pressure system; pressure regulators not adjusted; fuel valve assemblies mechanically imperfect; defective casting on regulator valve; stripped threads on barrel assembly; defective ignition shields; and improperly machined threads on fuel hose. Of the twenty-nine service kits received with this shipment, there were shortages in eight, and 14 percent of the bleeder valves or the charging lines leaked. 60/ These deficiencies continued to be found in shipments or new flame throwers until the end of the war. As previously noted, forty of the ninety-six M2-2's received by the 27th Infantry Division in 1945 contained major defects. 61/

58/
   Ltr, Cml O POA to C CWS, 9 Oct 43, sub: Defective Flame Throwers, M1A1. In CMLWG 470.71.

59/
   Ltr, Cml O POA to OC CWS, 12 Jan 44, sub: Report of Inspection of Flame Throwers. In CMLWG 470.71.

60/
   Ltr, Cml O CPBC to OC CWS, 24 Jul 44, sub: Defects of E-3 Flame Throwers and Service Kits. In CMLWG 470.71.

61/
   Rpt, Lt Col Wm. R. Maull to C CWS, 28 Sep 45, sub: Report of Official Travel, Sec III, p. 19. In CMLWG.

CHAPTER V

CHINA-BURMA-INDIA

A. Employment by the Chinese at Tengchung.

1. Situation. The Japanese offensive in 1942 resulted in closing the Burma Road and isolating China except for the thin line of air supply over the 500 miles of the Himalayan Hump between Assam, India, and the Yunnan Plateau. About the middle of 1943, the Combined Chiefs of Staff decided that an offensive should be undertaken in the winter of 1943 - 1944 to clear the way for extending the Ledo Road (later named the Stilwell Road), then under construction, from Assam to the old Burma Road at Mongyu. The preliminaries of this operation began late in October when the Chinese 38th Division, which had been trained and equipped in India, moved into Hukawng Valley. In February, the Chinese were joined by the 5307th Composite Unit, Provisional (Merrill's Marauders) which were especially trained for long range penetrations. In May they fought their way into the airfield at Myitkyina, the key to northern Burma; capture of the town of Myitkyina took place in August. These troops were then reinforced by the 14th and 50th Chinese Divisions which had been flown in from Yunnan, China.1/

2. Employment of Flame Throwers. During the battle for Myitkyina, attempts to employ flame throwers had met with failure, which resulted in the general attitude that it was a suicide weapon. From October 1943 flame thrower training for personnel of Chinese divisions had been conducted at the Ramgarh Training Center, in Bihar Province, India. This training, which consisted of a two-weeks course for ten officers and approximately twenty-five enlisted men and non-commissioned officers in each regiment, conformed generally to existing doctrine. The reasons for the reported ineffectiveness of flame throwers during the operation was not clear. It appears that either the trained regimental personnel failed to effect the necessary training of flame thrower squads or that flaming operations were not adequately planned. At any rate, future training included practical exercises with the flame thrower as part of organized assault squads and as a definite part of a tactical plan.

1/ C of S USA, Biennial Rpt, 1 Jul 43 - 30 Jun 45, pp. 57, 58.

The men, therefore, acquired increased confidence in the weapon when they saw the increased range possible with thickened fuel and that its use was based on carefully prepared plans in which all possible supporting fire was to assist the flame assault. 2/

In July 1944, while the 53d and 54th Chinese Armies were preparing for the battle of Tengchung, the U.S. Flame Thrower Liaison Team conducted schools to train 175 operators. The Chinese Armies consisted of five divisions, i.e., the 2d Reserve, the 36th and 198th Divisions of the 54th Army, and the 116th and 130th Divisions of the 53d Army. The students were from the engineers attached to the 2d Reserve and infantrymen from the 116th and 130th Divisions. Training was practical with very little emphasis placed on servicing and maintenance. Operation and tactical employment was stressed because the Chinese officers and men were to use the weapon in combat immediately after the training. Servicing and maintenance was to be handled by the American liaison team, thus enabling all trained Chinese personnel to be used in combat.

The main objectives were Laifengshan and Tengchung. Laifengshan was a strongly fortified hill position dominating the city of Tengchung. It was located about one mile southwest of the city and was garrisoned by about 400 Japanese. Tengchung was a walled city on the Burma Road and was important because of its position on the line of supply from India to China by way of the Ledo Road. The city was garrisoned by about 2,000 Japanese troops.

After several fruitless attacks, the 2d Reserve, the 36th and the 116th Divisions attacked Laifengshan on 26 July. The ground attack was preceded by a heavy aerial and artillery bombardment. Using five flame throwers very effectively, the assault engineer detachment gained a foothold on the large hill. Several pillboxes had to be cleared out before the crest was reached. Thickened fuel was used in the five flame throwers. Later refills were made with liquid fuel. By the morning of 27 July all flame thrower operations ended and the rest of the Japanese were mopped up by the infantry. The entire position was taken by 29 July. Simultaneously with the attack on the large hill, the small hill was stormed by an assault group employing two flame throwers, primarily to knock out several pillboxes which dominated the best route of approach up the slope. Once these strong points were reduced, the rest of the position was taken by the infantry.

2/ (1) Unit Hist CW Sect 5332d Brig (n.d., ca. 25 Mar 45), p. 2. In CMLWG. (2) Memo, Capt Louis J. Stefani for Hist Off OC Cml C, 12 Sep 49, sub: Flame Thrower Operations in the Chinese Theater. In CMLWG.

In the fighting in and around Tengchung the flame throwers were used initially as a defensive weapon to repel Japanese counterattacks. These Japanese attacks were launched against a position which the Chinese had gained on one corner of the city wall. Later the flame throwers were used offensively against the Customs House and British Consulate areas just outside the wall. These areas, consisting of fortified homes and compounds, dominated the approaches to the walls and prevented the Chinese on the wall from enlarging their positions and moving into the city. Trenches were dug and demolitions were used to approach and overcome these positions, after which the Chinese were able to move into the city. Within the city the Japanese had entrenched themselves in each house and compound, often digging deep into the ground and using the rooms of the buildings as dugouts and gun emplacements. To drive the Japanese out of these positions the Chinese used flame throwers, demolitions, bazookas, antitank guns and artillery. The flame throwers were used both as an assault weapon and in mopping-up operations. For mopping up, the Chinese reported that the flame throwers were excellent.

The flame thrower operators were able to approach many of the Japanese positions in the city by taking advantage of the ruins and rubble; however, some approach trenches had to be dug in order to get within firing distance. One compound was especially troublesome because it was large and well fortified. The Japanese had dug themselves under the steps and walls and had good fields of fire both in the courtyard and around the compound. This area was taken by first neutralizing the outer Japanese defenses with flame throwers and grenades. Then, about forty gallons of mixed fuel was thrown over the walls -- using jars, bottles and cans. After the inner Japanese dugouts were well soaked, flame throwers were used to ignite the fuel. The resulting heat and smoke killed most of the Japanese; others who tried to escape were disposed of with rifle fire and grenades. Finally, the Chinese mopped up all opposition in the city except that in one corner near the east gate. After flame throwers knocked out the pillbox guarding this gate the last position was taken and the battle for the city was over.3/

The troops were equipped with the old M1A1 flame thrower and several instances of the malfunctioning of equipment and other difficulties were noted. Pressure regulators were clogged by the overflow from tanks and caused relief valves to open and thereby exhaust the

---

3/ Ltr, Hq Y-Force Opns Staff USAF, CBI, 23 Oct 44, sub: Use of Flame Throwers in Lai Fung and Tengchung Campaigns. In AG Hist Records Sect.

pressure cylinder. Rubber diaphragms became soft due to the overflow of fuel. Fuel discharge valves failed to close properly; difficulty was encountered in obtaining a tight fit at the junction of gun and hose; and hydrogen trigger valves stuck. Ignition was faulty at times due to moisture collecting on spark plug gap. The recommended mixture of one can of napalm to twenty gallons of gasoline would not stay gelled. A mixture of two cans to thirty gallons stayed gelled for at least two days, but then tended to break down slowly from a thick gel to a progressively soupy liquid. On one nitrogen assembly, the nipple and the coupling nut on one hydrogen bottle charging line were cracked. Packing on hydrogen bottles was difficult to replace because of the poor design of the handwheel and the method of fastening to the valve stem. Only Bright Star batteries functioned well. In operation it was found that the trigger valve was difficult for the Chinese to operate because of their small hands. Hydrogen valves were too small and poorly placed for ease of operation.

3. <u>Supply for the Tengchung Operation</u>. Requisitions for fuel and equipment were sent in from the using units to Force Headquarters either by radio or telephone. These demands were routed to the Engineer School and filled from available stocks. If the Engineer School at Paoshan could not fill these requests or if the requests necessitated air dropping, the requisition was sent to Base Depot #2 at Yunnan Yi, where the balance of all flame thrower equipment and supplies were stored. The Air Dropping Section at Base Depot #2 would then deliver the material at the nearest air drop field. L-5 planes were also used from Paoshan to Tengchung. These planes carried commercial nitrogen and hydrogen cylinders, fuel, flame throwers and spare parts. The quantity carried by an L-5 was small, however, and these planes were used only in emergencies. Damaged flame throwers, empty gas cans and empty cylinders also were returned by L-5 planes. Pack transportation (coolie) was used to haul 2½ tons of equipment from an air drop field in the Shweli Valley to the site of the first school. Eighty coolies were needed to haul this equipment about fifteen miles.

Refueling points manned by the American liaison team were set up about one mile from the scene of action. At these refueling dumps the spare nitrogen and hydrogen bottles were filled, fuel was mixed and all service and maintenance work was done. Each regiment using flame throwers was given extra cans of fuel, nitrogen and hydrogen bottles, plus one set of wrenches for every two flame throwers, and a piece of wire to clean out the burner head holes.

4. <u>Comments on Employment at Tengchung</u>. The time allotted to training was too short. At least one week or more was necessary to

train Chinese not only in the operation, tactical employment and servicing, but also in coordination with infantry and engineers. With reference to tactical employment, thirteen complete shots were fired on Laifengshan and seventy to eighty shots in Tengchung. The latter figure was considered unusually high and could have been reduced by a longer and more complete training period. Infantry support was inadequate due to lack of coordinated training and poor leadership on the part of the higher ranking Chinese officers.

The following recommendation was made with reference to malfunctions and service kits:

> At least two 5/16" thin body engineers wrenches and two long-nosed pliers should be included in the service kit for disassembly of the hydrogen trigger valve. Only Bright Star or the equivalent batteries should be furnished. Some sort of baffle or method is needed to prevent overflow into pressure regulator. The hydrogen valve should be redesigned for easier operation. Long-handled construction wrenches should be replaced by # 706 wrenches. The latter can be used not only on the pressure cylinder nuts but also on the gun tube and hydrogen bottle coupling nut. More adjustable wrenches should be furnished - at least six per Kit, Service. Then, with six adjustable # 706 wrenches, six 3/8" wrenches and six of the three different sized Allen wrenches enough tools would be available for ten flame throwers, plus one set at the refueling point.

The most dependable means of supply was by air dropping, in which less than 3 percent loss was sustained in dropping fuel and equipment to the 53d Army. The usefulness of the L-5 planes was limited by the small carrying capacity of 200 pounds per plane. Pack transportation was slow but the only means of moving equipment over the narrow trails and difficult terrain. All flame thrower equipment, by suitable distribution of loads, could be carried by coolies.

It was the opinion of an observer that flame throwers could be employed effectively by Chinese troops if sufficient technical training were given the flame thrower teams, if the supporting troops were properly trained in coordinating the attack with flame throwers, and if weather conditions were favorable.4/

B. Plans for 1945.

On 26 January 1945 the Chinese Training Center, Provisional, was established for the purpose of providing training for thirty-six Chinese divisions comparable to that conducted at Ramgarh in India. Since these divisions were widely dispersed, mobile training units were organized and conducted training for the various divisions wherever they were located. One of these mobile training teams was a flame thrower team consisting of two officers and six enlisted men. From April until August 1945 the flame thrower training conducted by this team was approximately as follows:

			Personnel Trained		
Date	Units	Place	Chinese Officers	Chinese EM	U.S. Officers
Apr 1945	6th Chinese Army	Chen Yi	35	-	4
Apr 1945	8th Chinese Army	Chen Yi	35	-	5
May 1945	54th Chinese Army	Ann Jung	30	-	4
May 1945	71st Chinese Army	Chickiang	23	-	3
May 1945	13th Chinese Army	Chickiang	25	-	5
Jun 1945	207th Chinese Div	Yunan Yi	32	-	2
Jun 1945	30th Chinese Div	Yunan Yi	36	-	2
Jul 1945	18th Chinese Army	Chickiang	62 officers and EM		-
Jul 1945	74th Chinese Army	Chickiang	76 officers and EM		-
Aug 1945	73d Chinese Army	Ann Wei	86 officers and EM		-
Aug 1945	94th Chinese Army	(in the field)	10	32	-

With the exception of the last brief course conducted for the 94th Army, the personnel trained by this team were officers or warrant officers who were to conduct the training of flame thrower squads in their respective organizations.5/

A report dated 21 March 1945 described the preparation for further use of flame throwers. The two American regiments were each authorized eighteen M1A1 flame throwers. The 475th Infantry chose to use

---

4/ Ibid.

5/ Memo, Capt. Louis J. Stefani for Hist Off, 12 Sep 49, sub: Flame Thrower Operations in the Chinese Theater. In CMLWG.

them in the battalion pioneer and demolition platoons while the 124th Cavalry trained about four men from each rifle troop. Approximately twelve hours of instruction was given each team. Each man was given an opportunity to fire in a problem, and the instructions included complete servicing, maintenance and preparation of fuel. The 1st Chinese Regiment was authorized twelve flame throwers and received the same instructions as all of the other units. Appropriate training memoranda were issued, which outlined practical tactics based on experience in the South Pacific Theater. The coordination of all other weapons, particularly supporting mortar and rocket fire, was stressed. A typical squad organization in training included a sergeant in command, two flame thrower operators and two assistants, two sub-machine gunners, and two grenade throwers. The training also provided the personnel with considerable practice in the effective use of the white phosphorus grenade. Several good demonstrations were staged for the line units in both regiments. 6/

It was still necessary at this time to supply the troops by air drops from Advance Section No. 3 at Ledo. The weapons were dropped in pairs, with a spare nitrogen and hydrogen cylinder, spark plugs, tools, and three 4.5-gallon fuel charges. Thickened fuel was the most desirable because of its increased range. 7/

6/ Unit Hist CW Sect 5332d Brig (n.d., ca. 25 Mar 45), pp. 2-4. In CMLWG.

7/ Ibid.

CHAPTER VI

PLANS FOR EMPLOYMENT IN THE KYUSHU OPERATION

A. Situation.

By direction of the Joint Chiefs of Staff, General MacArthur assumed command of all United States Army Forces in the Pacific (AFPAC) on 6 April 1945. In June he created the new command of United States Forces in the Western Pacific (WESPAC) to replace the old SWPA and redesignated the Pacific Ocean Areas (POA) as Army Forces of the Middle Pacific (AFMIDPAC). Since operations in these two areas had been virtually completed, they were in the communications zone and corresponded to service commands in the United States. The American Sixth Army was assigned I Corps (25th, 33d and 41st Infantry Divisions), IX Corps (77th, 81st and 98th Infantry Divisions), XI Corps (1st Cavalry Division, 43d and Americal Infantry Divisions), V Marine Corps (2d, 3d and 5th Marine Divisions), the 11th Airborne Division and 40th Infantry Division (Army Reserve). The mission of Sixth Army was to make a three-pronged attack on the southern coast of Kyushu on 1 November for the purpose of establishing airfields and bases to support the attack on the main Japanese island of Honshu by the First, Eighth and Tenth Armies several months later.1/ The assault echelon for the Kyushu Operation included over 500,000 men and 61,000 vehicles with a follow-up of approximately 300,000 men and 89,000 vehicles of all types.2/

B. Training and Preparation.

All of these divisions were veterans, with the exception of the 98th which had been stationed in Hawaii since April 1944. Inspection of the 98th revealed that the training of flame thrower operators and assault parties was excellent. With the exception of the 81st, the flame thrower personnel in the remaining divisions had been depleted by casualties, rotation and promotion, and an extensive replacement training program was initiated in July. The Chemical Warfare Training Center at Manila established a five-day course for flame thrower technicians. Key flame thrower personnel from all

---

1/ C of S USA, Biennial Rpt, 1 Jul 43 - 30 Jun 45, p. 84.

2/ Hist CWS Mid Pac, Vol I, Sec 3, p. 45.

divisions were to be sent to this school to study servicing, maintenance, operation and fuel mixing. The second class had just begun when the Japanese sued for peace on 10 August. In addition, each division had started flame thrower technical and tactical training.

A study was made to determine the practicability of the current training doctrine as established by the training memorandum issued by Sixth Army on 22 June 1944 (See Appendix 9). Two glaring deficiencies in this doctrine were noted. It had been found impracticable to hold permanently organized battalion assault parties in reserve during combat when casualties had mounted and every available man was needed to perform the normal infantry functions in the battalion. Too, the assault party controlled by the battalions had not offered the flexibility required by rifle companies. In addition, experience had demonstrated the need of designating personnel to be made responsible for servicing and maintenance. As a result of these studies, Sixth Army published a new training directive in August 1945. This directive prescribed that training of assault squads would be conducted in accordance with War Department Training Circular No. 2, dated 25 January 1945, and that a minimum of two squads in each company would be organized and trained in accordance with Section II thereof. Pertinent extracts of Section II read as follows: 3/

> General. Protection and support are provided for the portable flame thrower on combat missions by a flame thrower squad. This is a rifle squad that functions as such until a specific situation arises in which the flame thrower can be used to advantage. All rifle squads should be trained to perform this additional mission. Flame throwers may be employed singly or in pairs. When available, the employment of mutually supporting flame throwers is desirable.
>
> Organization. a. The rifle squad lends itself readily to conversion into a flame thrower squad with a minimum of reorganization. Of the 12 men, eight retain the same designations and perform the same sort of duties as in the rifle squad. These are the squad leader, assistant squad leader, two scouts, the two-man BAR team, and two riflemen.

3/ See Appendix 12 for complete copy of the TM.

b. The remaining four riflemen are designated and given new functions. Two form a rocket-launcher team; one, armed with the rocket-launcher, becomes the rocket gunner, and the other, the assistant rocket gunner. Two comprise the flame thrower team, as operator and assistant operator. The operator carries the portable flame thrower; his assistant carries additional fuel and accessories to refill and charge the flame thrower.

c. When additional flame throwers are available, the two riflemen may be formed into a second flame thrower team.

d. Individual arms are retained by all members of the squad, except the flame thrower operators and the rocket gunner, who carry pistols.

e. If the flame thrower squad is operating over terrain containing many strong emplacements, it may be necessary to attach a party of trained demolition men equipped with bangalore torpedoes, pole charges, or other demolition material.

4. Additional equipment. In addition to individual arms and equipment prescribed for the rifle squad, conditions in the situation and terrain in specific theaters will dictate the additional equipment to be carried by the flame thrower squad. The following is one example of the use of additional equipment:

1	Squad leader	2 fragmentation hand grenades.
2,3	Scouts (each)	Launcher, grenade; 4 WP rifle grenades; 3 fragmentation hand grenades.
4	BAR	4 fragmentation hand grenades.
5	Asst. BAR	Launcher, grenade; 2 WP hand grenades; 3 WP rifle grenades.

6	Rocket gunner	Rocket launcher; 2 WP rockets.
7	Asst. Rocket gunner	3 2.36-inch HE rockets; 3 WP rockets.
8	FT operator	1 portable flame thrower; 1 can ignition cylinders; 2 WP hand grenades.
9	Asst. FT operator	Standard plywood backboard; 1-5 gal. can fuel; 1 charged pressure tank; 1 adjustable wrench; 1 heavy end wrench; 2 cans ignition cylinders; 2 incendiary hand grenades.
10,11	Riflemen	4 fragmentation grenades each.
12	Asst. squad leader	4 fragmentation hand grenades; 4 WP hand grenades (including launcher, grenade, if colored smoke rifle grenades are substituted.).

In addition, it was directed that the regimental and battalion gas officers would be designated as flame thrower officers and become advisers to their respective commanders on the technical aspects of the flame thrower. The battalion gas officer (ammunition and pioneer platoon leader) was made responsible for servicing and maintenance of the battalion flame throwers. It was directed that the battalion gas corporal be qualified as a flame thrower technician and turned over to the battalion flame thrower officer to assist in maintenance and servicing in addition to his duties in defense against chemical attack. This procedure facilitated the training of flame thrower technicians by the Chemical Warfare Service, which was responsible for such training.

C. Supply and Maintenance.

For the first time, allowances of accessory kits were established on such a basis as to make each infantry battalion and cavalry squadron self-sufficient. In previous operations the scarcity of accessory kits had necessitated servicing at the regimental level, which, in most cases, resulted in lack of sufficient flexibility. The allowance of flame throwers was set at thirty-nine per regiment (117 per division) to be distributed as the regimental commander saw fit. Six complete service kits were also authorized to each regiment. 4/ The portable flame thrower manifold, E4, was authorized on the basis of one per battalion. It was felt that the use of portable flame thrower fuel tanks with the E4 manifold did not meet the requirement for an extension hose and a number of units were built by mounting the 25-gallon fuel unit from the auxiliary tank flame thrower on a 4.2-inch mortar cart. The extension hose from the E4 manifold kit was attached to this unit and the M2-2 flame gun used. Several divisions had expressed a desire for this unit and it was planned to make a sufficient number for issue of one to each infantry battalion. 5/

A chemical service platoon was assigned to each Army division by GHQ, AFPAC, and a minimum of eight flame thrower technicians were to be trained in each platoon. When required, these technicians could be attached to battalions to assist in servicing flame throwers. Fuel, with specific properties, was to be prepared by the chemical service platoons.

4/
  Hist CWS Mid Pac, Vol II, Annex IIb, p. 6.

5/
  (1) Ltr, CG AFPAC to CG's Sixth Army and WESPAC, 16 Jul 45, sub: Kits, Manifold, Portable Flamethrowers E-4. (2) Ltr, CG Sixth Army to CG WESPAC, 21 Jul 45, sub: Issue of Flamethrowers, Portable, M2-2 and Accessories. AG 470.71. In Sixth A Cml Sect Records, 470.71, PFT, ORB.

CHAPTER VII

NORTH AFRICAN AND MEDITERRANEAN THEATERS

A. North African Operations.

At dawn 8 November 1942, U. S. Forces including the 1st, 3d, 9th and 34th Infantry Divisions and the 1st and 2d Armored Divisions landed simultaneously at Casablanca, Oran and Algiers on the north coast of Africa. Within three days the "Vichy" French had capitulated and the initial phase of the campaign was over. These forces then consolidated and converged on Tunisia where they were deployed against Rommel's Afrika Korps which was being reinforced by Von Arnim's Army from Italy. The fighting in Tunisia covered the period from January to 13 May 1943 when enemy forces in Tunisia surrendered.

Each engineer combat battalion, organic with the divisions, carried twenty-four of the early model (E1R1 and M1) portable flame throwers as part of their organizational equipment. These engineers had received superficial training with the flame throwers in both the United States and the British Isles prior to the operation. Training exercises had served to establish the technical deficiencies of the weapon and troops had little confidence in it. Thickened fuel was not yet available and the range of the weapon consequently was short. Because of the fast moving situation encountered during the first month in North Africa, flame throwers were usually left behind with organizational equipment and were not considered an essential weapon. However, situations did arise in which the use of flame throwers were indicated and attempts were made to bring them up. Three instances were reported where requests were made for flame throwers to be brought forward. In each case, delivery of the weapons was too slow and the positions had to be taken by hand-to-hand fighting. No instances were reported of the flame thrower actually being used in combat during the struggle for Morocco in Algeria.[1]

The operations in North Africa brought out the logistical problem which involved making portable flame throwers available to front line troops, serviced and ready to use at the critical moment. This

---

[1] Pers Ltr, Cml O Western Task Force to OC CWS, 2 Dec 42. SPCW 320.2/100. In CMLWG.

problem was never completely solved during the war. The flame thrower remained organizational equipment for which no provision was made for personnel in the tables of organization. It is true that in the Pacific many field expedients were established for the purpose of alleviating this situation. Nevertheless, there remained a tendency to discard equipment not required at the moment in order to get mobility. Following the experience in North Africa, a light, single-shot flame thrower similar to a roman candle was proposed as a solution to the problem.2/ Also, it was felt that such a flame thrower would not require continual maintenance and would solve the spare parts problem.

B. Sicily (10 July - 18 August 1943).

Early shipments of napalm arrived in the theater during the spring of 1943 and the first shipment of the new M1A1 flame thrower became available in June, on the eve of the invasion of Sicily.3/ The engineers had looked forward to the arrival of this new equipment in the hope that the improved model, operating with thickened fuel, would prove useful. The 39th Engineer Regiment conducted training at Chanzy, Algeria, during April.4/ The forty to fifty yard range obtained with thickened fuel was encouraging. In preparation for the operation, all combat engineer battalions conducted training and demonstrations with the portable flame thrower and thickened fuel. The serviceability of the new M1A1 flame thrower was disappointing, however, as it incorporated the same basic weaknesses found in the M1 model.5/ Division engineers were not impressed and the 15th Engineer Battalion (9th Inf Div) went so far as to turn their portables back to the base depot before leaving North Africa.6/ Theater status of equipment reports for the period indicate that a second division also turned in their flame throwers.7/

2/ Ibid.

3/ Status of Equipment Report, MTOUSA, 30 Jun 43. In CMLWG.

4/ Daily Jour, Cml O Fifth Army, 1, 27-30 Apr 43. In CMLWG.

5/ U.S. Seventh Army, Rpt of Opns, Sicilian Campaign, 10 Jul - 17 Aug 1943, p. H-3.

6/ 1st Ind, 3 Dec 43, on Ltr, C Cml O ETOUSA to C Cml O AFHQ, 18 Nov 43, sub: Use of Flame Throwers in Sicilian Campaign. In Seventh A Cml Sect Records, 470.71 FT Fuels, No. 1, 1 Jan 43 - Feb 45, ORB.

7/ Status of Class II, IV and V Supplies, MTOUSA, 31 Jul 43. In CMLWG.

Three hours before sunrise on the morning of 10 July 1943 assault troops of the 15th Army Group struggled through rough seas to land with little resistance along 100 miles of the southern coast of Sicily. The forces were made up of the British Eighth Army under Alexander on the right and the U. S. Seventh Army under Patton on the left. The Seventh Army was made up of II Corps, consisting of the 1st and 45th Infantry Divisions, and elements of the 82d Airborne Division, and a Provisional Corps made up of the 3d Infantry Division and a combat team of the 2d Armored Division. The Germans launched an armored counterattack against the 1st Division northeast of Gela, on D plus 1. It was during this engagement that the 1st Battalion, 39th Engineer Combat Regiment, as part of a special ranger force attached to the 1st Division, employed portable flame throwers to burn off a wheat field from which enemy infantry were resisting.8/

Allied aircraft, flying up to 1200 sorties each day, gave close support to the ground operations and the troops forged steadily ahead. Within a week one-quarter of the island had been taken. The northern side of the island offered rugged mountainous terrain which was stubbornly defended by the enemy. Where flame throwers would have normally been used in attacking a pillbox or similar fortification, high explosives and white phosphorus were effectively used to route the enemy before our troops came close enough to use their flame throwers. Flame throwers, therefore, were not used again throughout the operation which ended on 18 August 1943.

At a critique held following the Sicilian campaign, spokesmen for the various infantry divisions stated that their engineers did not use flame throwers and that they were not only useless but occupied valuable shipping space on amphibious operations. It was recommended that they be made Class IV (optional) items carried in army or base depots for use on special occasions, which were planned considerably in advance. The lack of use by the enemy was cited as evidence of their having little tactical value.9/

C. Operations in Italy (9 September 1943 - 2 May 1945).

    1. To the Fall of Rome (Salerno, Anzio and Cassino). After the Sicilian campaign, the attitude toward portable flame throwers hit an

---

8/ Cml O Seventh Army, Rpt of CW Opns - Opn Husky, n.d. In MTOUSA Cml Records, 370 Empl, Opn and Move of Troops, 1942-44, ORB.

9/ Conf of Army, Corps and Div Cml O's and CO's of all CWS Units in the Seventh Army, 28 and 29 August 1943. In CMLWG.

all time low. Training by Fifth Army units prior to landings at Salerno and Anzio consisted of little more than demonstrations and technical training sufficient to familiarize operators with the weapon. In fact some units did not go to the trouble of exchanging their old M1 models for the new M1A1.[10]/ However, engineers embarked for Salerno with their full allowances of twenty-four flame throwers per combat battalion. The landing was made by Fifth Army, consisting of British X Corps on the left and U.S. VI Corps on the right. VI Corps was made up principally of the veteran 45th and the untried 36th Infantry Divisions. The Germans had anticipated an amphibious operation against Naples and their resistance at the beach was strong. Vigorous counterattacks started the same day. The veteran 3d and 34th Infantry Divisions were rushed into the area. By 15 September high ground commanding the beaches had been taken and contact was made with the British Eighth Army forty miles southwest of Salerno, on 16 September. By 1 October Naples was ours.

Progress continued to be satisfactory and the first crossings of the Volturno River were forced on the night of 12 - 13 October. The Germans, however, had been developing winter defenses along the Garigliano and Sangro Rivers, about seventy-five miles south of Rome. Here they constructed strong points of log and earth emplacements and even dug into solid rock. This defense line became known as the Gustav Line. 240-mm. howitzers and 8-inch guns were rushed from the United States to deal with the situation. At this time interest was revived in the possible use of portable flame throwers. For example, these weapons were issued to the engineer battalion of the 2d Moroccan Infantry Division and on 21 December VI Corps called upon the chemical officer, Fifth Army, to conduct a two-day school to familiarize its personnel with loading, firing and employment.11/

In an attempt to break the Gustav Line and roll up the German left flank, VI Corps was pulled from the line and prepared for landing fifty miles behind the enemy lines on the beaches of Anzio-Nettuno, twenty-five miles south of Rome. The task force embarked from Naples after a short amphibious training program. The landing was made in the early morning hours of 22 January 1944 with U.S. troops on the right and British troops on the left flank. U.S. assault troops con-

---

10/ Routing Slip, Cml O NATOUSA to Engineer, G-4, 14 Nov 43, sub: Flame Throwers. In MTOUSA Cml Sect Records, 470.71 Apparatus for Using, ORB.

11/ Daily Jour, Cml O Fifth Army, 21 Dec 43. In CMLWG.

sisted of the 3d Infantry Division, the 6615th Ranger Force (Provisional), the 83d Chemical Mortar Battalion, and the 509th Parachute Infantry Battalion. The landing was co-ordinated with a strong attack by the remainder of the Fifth Army, reinforced by two fresh divisions from the British Eighth Army, whose mission was that of breaking the Gustav Line and driving up the Liri Valley to make contact with VI Corps. The Germans held, and for the next four months both sides were deadlocked in a battle of attrition. During this time U.S. reinforcements, consisting of the 45th and 34th Infantry Divisions, 1st Armored Division, 100th (Nisei) Infantry Battalion, 36th and 39th Engineer Combat Regiments, and 504th Parachute Infantry (82d Div)12/ were brought into the Anzio beachhead. On 25 May a junction was made with Fifth Army forces pushing up from the south, which forces included the 88th and 85th Infantry Divisions, which had been committed to action for the first time in March and April, respectively. A coordinated attack found Rome in the hands of our troops on 4 June 1944.

    The engineers of the 85th Infantry Division had received sporadic training with the flame thrower both in the United States and while staging in North Africa. When the division arrived in Italy, flame thrower training and supply was transferred to the division chemical officer in accordance with the new Fifth Army policy, which left the engineers free for other duties such as building roads, bridges, clearing mine fields, and planting mines. Flame throwers were maintained and serviced by chemical personnel at a forward supply point and furnished to the infantry as required. An instance which involved the first use of the flame thrower by a member of the 85th Division occurred during the fighting at Tremensouli in attacking the Gustav Line. Under cover of an artillery barrage on 11 May 1944, the 1st Platoon, Company G, 339th Infantry Regiment, proceeded west along the Capo D'Aqua until its advance was stopped on the reverse slopes of Hill 79. A series of enemy pillboxes was stretched across dominant high ground, and the platoon was pinned down. It remained in this position until the morning of 13 May when the platoon leader, determined to obtain a flame thrower in order to carry out an attack on the key fortification. He made his way back some 500 yards to the regimental command post where he obtained a flame thrower. He returned to his platoon, formed an assault party, and directed the attack against the opposing pillboxes. His regular flame thrower operator had been wounded so he detailed his sergeant, an assistant squad leader, to use the weapon. Fire from small arms and automatic weapons kept the key pillbox sealed

---

12/ The 36th Infantry Division arrived at Anzio on 22 May and the 361st RCT (91st Div) on 1 June 1944. (1) Hist Div, DA, Anzio Beachhead, p. 117. (2) Combat Chronicle - An Outline History of U.S. Army Divisions, p. 76.

up until the sergeant was within 15 yards of the emplacement. With three short bursts of flame he killed all of the occupants. After this pillbox was silenced, the platoon swiftly took over the other enemy positions with white phosphorus grenades. The sergeant was awarded the Distinguished Service Cross for this action.13/

During this period, the 11th Chemical Maintenance Company operated with a detachment of one officer and thirty enlisted men at Anzio, and their duties included that of maintaining flame throwers. The remainder of the company supported the main Fifth Army forces on the Gustav Line. Chemical technicians were available on call to take complete flame thrower equipment to any unit and assist in putting on an attack as desired.14/ At Nettuno (Anzio beachhead) several units, each consisting of a 1-ton trailer, loaded with ten M1A1 flame throwers, 100 gallons of thickened fuel, and one filling and service kit, were held available for tactical units on call. These units were accompanied by experienced technicians.

Combat engineers did not ignore the possibility of employing flame throwers to neutralize German defensive positions. On 3 February 1944, the 34th Infantry Division requested that six flame throwers be made ready for action. These were prepared, filled with thickened fuel and delivered to Capua. The 34th was prepared to use them in the fighting around Cassino. They were tested before they went into the line and were in operating condition, but failed to ignite when in position and ready to fire, leaving the operators exposed to enemy machine-gun fire.15/ This Division attempted to employ flame throwers later at Anzio and they again failed to fire. It was concluded that the electrical ignition system was unsatisfactory for use in rainy weather.

Before the battle for Mount Cassino, the Polish divisions were each issued eight flame throwers, serviced and ready for use. After a brief period of training in using the weapon, operators picked them up and jumped off with the infantry, intending to employ the flame throwers as weapons of opportunity. The results, in part, were most unsatisfactory. Several flame throwers were destroyed in the concentration area by artillery and mortar fire. After jumping off from the starting line,

---

13/ Interv, Hist Sect, with Lt Col H.C. Joyner, formerly Cml O 85th Inf Div, 2 Aug 48.

14/ (1) Hq Fifth Army, Report of CW Activities, 19 Feb - 3 Mar 1944, 4 Mar 44. In Cml C Sch Lib. (2) Ltr, Cml O, Fifth Army to C CWS thru Cml O NATOUSA, 14 Apr 44, sub: (?). In MTOUSA CW Records, General, ORB.

15/ AGF Board, MTOUSA, Report No. 359, sub: Current Questions Regarding Infantry Operations, 27 Mar 45.

two flame throwers were set on fire by hits from enemy machine guns. Because of the excess weight, operators experienced difficulty in keeping up with the riflemen. In a few cases, however, operators got into position and successfully fired their weapons with good effect. Polish officers were favorably impressed but immediately recommended a change in tactical employment.[16]

2. Pursuit to the North. Cumulative experience in the theater had revealed that the prescribed allowances for flame throwers were unsatisfactory. It had been demonstrated that chemical technicians were required to maintain and service the weapon. Furthermore, the numbers required by any unit depended upon the situation. It had become apparent that infantry units should be equipped with flame throwers if they were to be exploited to their full advantage. On 5 April 1944, Fifth Army issued Training Memorandum No. 8 prescribing the technique and tactics of flame throwers. (See Appendix 18.) This directive was followed in May by a series of two-day schools conducted by the 11th Chemical Maintenance Company at Francolise, Italy. One-half of the time was devoted to mechanical details, one-quarter to practice firing and one-quarter to tactical employment. A separate class was conducted for each American and Allied division, which necessitated giving instruction in English, French, Arabic, Polish, and three Indian dialects.[17] Fifty men in each division were trained as operators in these two-day schools. War Department Circular 204, IV, 23 May 1944, deleted all flame throwers and accessories from the Tables of Basic Allowances and made them items of Class IV (Optional) supply. This directive enabled commanders in the field to determine their own basis of issue and to promulgate their own tactical doctrine. During the last year of the Italian campaign, portable flame throwers were issued to divisions on the basis of four per infantry regiment and these in turn were apportioned out through the infantry battalions to front line companies as desired by the respective commanders.[18]

There was no standard method prescribed in the theater for organizing and equipping flame thrower teams. In all cases at least one operator and one assistant operator was trained for each apparatus issued. The remainder of the assault team was provided according to availability and to the desires of the commanding officer concerned.

---

[16] Ltr, Main Hq 2 Polish Corps, to Main Hq AAI, Jul 44, sub: Flame Throwers. In MTOUSA CW Records.

[17] A Study of Portable Flame Throwers, 16 Jan 46. In Cml C Sch Lib.

[18] AGF Board Rpt, MTOUSA, No. 283, 31 Jan 45.

The 1st Armored Division prescribed an assault team of twelve men consisting of one flame thrower operator, one assistant operator, and ten men armed with M1 rifles and Browning automatic rifles. All members of this team were trained to operate the flame thrower. A training memorandum issued by the commanding general, 88th Infantry Division, prescribed that a flame thrower squad be available to the ammunition and pioneer platoon in each battalion. Each squad was to be manned and armed as follows:

Personnel	Armament
1 Flame Thrower Operator	Flame Thrower and Pistol, Cal..45
1 Asst Flame Thrower Operator	Flame Thrower and Pistol, Cal..45
1 Squad Leader	M1 Rifle and 2 Thermate Grenades
3 Tommy Gunners	SMG Cal..45 and 2 White Phosphorus Grenades, each
3 Riflemen (1 Asst BAR man)	M1 Rifle and Launcher and 2 Rifle Smoke Grenades
1 BAR man	BAR
1 Bazooka man	Rocket Launcher and Carbine M1 Rifle
1 Asst Bazooka man	Rocket Launcher and Carbine M1 Rifle[19]

The following extract of a divisional training memorandum indicates how it was expected that flame thrower assault teams would be employed tactically:

> Tactics: One man carries and operates the flame thrower but the weapon is such that operator is vulnerable and completely impotent unless his effort is preceded by and coordinated with an infantry team assault upon the obstacle encountered. Normally, ample fire support must be rendered to permit the flame thrower operator to close to within 25-30 yards of the target without being observed from the target. Well-placed rifle smoke grenades and smoke hand grenades can be useful for this purpose. In any case, it is essential that a high volume of small arms fire be directed at enemy peep-holes and weapon openings so as to keep the enemy pinned down during the advance of the flame thrower operator.[20]

Assault teams armed with rifles, automatic rifles, and bazookas, were employed to a great extent against fortified houses and dugouts throughout the fighting in Italy. The automatic rifle formed the nucleus of the team, which usually employed few riflemen as a base of fire

---

[19] Ibid.

[20] Ibid.

while a reconnaissance was being made. Flame throwers were seldom used as an additional weapon in such assault teams. It was found that they were not essential in attacking houses since the bazooka rocket or anti-tank grenade, fired through the door or window of the house, usually sufficed. In a few cases, however, the flame thrower was reported to have been used to great advantage in assaulting pillboxes or well-protected dugouts where the bazooka and anti-tank grenade were ineffective.[21] One reason for not employing the flame thrower to a greater extent was the lack of trained specialist operators. Because of the complicated nature of the weapon, an operator had to be proficient. As a result of casualties, transfers and promotions, operators trained prior to a certain operation were seldom available when the need for them arose.[22] In the 92d Infantry Division this problem was solved theoretically by keeping the flame throwers in the engineer battalion with trained personnel. When a flame thrower team was required by an infantry assault group, the engineer battalion was to send up the weapons with a trained crew to operate with the infantry. However, there is no record of flame throwers ever having been used by this division.[23]

The general plan for refueling was to have the servicing kits at refilling points which were located as far forward as possible. All operators were informed of the location of such points and were instructed to take their flame throwers to these places when they required refilling. Of the six divisions in the theater in January 1945, three utilized personnel of the division chemical section to operate refilling points, two utilized engineer personnel, and one placed the responsibility on the using units, assisted when necessary by personnel of the division chemical section. First echelon maintenance was usually performed by the operators themselves or by the technicians located at the refilling points. For higher echelon maintenance, flame throwers were turned in to the chemical maintenance company at the army depot.[24] In spite of the strict surveillance maintained by chemical technicians, the M1A1 flame thrower never functioned properly for the troops. It should be noted that in spite of numerous instances reported of misfires, no means was ever devised

---

[21] Hq 15th Army Group, *A Military Encyclopedia Based on Operations in the Italian Campaign, 1943-45*, p. 187.

[22] Ibid.

[23] AGF Board Rpt 359, MTOUSA, 27 Mar 45.

[24] Ibid.

for waterproofing the ignition as was done in the Southwest Pacific Area, where climatic conditions were such that the flame thrower would never have functioned had it not been for modifications which included waterproofing. The new M2-2 cartridge ignition flame thrower did not reach Italy until March 1945 and they were being issued with a maximum allowance of thirty-six per division 25/ when the German forces in Italy surrendered 2 May 1945.

D. Critique.

The lack of importance of the portable flame thrower as a weapon in the North African and Mediterranean Theaters may be traced to the basic deficiencies of the weapon itself. When a weapon fails to function in combat, the news travels fast and troops lose confidence in it. The M1A1 flame thrower was by no means a "foolproof" weapon and its delicate electrical ignition system, as issued, was absolutely unreliable for field use. There is no record of chemical service troops attempting to correct this condition in these theaters. Had the more reliable M2-2 model been available at the beginning of the war, it is entirely possible that a tactical requirement for the portable flame thrower would have evolved.

The logistical problems encountered in employing the portable flame thrower limited its usefulness in either a fast-moving situation or on mountainous terrain. It was too cumbersome for the soldier to carry long distances and fuel had to be made available. In cases where transportation was at a premium, heavy equipment that was not used regularly had to be left behind. The chemical officer, Fifth Army, strongly recommended the development of a light, single-shot, expendable flame thrower to meet the objections of the M1 model. Although this recommendation was made in December 1942, 26/ development of such a model had not proceeded beyond the experimental stage when the war ended. 27/

As on all battlefields of the war, it was learned that once the flame thrower was filled and serviced, it could not be depended upon to function a few days later when it was placed in action against the

---

25/ (1) Historical Report - Chemical Section, Fifth Army, 1 Mar 45. In Cml C Sch Lib. (2) 1st Ind, Hq MTOUSA, to CG AGF, AC of S G-2, 5 Apr 45. In MTOUSA CW Records, 319.1 AGF Rpts, ORB.

26/ Pers ltr, Cml O Western Task Force to C CWS, 2 Dec 42. In CMLWG.

27/ Rpt of Activities of Tech Div, p. 139.

enemy. In addition to being subject to misfires, gas leaked out from the pressure cylinders and upon being fired a short stream of fuel would dribble from the flame gun leaving the operator in a most embarrassing, and frequently vulnerable, position.[28]

---

[28] Comments on Conference of CW Officers, Seventh Army, 28-29 August 1943, p. 2. In CMLWG.

CHAPTER VIII

EUROPEAN THEATER OF OPERATIONS

A. Pre-operational Training and Plans.

    1. <u>Training Conducted</u>. The Command Post, First U. S. Army, opened at Clifton College, Bristol, England, on 20 October 1943, and American troops stationed in England were assigned to the Army for training. The program was directed toward the specific task of invading the Continent. The 1st and 9th Infantry Divisions, and the 82d Airborne Division were veterans of the North African Theater. The remainder of the divisions making up the Army's assault force (2d, 4th, 29th, and 90th Infantry Divisions and 101st Airborne Division) had been well-trained by maneuver exercises in the United States. The status of training of flame thrower operators, however, was poor, not only in the new divisions but in the veteran divisions. Divisional and separate combat engineer battalions had received a limited amount of training with flame throwers in connection with the assault of fortified positions. The infantry, however, was unfamiliar with both the technical and tactical employment of the weapon.1/ Critical shortages of training allowances in the U. S. had restricted training to little more than dry runs.

    On 6 October 1943, the Commanding General, ETOUSA, issued Training Memorandum No. 33, Section II of which covered training with portable flame throwers. This directive supplemented War Department Training Circular No. 33, "Attack on Fortified Positions," which had been issued in March 1943. It was prescribed that a minimum of two 3-man teams for each authorized flame thrower be trained in all phases of repair, maintenance, operation and employment of the equipment. British "K" FTF (Flame Thrower Fuel) was prescribed. This fuel had been developed by the British for use in the M1A1 flame thrower, and consisted of ready-mixed thickened fuel made by thickening gasoline with aluminum stearate, with xylenol (or cresol) added as stabilizer. In order to get optimum performance with this fuel it was necessary to reduce the working pressure from 375 p.s.i. to 275-300 p.s.i. The directive also stated that a portable pack carrier which contained everything for one complete refill had been developed in the theater and would soon be ready for issue. The filled pack weighed about 20

1/
  Interv, Hist O with Lt Col W. H. Greene, formerly Cml O, 26th Div and XX Corps, 12 Jul 46.

pounds.2/

At this date flame throwers were authorized on the basis of twenty-four to each combat engineer battalion and twelve to each parachute infantry regiment. However, it was believed that these allowances were insufficient and each assault infantry division was later equipped with 150 for the landing. In addition to division schools for training flame thrower operators, each regimental combat team successively carried out tactical exercises at the Assault Training Center located at Ilfracombe on the northwest coast of Devonshire.3/ On 5 April 1944 ETOUSA issued Training Memorandum No. 10 (See Appendix 20), which rescinded Training Memorandum No. 33. This directive was little more than a repetition of the previous training memorandum (No. 33, 6 October 1943) and the scope of training remained the same. It was noted that fuel K had been redesignated FTF, Heavy No. 1. By this time napalm had become available and directions were given for mixing in the field (5.2 pounds napalm to twenty gallons of dry gasoline). The Third U.S. Army had been established in England in February 1944, but priority for flame throwers had been given the First Army, with the result that these critical items were not available to units of Third Army for training purposes. The status of training in the divisions of the Third Army was, therefore, poor when they later embarked for the Continent.4/

2. **Plans for Employment.** Prior to the Normandy landing, flame throwers had been made items of Class IV issue.5/ Upon receipt of this War Department directive the following basis of issue was suggested:

Type Unit	Allowance, PFT
Airborne Division	15
Assault Division (First Army only)	108

2/ For Sect II of Tng Memo 33, Hq ETOUSA, 6 Oct 43, see Appendix 19.

3/ First U.S. Army, Rpt of Opns 20 Oct 43-1 Aug 44, Book VII, p. 190.

4/ Interv, Hist O with Lt Col W. H. Greene, formerly Cml O 26th Div and XX Corps, 12 Jul 48.

5/ WD Cir No. 204, Sec IV, 23 May 44.

Armored Division	18
Special Armored Division	24
Infantry Division	24
Parachute Regiment	12
Ranger Battalion	6
Engineer Combat Battalion	24 6/

This basis of issue was used primarily by the supply people for the purpose of establishing theater levels and was never adopted by combat forces. As stated above, assault divisions of the First Army were each equipped with 150 flame throwers for the landing operation. After establishing the beachhead, all flame throwers in excess of those required for continued operations were to be turned in to army depots. The number of flame throwers to be carried by reinforcing divisions was to be determined by the respective commanders.7/ It was hoped that this arrangement would prevent excess stocks in the hands of troops and at the same time provide for serviceable equipment that could be made available by army supply points when the need arose. The plan for servicing and maintenance called for all refilling to be accomplished by army chemical depot detachments which were to operate far enough forward for infantry regiments to exchange spent weapons for those that were charged and ready to use. During the early phases of the operation a minimum of fifty flame throwers, serviced and ready for instant use, were to be maintained at all times in each of two army distributing points.8/

6/ Ltr, Hq SOS, ETO, O Cml O to Hq FUSAG, O Cml O, 5 Jun 44, sub: Flame Throwers. In 12th Army Gp Records, 470.71 Apparatus, Hist Records Sect, AGO.

7/ Interv, Hist O with Lt Col W. H. Greene, formerly Cml O 26th Inf Div and XX Corps, 12 Jul 48.

8/ First U.S. Army, Rpt of Opns 20 Oct 43-1 Aug 44, Book VII, p. 200.

B. The Normandy and Northern France Campaigns.9/

1. <u>Landing and Early Operations</u>. At 0130 hours on the morning of 6 June 1944 troops of the 101st Airborne Division started dropping in an area about three miles south of Utah Beach. An hour later the 82d Airborne started landing west of Ste. Mere-Eglise which was located about eight miles southwest of Utah Beach. The sea-borne landing began shortly after daylight with the British Second Army on the left and U.S. First Army on the right. The American force landed on two beaches, separated by the Vire River, and designated as Omaha (left) and Utah (right). Assault forces for each beach totaled about 30,000 men. The initial wave, consisting of the 18th Infantry (1st Division) and 116th Infantry (29th Division), reached Omaha Beach at 0635 hours. Three companies of Rangers accompanied the 18th and one company of Rangers came in with the 116th. At Utah Beach, the 4th Infantry Division spearheaded the assault with men of the 8th Infantry in the lead, reaching shore at 0630. By midnight, the 1st Infantry Division and two regimental combat teams of the 29th Infantry Division were ashore on Omaha Beach (V Corps sector), and the 4th Infantry Division, with the 359th Regiment (90th Division) attached, had been put ashore on Utah Beach (VII Corps sector). The seas were rough and the landings were opposed by automatic weapons, snipers and artillery fire, and resulted in the loss of much equipment. Heavy infantry weapons, such as flame throwers, had to be abandoned. However, the type of opposition encountered did not lend itself to the use of portable flame throwers. At the end of the first day our troops occupied a beachhead 5 miles long and 1½ miles deep at Omaha, and 2½ miles long by 6 miles deep on Utah. By 10 June three divisions (1st, 2d and 29th) were ashore in V Corps sector (Omaha) and five divisions (4th, 9th and 90th Infantry Divisions and the 82d and 101st Airborne) in VII Corps sector. Progress was rapid although casualties were high, a total of 2,824 having been evacuated from Omaha and 3,853 from Utah in the first four days of fighting.10/

Detachments of chemical service troops were ashore by 10 June and were attempting to collect chemical supplies and equipment that had

---

9/
Operations in Europe were divided into six campaigns: (1) Normandy Campaign, 6 Jun-24 Jul 44; (2) Northern France Campaign, 25 Jul-14 Sep 44; (3) Southern France Campaign, 15 Aug-14 Sep 44; (4) Rhineland Campaign, 15 Sep 44-21 Mar 45; (5) Ardennes - Alsace Campaign, 16 Dec 44-25 Jan 45; (6) Central Europe Campaign, 22 Mar-11 May 45. See WDGO No. 24, 4 Mar 47.

10/
First U.S. Army Rpt of Opns, 20 Oct 43-1 Aug 44, Book I, pp. 39-56.

been discarded. During the early stages of the operation over 100 abandoned flame throwers were collected for salvage. Most of these, however, were repaired and returned to depot stock upon arrival of the 14th Chemical Maintenance Company on 30 June.[11]

As U. S. troops spread out over Normandy, reinforcements continued to arrive. By the end of June, fourteen divisions (1st, 2d, 4th, 8th, 9th, 29th, 30th, 79th, 83d, and 90th Infantry; 2d and 3d Armored; and 82d, 101st Airborne) were ashore operating under four corps (V, VII, VIII and XIX). The fields of Normandy were small and surrounded by rows of trees and brush hedges, along the bases of which earth had been heaped to form parapets from three to ten feet thick and from three to four feet high. The enemy defended from these hedgerows in a tenacious manner. This situation made bitter and difficult the advance of small subordinate units and required careful and determined application of minor tactics by units of company size and smaller. Careful use of cover and aggressiveness were necessary in order to move forward from one hedgerow to the next.[12]

During the fighting in Normandy in July, portable flame throwers were employed on several occasions with results that were usually described as "generally successful." The weapon proved helpful in reducing certain pillboxes and strong points that could not be reduced by other weapons. In taking St. Jean De Daye on 7-8 July, the 30th Infantry Division used twenty-four flame throwers with satisfactory results.[13] On 8 July the 23d Infantry (2d Division) encountered a series of dwellings on the outskirts of St. Germain d'Elle that were protected and heavily defended. An assault party made up of two flame thrower teams, each consisting of an operator and an assistant operator, four Browning automatic riflemen and four rifle scouts, worked their way to within fifty

---

[11]
(1) First U. S. Army, Rpt of Opns, 20 Oct 43-1 Aug 44, Book VII, p. 197. (2) Informal comments of CWS O, 21 Jun 44. In CMLWG.

[12]
Ltr Cml O 12th A Gp to Comdt CW Sch, 14 Nov 44, sub: Flame Thrower Rpts. See inclosures for extracts from reports received from units of First U. S. Army, pursuant to questionnaire of Col St. John, of 4 Aug 44. In CMLWG.

[13]
Rpt, 2d Lt Thomas W. Leland to Cml O, First Army, n.d., In Cml C Sch file 319.1/208, Misc Rpts - E4-5R1 FT, 12 A Gp.

yards of the buildings and were successful in directing flame into the windows of the houses. The enemy evacuated the positions immediately and the mission was reported successful.14/ Although detailed reports of individual flame thrower actions occurring during the month of July were not made, the 2d Armored Division reported that the weapon was successfully employed; the 3d Armored Division stated that flame throwers were used occasionally against pillboxes by the engineers who accompanied the infantry; the 4th Infantry Division employed them against fortifications and fortified houses; and the 15th Engineer Battalion (9th Division) reduced several pillboxes with flame. In one instance a critical fortification had held out against the 4th Infantry Division for three days. The engineers brought up a single flame thrower and, when it failed to ignite, the operator ignited the fuel with a match and quickly reduced the position.15/

2. **Brittany.** At noon 1 August 1944, 12th Army Group, under Lt General Omar N. Bradley, became operational and assumed command of the First and Third U. S. Armies. The Third Army became operational at the same time as the Army Group. The VIII, XII, XV and XX Corps were assigned to Third Army while V, VII and XIX Corps remained with First Army. All forces, except VIII Corps, were assigned the task of encircling the German Seventh Army and Panzer Group West. Consequently, the Falaise-Argentan pocket, by 22 August, became the graveyard of enemy forces who, a short time before, had confidently waited to smash the Allied invasion on the Normandy beaches. Because of the nature of this operation flame throwers were not used.

The VIII Corps was assigned the mission of securing the Brittany Peninsula. On 5 September 1944 the forces in Brittany were turned over to the newly created Ninth Army. Although the peninsula was cleared of organized resistance by 8 August, the port areas of St. Malo, Brest, Lavent, St. Nazaire, and Quiberon Bay were fortified and held tenaciously by die-hards who had given Hitler their pledge not to surrender. St. Malo capitulated 17 August while Brest with 30,000 men under General Ramcke did not fall until 18 September, at which time the First and Third Armies had completed their race across France to the German border. It was during this fighting in the peninsula of

---

14/
   1st Ind, on ltr, Cml O VIII Corps to Cml O 2d Inf Div, 25 Sep 44, sub: Rpt of FT Activities. In Ninth Army Cml Sect files, T-17, PFT (Tactical). In Cml C School Lib.

15/
   Ltr, Cml O Twelfth Army Gp to Commandant CW School, 14 Nov 44, sub: Flame Thrower Rpts. See inclosure for rpt from 4th Inf Div. In CMLWG.

Brittany, with an enemy who refused to surrender, that flame throwers were employed to advantage in a few instances.

On 27 August 1944, the 38th Regimental Combat Team (2d Division), operating on Daculas Peninsula, encountered a series of strong enemy positions dominating the terrain in the area of Hill 154. The majority of these strong points consisted of heavily reinforced concrete pillboxes, well-protected by interlocking bands of fire from adjacent positions. Attempts to blast the Germans out of these strong points by artillery fire were of no avail. The only suitable weapon available was the portable flame thrower. Three teams, each consisting of a flame thrower operator, assistant operator, and two automatic riflemen were sent forward under the cover of fire from their own unit. Team No. 1 reached its contact point but the operator was killed by machine-gun fire which also punctured the fuel tanks of the flame thrower, which prevented the assistant operator from taking over. Team No. 2 reached its contact point but when the operator tried to fire, it was found that the hydrogen line had been torn loose enroute to the objective and the team had to be withdrawn. Team No. 3 reached its objective and fired flame through the aperture eliminating this obstacle.16/

During the fighting in Brest on 9 September 1944, the 23d Regimental Combat Team (2d Division) encountered heavy machine-gun fire from one corner of the city square. The obstacle consisted of a heavily reinforced dugout on one corner of the street, with the opening on street level and the top about ten inches above ground. An assault party was made up of two flame thrower operators, two assistant operators, one bazooka team and two automatic riflemen. This party moved around one flank and, by neutralizing a small strong point enroute, was able to come up behind the pillbox. Both flame throwers functioned perfectly and the thirteen enemy occupants, although not killed, gave up immediately.17/ The 2d Infantry Division also used flame to burn down buildings in Brest when the enemy persisted in holding the top floors even after our forces had occupied the lower floors. Setting fire to the buildings with flame throwers solved the problem in several instances.18/

16/
 Ltr Hq 2d Inf Div to Cml O VIII Corps, 25 Sep 44, sub: Use of Flame Throwers During the Brest Campaign. In Ninth Army Cml Sect files, T-17B, PFT (Tactical), Cml C Sch Lib.

17/
 Ibid.

18/
 Ibid.

On another occasion during the fighting around Brest, the 1st Battalion, 121st Infantry (8th Division) was stopped by a fortified locality consisting of three concrete embrasures. Artillery had failed to reduce the positions but had left large craters on the surrounding grounds by which flame thrower crews could advance to within effective range without being overly exposed to fire. Special assault parties were not organized. Instead, two men from Company B were armed with flame throwers and, supported by small-arms fire from about ten men, crawled out from the cover of the hedgerow 200 yards from the nearest embrasure. By crawling from crater to crater, they were able to get within thirty yards of the positions and gave each embrasure a short squirt of flame. The Germans quickly ran out and surrendered. Since none of them were burned it was believed that the sight of the flame rather than the actual heat had converted them from Hitler's die-hard policy. Both infantrymen who operated the weapons were wounded during the approach.

Another case, involving the 8th Infantry Division, occurred during the operations on Pte. de Espagnols Peninsula. The 3d Battalion, 13th Infantry, was carrying two filled flame throwers in each company in order that they might be immediately available should a strong point be encountered that could not be neutralized by any other means. A platoon of Company L was pinned down by fire from a concrete emplacement. A flame thrower operator worked his way through a briar patch to get within effective range and relieved the situation by burning out the position.[19]

While the 29th Infantry Division was fighting near Brest, the 116th Infantry ran into a pillbox and, after working on it for a half-hour with hand grenades and small arms without success, brought up a flame thrower. The weapon had been partially spent. However, the operator crawled to within about twenty yards of the position and placed a burst of flame in one doorway, a second burst in another opening and the third burst back in the first doorway. The pillbox was covered with a camouflage net which caught fire and added to the flame. The five Germans inside immediately began to yell and scream but could not come out because of the fire. It took about ten minutes for the flames to subside sufficiently to allow them to come out and surrender. They were only slightly burned but their nerves were shattered and they shook their heads dismally as they passed the flame thrower sitting outside on the ground.[20]

---

[19]
  Ltr CG 8th Inf Div to CG VIII Corps, 23 Sep 44, sub: Employment of Vehicular and Portable Flame Throwers. In CMLWG.

[20]
  Ltr Cml O 29th Inf Div to Hq Ninth Army, 21 Oct 44, sub: After Action Report on Portable Flame Throwers. In CMLWG.

C. Southern France.

1. **Preparation**. After the Sicilian Campaign which terminated on 18 August 1943, Seventh Army Headquarters became inoperational. The Army was stripped of its combat troops, and at the end of the year Lt. Gen. Patton was relieved of command, taking with him many of his key staff officers. During this time the Army Headquarters was stationed at Palermo, Sicily. In December 1943, the Army Headquarters received directions to start planning for an invasion of southern France. The planning group then moved to Algiers in order to be near Allied Force Headquarters. On 2 March 1944, Major General Alexander M. Patch, a veteran of Guadalcanal, took command of the Seventh Army. On 15 June, Headquarters VI Corps, 3d, 36th and 45th Infantry Divisions, and two French divisions were withdrawn from the fighting in Italy and were assigned to Seventh Army for the invasion of southern France. Seventh Army Headquarters moved to Naples early in July and initiated an intensive training program to prepare the troops for an assault landing. [21]

Seventy-two portable flame throwers (M1A1 model) and accessories were issued to each U. S. division for use by the infantry in assault operations.[22] Plans called for a reserve stock of twenty-four additional flame throwers for each U. S. and French division participating in the operation. This reserve was scheduled to arrive during early phases of the operations.[23] Plans for the invasion called for one flame thrower with each assault boat. Also, there were to be three trained flame thrower teams in each infantry rifle company, each to consist of an operator, assistant operator, and a replacement operator. In addition a number of noncommissioned officers in each regiment were trained in the operation, care and maintenance of the weapon. This flame thrower training program was undoubtedly the most ambitious carried out by any task force in the European or Mediterranean Theaters prior to an operation during the entire war. For example, 271 operators were trained in the 36th Infantry Division alone.[24] To implement

---

[21]
Seventh Army, Rpt of Opns in France and Germany, 1944-1945, Vol. I, pp. 1-22, 71-89.

[22]
Hq Force 163, Annex No. 7 to Admin Instructions #1, p. 3. In CMLWG.

[23]
Hist Rpt, Cml Sect Seventh Army, 1 Jan-31 Oct 44, p. 6. In CMLWG.

[24]
Interv Hist O, with Lt Col Claude J. Merrill, 24 Aug 48.

this training program the 11th Chemical Maintenance Company established a mobile training team which conducted 3-day schools for Seventh Army Units. The chemical sections and engineers of divisions also conducted schools. At the Invasion Training Center, Salerno, Italy, the program included organizing boat teams and infantry demolition squads, wire breaching by boat teams, and the use of flame throwers. 25/

    2. *The Operation*. At 0800 hours 15 August 1944, the infantry started landing along a 40-mile stretch of the coast southwest of Cannes, France, with three infantry divisions abreast, the 3d on the left, 45th in the center and 36th on the right. Although the beaches were heavily mined, resulting in some casualties, enemy resistance was light. By midnight, 2,041 prisoners of war had been taken and our casualties had been almost negligible. Since the enemy offered only scattered resistance the flame throwers were not used to any great extent.26/ Tanks and artillery were brought ashore early and strong points were neutralized quickly without resorting to the use of flame.

    The rapid development of the beachhead and the scattered enemy opposition indicated a rapid moving operation in the offing. Flame throwers were dropped according to plan and picked up by army chemical depot units. During the advance up the Rhone Valley, flame throwers were kept available on a Class IV basis. For example, the 36th Division Chemical Section kept six charged flame throwers available and ready for issue but they were not required.27/ The 11th and 12th Chemical Maintenance Companies supported the Seventh Army during operations in Southern France. These companies carried spare parts for flame throwers and maintained a detachment at army supply points for the storage and issue of flame throwers and fuel. 28/

    On 16 September 1944, 6th Army Group (also called the Southern Group of Armies) became operational and assumed command of the U. S. Seventh Army and the First French Army.

25/
  Seventh Army, Rpt of Opns in France and Germany, 1944-1945, Vol. I, p. 83.

26/
  Ibid., p. 145.

27/
  Interv, Hist O with Lt Col Claude J. Merrill, former Cml O 36th Div, 24 Aug 48.

28/
  Seventh Army, CW Cir No. 1, 24 Jul 44. In CMLWG.

D. Siegfried Line.

After sweeping across France, Belguim and Luxembourg against the remnants of Germany's broken armies in France, First Army troops crossed the German border at several points on 11 and 12 September 1944. These troops easily penetrated the outer defenses of the Siegfired Line south of Aachen. At the same time Third Army had come to a halt along the Moselle River. These armies were ordered to consolidate their positions and improve their supply status while a main effort was to be made across the lower Rhine beyond the main fortifications of the Siegfried Line.29/

During October and November, considerable training and practical exercises were conducted by divisions and combat engineers. These exercises were directed toward breaching the Siegfried Line. In XX Corps sector this training was carried out on captured Maginot Line fortifications.30/ Portable flame throwers were included in this assault training. Divisions obtained additional flame throwers from the army depots during this period, the number drawn varying with the different divisions. For example, the 30th Infantry Division operating under First Army secured ninety-nine flame throwers and 2,700 gallons of British K fuel. It was found that none of the operators trained in England were available and a school was conducted by members of the chemical warfare section and engineer battalion. Each infantry regiment was then issued twenty-five filled flame throwers which were assigned to designated, trained members of assault groups. Each engineer letter company supporting an infantry regiment received eight flame throwers as a reserve, along with one fuel-filling kit, fuel, hydrogen and nitrogen. Supply and servicing was to be a function of the engineers supporting the infantry. After the infantry had used the weapons they were to be collected and turned over to the engineers for refilling and checking. At the end of three weeks fighting in and around the Siegfried Line, only one flame thrower operation was reported by this division. In this instance flame was not used against the pillbox but against the trenches which surrounded it. The trenches were sufficiently filled with flame to dislodge the enemy.31/

29/
  (1) 12th Army Group, G-3 Sect, Final After Action Rpt, Part II, p. 8.
  (2) First Army Rpt of Opns, 1 Aug 44-22 Feb 45, Vol. I, pp. 39-45.

30/
  Interv, Hist O with Lt Col W. H. Greene, formerly Cml O XX Corps.

31/
  Ltr, Cml O 30th Inf Div, 30 Oct 44, sub: Report on Use of Flame Throwers on the Siegfried Line.

Figure 30. American Infantrymen of the 28th Infantry Division Employ Flame Throwers To Mop Up Enemy Resistance in Siegfried Line Defenses Near Elsemboen, Germany, 9 October 1944.

On the afternoon of 22 September, Company K, 39th Infantry (9th Div) encountered a bunker located on the reverse slope of a hill. It had been built primarily for the purpose of housing personnel, hence its location. It was mostly recessed in the steep hillside and was accessible only by steps cut in the incline. The bunker was constructed of concrete with eyebeams forming the inside ceiling. The reinforced concrete was six feet thick with five feet of earth on top. This bunker could not be readily by-passed because it commanded the main road from Lammersdorf to Rollersbroich. There were two doors in front with slots or apertures through which machine guns were fired. Men were able to get on top and around the sides where they fired bazookas and placed pole charges against the doors. After this failed to dislodge the occupants, gasoline was poured under the door and ignited with a thermite grenade. The occupants still fired from the inner compartment doors. Next morning, further attempts to capture the strong point were met by bursts of machine-gun fire. A teller mine and a beehive charge were placed on the ventilator and the pipe was blown off. Twelve teller mines were then placed on the opening where the ventilator had been. This was followed by another charge of twenty-four teller mines. Next, the earth was blown off the top to get at the concrete. Then, six or eight single beehive charges were used in succession. Finally, three beehives were placed in the hollow created by the previous charges. Although a single charge is calculated to blow through $2\frac{1}{2}$ feet of concrete, the total penetration of all of these charges was no more than $2\frac{1}{2}$ feet. Bazookas and flame throwers were used against the apertures and ignited oily waste was stuffed into the vents. Finally a charge of 300 pounds of TNT was tamped into the hole formed by the beehive charges and set off. Following this explosion, thirty men came out with their hands up.

Upon interrogation, the German lieutenant reported that on 22 September some smoke entered through the apertures, but none through the vents or door. Flame throwers had no effect, although the odor of burning phosphorus was detected and the candlelight dimmed and went out several times from lack of oxygen. On 23 September, twenty to thirty explosions were heard and the air again became foul, this time with the odor of gasoline. However, sufficient air entered through the firing apertures to keep the men alive. All other holes were plugged from the inside. They surrendered, not because of the concussion of the final TNT charge but because the lieutenent believed that one of the entrances was blocked and that the other was sufficiently blocked to make their fire ineffective, thereby making it possible to place charges next to the door.[32]

---

[32] Ltr, CO 39th Inf to CG 9th Div, attn: ACofS, G-2, 23 Sep 44, sub: Reduction of Bunker by Co. K, 22-23 September 1944. In First Army Records, Documents of Siegfried Line, ORB.

The 117th Infantry (30th Division) also reported that their portable flame throwers were of no value against two large bunkers encountered in their zone of advance. These bunkers contained heavy machine guns only and were protected by wire, communication trenches, and additional fire trenches located outside the pillbox. 33/

The 15th Engineer Battalion (9th Division) reported that flame throwers were ineffective against large pillboxes. The heat generated was insufficient to drive out the occupants and the duration of the flame was too short to deny the enemy the use of the firing ports while demolition parties were moving up. In only one instance, where flame was played through a port which had been jammed open, was the flame thrower of any value. Before employing the flame thrower, the ventilator and all likely sources of air were closed off with sand bags and the occupants were partially suffocated, causing them to vacate the position. 34/

In the Seventh Army zone of action, the 2d French Armored Division entered Strasbourg on the Rhine 23 November 1944, and on 16 December the 45th, 79th and 103d Infantry Divisions of VI Corps crossed the Franco-German border northeast of Wissembourg. On 17 December, VI Corps launched an attack on the Siegfried Line with the 45th, 79th and 103d Infantry Divisions and 14th Armored Division. The Line consisted of tank traps, intensely defended bunkers, and barbed wire. The pillboxes were usually impermeable to artillery and generally could not be approached closer than 100 yards, but in a few cases they were approached after the artillery and bombers had driven the defenders from the supporting trenches to the bunkers. For example, a platoon leader of Company K, 180th Infantry (45th Division), climbed to the roof of a pillbox, lifted the concrete ventilator cap and dropped in a phosphorus grenade. Fifteen minutes later four Germans came out with their hands up and their gas masks on. 35/ The use of flame throwers was, therefore, indicated, but no attempt was made to use them. Because of the German Ardennes offensive at this time, the attack was called off and

---

33/
Ltr, S-3, 2d Bn, 117th Inf to ACofS, G-2, 30th Inf Div, 14 Oct 44, sub: Documentation of Siegfried Line. In First Army Records, Documents of Siegfried Line, ORB.

34/
Memo, S-3, 15th Engr Bn for ACofS, G-3, 9th Inf Div, 23 Oct 44, sub: Assault Methods Employed by Engineers on Siegfried Line. In First Army Records, Documents of Siegfried Line, ORB.

35/
Seventh Army. Rpt of Opns in 1944-45, Vol. II, p. 493.

Seventh Army troops took up a defensive position and were unable to resume the attacks on the Siegfried Line until nearly three months later.

Prior to reopening the assault on the Siegfried Line on 15 March, all divisions of the Seventh Army conducted extensive training programs on flame thrower operation and maintenance. The new M2-2 flame thrower was becoming available at this time and it was hoped that it would prove more useful.36/ In January, training in the operation, use, and maintenance of portable flame throwers was made a responsibility of organization chemical officers. To assist in carrying out this directive, the army chemical officer made available a team of qualified personnel from the 11th Chemical Maintenance Company to assist division chemical officers in conducting schools.37/ During February, this team conducted four schools in which twenty officers and 150 enlisted men were trained.38/ On 22 February 1945, flame throwers were being carried by each division of the Seventh Army as follows:

Unit	On Hand
36th Infantry Division	6
42d Infantry Division	0
44th Infantry Division	4
45th Infantry Division	6
63d Infantry Division	6
70th Infantry Division	34
100th Infantry Division	12
103d Infantry Division	0
14th Armored Division	12
2d French Armored Division	24 39/

Although considerable preparation had been made and ETOUSA had issued a supplementary training memorandum (see Appendix 21), the

---

36/ Hist Rpt, Cml Sect Seventh Army, 1-31 Mar 45, p. 4. In CMLWG.

37/ Seventh Army, Cml O's Circular ltr No. 6, 30 Jan 45. In CMLWG.

38/ Hist Rpt, Cml Sect Seventh Army, 1-28 Feb 45, p. 11. In CMLWG.

39/ IOM, Cml O to G-4, Seventh Army, 22 Feb 45, sub: M2-2 Portable Flame Throwers. In CMLWG.

portable flame thrower was not found useful in assaulting the Siegfried Line. The only recorded instance of employment by Seventh Army troops at this time occurred against a Maginot Line blockhouse, near Fidenberg Farm in the Bitche sector. The weapon was used by a raiding party from Company K, 399th Infantry (100th Division) at 0415 hours, 12 February 1945, and the flame killed the lone sentry while the patrol sustained no casualties. 40/

E. Comments and Critique.

The portable flame thrower was not used extensively in Europe. The primary reason for this lack of employment was that other weapons which could do the job more efficiently were available. There were a number of instances, however, where positions could not be reduced by the conventional weapons and resort was made to the flame thrower. In such cases the approaches were often covered by interlocking fire for considerable distances. Attempts to employ flame throwers, therefore, frequently resulted in a high rate of casualties among operators. In fact, this vulnerability was a standard complaint with infantry commanders. Yet, few of them used smoke to screen the approach of the operator. Many of the criticisms brought forth by tacticians do not stand up against a critical analysis. For example, in February 1945 the G-3, 76th Infantry Division, made the following comments relative to the use of flame throwers in assaulting pillboxes:

> Although 52 flame throwers were available, not one of them was used in the reduction of pillboxes. Flame throwers in their present state of development are believed ineffective against pillboxes for the reasons hereinbelow:
>
> 1. Ease with which embrasures can be neutralized by small arms fire,
> 2. Difficulties involved in long carry,
> 3. Short life of fuel load,
> 4. Difficulties of resupply and recharging, and
> 5. Size of silhouette, making carrier a conspicuous target. 41/

Obviously, if positions can be neutralized by small-arms fire, a flame thrower is not indicated. Comments 2, 3 and 5, above, establish a requirement for a mechanized flame thrower. No. 4 is a problem that was solved in areas where flame throwers were used frequently.

40/ Hist Rpt, Cml Sect Seventh Army, 1-28 Feb 45, p. 3. In CMLWG.

41/ 76th Inf Div, A A Rpt, 31 Mar 45, p. 18.

In another report, the startling statement was made that "the portable flame thrower has been used only after all other means have failed."42/ This statement would have been true throughout the war and in all theaters. It must be noted that the complaint against the high and distinctive silhouette of the portable flame thrower was more frequent in the ETO than in any other theater. The complaint was justified, if for no other reason than that such a silhouette is unnecessary. The Russians long before had corrected the silhouette of their portable flame thrower to make it look like an ordinary infantry pack.

In the Seventh Army, considerable technical training with portable flame throwers was conducted prior to assaulting the Siegfried Line. However, reports do not indicate extensive tactical training with this weapon. Such training cannot stop with the technical aspects. It is imperative that both men and commanders know how to exploit the weapons at their disposal.

The following account prepared by the VII Corps Engineer describes successful tactics employed by First Army units to fully utilize the troops and weapons at their disposal: 43/

> Information gathered from the Divisions participating in breaching the Siegfried Line reveals that, although four different circumstances existed on the Corps front, the general methods of breaching the line were the same, whether carried out by infantry or armored divisions, in wooded or open country, on roads or cross-country.
>
> The initial attack to establish a bridgehead was made by infantry, supported by an artillery preparation to drive the defenders inside the pillboxes, to damage the crews and weapons of antitank positions, and to neutralize the fire of the bunkers. At the same time suspected OPs were smoked by the artillery and close in targets smoked by 81mm and 4.2" mortars.

42/
  Ltr, CG 8th Inf Div to CG VIII Corps, 23 Sep 44, sub: Employment of Vehicular and Portable Flame Throwers. In CMLWG.

43/
  Ltr, CG FUSA to CG's V, VII and XIX Corps, 4 Oct 44, sub: Discussion of the Siegfried Line; and 1st Ind from CG, VII Corps to CG, FUSA. In CMLWG.

Under cover of the smoke and artillery and mortar fire, the infantry assault group (usually a platoon) and tanks moved forward, preferably at a point where a road passed through the defense line. Immediate advantage could then be taken to exploit the penetration by sending tanks through to fan out and take the line from the rear.

Covered by this action, engineers and infantry demolished barriers and removed obstacles, while the assault groups took up the attack of the pillboxes, supported by direct fire of tanks and tank destroyers against the embrasures. When a passage had been cleared through the barrier, tanks were sent through, deploying and attacking the defenses from the rear.

Direct fire from high velocity, flat trajectory guns was found to be most effective against concrete and masonry bunkers. Fire from light and medium artillery did not damage the closed emplacements to any extent, but did destroy weapons and personnel in open emplacements and drove personnel inside the pillboxes, where their effective fire was limited by the direct fire against embrasures.

In cases where direct fire did not bring the occupants to surrender a small force was left to contain the obstacle, while engineers employed flamethrowers, beehive charges, and demolition charges against the ventilator and doors. In several cases, tankdozers or bulldozers were utilized to cover all exits with dirt, sealing the occupants inside the pillboxes for later treatment.

CHAPTER IX

EMPLOYMENT OF THE PORTABLE FLAME THROWER BY THE ENEMY

A. Japanese.

The Japanese first employed the portable flame thrower against American troops on Bataan on or about 10 February 1942 and killed several American soldiers with the weapon. [1] The characteristics of the enemy's weapon became known when a complete unit was captured on Bataan in 1942. It possessed a positive cartridge ignition system, the principle of which was superior to the troublesome electric ignition system used on the M1A1 flame thrower. Fortunately, however, the ignition cartridges contained a paper case which was subject to deterioration by moisture and several instances were reported throughout the war of its use on our troops where the fuel failed to ignite because of a misfire. During the New Georgia operation one of our tanks was thoroughly covered with fuel from a Japanese flame thrower but the fuel failed to ignite.

The Japanese recognized the weapon as being designed primarily for assault operations against pillboxes and similar fortifications but, fighting almost entirely on the defensive, they lacked opportunities for extensive offensive employment. During an amphibious counter-attack made by the Japanese against our troops at Finschafen, New Guinea, the first Jap soldier to leave the assault boat was a flame thrower operator who charged forward toward a machine gun emplacement defending the beach. He was killed instantly by a soldier from the 2d Engineer Special Brigade who was located in the machine gun emplacement.

---

[1]
(1) Memo, Cml O Philippine Dept to Asst CofS, G-2 and CofS, USAFFE, 16 Feb 42, sub: Reported Use of Flame Throwers by Japanese Forces on Bataan. In CMLWG. (2) "CWS Studies Flame Deaths," CW Bull, Vol. 30, No. 2, Apr - May 44, p. 32. (3) Col S. A. Hamilton, "Activities of CWS, Philippine Islands, World War II, Sec B, pp. 21, 22.

The Japs also stressed the use of the flame thrower as an anti-tank weapon in defensive warfare. An example of this tank-against-flame thrower conflict, which usually resulted in defeat for Japanese troops, was reported in the Leyte Operation. In this instance, elements of U.S. forces were held up by a Japanese road block during an advance along a Leyte road. The approach to the road block was protected by groups of fox holes and machine gun emplacements dug into the bank along the side of the road. A tank was sent along the road to reduce the Japanese positions. As the tank approached the road block, a single Japanese stepped out on the road with a flame thrower. A Japanese officer, waving his sword and urging the attack forward, followed the flame thrower operator. It was evident that the operator had not been properly trained in the use of his weapon, because no attempt was made to approach the tank quietly and unobserved by using the ditch alongside the road. Both the operator and the officer were killed before the flame thrower was fired. 2/

About 0400 on 12 April 1945 five Japanese soldiers attempted to eliminate a light machine gun set up by Company C, 128th Infantry (32d Division) during the fighting along the Villa Verde Trail on Luzon. The men at the machine gun did not know that an attack with a flame thrower was being made. The first indication of an attack on the position was an explosion about fifteen yards to the front, which was subsequently determined to be from a pole charge. Our troops fired at the attackers and when daylight came five dead Japs and a flame thrower were found. Fuel had been discharged in the area in front of the position but had not ignited. The remains of three pole charges were found where they had been thrown forward, missing the area over which the fuel had been spread. It could not be determined whether or not the flame thrower misfired as it may have been planned to ignite the fuel with the pole charges. Shortly afterwards, a large cave was located some thirty yards from the gun position. Seven Japanese were killed inside the cave and it was decided that the attack had originated from this position, employing two men with the flame thrower and three with the pole charges. 3/

2/
MID, Tactical and Technical Trends, No. 58, May 45, p. 37

3/
(1) Ltr, CWS Sec Tech Intell Field Unit No. 8 to Cml O, I Corps, 14 Apr 45, sub: Report on Jap Use of the Flame Thrower. (2) Cml O I Corps, Cml Intell Period Rpt No. 1 to CG Sixth Army, 16 Apr 45. In CMLWG.

Figure 31. A Japanese Flame Thrower in Action.

Figure 32. Jap Use of Portable Flame Throwers, a Rehearsed Action, After the Fall of Corregidor, for Use as Propaganda.

The following is a report submitted by the 382d Infantry (96th Division) of an instance in which the Japanese used a flame thrower on Okinawa:

> At 100645 the 3d Battalion jumped off to secure the small hills on the left boundary overlooking the approaches to Tombstone Ridge. At 0700 the 1st and 2d Battalions began the attack. Initially Company "A" met no strong opposition and moved forward to the base of the ridge. Here it was stopped by extremely heavy fire coming from the face of the cliff, which almost completely surrounds the ridge. Great volumes of artillery and mortar fire, including several rounds of 320mm spigot mortar fire halted the advance of Company "A".
>
> It was evident that an attack from the north end of the ridge was not feasible, so Companies "B" and "C" were ordered to make an envelopment around the right. These companies moved to the west in the draw which runs north of Kaniku and into the village without meeting resistance. In the village a concentration of artillery fire was received but light small arms fire. By 1200 the attack was still progressing satisfactorily and troops were about half way up the ridge. At 1350 elements of both companies were approaching the top of Tombstone Ridge. At 1430, following a 15 minute concentration of artillery and mortar fire of all calibers, the Japs staged a strong counter-attack. Just as the shelling lifted, the advance elements of "B" Company were cut off from the rest of the company by continuous fire from six machine guns emplaced in pillboxes on both flanks. The enemy then counter-attacked this isolated section with bayonets, grenades, <u>flame throwers</u>, and machine guns. The left flank was overrun and one LMG section of Company "B" wiped out. Companies "B" and "C" fought desperately to gain a substantial foothold on the ridge but the suicidal defense of the Japs prohibited the capture of the objective. 4/

4/ 382d Inf (96th Div), Opns Rpt, Okinawa, 1 Apr - 30 Jun 45.

Hundreds of Japanese portable flame throwers were captured during the war. For example, I Corps captured over sixty during its operations on Luzon to 21 April.5/ A prisoner from the 10th Division Engineer Regiment (Luzon) stated that each of the three companies of the regiment was normally equipped with one Type 93 flame thrower.6/

Two models of flame guns were found. Type 93 and Type 100. Type 100 being the later model was essentially the same as the older model. It was shorter, lighter and contained some refinements in the ignition head. The major difference in the principles of the Japanese flame thrower and the U. S. model M2-2 is in the pressure system. The Japanese avoid the high pressure system by employing a larger pressure tank of 350 pounds per square inch operating pressure, thereby eliminating the need of a pressure regulator valve. Tests have demonstrated that in the Japanese flame thrower a maximum range of 30 yards is obtained only on the initial burst because of the rapidly diminishing pressure in the pressure tank.7/ The high pressure system employed in all U.S. flame throwers provides a maximum range for the entire fuel load.

B. German.

1. The Fougasse Type. This defensive or static type flame weapon was reported as first employed by the Germans in Italy. The model encountered there was copied from an apparatus originally devised by the Russians.8/ United States forces encountered these flame throwers for the first time when the Fifth Army was in the Castelforte Area, Italy.9/ Also reported from Italy was an example of actual employment of fougasse emplacements, by the Germans, in the defense at Colle Cerasols. Four were found in one location, concealed in piles of rocks behind mines and wire. Two of them had been fired. One fatality resulted and one man

---

5/ Cml O I Corps, Cml Intell Period Rpt No. 2, 24 Apr 45. In Sixth Army Cml Sec Records, 319.1 Cml Intell Period Rpts, ORB.

6/ Cml O I Corps, Cml Intell Period Rpt No. 5, 15 May 45. In Sixth Army Cml Sec Records, 319.1 Cml Intell Period Rpts, ORB.

7/ MID, Tactical and Technical Trends, No. 18, 11 Feb 43, pp. 8-10.

8/ MA Rpt, Germany, 62794, 16 Nov 43. In AGF G-2-DD.

9/ Legend on official photograph dated 15 May 1944. The information is credited to CW Sect, Fifth Army. A description and evaluation of the German Fougasse is in Military Reports from the United Nations No. 20, 15 July 1944. In AG Hist Records Sect.

was seriously burned. In the same area as many as seven were found in one defensive position.10/ On the Rimini Front, heavy flame throwers had been used in fixed installations. The chief disadvantage of this type was that a large amount of fuel was consumed and it was relatively difficult to refuel the units.11/ In comparison with the known range of all other type flame throwers, the reported range of 300 meters by these units appears doubtful. These and other intelligence reports indicated that the fougasse had to be considered in Allied planning for operations against defenses on the Continent. The available information suggested that these flame throwers were being installed in the defense of German concrete pillboxes; and the range of the weapon was unknown.12/

Subsequently it was learned that the fougasse had been incorporated in German defenses on the Continent. Installations had been made at many of the beaches in France. At Cherbourg, for example, at least thirty were installed along ten miles of the coast west of the city.13/ At Marseille, about fifty were installed on both sides of the Prado.14/ On the shoreline at Dinard there was an arrangement whereby, from a central switchboard, the emplaced flame throwers could be fired so that the flame would contact naval shells and detonate them.15/ Another arrangement was found whereby flame throwers emplaced on the seabed could be fired electrically, and the flame emitted over the water from jets. Fuel floats for the same purpose were devised.16/

10/
Tech Intell Rpt No. 797, North Africa and Central Mediterranean, 3 Jun 44. In AGF G-2-DD.

11/
CWS, Intell Div Rpt, ETO, No. 3237, 28 Nov 44.

12/
U.S. Assault Training Center, ETO, Conference on Landing Assaults, 24 May - 23 June, Vol. I, p. 13. In AGF, G-2, DD.

13/
Reported from an interrogation of a PW who had helped to install them. CW, Digest of Intelligence Reports No. 10, 11 Jul 44.

14/
MA Rpt, S/384/43, Madrid, 14 Dec 43. In AGF G-2-DD.

15/
ASF Report No. 35, 3 Oct 44. SPEIN 2AA9-7.

16/
MA Rpt, Great Britain, No. 61021, 17 Sep 43. In AGF G-2-DD.

At Dieppe the Germans had emplaced flame throwers east of the harbor, overlooking the beach. Only a few of them functioned when the Germans attempted to fire as they were leaving the area.17/ A few had been fired at Le Havre.18/ These were not merely sporadic attempts to use the fougasse in German defense tactics. They developed standard models for which numerous uses were planned. In the last phase of the war tactical experiments were still being conducted.19/ One plan was to install flame throwers in the defense of airfields after attack from low-flying American fighter planes had reduced other types of defense. Between April 1944 and 12 January 1945, flame thrower defenses were completed on airfields at Goppingen and Crailsheim. Finally, a German memorandum was found, dated 27 March 1945, which proposed a plan to mount five static flame throwers on a locomotive; these were to be fired simultaneously when the locomotive was attacked by American aircraft.20/

2. **The German Portable Flame Thrower.** The German Army was equipped with several types and models of portable flame throwers, all of which had American or British counterparts. Reliable reports on German tactical employment of the portable flame thrower were not available to American and British Armies up to the middle of 1941. The reports which did come to hand were based on tactics used on both the Polish and Russian fronts and justified the expectation that the Germans would use flame extensively in the war in the west. One of the first reliable reports was a detailed analysis of German tactics, using flame, before Fort IX, at Warsaw, in the Polish campaign.21/ In the German advance from the west of Stalingrad, flame throwers played an important part in street-fighting where every house had to

---

17/
  21st Army Gp, CWS Intell Rpt No. 3092, 6 Oct 44. In Intell Br, OC CmlC.

18/
  1st Canadian Army, CW Weekly Rpt No. 5, 22 Sep 44, "Extracts." In Cml C Tech Div.

19/
  1st Army, Engineer Intell Memo No. 4, 29 Jan 45.

20/
  CWS Intelligence Division Report, ETO, No. 3747, 8 May 45. In Intell Br, OC Cml C, 390.05/3215 MA.

21/
  General Staff, War Office, London, Summary of Intelligence Regarding Weapons, War Industry, and Transportation, No. 35, 9 Mar 41, pp. 6-7. In Intell Br, OC Cml C, SPEIN 64-B-1917.

be taken separately.22/

Although Intelligence reported a very limited German employment of portable flame throwers in North Africa, the Germans used flame in Italy to a greater extent than either the Americans or the British, employing them principally against Allied troops on the beachheads.23/ A report on the employment of portables in the west sector of the Anzio beachhead, 1 April 1944, evaluated their effectiveness in terms of a slight psychological and morale advantage when used against Allied troops who had not encountered them before. It was said that they created "a certain amount of dismay mixed with astonishment and curiosity."24/ According to the accounts of war correspondents, the German not infrequently used the portable in Italy as a weapon of opportunity, for example, in dispatching Allied parachutists caught in trees.25/

From German documents captured in Tunisia it was learned that the tactical doctrine formulated by the Germans was similar to that evolved by the Allies.26/ The earliest German portable, the model 35, had serious tactical limitations because three men were required to man the apparatus.27/ A large stock of later German models was found in Paris. It consisted of 4,000 complete flame throwers, 4,000 fuel tanks, and 15,000 ignition cartridges.28/ The discovery of these

---

22/ Intelligence Report, from Naval Attache, Madrid, 14 Dec 43. In Intell Br, OC Cml C, 350.05/2411 MA.

23/ Memo Dr. George Broughton, OSRD Liaison Office, London, Eng., to OC CWS, 13 Oct 44, sub: Weekly News Letter No. 19A (hereinafter, Broughton's Weekly News Letter.) In files of Tech Div, Cml C.

24/ SHAEF, Report on Use of Flame Throwers, 5 Apr 44. AGF G-2 - DD.

25/ See newspaper clippings on the subject of flame throwers, in the Information Br, OC Cml C.

26/ MA Rpt, Cairo, No. 4479, 18 Jun 1943.

27/ MA Rpt, Cairo, No. 5643, 20 Sep 43.

28/ Rad, CM-IN-1029, 1 Oct 44.

weapons may well have spurred Allied counter-developmental work on flame throwers, especially when the statement was made that "widespread use of (German) flame throwers," was to be anticipated "in the very near future."29/ Moreover, it was not then known what to expect in the military capacity of the German models. Tests by the 1st Canadian Army revealed that the German model 42, captured at Caen, had a maximum range of thirty-two yards, using either German or British fuels.30/ An unusual comment on the German portable flame thrower was made by the commanding officer of an American infantry battalion, to the effect that whenever he needed a flame thrower he tried to find a German model because it was lighter and had more range.31/ The range of the flame gun was estimated as between fifty and sixty yards. The tanks were employed, tactically, to flame out enemy personnel otherwise inaccessible, especially among rocks, and in trenches and dug-in positions.32/ Another use was in spearheading counterattacks.33/

C. Italian.

Although pioneers in the endeavor to make flame an important weapon of modern warfare, Italian equipment was reported as replete with "gadgets" which made its use doubtful. In MTO samples of their equipment were found and tested early in the conflict;34/ and it was known that in both North Africa and Sicily that the Italian Army organization made provision for flame thrower companies. According to one document, of late 1942, the company strength was 150 men, equipped

---

29/ Office of Strategic Services, Rpt No. J-2632 PT, 18 Oct 44. In Intell Br, OC Cml C.

30/ Broughton's Weekly News Letter No. 17, 29 Sep 44. In Tech Div, Cml C.

31/ Immediate Report, ETO, No. 4, 29 Nov 44. In Hist Records Sect, AGO.

32/ MID, Tactical and Technical Trends, No. 19, Feb 43, p. 9.

33/ Associated Press Cable from Allied Hqs, Algiers, 29 Nov 43. SPCWN G-0/W-5. Employed so against the Eighth British Army near Langro, Italy.

34/ MEF, Technical Intelligence Summary, No. 12, 27 Dec 40, p. 3. Ibid., No. 12, 4 Feb 41.

with at least forty-five portable flame throwers.35/ It appears that their T/O and E's were never filled, and that the Italian Army never employed a flame thrower in action.

35/ MA Rpt, Egypt, No. 947-43, 16 Jan 43, and MA Rpt, Italy, No. 160, 5 Aug 43.

CHAPTER X

SUMMARY AND EVALUATION

A. Tactical Doctrine

Consideration was given to the tactical place of the portable flame thrower well before United States participation in World War II. Enemy successes with flame had prompted intelligence reports that the weapon could be used against mechanized vehicles and permanent and semi-permanent fortifications; and the conclusion was that the weapon would be desirable as an item of equipment for engineer combat troops.1/ Later, the agencies concerned in the development of the flame thrower decided that a requirement did exist with Engineers for the portable flame thrower, that the Marines had the same requirement, and that although the weapon was needed for infantry operations the Corps of Engineers would be the primary using arm.2/ Accordingly, in December 1942, the portable flame thrower was included in Tables of Basic Allowances for Engineers as follows:

```
Headquarters, Service Company, Combat Regiment........ 24
Parachute Company, Airborne Battalion................. 27
Headquarters Company, Armored Battalion............... 24
Headquarters, Service Company, Combat Battalion....... 24
Headquarters, Service Company, Mountain Battalion..... 24
Headquarters, Service Company, Motorized Battalion.... 24
Headquarters, Service Troops, Squadron................ 24  3/
```

As a result, the Corps of Engineers was charged with the tactical use of flame throwers, and it was recommended that the weapon be used only by properly trained engineer troops.4/

At the beginning of the offensive against the enemy in the Pacific and North Africa flame throwers were carried by the engineers but no firm

---

1/ Ltr, C Engr to TAG, 24 Jul 40, sub: Flame Thrower for Individual Use. CWS 470.71/52.

2/ AD Hoc Committee on Flame Throwers, 8 Jun 1942 (2d meeting). In GNRGT.

3/ T/BA 5, "Engineers," 1 Dec 42. The requirement set up was for the M1 model. Change No. 2 to this T/BA, dated 1 Jun 43, provided the M1A1 as the model to be supplied to Engineers.

4/ IOM, C Fld Req Br to C War Plans and Theaters Div, OC CWS, 8 Apr 43.

doctrine had been established. Neither the British nor the Americans had worked out the full tactical use of flame and uncertainty continued as to how and when the portable should be used. The British belief was that flame throwers would almost always be used under cover of smoke.5/ Published doctrine defined the type targets against which flame could be used but without explicit directions for tactical employment by the using troops. In the CWS Manual, Tactics of Chemical Warfare,6/ permanent field fortifications were specified as prime targets. The precaution was added that operations with flame against fortifications should be well rehearsed against a dummy fortification in terrain similar to that of the target. Another use was as an incendiary against woods, wooden buildings, ripe grain fields, etc. In the Engineer Field Manual,7/ the assault of a permanent fortification was defined as an infantry mission, but it was indicated that, after suitable training, engineers should participate. This doctrine was developed around the statement that the portable flame thrower should be used to protect men placing the demolition charges against a fortification after direct fire had covered the approach to an embrasure. For such an operation an assault detachment of sixteen men, including two flame thrower operators, was advised. Mention was made that the flame thrower could be used as a casualty-producing weapon.

When the manual for the M1 and M1A1 flame throwers 8/ was published it included an appendix on "Technical employment," which stressed the fact that the flame thrower was primarily an offensive weapon and was not a weapon of opportunity. The primary use of the weapon was to be in the assault upon fortifications. This manual also included two directives, not otherwise published, for tactical employment. Refilling of the flame thrower while in combat should not be attempted. Instead, filled flame throwers should be on hand and empty weapons could be discarded if necessary. It was also pointed out that the use of portable flame throwers in large numbers would be very demoralizing to the enemy. FM 31-50 9/ repeated the directions for the effective use of the weapon. Close-in protection for the flame thrower operator was to be provided while breaching charges were placed against a fortification and during mopping-up

---

5/ "Notes in Col Gerhard's Discussion with Personnel of the Petroleum Warfare Department," 26 Mar 43. In CMLWG.

6/ FM 3-5, 20 Jul 42, Sec VI, "Engineer Troops," pp. 76-78.

7/ Operations of Engineer Field Units, 23 Apr 43, pp. 80-82.

8/ TM 3-375, Portable Flame Throwers, M1 and M1A1, May 43, which superceded TC 17, 1943.

9/ Attack on a Fortified Position and Combat in Towns, 31 Jan 44.

operations after a bunker had been breached. A 12-man assault squad, and similarly an assault platoon, were described with emphasis on flexibility of organization, depending on the tactical situation. This manual, FM-31-50, was also the basic reference for tactical doctrine for employment of the M2-2. It was also stated that the portable could be used to eliminate enemy strong-points in street or jungle fighting.[10]
In the manual on "Operations,"[11] only casual mention was made of the possible use of flame throwers in a special operation for the attack of a fortified locality.

After the Papuan Campaign and the battle of Guadalcanal, a great deal of thought was given to the development of tactics and technique of overcoming the type of defenses employed by the Japanese. One of the weapons that appeared to have possibilities was the flame thrower. By the middle of 1943, it was the concensus that the primary mission of combat engineers in jungle operations was that of construction and that flame throwers should be issued to infantry units. A study of the early plans for the employment of portable flame throwers by infantry units reveals that operators were trained not only in the functioning of the weapon but also in maintenance and servicing. It was intended that flame throwers and accessories would be held in nearby regimental or battalion supply to be issued to operators as a secondary weapon when the situation favored its employment. This system failed during operations in New Britain, the Admiralty Islands, and in the early phases of the New Guinea Campaign. In these cases, operators had been thoroughly trained several months prior to the operations and the flame thrower equipment carefully stored away in supply rooms. When the occasion arose for their use in combat, operators very often found the equipment in an unsatisfactory condition and also had forgotten how to service and maintain the equipment. This situation was not particularly applicable to combat engineers who were able to furnish qualified flame thrower teams to the infantry when called upon to do so during operations in the Gilbert, Marshall, Admiralty and Wakde Islands.

As a result of the above experience, units in the Pacific turned toward assault organizations such as the "flame thrower platoons" in the South Pacific and "assault parties" in the Southwest Pacific and Central Pacific. These organizations performed well in combat because they had been trained to fight as a team and each individual knew what the other was to do, in the same manner as a football team. It was found, however, that in sustained combat when casualties began to mount, a regiment or battalion could not afford to hold such an organization in reserve for

---

[10] In TM 3-376A, Portable Flame Thrower M2-2, 16 May 44, p. 87.

[11] FM 100-5, 15 Jun 44, p. 219.

special assault use against fortifications, and it was soon broken up with the result that assault groups were formed "on the spot" when the situation demanded the employment of flame throwers or other special infantry assault weapons. This procedure, therefore, often resulted in improper employment of the flame thrower, insufficient infantry support and use of improperly trained flame thrower operators.

War Department Circular No. 2, dated 25 January 1945, became available early in 1945 and a study of past operations revealed that the policies prescribed therein were sound, provided that sufficient flame throwers and accessory equipment were available to make each infantry battalion and cavalry squadron (dismounted) self-sufficient in servicing, maintenance and operation. Also, to establish this tactical doctrine, it had been found necessary to furnish each infantry division sufficient CWS technical personnel to provide adequate technical assistance. This doctrine was accepted by Sixth Army for the Kyushu operation and, although it was never tried out in combat, it was believed to be sound because those units which had been fortunate enough to acquire sufficient flame thrower equipment, especially in the Central Pacific Area, had evolved into this doctrine during the latter stages of the war.

A satisfactory tactical doctrine, such as that which evolved in the Pacific, was not developed in the European theaters. In general, the tactical doctrine furnished to troops in these theaters was copied from that developed in the Pacific[12]/ and it did not find extensive application. There were, however, attempts to introduce new concepts applicable to the situation. For example, prior to the invasion of Sicily a tentative plan was proposed for the use of flame throwers in the attack of a fortified beach, which would include two flame throwers in the assault platoon of an assault company. It was believed that such employment would be feasible because of the increased range possible with thickened fuel in the M1A1.[13]/ Special assault parties were to be built around the approach of the portable flame throwers, before demolition charges were placed, in the reduction of obstacles and fortifications.[14]/ After the Sicilian campaign, however, it was "observed that the flame thrower did not have sufficient tactical value to warrant its retention as standard

---

[12]/ See ETOUSA TM's, Appendices Nos. 19, 20 and 21.

[13]/ U.S. Assault Training Center, ETO, "Conference on Landing Assaults, 24 May - 23 Jun 1943," Vol II, p. 16 and pp. 32-34. In AGF G-2, DD.

[14]/ Ibid., Vol I, p. 12.

equipment for engineer troops.15/ Logistical problems which surrounded the employment of the M1 and M1A1 in the field dictated that conclusion. In a conference, following the Sicilian campaign, the question was posed as to whether or not the portables should be carried forward with the using troops. It was stated that the weapon had very little tactical value, and if carried at all it should be held well back for use on special occasions only; and not employed except after considerable tactical planning in advance of an operation. Actual combat use of the weapon was to be entirely a matter of discretion of the commanding officer.16/ These conclusions were based, in part, on the fact that during the Sicilian Campaign flame throwers had been carried, among other CWS items, with no tactical plan for their use. It was recommended that a prior determination be made of the weapons to be tactically employed in an operation and that division and corps chemical officers should be fully advised of these plans at the earliest opportunity.17/

  A proving ground for development of all phases of doctrine affecting assault operations was established for ETO - the U.S. Assault Training Center, ETOUSA, at Ilfracombe, England.18/ Possible employment of portable flame throwers in beach operations was further considered. In the midst of the Italian Campaign it was stated that both British and American assault training authorities had decided that the man-pack flame throwers were too heavy for beach operations.19/ Up to and including the allied invasion of the continent, the tactical use and advantage of the flame thrower had not been appreciated or exploited.20/

  In May 1943, the War Department, on the basis of lessons learned in the theaters, decided to delete portable flame throwers and kits therefor, from all Tables of Basic Allowances for the Corps of Engineers. The weapon and accessories were made items of Class IV supply.21/ Theater

---

15/ Lt Gen George S. Patton, "Notes on the Sicilian Campaign," 10 Jul - 11 Aug 1943. In Hist Records Sec AGO.

16/ 7th Army, "Conclusions and Recommendations from Conference Notes," Conference of Army, Corps and Division Chemical Officers and Commanding Officers of All CWS Units in the Seventh Army, 28 and 29 Aug 43. In CMLWG.

17/ Cml O Seventh Army, "CW Operations, Sicilian Campaign," 24 Sep 43. In CMLWG.

18/ "Observers Board Rpt No. 4, ETOUSA," 1 Mar 1944. In AGF G-2, DD.

19/ Rad, CM-IN-8848, 14 Nov 43.

20/ Ltr, OC CWS to CG ASF, 13 Jun 44, sub: Replacement Factors. In CMLWG.

21/ WD Circular 204, 23 May 44.

commanders were therefore enabled to determine the basis of issue within the theater, to promulgate tactical doctrine for the theater, and to arrange for training of using troops in the operation, use and maintenance of the portable flame thrower. In Europe the basic doctrine, applicable to the use of the M1A1, for that theater was published by Headquarters, ETOUSA, on 6 October 1943.[22]/ Therein it set forth that the most important use of the weapon was in the neutralization of pillboxes and other fortifications. The technique described called for the employment of a three-man flame thrower team in the assault of a fortification. The team was composed of an operator, an assistant, and a refill carrier.[23]/ Small arms covering fire and/or smoke was to give protection to the flame thrower team. More complete directions for all phases of portable flame thrower activity were issued later in a training memorandum, dated 5 April 1944, which appears to have remained as the basis for all such activity in the theater.[24]/ More detailed instructions were provided for demolition parties in cases where flame throwers were to be utilized. However, contrary to other published doctrine it was suggested that the weapon might have a use in the defense; and the references given for additional material regarding the flame thrower and its operations contained nothing applicable to tactical experience in that theater.

The tactical doctrine published by the War Department in January 1945[25]/ was based on experience in the Pacific and stressed the approach of the flame thrower for the purpose of firing directly into an opening in an emplacement. This was in contrast with the doctrine that the flame thrower should fire from the flank across an embrasure or opening in order to blind and demoralize the occupants while demolitions were placed, thus providing more protection to both flame throwers and demolition men. This doctrine was subject to criticism by proponents of the psychological value of flame. Although prisoners were the normal results of most flame actions in Europe, few, if any, prisoners were taken in the Pacific and a

---

[22]/ ETOUSA Training Memorandum No. 33, 6 Oct 43. In CMLWG.

[23]/ The adoption of British type Fuel K, pourable and ready-mixed, improved the tactical conception of an advantageous employment of the weapon.

[24]/ ETOUSA, Training Memorandum No. 10, 5 Apr 44. In CMLWG.

[25]/ WD TC No. 2, 19 Jan 45, II, "Employment of Portable Flame Throwers."

position was not neutralized until its occupants were annihilated.[26]/ It appears, therefore, that whether the casualty producing effect of flame or its demoralizing and psychological value is more important depended upon the stamina and determination of the enemy against which it was being employed and upon the degree of his reaction to the threat of fire.

B. Training Problems in the Theaters

Both technical and tactical training for the employment of the portable flame thrower was a major problem for the Chemical Warfare Service throughout the war in the Pacific. Technical training was primarily a CWS responsibility. However, in many instances chemical officers were called upon for assistance in tactical training. Chemical warfare officers put on many tactical demonstrations for units, and especially for infantry officers of company, battalion and regimental grade, for the purpose of illustrating the proper employment of smoke and flame throwers in the assault of fortified positions. Division chemical officers conducted schools to train flame thrower operators and technicians after each operation in the Pacific and sometimes even during operations. Schools were also conducted by corps, army and higher commands. I Corps and XIV Corps conducted several flame thrower schools and field exercises from time to time. Sixth Army provided a traveling training team during the latter part of 1943 and the first half of 1944. The Chemical Warfare Training Center, Southwest Pacific Area, conducted schools to train operators and instructor personnel and also provided traveling demonstration and instruction teams. The Hawaiian Department conducted numerous schools to train operators, maintenance men and instructor personnel. The loss of operators and technicians through casualties, illness, transfers, promotions and rotation caused the training of individuals to be a never ending process.

Less effort was expended in continuous training of operators in the European theaters. In general, technical training was prescribed and schools for the training of operators were conducted from time to time. However, the standard of tactical training was low when compared to that required in the Pacific areas. This situation was, of course, the result of the relative unimportance attached to portable flame throwers in Europe, an attitude which did not justify a greater expenditure of time and effort by commanders. This lack of proficiency of tactical commanders undoubtedly encouraged less use being made of the weapon than if its employment had been thoroughly understood. There were numerous examples throughout the war to provide evidence for this presumption. The success achieved by any weapon depended upon the ability of commanders to employ it to the best advantage.

---

[26]/ Review Sheet: "TC 2 Employment of Portable Flame Throwers, M1A1 and M2-2." In Inspection Div, OC CWS.

It is very possible that if the employment of flame throwers had become a normal squad function in accordance with War Department Training Circular No. 2, 1945, the specialized training of flame thrower operators would have been accomplished during basic infantry training and would not have remained a burden on the theater of operations. This system would have been practicable if flame thrower technicians for servicing and maintenance had been provided by tables of organization and made an organic part of a division. Such a policy would also have furnished to the theaters officers thoroughly schooled in the employment of the weapon and a flame thrower situation would have been quickly recognized when it presented itself.

C. Employment

A study of the employment of the portable flame thrower reveals that it was used both in assault and for mopping up. Tactical doctrine envisioned its employment primarily as an assault weapon. It nevertheless received extensive use in mopping up by-passed positions manned by an enemy that refused to surrender even though his situation was hopeless. When the enemy was prone to surrender after his position became untenable, there was less demand to resort to the use of flame throwers.

The progressive use of the flame thrower in the Southwest Pacific Area is best illustrated by following the campaigns of the 32d Infantry Division. This division first tried to employ the flame thrower at Buna in December, 1942 before tactical doctrine suitable for jungle warfare was developed. Further operations at Saidor and Aitape, New Guinea, and Morotai Island saw little use of the flame thrower because of the nature of the operations. In Leyte the flame thrower was used extensively during the fighting for the Ormac Corridor. In Luzon this division employed the portable flame thrower more than 200 times.

Owing to the heavy weight of the flame thrower, its use was limited to either stabilized situations or to terrain where the equipment could be brought forward in vehicles or by native carriers. During the amphibious operations in the Pacific the Japanese were never able to seriously oppose a landing except on small islands such as Tarawa and Iwo Jima. This failure on the part of the enemy was primarily caused by the fact that he was rarely able to predict the landing beaches and the intense, murderous barrages laid down on the beaches by the Navy and Air Forces either destroyed the defenses or caused the defenders to withdraw. As a result, the flame thrower was rarely used extensively during landing operations. Each time the situation became stabilized and the attackers were forced to advance against dug-in positions, the flame throwers came into use both in the assault and in mopping up. For example, one battalion commander reported after the Iwo Jima operation that the portable flame thrower was the one indispensable infantry weapon.[27]

---

[27] Hist CWS Mid Pac, Vol IV, Annex IIc3, p. 26.

In Europe the portable flame thrower was used less than in any other area. Although tactical targets were infrequent, there was much less frequent employment of the portable than might have been true otherwise because of the technical deficiencies and limitations of the weapon and because of the **logistical** and maintenance problems encountered, especially with the M1 and M1A1. An illustration of the tactical repute of the M1 is in a comment by an officer of an Engineer regiment who served from the landing date in North Africa through the Sicilian and Italian Campaigns. The impression held by this officer was to the effect that the M1 was not used because, with the attendant problem of supply, to use the weapon was like employing "two tons of fire-crackers to blow open a door when it could be done with ten pounds of high-explosives."28/ A report illustrative of the repute of the weapon in Italy asserted that only two of the eleven portables in a unit could be made to work and that the men had no confidence in the weapon.29/ As many as twenty pillboxes were taken in a day and successful capture of pillboxes was carried out by infantry without the use of bangalores or flame throwers.30/

Commanders and staff officers in Italy often rationalized the lack of employment of flame throwers by citing the fact that the Germans were not using them to any great extent. They failed, however, to note that the Japanese also were not successful in employing flame. They also failed to appreciate the fact that flame throwers are primarily an offensive weapon and that an enemy on the defensive was not in a position to exploit flame. This deduction is further substantiated by the successful use of flame by the Germans in their "blitz" across Europe in 1940.

D. Maintenance and Servicing

During the latter part of 1943 when flame throwers were issued to the infantry, division chemical officers found themselves responsible for the maintenance of equipment for which they had inadequate personnel. Attempts to solve this problem varied with divisions. In some instances operators performed their own maintenance. This system did not work because the flame thrower was a secondary weapon and was not issued to

---

28/ Interv, Hist Br with Capt L. Freemire, formerly of the 540th Eng Regt, Fort Belvoir, Va, 15 Jun 45.

29/ TIR No. T/PFI-390, SPEIN 62.2 - US - 1902, 2 Oct 44.

30/ Rpt, 105th Eng Combat Bn, "Breaching of the Siegfried Line by 30th Infantry Division," 18 Oct 44.

operators. In some divisions maintenance and servicing was charged to personnel in the regimental or battalion headquarters company. This system often broke down because of lack of supervision and lack of training, resulting in charged flame throwers being issued to operators in an unserviceable condition. In some divisions, these duties were performed by engineers. This method was successful during training periods but often failed in combat because engineers were not available for attachment to the infantry. In other divisions, servicing and maintenance was performed by the division chemical section and regimental or battalion gas personnel. Misfires and unsatisfactory performance of the flame throwers could nearly always be traced to improper maintenance and servicing. It, therefore, became evident that if the flame thrower was to be successfully employed, it was necessary to provide properly trained CWS technicians and make some officer in the regiment or battalion responsible for proper servicing and maintenance. This problem was solved in Sixth Army by attaching a chemical service platoon to each division and designating the battalion and regimental gas officers as flame thrower officers. The battalion gas corporal was also required to be a qualified flame thrower technician.

E. Supply and Logistics

The M1 portable flame thrower was replaced by the M1A1 about the middle of 1943. The only substantial improvement offered by the M1A1 was its ability to employ thickened fuel. There was no improvement on the unsatisfactory electrical ignition system which was a source of trouble throughout the war. Batteries deteriorated in storage in the tropical climate and were undependable. Moisture shorted out the electrical spark assembly in spite of all possible precautions of waterproofing. There was always a shortage of accessory kits with the M1A1. This required servicing and maintenance at the regimental or even division level instead of in battalions or companies, thus limiting the flexibility of employment. Also, throughout the war there existed a critical shortage of spare parts which necessitated cannibalization of new flame throwers to maintain serviceable weapons in the hands of combat troops.

The M2-2 flame thrower started arriving in the Pacific areas about the middle of 1944. The 77th Infantry Division was equipped with this model for the Guam operation (July, 1944), in which it was first employed in combat by an army division. The XXIV Corps was equipped with the M2-2 for the Leyte operation and units of the Southwest Pacific Area were partially equipped with this model for the Luzon operation. However, issue was not completed until after the end of the war. For example, the 31st, 40th and 41st Divisions never had an opportunity to employ the new flame thrower and their last campaigns were fought with the M1A1. Sufficient flame throwers, accessory kits and spare parts would have been available for the first time for the Kyushu operation.

Napalm first became available for combat during the latter part of 1943. The supply of napalm was adequate from the time it became available until the end of the war. However, had the infantry learned to use thickened gasoline earlier, stocks during the first part of the war would have been inadequate. It is true that shortages of napalm existed at various localities during certain periods, but this condition was primarily a result of distribution and not caused by a shortage in the theater.

G. Evaluation.

Portable flame throwers are close-range weapons, more comparable to the bayonet and grenade than the rifle and machine gun. They are essentially offensive weapons and, if used in the defense, their normal role is in counter-attacks or in defense of a position. Their greatest use was against isolated centers of resistance. However, when used aggressively, they proved successful against organized defensive positions. They were found extremely useful in close country where normal support weapons were handicapped, such as jungles, mountains, wooded areas and towns or villages. The choice and size of targets was restricted by the small fuel capacity of the weapon. When vehicular flame throwers are available, the portable should be used only in terrain where vehicles cannot operate.

Many instances occurred during the war where the infantry was able to advance to within 10 to 40 yards of a position and were then forced to retire, usually with casualties, because they had no weapon that would neutralize the position. Where portable flame throwers were brought up, such positions were usually taken. Such occasions were special ones and as a result the flame thrower became a special weapon. The record shows that flame was a valuable weapon when placed into the hands of infantrymen at the right time at the right place.

Valuable as the flame thrower was when properly used, none of the models available during the war met the full requirements of the infantry. The logistics of the weapon hindered employment by foot-soldiers. It was too complicated and too fragile for combat use and required constant care and maintenance by experts in order to keep it in operation. Servicing and refilling was too involved, especially when non-pourable thickened fuel was used. Thickened fuel was too slow-burning to produce the required concentration of heat in a short time. The range was limited by the complicated high-pressure system used for propulsion. All of these limitations must be corrected if the weapon is to be exploited by the infantry. A simple, fool-proof, portable flame thrower that can be held by divisions and regiments ready for instant use is required. It should either be expendable or lend itself to simple reloading by insertion of cartridges. The range must be increased by using either solid or gelled fuel with rapid burning qualities and increased heat capacity characteristics; also the propellant should depend on a chemical reaction instead of on the expansion of compressed gases. The weight must be decreased by using lighter alloys and by decreasing the fuel capacity. The decreased fuel capacity would necessarily require tactical employment of several units in order to place adequate flame on the target. Studies have shown that one and one-half gallons of fuel delivered into an average poorly ventilated pillbox or bunker of 1,000 cubic feet capacity will kill the occupants. It has also been shown that an horrific burst of flame on the outside or against a closed embrasure has little effect upon the occupants.[31]

---

[31] CWS T of Opns Ltr, No. 25, 30 May 45, Rpt of Flame Attack Section of Medical Division, OC CWS. In CMLWG.

APPENDIX 1

HEADQUARTERS
25TH INFANTRY DIVISION
APO 25

27 March 1943

TRAINING MEMORANDUM)
:
NUMBER   6)

        SECTION I FLAME THROWER SCHOOL
        SECTION II DESCRIPTION, OPERATION, USE
                    AND SUPPLY OF PORTABLE FLAME
                    THROWER, M1

        SECTION I <u>FLAME THROWER SCHOOL</u>

    1. A one-day school for training flame thrower operators and assistants will be conducted by the Division Chemical Officer for each infantry regiment while that unit is on the Division Combat Range. Eight (8) men from the pioneer platoon of each battalion will attend. Attendance of a limited number of additional men may be arranged with the Division Chemical Officer. Units Commanders will make arrangements with the Division Chemical Officer concerning the date and details of the school.

        SECTION II <u>DESCRIPTION, OPERATION, USE AND
                     SUPPLY OF PORTABLE FLAME THROWER, M1</u>

    2. <u>DESCRIPTION, OPERATION AND CARE</u>. The description, operation and care of the Portable Flame Thrower M1 are given in detail in the attached Tentative Chemical Warfare Technical Manual, 12 March 1942.

    3. <u>TACTICAL USE</u>. a. <u>Advantages and Limitations</u>. The tactical use of the Portable Flame Thrower is in the development or experimental stage. Plans for its use must consider the factors of weight (portability); range, limited time of fire, availability of additional charges, security, and whether it is the best weapon to accomplish a given mission. Weight of the equipment severely limits the mobility of the weapon, particularly in jungle operations. This limitation is increased by the weight and bulk of the additional gas charges and fuel if they also must be taken forward. The comparatively short range limits use of the weapon to situations where it can be brought to within 20-25 yards of the target, and its short duration of fire requires that the target be brought under attack promptly. In order to bring the weapon close enough to be effective, security must be obtained by the use of cover or smoke

Trng Memo #6, Hq 25th Inf Div, 27 Mar 43--Contd.

or by supplementary fire power forcing the enemy to seek cover. The advantage of the flame thrower over other weapons lies in both its demoralizing and its incendiary effect. It is highly destructive against any combustible material, ammunition, and especially against personnel. The incendiary effect can be obtained along curved as well as straight lines of fire, making the weapon particularly suitable for use against moderately curved passageways into dugouts and emplacements, or against tanks and other vehicles where it is desired to obtain penetration into interior parts. Secondary but tactically important effects are the devitalizing of the air in a close space and the radiated heat which is intolerable for several feet distance from the flame. Both these secondary effects will cause casualties.

       b. Operation. Limited experience in use of the flame thrower in offensive jungle operations indicates it is most useful in mopping-up operations, particularly against well-prepared dugouts in rocky hillsides or under large trees. The weapon is kept in readiness at a convenient point in the battalion area. Usually near battalion headquarters, until an obstacle is encountered which cannot be reduced readily by ordinary attack. The obstacle is by-passed and enemy resistance in the vicinity is eliminated by fire. The flame thrower operator and accompanying security detachment advance toward the obstacle, preferably from a flank, making maximum use of cover. A suitable security detachment consists of 2 BAR--men and 2 riflemen who eliminate snipers in the vicinity of the obstacle, force the enemy in the dugout to seek cover, and definitely locate the target. A frontal holding attack (fixing force) by two riflemen on the dugout is desirable. Upon approaching the target, the nitrogen, fuel-line, and hydrogen valves of the flame thrower are opened, the ignition system is given a final test, and the operator crawls forward, holding the flame gun in one hand and dragging the fuel tank assembly behind him. When he had obtained a position within 20 yards of any opening in the dugout, a 1 to 2 second blast of the flame directed into the opening will usually eliminate all resistance, either by killing the occupants or by forcing them to evacuate, in which case they can be disposed of by the security detachment. A single charge of fuel should suffice for 5 or 6 two-second flames.

  4. SUPPLY. a. Basis of Issue. The present plan is to issue 2 Portable Flame Throwers M1, complete with supplementary equipment, to each infantry battalion. It is expected that these flame throwers will be used by personnel of the pioneer platoon, anti-tank platoon or such other trained personnel as may be available when need for them arises.

       b. Unit of Issue. The complete unit of issue consists of the following items:

Trng Memo #6, Hq 25th Inf Div, 27 Mar 43--Contd.

    (1) 1 Portable Flame Thrower, complete with fuel tanks, charged nitrogen cylinder, shoulder harness, and flame gun with charged hydrogen cylinder.

    (2) 1 Accessories Kit containing:
      5 charged nitrogen cylinders
      5 charged hydrogen cylinders
      1 Crescent wrench, 6-inch
      1 End wrench, 1-inch
      1 End wrench 7/16-inch
      2 Ignition batteries
      1 Funnel

    (3) 5 gasoline cans, 5-gallon capacity, for carrying extra fuel.

    (4) 1 flexible metal spout for pouring fuel from cans.

    (5) 1 30-gallon drum of flame thrower fuel.

  c. *Servicing.* In most cases, it will be possible for the flame thrower to be refilled at the battalion supply dump. If the situation requires considerable continuous use of the weapon, the accessories kit and additional fuel in 5-gallon cans can be brought forward by a suitably protected detail, the nitrogen and hydrogen cylinders replaced and the fuel tanks refilled using any available shelter, such as a large buttressed tree.

  d. *Recharging.* After using 6 complete charges, the complete assembly (par 4.B. (1) and (2)) should be exchanged for another assembly, which will be delivered on call to the regimental supply dump by the Division Chemical Section. The used weapon is taken to the Division Chemical Section's Shop where it is thoroughly cleaned and checked, the gas cylinders recharged, and prepared for issue.

  e. *Caution.* Since there is no supply of spare parts, all personnel are requested to take every precaution to prevent losing, breaking or abandoning any parts of the flame thrower.

  By command of Major General COLLINS:

            /s/ Wm. P. Bledsoe,
            WM. P. BLEDSOE,
A TRUE COPY /s/ W. A. Sweeten, Colonel, General Staff Corps,
    W. A. SWEETEN,   Chief of Staff.
 Lt. Colonel, Adjutant General's Department
   Adjutant General.

APPENDIX 2

HISTORICAL STATEMENT
ON THE
FLAMETHROWER PLATOON
OF THE
132D INFANTRY REGIMENT

April 1944

Table of Contents

	Pars.
SECTION I - History and Reason for Existence	1 - 2
SECTION II - Introduction	3 - 4
SECTION III - Organization	5 - 8
SECTION IV - Formations	9
SECTION V - Importance of Mobility	10
SECTION VI - Tactical Employment of Platoon	11 - 12
SECTION VII - Training Schedules	13

PROVISIONAL FLAME THROWER PLATOON
132d Infantry
APO 716

SECTION I - History and Reason for existence:

1. Reason:

The frequency of enemy fortified positions and the tenacity of the Japanese in occupying them in the South Pacific theatre almost demand that a special unit be formed that can effectively neutralize these with speed and with as few casualties on our side as possible. Flamethrowers were issued to the battalions and, when needed, would be placed in the hands of a hastily trained soldier who neither knew how to operate the weapon effectively nor had any particular desire to learn. The rifle units were not cognizant of the support to be given the operator and the flamethrower consequently has never had a fair trial.

2. History:

On 18 February 1944, a provisional flamethrower platoon was formed and assigned to Regimental Headquarters Company, 132d Infantry. It was organized with the aim of offering a solution to the problem of reducing enemy installations quickly and effectively. This was to be accomplished by training a group of men as a team with the ultimate aim always in mind.

The report given below is the result of much thought and many conferences among the Regimental Commander, the Regimental S-3, the platoon leader, and the enlisted men of the platoon. It has been tried in battle and was highly successful. It has been proved to the satisfaction of all concerned that the plan will work.

SECTION II - Introduction.

3. Mission of training and employment:

The flame thrower platoon of the 132d Infantry is a newly formed unit to be used primarily for successful annihilation of enemy strong points in conjunction with the rifle units. The theory that the flame thrower should be manned by an experienced operator has now become a principle with us. Not only must he be able to fire the weapon effectively, but he must also know all its capabilities and limitations. This result can only be obtained by an intensive training program controlled by competent instructors. The manual operation of the piece is reasonably simple but to make a properly functioning unit the training must go beyond that usually given the operator. The schedule must include: comprehensive training in assembly, disassembly, and functioning; firing the piece into prepared positions of various construction to observe the effect;

Historical Statement on the Flamethrower Platoon of the
132D Inf Regt, Apr 44--Contd.

development of tactics of the squad and platoon to get the desired teamwork; and, parenthetically, close coordination between the rifle units and flame throwers.

4. Effectiveness.

Although the platoon had received only a sketchy training prior to its first commitment in battle, it proved extremely effective by reducing eight (8) pillboxes in 100 seconds of actual firing. How many more can it neutralize after it is completely trained? We have found that only volunteers should be used in the platoon. Because of the comparative danger in action, unwilling operators are a detriment to a smoothly coordinated unit.

SECTION III - Organization of Platoon.

5. Original T/O:

The original T/O called for 26 men consisting of a platoon leader (1st or 2d Lt.); platoon sergeant (T/Sgt); 6 squad leaders (Sgts); 6 assistant squad leaders (Cpls); 6 automatic riflemen; and 6 shot gunners. It was observed that under the strenuous conditions of combat the size of the platoon was too small. It had to be enlarged to provide frequent reliefs for the squad leader (the flame thrower) in transport of his 70 pound weapon.

6. Present T/O and T/E:

On the attached diagrams are shown the present T/O of the platoon and the weapons carried by each individual, and the T/E of a completely equipped unit.

7. T/O and weapons of Flame throwers:

    a. Platoon Headquarters:

        (1) Platoon leader, a 1st or 2d Lt. - carbine, one fragmentation, and one smoke grenade.
        (2) Platoon sergeant, a technical sergeant - carbine, one fragmentation and one smoke grenade.
        (3) Two messengers, Pfc's - M1 rifles, one fragmentation and one smoke grenade each.
        (4) One driver, Pfc - M1 rifle, one fragmentation and one smoke grenade.

    b. Six squads - each consisting of:

Historical Statement on the Flamethrower Platoon of the
132D Inf Regt, Apr 44--Contd.

   (1) One squad leader, a staff sergeant - flame thrower and caliber 45 pistol.
   (2) One assistant squad leader, a technician 5th grade - M1 rifle, one fragmentation and one smoke grenade.
   (3) Two automatic riflemen, a Pfc and a Pvt - Browning Automatic Rifle, one fragmentation and one smoke grenade.
   (4) Two shotgunners, a Pfc and a Pvt - M97 Remington Shotgun, one fragmentation, one thermite, and three smoke grenades.

  c. General notes on weapons and ammunition:

  The shotgun has been found very effective in close combat. It is light, as is the ammunition, and has a tremendous casualty producing effect up to 50 yards. By taking the contents of a red Very pistol shell in its entirety from the cartridge and inserting them in an emptied 12 gauge shell, one may use it very effectively in target designation. With the increased pressure produced in the long barrel, one can get up to 75 yards of comparatively flat trajectory fire. It is fired directly at the installation and drops to its base on impact. It burns long enough to greatly aid the operator in getting into a favorable location for firing. Even if the red glow is obscured by intervening brush, the smoke produced by the burning is sufficient to point out the target definitely. The normal distribution is two Very pistol shells to 5 "00" buck-shot shells.

  Smoke grenades are issued to each man for his own protection in addition to those issued to the shotgunners for laying a smoke screen. Many times sniper fire has held a man pinned down for many minutes. However, if each man has a smoke grenade he can toss it in front of him and retire under screen of the resulting smoke.

  The three smoke grenades issued to each shotgunner are to be used to lay smoke screens which will deny enemy riflemen aimed fire on the advancing squad. The automatic weapons and riflemen inside the pillbox can be held under control by the mass of fire and the automatic weapons in the maneuvering force. The supporting enemy riflemen around the pillbox, however, are seldom visible, hence the use of smoke as a passive defense measure against them. The six smoke grenades in the squad have been found effective for approx. 15 yards on each side of the position.

  The thermite grenades carried by the shotgunners are issued as a precautionary measure. There is always the possibility that the ignition system on the flamegun will not operate satisfactorily. In this event the fuel may be ejected from the gun; and, after the desired amount has covered the installation, the thermite grenade is thrown into the fuel. It promptly ignites and is as effective in setting the fuel on fire as it would be if the ignition had worked.

Historical Statement on the Flamethrower Platoon of the
132D Inf Regt, Apr 44--Contd.

8. Organization of the Flame Thrower Platoon and principal duties of individuals:

   a. General: Platoon headquarters will consist of a command group:

      (1) The platoon leader, a 1st or 2d lieutenant, is responsible for the training, and tactical employment of the platoon. He is a member of the Regimental Special Staff and serves as the Regimental Flame Thrower Officer. He divides the time with the unit commander of the unit being supported and the flame thrower platoon. He designates the refueling point and coordinates the tactical disposition of the flame thrower squads and maintenance of flame throwers.

      (2) The second-in-command, a technical sergeant, is the principal assistant to the platoon leader. He is kept abreast of the tactical situation and replaces the platoon leader in the event the platoon leader becomes a casualty. His position is at the refueling point where he assists the platoon leader in controlling the platoon. He assists him by supervising the work of the corporal technicians who are refueling the extra flame throwers. He is responsible to the platoon leader for the security of the refueling point. He also assists the platoon leader in seeing that needed supplies are requisitioned and brought up from the rear.

      (3) One messenger who reports to the CO of the unit being supported.

      (4) One messenger who accompanies the platoon leader.

      (5) One messenger who drives the $\frac{1}{4}$-ton truck.

   b. The Flame Thrower Squad consists of:

      (1) The squad leader, a staff sergeant, commands the squad and operates the flame thrower.

      (2) Two automatic riflemen who are tactically disposed by the squad to cover the enemy by fire so that the flame throwers may be brought into action.

      (3) Two riflemen whose function is to secure the flame throwers, act as target designators, and lay smoke screens at the direction of the squad leader.

Historical Statement on the Flamethrower Platoon of the
132D Inf Regt, Apr 44--Contd.

        (4) Corporal technician who is responsible to the squad leader for maintenance and refueling of the flame throwers. His position is at the refueling point where he works under the supervision of the platoon sergeant.

SECTION IV - Formations:

    9. The following diagrams show various formations which may be used. (See page 241). These are to be taken as guides only as they must often be changed in appreciation of terrain and situation. It must always be kept in mind that the organic transportation of the regiment should be used on all possible occasions due to the weight of the equipment and the desire to keep the men as fresh as possible for the work ahead. It must be remembered that the flame thrower squad is never used as a separate unit but always in conjunction with supporting riflemen.

SECTION V - Importance of mobility:

    10. Because of the highly specialized use of the platoon it should be held in a highly mobile state at all times. This position of readiness includes: all men must have their belts loaded with the full allowance of ammunition; canteens must be full and attached to belt at all times, except when in use; packs should be kept rolled with shelter half, blanket, and 1 day's ration. All organizational equipment should be kept in truck piles so that rapid loading may be facilitated. Included in these piles are spare fuel cans (5 per gun), spare Hydrogen cylinders (5 per gun), spare Nitrogen cylinders (5 per gun), and all tools and extra ammunition. The order of loading is governed by the necessity of having the most vital equipment at the rear of the truck so that immediately upon detrucking the unit can move into battle if the situation demands. With practice the platoon should clear its area 15 minutes after the transportation has been ordered, 3 minutes after the trucks have arrived.

SECTION VI - Tactical Employment of Platoon:

    11. Tactics:

        Immediately upon arrival at the assembly area the platoon leader, accompanied by two runners, reports to the commander of the unit to which the flame thrower platoon is attached and accompanies him on his reconnaissance. After locating the refueling point the platoon leader should be present at the recital of the Field Order in order that he may fully understand the situation. Upon completion of the order he submits his plan to the commander. After a short conference a perfect coordination should be agreed on between the rifle and flame thrower units. While the order is being given the platoon sergeant supervises the unloading of the vehicles, the

Historical Statement on the Flamethrower Platoon of the
132D Inf Regt, Apr 44--Contd.

disposition of the personal equipment, and posting of security. The squad leaders orient their men as much as possible, and the asistant squad leaders make a last minute check of the flame throwers. The runner picks up the platoon here and leads the platoon to the refueling point. Communication is established between the refueling point and the Company CP. Platoon sergeant disperses the platoon and equipment and in general prepares the platoon for combat. The platoon leader must be at the refueling point at some time prior to action to issue his order. This is a normal 5 paragraph Field Order applied to the platoon's specialized tactical employment. Under ordinary circumstances in the jungle the entire platoon is seldom committed at once. Three flame throwers to a rifle platoon are all that the rifle platoon can effectively use; and in this theatre, a squad or a platoon is usually the maneuvering force. However, in the event that the entire flame thrower platoon is committed, additional riflemen must be detailed to secure the refueling point manned by the assistant squad leaders who are refueling and servicing the pieces. The flame thrower squad(s) is normally sent with the maneuvering force. Here they have protection from the base of fire set up by the riflemen, the covering fire by the maneuvering force in the event of enemy surprise attack, and are best able from this approach to work themselves in close enough to the installation to place effective flame on it. The platoon leader of the flame throwers remains at the Co. CP and holds one squad in readiness there. After an enemy location has been located which is holding up the advance the CO will probably request flame throwers, the number sent depending on the number of squad in the maneuver. The platoon leader sends his one available squad to the maneuvering force and if more are needed calls for them on the sound power phone which is established between the CP and the refueling point. The flame thrower remains slightly in rear of the maneuvering force after it is deployed and begins to move in to attack. Flame throwers are only brought into the point after a target has definitely been found. After the squads that are committed have expanded their fuel, one of them sends a shotgunner back for more flame if it is needed, then the squad either remains to assist the riflemen in fixing the enemy in position or they retire for refueling. If they all retire, the withdrawal is accomplished in the following manner: First the flame thrower, covered by the automatic rifles and shotguns, withdraw; second the automatic rifles under cover of the shotguns, then the shotguns one at a time. They then reorganize and take up the same formation used in the approach march and return to the rear. The flame thrower platoon is contacted by the shotgunner who requests more flame throwers and then guides them into position. After the installation has been neutralized the <u>maneuvering force</u> envelops it to deny its reoccupancy by the enemy. The value of the flame thrower is lost if the enemy is allowed to reoccupy the position. This point must <u>always</u> be kept in mind. The original base of fire holds its position. They do this in order to cover the assaulting force and to deliver fire in the event of a counter attack. After the forward

Historical Statement on the Flamethrower Platoon of the
132D Inf Regt, Apr 44--Contd.

position has been secured they may then move forward and continue the advance. If a series of installations are encountered it is advisable to approach them, if possible, from a direction which will offer infilade fire on the enemy. This will also alleviate the danger of the enemy's cross fire in front of their positions. The pillboxes may then be taken singly and in bounds, knock out one, secure it, move on to the next. This will not always be possible due to the difficulty of locating the pillboxes. The enemy is skillful in the use of camouflage and seldom gives its position away by firing until we are extremely close - sometimes not more than a few feet. When the friendly forces are confronted with the situation that they are moving frontally into a group of boxes and are unable to maneuver to the flanks, one flame thrower should be delegated to each installation; i.e., three pillboxes - three flame throwers. It is not practicable to attempt to knock out one at a time in a frontal attack because the support-installations can deny us the ground by cross fire. Hence the necessity of a larger force in a coordinated attack to reduce all installations simultaneously. After the fuel of a unit is expended the operator returns to the refueling point for filling and servicing. When the flame has been fired it is usually the target of intense enemy fire: mortars, rifles, machine guns, grenades, and even artillery. The difficulty of carrying and maintaining the flame thrower coupled with the concentration of fire the enemy can be expected to bring on the group make it necessary to withdraw the flame thrower as soon as possible after the completion of its mission.

12. Supply:

    a. In using flame throwers much consideration must be given to the problem of supply. Carrying parties from units other than the flame thrower platoon must be available to bring supplies to the refueling point. After the arrival of supplies at the refueling point the platoon can supply itself from there to the point of contact.

    b. To take care of all 2d echelon maintenance of the flame throwers we call upon the Chemical Warfare Service. They have additional tools and spare parts in rear of the platoon refueling point. They also fill the Nitrogen and Hydrogen cylinders, and mix the fuel.

SECTION VII - Training schedule:

13. The accompanying schedules may be of value in planning the first three weeks of training for a newly formed Flame Thrower Platoon.

T/O & T/E - PROVISIONAL FLAME THROWER PLATOON

	PLAT. HQ.	6 SQDS (EA)	TOTAL PLAT.	REMARKS
Lieutenant, 1st or 2d	1 (c)		1	
Technical Sergeant (651) (2d in command)	1 (c)		1	
Staff Sergeant (653) (squad leader)		1 (p)	6	
Tec 5th Grade (653) (2d in command, squad)		1 (p)	6	
Privates 1st Class and Privates				
Messenger (675)	2 (r)		2	1 Private lcl, 1 Private
Driver, Truck, ½-T (345)	1 (r)		1	Private lcl
Rifle, Auto-BAR (746)		2 (ar)	12	6 Pvts, 6 Pfcs
Riflemen (745)		2 (s)	12	6 Pvts, 6 Pfcs
Rifle, Cal..30, M1	3	1	9	1 per msgr; 1 per T/5 asst sqd ldr; 1 per driver
Carbine, Cal..30	2		2	1 per plat ldr; 1 per plat sgt.
Pistol, Cal..45		6	6	1 per sqd ldr
Rifle, Auto-BAR, Cal..30		2	12	2 per sqd
Shotgun, model 97 riot type		2	12	2 per sqd
Flame thrower, port. M1A1		2	12	2 per sqd
Truck, ¼-T, 4x4, C&R	1		1	1 per Plat Hq
Trailer, ¼-T, 2-wheel	1		1	1 per Plat Hq
Compass, lensatic, with luminous dial	2		2	1 per plat ldr; 1 per plat sgt.
Compass, watch		6		1 per sqd ldr
Binoculars, M3	1		1	1 per plat ldr
Knife, trench, M3, with scabbard, M8	5	27	32	1 per ind. armed w/ carb, pistol, shotgun, & Auto-rifle
Watch, wrist, 7-jewel	1		1	1 per plat sgt
Mask, gas, service	5	36	41	1 per individual

Quartermaster Individual Equipment issued as per T/E 7-17.
Code: (c) Carbine, (p) Pistol, (r) Rifle, (ar) Auto-Rifle, (s) Shotgun.

FLAME THROWER PLATOON
Training Schedule - 1st week.

Day	TIME	PERSONNEL	SUBJECT	AREA	INSTR EQUIPMENT	REF
1st	0800	Entire Plat	Assembly & disassembly of BAR	Instr. tent	Plat ldr BARs, cleaning material	FM 23-15
	0930-1030	"	Functioning & stoppages of BAR	"	Plat ldr BARs	" "
	1030-1145	"	Assembly & disassembly of M97 shotgun	"	Plat ldr Shotguns	None
	1300-1400	"	Assembly & disassembly of 45 pistol	"	Plat ldr Pistols	FM 23-45
	1400-1500	"	T/O & T/E of flame thrower platoon (review)	"	None	None
2nd	0800-1500	"	Assembly, disassembly, nomenclat., functioning, use of f.t. (M1A1) (Review)	"	" None	None
3rd	0800-0930	"	T/O & T/E & designation of individual duties	"	" None	None
	0930-1145	"	Discussion of sqd tactics	"	" None	None
	1300-1500	"	Sqd combat exercise	Tng area	" None	None
4th	0800-1500	"	Discussion & plat combat exercise critique	"	" None	None
5th	0800-1145	"	Test firing of all weapons	Range area	" All wpns	None
	1300-1500	"	Review of all previous work	Instr. tent	" None	None
6th	0800-1500	"	Plat combat firing exercise (situation tactical fr. Co. area. Emphasis on loading)	Tng area	" Trans., Ammo., Wpns, Packs	None

/t/ THOMAS B. ALLEN
2d Lt., Infantry
Flame Thrower Plat ldr

TRAINING SCHEDULE
Provisional Flame Thrower Platoon
2nd week

Day	TIME	PERSONNEL	SUBJECT	AREA	INSTR	EQUIPMENT	REF
1st	0745-0815	Entire Plat	Review; Nomenclat., functioning, care, cleaning, stoppages	Instr tent	Plat ldr	None	FM 3-376 Pars 2-18, 44, 45
	0815-0915	"	Review: Tactical use of wpns & sqd, tactics of plat	"	"	None	None
	0915-1600	"	Construction of Jap pillboxes (2)	Tng Area	"	Machettes axes, shovels	None
2nd	0745-1500	"	Effect of f.t. on Jap pillboxes (experimentation)	"	"	F.T.'s	None
3rd	0745-0900	"	Repair of burned pillboxes	"	"	Machettes axes, shovels	None
	0900-1500	"	Demolition & neutralization of pillboxes by F.T.'s & Bazookas	"	"	AT gren, M7 launchers, f.t.'s	None
4th	0745-1500	"	Sqd tactics in support of rifle sqd	"	"	F.T.'s & weapons	None
5th	0745-1500	"	Plat tactics in support in rifle comp.	"	"	F.T.'s, wpns, AT gren, M7 launchers smoke grenades	None

- 243 -

TRAINING SCHEDULE
Provisional Flame Thrower Platoon
2nd week Contd.

Day	TIME	PERSONNEL	SUBJECT	AREA	INSTR	EQUIPMENT	REF
6th	0745-0945	Entire Plat	Creeping & crawling with F.T. Practice in removing f.t. from wounded gunner & Continuing advance by assistant	Tng Area	Plat ldr	F.T.'s	None
	0945-1045	"	Review of week's work	Instr tent	"	None	None
	1045-1145	"	Orientation lecture	"	"	None	None

/t/ THOMAS B. ALLEN
2d Lt., Infantry
Flame Thrower Plat Ldr

FLAME THROWER PLATOON
Training Schedule - 3rd Week

Day	TIME	PERSONNEL	SUBJECT	AREA	INSTR	EQUIPMENT	REF
1st	0745-0815	Entire Plat	Introduction, necessity for flame thrower plat	Inst tent	Plat ldr	Notebook pencil	None
	0815-0915	"	Nomenclat. of port. f.t. M1A1	"	"	"	FM 3-375 par. 2-7
	0915-1145	"	Functioning, assembly & disassembly	"	"	f.t. "	"
	1300-1330	"	Safety precautions	"	"	"	Pars. 18, 44 & 45
	1330-1430	"	Operation-care, cleaning, stoppages, tech. employmt.	"	"	"	Pars. 8-18
	1430-1500	"	Review, examination	"	"	"	Review pars.
2nd	0745-0815	"	Review-nomenclature	"	"	"	"
	0815-0915	"	Review-functioning, assembly, disassembly	"	"	"	"
	0915-1030	"	Review-operation, care, cleaning, stoppages, tech. employment	"	"	"	Review
	1030-1145	"	Fuel-tanks-mixture, operation	"	"	"	Pars. 19-28
	1300-1330	"	Review-fuel tanks, mixtures, operation	"	"	"	Review pars.
	1330-1400	"	Charging of pressure cylinder	"	"	"	Pars. 29-32
	1400-1430	"	Charging of hydrogen cylinder	"	"	"	Pars. 33-36
	1430-1500	"	Care & maintenance	"	"	"	Pars. 46-58

FLAME THROWER PLATOON
Training Schedule - 3rd Week Contd.

Day	TIME	PERSONNEL	SUBJECT	AREA	INSTR	EQUIPMENT	REF
3rd	0745-0815	Entire Plat	Review, care, maintenance	Inst tent	Plat ldr	f.t.	Review
	0815-0845	"	Equipment & material	"	"	"	Pars. 59-64
	0845-1015	"	Written examination of all previous instructions	"	"	"	Review all prev. pars.
	1015-1145	"	Make of sqd equipment & wpns carried, duties	"	"	Blackboard chart	Unnum. memo Hq 132d 4 Feb 44
	1300-1500	"	Test firing, all platoon personnel	Tng Area	"	"	Pars 2-7 " 8-18
4th	0745-0815	"	Review—make-up of sqd eqpmt & wpns carried, duties, etc.	"	"	"	Memo, unnumbered Hq 132d 4 Feb 44
	0815-0930	"	Target designation, methods to be used	"	"	"	None
	0930-1030	"	Blackboard lecture showing operation of target designation	Inst. Tent	"	"	None
	1030-1145	"	Discussion by entire plat personnel on best tactical principles to be used.	"	"	"	None
	1300-1500	"	Complete review—sqd make-up, eqpmt, wpns, duties, target designation, tactics, etc.	"	"	Notebook pencil	Review
5th	0745-1500	"	Practice ex. of 1 inf. rifle sqd w/F.T. plat in assault on fortified positions	Tng Area	"	F.T. & necessary equipment	None

- 246 -

FLAME THROWER PLATOON
Training Schedule - 3rd Week Contd.

Day	TIME	PERSONNEL	SUBJECT	AREA	INSTR	EQUIPMENT	REF
6th	0745-1500	Entire Plat	Practice ex. of f.t. plat with rifle co.	Tng Area	Plat ldr	F.T. & necessary equipment	None

/t/ THOMAS B. ALLEN
2d Lt., Infantry
Flame Thrower Plat Ldr.

APPENDIX 3

HEADQUARTERS
XIV CORPS
APO 453

29 April 1944

ANNEX NUMBER 3 TO)

TRAINING MEMORANDUM)

NUMBER   8)

Training in the Use of Flame Throwers.

1. General:

While recent operations in this as well as previous campaigns have demonstrated the value of flame throwers in jungle combat, the tactical capabilities of this weapon have not yet been fully developed. Its use, therefore, must be considered as being in the experimental stage. The weapon has functional and mechanical limitations which are in the process of correction and improvement. Continuous training, observation, and initiative are necessary to obtain maximum usefulness of flame throwers in combat.

2. Principles governing employment of flame throwers:

The principles described in this memorandum governing the use and employment of flame throwers are based on limited combat experience. As a result they cannot be considered as the best or only solution nor accepted as final. They do, however, form a basis upon which infantry training and operations may be conducted and from which specific, clear cut principles and technique may be evolved. In order that this may be obtained the principles stated must be adapted to the specific tactical and terrain conditions under which the weapon is employed. The following is a brief summary of general principles:

    a. In general, flame throwers are used to support the infantry advance by helping in the neutralization and destruction of fortified obstacles and in mopping up operations. They may also be used in helping break up an enemy attack.

    b. The weapon should be used only when the location or construction of fortified obstacles precludes the effective use of other available weapons.

    c. All elements using the flame thrower should consider all the limitations of the weapon so that its use may be fully exploited.

- 248 -

Annex #3 to Trng Memo #8, Hq XIV Corps, 29 Apr 44--Contd.

These limitations include:

        (1) Portability and mobility

        (2) Range

        (3) Limited time of fire

        (4) Availability of additional gas charges

        (5) Security

    d. The advantage of the flame thrower over other weapons lies in both its demoralizing effect and its incendiary effect. It is highly destructive against any combustible material or ammunition, and especially against personnel.

    e. Tactics should conform in general to basic infantry principles of fire and movement as applied to the particular situation.

    f. Flame thrower teams and infantry as well must develop perfect teamwork. The flame thrower must provide accurate direct fire against resistance holding up the infantry. The security detachment and infantry elements must provide close in security for the flame thrower during the approach, attack, and withdrawal.

3. Advance preparation for a flame thrower attack.

    The flame thrower should be kept in readiness at a convenient point in the battalion area, usually near the battalion headquarters, until an obstacle is encountered which cannot be reduced by ordinary attack.

    a. Even before it has been decided to use flame throwers in any operation the flame thrower must be given a final maintenance check to insure adequate operation. Fuel tanks must be filled, and additional fuel placed in readiness. The charged nitrogen and hydrogen cylinders must be inspected, or replaced, and the valves tested. The ignition system must be given a final test and batteries replaced if necessary. The accessories kit must be available for use in case of hasty and minor maintenance.

    b. When the use of flame throwers is deemed feasible the flame thrower commander and his subordinates will make a detailed reconnaissance in conjunction with the proper infantry personnel and will complete the detailed plans for the attack. These plans should include:

Annex #3 to Trng Memo #8, Hq XIV Corps, 29 Apr 44--Contd.

      (1) Number of teams to be employed.

      (2) Selected routes of approach for flame thrower team or teams.

      (3) Location of reservicing point or points.

      (4) Selection of attack positions.

      (5) Conduct of the attack.

      (6) Location or reorganization point or points.

    4. In jungle operations the following installations will prove useful:

      a. Location of reservicing point or points -- This point must be near enough to the front line to enable continuous use of the flame thrower, and must give protection to personnel and equipment from effective small arms fire. If the situation requires considerable use of the weapon, the accessories kit and additional fuel must be maintained at this point. Emergency minor maintenance crews should also be available here.

      b. Attack position -- This is a convenient place as near to the front line as possible where the flame thrower can be placed in the attack formation. In this position last minute instructions will be issued and final coordination with the infantry be assured. Also, additional information concerning enemy targets can be obtained.

      c. Conduct of the attack:

      (1) During the attack the security detachment and infantry must give close and continuous support to the flame thrower. A suitable security detachment consists of two BAR's and two riflemen who eliminate snipers in the vicinity of the obstacle and force the enemy in the fortified position to take cover.

      (2) Flanking attacks are usually preferable. When frontal attacks must be made, it may be necessary to increase the size of the security detachment, thereby giving additional supporting fire. In the absence of natural cover, smoke should be employed. A special smoke man should be designated for this.

      (3) Before approaching the target, the operator should open the nitrogen, hydrogen and fuel line valves, and test the ignition system to assure the operation of the flame thrower. The assistant flame thrower operator should always carry one or more thermite grenades to insure ignition of the fuel after it has been placed upon the target if the ignition system proved faulty upon testing. Others in the team may also carry such grenades.

Annex #3 to Trng Memo #6, Hq XIV Corps, 29 Apr 44--Contd.

(4) Upon reaching a selected position within effective target range a one to two second burst of flame directly into the position will usually eliminate all resistance within, and those of the enemy who are able to come out of the emplacement can then be disposed of by the security detachment.

(5) When the enemy fire has been reduced the security elements should occupy the position until relieved by the infantry. After relief has been made, the flame thrower team should be reorganized and if necessary flame throwers should be reserviced and given minor maintenance at the reservicing point.

5. a. With the above thoughts in mind it is considered highly important that flame thrower operators be thoroughly trained in the operation, functioning, maintenance, and tactical employment of the flame thrower. Also it is essential that a sufficient number of highly trained operators be maintained at all times.

b. In order that an operator be considered as qualified in the operation, functioning, maintenance, and tactical employment of the flame thrower, the following minimum standard of training is established:

(1) Nomenclature and functioning of the flame thrower-- 2 hours.

(2) Operation, refueling, and mixture of fuels--3 hours.

(3) Maintenance --3 hours.

(4) Combat training --20 hours.

(a) This will include a series of five realistic problems emphasizing briefing of situation, reconnaissance, approach, use of smoke, use of supporting fires, replacement in case of casualties, the assault, withdrawal, reorganization, and refueling in the field.

6. a. Based on the principles described above the 37th and Americal Divisions, 25th RCT, and 1st Bn 24th Inf will conduct training in the operation and tactical employment of the flame thrower as soon as practicable.

b. Training will provide for brief lectures and demonstrations followed by practical field exercises. Each exercise will be followed immediately by a short critique.

c. Training schedules will be submitted by the 37th and Americal Divisions, 25th RCT, and 1st Battalion, 24th Infantry a minimum of two days before training is begun.

Annex #5 to Trng Memo #8, Hq XIV Corps, 29 Apr 44--Contd.

          d. The Commanding General 37th Division, the Commanding General Americal Division and the Commanding Officers of the 25th RCT and 1st Battalion, 24th Infantry will submit a report of training with recommendations for changes and additions in the principles, tactics and technique of the use of flame throwers in jungle operations within 10 days after the completion of the training period.

                          By Command of Major General GRISWOLD:

                          W. H. ARNOLD,
                          Brig. Gen., G.S.C.,
                          Chief of Staff.

OFFICIAL:

/s/ James T. Walsh
/t/ JAMES T. WALSH,
    Lt.Col., A.G.D.
    Adjutant General.

DISTRIBUTION:
2- COMGENSOPAC
2- COMGENSOPAC ADV
5- CG, 37th Div
5- CG, Americal Div
1- C/S, XIV Corps
3- CO, 25th RCT
2- CO, 1st Bn 24th Inf
1- Cml O
1- G-2
1- G-4
1- AG
2- G-3 file

APPENDIX 4

HEADQUARTERS
37TH INFANTRY DIVISION

26 September 1944

Inclosure No. 2   )
        to   )
TRAINING MEMORANDUM NO. 7)

Training in the Use of Flamethrowers

1. In accordance with Annex #5 to TM #8, Hq XIV Corps, dated 29 April 1944, the 37th Division will conduct training in the operation and tactical employment of the flamethrower.

2. Objective:

    a. To qualify flamethrower teams in the operation, functioning, maintenance and tactical employment of the flamethrower. A minimum of one flamethrower team will be qualified in each of the following units:

        (1) Infantry Rifle Company
        (2) Infantry Battalion ammunition and pioneer platoon
        (3) Engineer Company

    b. To familiarize all infantry and engineer personnel with the capabilities and limitations of flamethrowers.

3. Methods: Training will provide for brief lectures and demonstrations followed by practical field exercises. Each exercise will be followed by a short critique.

4. Time: Training will be completed prior to June 30, 1944.

5. Detailed Schedules: Infantry regiments and the 117th Engineer Battalion will submit detailed schedules covering the foregoing training to this headquarters in triplicate, at least one week prior to the effective date thereof.

6. Principles Governing Flamethrower Operations:

    a. The principles described in this memorandum governing the use and employment of flamethrowers are based on limited combat

Incl #2 to Trng Memo #7, 26 Sep 44--Cont'd.

experience. As a result they cannot be considered as the best or only solution nor accepted as final. They do, however, form a basis upon which infantry training and operations may be conducted and from which specific, clear cut principles and technique may be evolved. In order that this may be obtained the principles stated must be adapted to the specific tactical and terrain conditions under which the weapon is employed. The following is a brief summary of general principles:

(1) In general, flamethrowers are used to support the infantry advance by helping in the neutralization and destruction of fortified obstacles and in mopping up operations. They may also be used in helping break up an enemy attack.

(2) The weapon should be used only when the location or construction of fortified obstacles precludes the effective use of other available weapons.

(3) All elements using the flamethrower should consider all the limitations of the weapon so that its use may be fully exploited. These limitations include:

    (a) Portability and mobility
    (b) Range
    (c) Limited time of fire
    (d) Security

(4) The advantage of the flamethrower over other weapons lies in both its demoralizing effect and its incendiary effect. It is highly destructive against any combustible material or ammunition, and especially against personnel.

(5) Tactics should conform in general to basic infantry principles of fire and movement as applied to the particular situation.

(6) Flamethrower teams and infantry as well must develop perfect team work. The flamethrower must provide accurate direct fire against resistance holding up the infantry. The security detachment and infantry elements must provide close in security for the flamethrower during the approach, attack, and withdrawal.

b. Advance preparation for a flamethrower attack.

(1) The flamethrower should be kept in readiness at a convenient point in the battalion area, usually near the battalion headquarters, until an obstacle is encountered which cannot be reduced by ordinary attack.

Incl #2 to Trng Memo #7, 26 Sep 44--Cont'd.

(2) Even before it has been decided to use flamethrowers in any operation the flamethrower must be given a final maintenance check to insure adequate operation. Fuel tanks must be filled, and additional fuel placed in readiness. The charged nitrogen and hydrogen cylinders must be inspected, or replaced, and the valves tested. The ignition system must be given a final test and batteries replaced if necessary. The accessories kit must be available for use in case of hasty and minor maintenance.

(3) When the use of flamethrowers is deemed feasible the flamethrower commander and his subordinates will make a detailed reconnaissance in conjunction with the proper infantry personnel and will complete the detailed plans for the attack. These plans should include:

    (a) Number of teams to be employed
    (b) Selected routes of approach for flamethrower team or teams
    (c) Location of reservicing point or points
    (d) Selection of attack positions
    (e) Conduct of the attack
    (f) Location or reorganization point or points.

c. In jungle operations the following installations will prove useful.

(1) Location of reservicing point or points - This point must be near enough to the front line to enable continuous use of the flamethrower, and must give protection to personnel and equipment from effective small arms fire. If the situation requires considerable use of the weapon, the accessories kit and additional fuel must be maintained at this point. Emergency minor maintenance crews should also be available here.

(2) Attack position - This is a convenient place as near to the front as possible where the flamethrower can be placed in the attack formation. In this position last minute instructions will be issued and final coordination with the infantry be assured. Also, additional information concerning enemy targets can be obtained.

(3) Conduct of the attack.

(a) During the attack the security detachment and infantry must give close and continuous support to the flamethrower. A suitable security detachment consists of two BAR's and two riflemen who eliminate snipers in the vicinity of the obstacle and force the enemy in the fortified position to take cover.

Incl #2 to Trng Memo #7, 26 Sep 44--Cont'd.

(b) Flanking attacks are usually preferable. When frontal attacks must be made, it may be necessary to increase the size of the security detachment, thereby giving additional supporting fire. In the absence of natural cover, smoke should be employed. A special smoke man should be designated for this.

(c) Before approaching the target, the operator should open the nitrogen, hydrogen and fuel line valves, and test the ignition system to assure the operation of the flamethrower. The assistant flamethrower operator should always carry one or more thermite grenades to insure ignition of the fuel after it has been placed upon the target if the ignition system proves faulty upon testing. Others in the team may also carry such grenades.

(d) Upon reaching a selected position within effective target range a one or two second burst of flame directly into the position will usually eliminate all resistance within, and those of the enemy who are able to come out of the emplacement can then be disposed of by the security detachment.

(e) When the enemy fire has been reduced the security elements should occupy the position until relieved by the infantry. After relief has been made, the flamethrower team should be reorganized and if necessary flamethrowers should be reserviced and given minor maintenance at the reservicing point.

d. (1) With the above thoughts in mind it is considered highly important that flamethrower operators be thoroughly trained in the operation, functioning, maintenance, and tactical employment of the flamethrower. Also, it is essential that a number of highly trained operators be maintained at all times.

(2) In order that an operator be considered as qualified in the operations, functioning, maintenance, and tactical employment of the flamethrower, the following minimum standard of training is established:

(a) Nomenclature and function of the flamethrower - 2 hours
(b) Operation, refueling, and mixture of fuels - 3 hours
(c) Maintenance - 3 hours
(d) Combat training - 20 hours

(1) This will include a series of five realistic problems emphasizing briefing of situation, reconnaissance, approach, use of smoke, use of supporting fires, replacement in case of casualties, the assault, withdrawal, reorganization, and refueling in the field.

Incl #2 to Trng Memo #7, 26 Sep 44--Cont'd.

    e. Suggested organization for a flamethrower team is as follows:

Team Leader	1 man
Asst Team Leader	1 man
2 BAR Groups	4 men
2 Flamethrower Groups	4 men
1 Smoke Group	2 men
	12 men

7. **Reports.** Units will submit reports of training with recommendations for changes and additions in the principles, tactics, and technique of the use of flamethrowers in jungle operations within 5 days after the completion of the training period.

APPENDIX 5

HEADQUARTERS
SIXTH ARMY
Office of the Commanding General
APO 442

1 October 1943

TRAINING MEMORANDUM)
:
NUMBER   8)

TRAINING IN USE OF FLAMETHROWERS

This training directive prescribes a program for technical and tactical training with the portable flame thrower. Detailed instructions covering its operation and employment, extracted from TM 3-357, are included in Annex 1.

1. OBJECTIVES:

    a. Proficiency in the service, operation, firing, maintenance and repair of flame throwers.

    b. Proficiency in the tactical employment of flame throwers.

    c. Coordinated employment of all weapons of assault parties including flame throwers in the attack of fortified positions.

2. PERSONNEL TO BE TRAINED:

Flame thrower operators should be selected for coolness, determination and resourcefulness. An operator and an assistant will be trained as a team for the operation of each weapon. The units listed below will train flame thrower teams in the numbers indicated. This is to be considered a minimum and does not preclude the training of additional personnel.

    a. Parachute infantry regiments, and combat engineer separate companies and battalions - two teams for each authorized flame thrower.

    b. Ammunition and pioneer platoons, infantry battalions - two teams each.

    c. Pioneer and demolition section of the service troop, cavalry regiment - four teams each.

    d. Rifle company or troop - two teams each.

Trng Memo #8, Hq Sixth Army, 1 Oct 43--Contd.

3. TRAINING:

Thorough technical and tactical training of operators is necessary to insure maximum operating efficiency and satisfactory employment of the flame thrower in the attack of fortified positions. Individual technical training will be completed prior to participation in field exercises. When proficiency in the handling, operation, and firing of the weapon is attained, flame thrower teams will be included with specially organized assault parties for tactical training. Subsequently, field exercises involving the coordinated attack on fortified positions by assault parties will be conducted with other combined training.

    a. Technical Training:

Proficiency in technique of fire is required to obtain a maximum effect on a target with a minimum of fuel wastage. Training in firing the weapon should emphasize accurate range estimation, correct windage allowances, and proper elevation of the gun. Practice firing should be conducted under varied light and weather conditions. All instruction will be thorough and practical and will include:

        (1) Mechanical training:

            (a) Disassembly and assembly.
            (b) Care and cleaning.
            (c) Maintenance and repair.
            (d) Functioning.
            (e) Mechanical operation and adjustment.

        (2) Preparation of fuels.

        (3) Servicing and filling fuel tanks in preparation for firing.

        (4) Charging pressure and hydrogen cylinders.

        (5) Technique of firing flame throwers.

    b. Tactical Training:

The flame thrower is primarily an offensive weapon to be used in specific situations. Its principal employment in this theater is that of an auxiliary weapon in neutralizing bunkers and dugouts. To coordinate the employment of the flame thrower with other weapons, special assault parties, which may vary with the mission and the availability of weapons, will be organized and trained as units. A minimum of three flame throwers will be included with each party, the assistant operator of each being armed with either a submachine gun or a rifle. Close coordination, mutual support and control of all elements of the assault party must be emphasized.

Trng Memo #8, Hq Sixth Army, 1 Oct 43--Contd.

    (1) A type assault party is listed below for use as a guide:

Personnel	Number
Detachment leader	1
Assistant leader	1
Rocket launcher personnel	2
Flame thrower party	6
Demolition party	2
Automatic riflemen	2
Riflemen with bayonets and grenades	4

    (2) Arms and equipment used by assault parties may include:

- Submachine guns
- Automatic rifles
- Rifles and bayonets
- Carbines
- Demolition charges
- Bangalore torpedos
- Rocket launchers
- Flame throwers
- Smoke grenades
- Hand grenades
- Rifle grenades
- Wire cutters
- Signal projectors

    (3) Tactical training will include:

    (a) Methods of approaching fortified positions consisting of mutually supporting bunkers and dugouts.

    (b) Field exercises involving the employment of assault parties, in the attack on Japanese type bunkers and pillboxes.

    (c) Close coordination and mutual support by all weapons of the assault parties.

    (d) Mopping up of fortified positions.

    (4) **TESTS:**

    Division and separate unit commanders will determine by appropriate tests that satisfactory progress in the assault technique prescribed above is being made and that the desired objectives are being attained.

    By Command of Lieutenant General KRUEGER:

APPENDIX 6

HEADQUARTERS
24TH INFANTRY DIVISION

5 November 1943

TRAINING MEMORANDUM)
:
NUMBER   54)

TRAINING IN THE USE OF FLAME THROWERS

REFERENCES: TM #8, Hq Sixth Army, 1 Oct 43
Annex #1 to TM #8, Hq Sixth Army, 1 Oct 43
Notes on Employment of Flame Throwers in
 Jungle Operations. (Inclosure #1 & 2 to
 Confidential Letter 470.7 Hq I Corps, dated
 27 Sep 43.)
Conference Course Tng Bulletin GT-19A dated
 1 June 1943.

1. GENERAL: Infantry and Engineer units of the Division will receive special training in the technical and tactical operation and employment of flame throwers during the periods indicated below:

    a. 19th Inf - - - - - - - - - - - 22 Nov - 27 Nov

    b. 21st Inf - - - - - - - - - - - 29 Nov - 4 Dec

    c. 34th Inf - - - - - - - - - - - 13 Dec - 18 Dec

    d. 3d Engr Bn - - - - - - - - - - 22 Nov - 18 Dec

2. OBJECTIVES:

    a. To train a limited number of men in servicing, operating, firing and repairing the flame thrower.

    b. To familiarize Infantry personnel with the characteristics and limitations of this weapon and its coordinated employment with the Infantry and Engineer assault teams.

3. DEFINITIONS:

    a. Flame Thrower team: A flame thrower operator and an assistant operator who is armed with either a submachine gun, carbine, or rifle.

Trng Memo #54, Hq 24th Inf Div, 5 Nov 43--Contd.

      b. <u>Flame Thrower group</u>: More than one flame thrower team, normally organized to consist of 3 flame thrower teams one of which is a reserve or replacement unit and not employed in the initial assault.

      c. <u>Assault party</u>: A composite force organized, trained and equipped to play a special part in the attack on a fortified position. It will normally be organized as follows:

PERSONNEL	NUMBER	ARMS AND EQUIPMENT
Flame Thrower group	8	3 Flame Throwers. 3 sub MGs, carbines or rifles.
Command group	2 (1) Ldr-O or NCO	Pyrotechnic pistol, and sound powered telephone or SCR 536 radio.
	(1) Asst Ldr NCO	Individual arms plus a quantity of hand grenades.
Demolition party	2	Each man to carry individual arm, one pole charge (15-20 lbs HE) and a quantity of hand grenades (smoke and fragmentation).
Rocket party	2 (1)	One rocket launcher and a supply of AT rockets.
	(1)	Individual arm, a supply of AT rockets and hand grenades (smoke and fragmentation).
Support party	2 auto riflemen	1 AR and a supply of hand grenades each.
	4 riflemen (2 Asst auto riflemen) (2 riflemen)	Each carries 1 M1 rifle and a supply of hand grenades, 1 wire cutter.

Note: It should be noted that the above is considered a <u>normal</u> organization of an assault party. The organization and composition may, however, be varied to fit each situation. It should seldom be less than eighteen (18) men.

Trng Memo #54, Hq 24th Inf Div, 5 Nov 43--Contd.

   4. PERSONNEL TO BE TRAINED:

      a. Each rifle company and each battalion A & P platoon will organize and train three (3) flame thrower teams.

      b. Each Engr Company will organize and train two (2) flame thrower teams for each flame thrower authorized by T/E.

      c. Each Inf battalion will organize and train three (3) assault parties.

   5. TRAINING PHASES: Training in the use of flame throwers will be divided into two phases.

      a. Technical training - - - 16 hours.

         (1) Mechanical training:

            (a) Disassembly and assembly.

            (b) Care and cleaning.

            (c) Maintenance and repair.

            (d) Functioning.

            (e) Mechanical operation and adjustment.

         (2) Preparation of fuels.

         (3) Servicing and filling fuel tanks in preparation for firing.

         (4) Charging pressure and hydrogen cylinders.

         (5) Technique of firing flame throwers.

      b. Tactical training - - - 8 hours.

         This training will be coordinated with assault parties in attacking fortified positions and dugouts, and will include:

            (1) Methods of approaching fortified positions consisting of mutually supporting bunkers and dugouts.

Trng Memo #54, Hq 24th Inf Div, 5 Nov 43--Contd.

          (2) Field exercise involving the employment of assault parties in the attack of Japanese type bunkers and pillboxes.

          (3) Close coordination and mutual support by all weapons of the assault parties.

          (4) Mopping up of fortified positions.

    c. Upon the completion of flame thrower training the Division will select and test an assault party from each Infantry Regiment.

6. **INSTRUCTION:**

    a. The Division Chemical Officer will be responsible for technical advice and assistance in the training of flame thrower teams. Maximum use will be made of a demonstration team from the Chemical Warfare Service.

    b. Unit Commanders will be responsible for the training of assault parties.

    c. The Division Chemical Warfare Officer is authorized direct liaison with Infantry Regiments and the 3d Engineer Battalion to arrange details concerning equipment and schedules of instruction.

    By command of Major General IRVING:

APPENDIX 7

HEADQUARTERS I CORPS
Office of the Commanding General

10 December 1943

TRAINING MEMORANDUM)
:
NUMBER   17   )

TRAINING IN USE OF FLAME THROWERS

1. **General:** a. This training directive prescribes principles of organization and tactical employment of flame thrower assault parties and is supplementary to TM 3-375, Training Memorandum Number 8, Headquarters Sixth Army, dated 1 Oct 43, and letter Headquarters I Corps, file 470.7, subject: Employment of Flame Throwers, dated 27 Sep 43.

b. Experience has demonstrated the value of the flame thrower in jungle combat. Its tactical capabilities have not yet been fully developed. The weapon has functional and mechanical limitations which are in process of correction. Continuous training, observation and initiative are necessary to obtain maximum usefulness of flame throwers in combat. The principles stated in this and reference directives must be adapted to the specific tactical and terrain conditions under which the weapon is employed.

2. **Flame Thrower assault parties:** a. The flame thrower assault party will consist of a flame thrower detail, a security detail and a communications detail. The communications detail may also have flame thrower or security functions. The party may in addition include rocket, demolition and bangalore torpedo or wire-cutting details.

b. Type parties may range in strength from eight to twenty.

c. (1) The flame thrower detail will include at least two operators each with one flame thrower; and will also include two alternate operators.

(2) The security detail will consist of automatic riflemen and riflemen.

(3) The communications detail will consist of one or two men, with sound-power telephone, radio, or visual signal equipment; or of connecting files.

d. Equipment may include a sound-power telephone and radio in addition to such of the items listed in par. 3b (2) Training Memorandum Number 8, Headquarters Sixth Army as are appropriate to the mission.

Trng Memo #17, Hq I Corps, 10 Dec 1943--Contd.

"e. Two flame thrower assault parties will be trained in each rifle battalion headquarters company and lettered combat engineer company, in addition to the elements prescribed in par. 2 of Training Memorandum Number 8, Headquarters Sixth Army.

3. <u>Distribution of flame throwers</u>: Sixty flame throwers are authorized for issue to elements of each infantry division. Division commanders are encouraged to use latitude in distribution of flame throwers to insure availability of the weapons to meet tactical requirements.

4. <u>Training, maintenance, repair and fueling</u>: The chemical officer of the division is responsible for supervision of training of flame thrower assault parties and provision for maintenance, repair and fueling.

5. <u>Principles of tactical employment of flame throwers</u>: a. Flame thrower assault parties should be used only when the location or construction of bunkers precludes the effective use of other available weapons.

b. All elements using the flame thrower should know all capabilities and limitations of the weapon so that its use may be fully exploited.

c. Tactics should conform in general to basic infantry principles of fire and movement as applied to the particular situation. Smoke should be employed whenever it will aid the successful completion of the mission.

d. Thorough reconnaissance is necessary to determine the composition of the flame thrower assault party, whether one or more parties should be used, and so that, before the assault, these parties may have all available information affecting the mission.

e. A holding force should, when practicable, neutralize fire of the objective bunker and its support during the approach of the flame thrower assault party, and neutralize enemy supporting fire during the assault.

f. Flank attacks are usually preferable. When frontal attacks must be made, it may be necessary to increase the size of the party or the number of parties; and, in the absence of natural cover, the need for smoke will be greater.

g. Single parties should only be used for the reduction of single bunkers. Several assault parties should be used for reduction of strong points or defensive perimeters. These parties should attack selected bunkers simultaneously.

h. There is no fixed pattern of assault. Types satisfactorily for training include, among others:

Trng Memo #17, Hq I Corps, 10 Dec 1943--Contd.

"(1) The first burst is fired across port from flank by operator No. 1. Second burst is fired obliquely at port by operator No. 2. Third burst is fired from front into port by operator No. 1.

(2) Operator No. 1 fires across port from flank and remains there firing additional bursts as needed to protect operator No. 2. Operator No. 2 moves into position under cover of fire by operator No. 1 and fires into the port, first from the oblique and then from the front.

(3) In the foregoing and other types of assault patterns in which the simultaneous employment of two flame throwers is planned, one weapon may fail to function. Therefore, each operator must be prepared to accomplish with his weapon, the fires of both weapons, or to bring the plan of assault within the capabilities of one weapon. In this case, the decision must be made on the spot by the operator of the efficient weapon. The occasion for such decision is probable. All operators must be trained to make it quickly.

i. All security elements of the party not engaged in protection of flame thrower operators, pin occupants of bunker.

j. Demolitions should be employed to prevent enemy re-occupation of the objective bunker. Demolition charges are placed promptly upon completion of flame thrower fire.

k. Security elements of the flame thrower assault party establish perimeter defense of the reduced position until relieved.

By command of Lieutenant General EICHELBERGER:

APPENDIX 8

HEADQUARTERS 41ST INFANTRY DIVISION

TRAINING MEMORANDUM: 31 December 1943

NUMBER   19:

USE OF FLAME THROWERS

1. **General.** The flame thrower is primarily an offensive weapon to be used in specific situations. Its principal employment in this theater is that of an auxiliary weapon in neutralizing bunkers and dugouts. Experience has demonstrated the value of the flame thrower in jungle combat. Its tactical capabilities have not yet been fully developed. The weapon has functional and mechanical limitations which are in process of correction and which must be thoroughly understood by all personnel. Continuous training and initiative are necessary to obtain maximum usefulness of flame throwers in combat. The principles stated in this directive must be adapted to the specific tactical and terrain conditions under which the weapon is employed.

    2. **Objectives.** The objectives to be attained in training are:

        a. Proficiency in the service, operation, firing, maintenance and repair of flame throwers.

        b. Proficiency in the tactical employment of flame throwers.

        c. Coordinated employment of all weapons of flame thrower assault parties in attack of fortified positions.

        d. Coordinated employment of fixing or supporting fires to assist the flame thrower assault party in the accomplishment of its mission.

        e. Coordinated use of smoke by flame thrower assault parties and supporting elements.

    3. **Training Responsibility.** a. Units listed below will qualify flame thrower operators in the numbers indicated at the Division Schools conducted by the Division Chemical Officer. This is to be considered a minimum requirement and does not preclude the training of additional personnel:

           (1) 32 operators per Combat Engineer Company.
           (2) 12 operators per Infantry Rifle Company.
           (3) 12 operators per Infantry Anti-Tank and Cannon Company.
           (4) 8 operators per Infantry Battalion Headquarters Company.

    b. Infantry Regimental and Engineer Battalion Commanders are responsible for attaining training objective listed in paragraph 2 above. One flame thrower assault party will be trained in each Infantry and Engineer Platoon. Tactical training will include:

"(1) Methods of approaching fortified positions consisting of mutually supporting bunkers and dugouts.

(2) Field exercises involving the use of flame throwers in the reduction of Japanese type bunkers, pill boxes and dugouts.

4. <u>General Data Concerning Flame Throwers</u>:

    a. Weights:

Complete apparatus, filled	68 lbs
Fuel unit, complete, filled	60 lbs
Gun unit, complete	8 lbs
Complete apparatus, empty	32 lbs

    b. The effective range of the flame thrower is dependent upon the type of fuel used and will vary with each type according to the composition of the mixture used. In general, various mixtures of thickened fuel will give an effective range of 40-50 yards. Mixtures of liquid fuel will give an effective range of 20-25 yards.

    c. The limited total length of fire of 10 seconds should be kept in mind. However, experienced operators are able to fire 15-20 short effective bursts capable of neutralizing bunker positions.

    d. The flame thrower should not be fired into wind having a velocity greater than 10 mph.

    e. The use of liquid fuel gives large volumes of smoke and flame, thus affording protection for the assault party. The large, brilliant flame exercises a powerful demoralizing effect on the enemy, blinds them and the intense heat drives them away from their weapons. The flame thrower, using liquid fuel, fires a flame which rolls and billows into all cracks and corners. Liquid fuel is more easily transferred into the flame thrower tanks than is the thickened fuel, however, due to the shorter range, the operator must approach closer to the target before opening fire. In the case of thickened fuel the range is approximately twice that obtainable from liquid fuel. In addition, more fuel can be placed on the target than is possible with liquid fuel. The burning thickened fuel sticks to the clothing, skin and weapons because of its glue like consistency. Because of the decreased dispersion of the thickened fuel, more skill is required to hit a small target such as a weapons port. Final choice of fuel depends upon the situation, such as the angle from which the bunker can be approached and the range from which fire can be delivered.

5. <u>Flame Thrower Assault Parties</u>. a. The flame thrower assault party will consist of a flame thrower detail, a security detail and a communications detail. The communications detail may also have security functions. The party may, in addition, include rocket, demolition and bangalore torpedo or wire cutting details.

"b. Type parties may range in strength from eight to an entire platoon.

    c. (1) The flame thrower detail will consist of two operators, two alternate operators, and two flame throwers.

       (2) The security detail will consist of riflemen and automatic riflemen. The firepower of the detail to be consistent with the mission.

       (3) The communications detail will consist of one or two men equipped with one or more of the following devices: sound-power telephone, radio, visual signal equipment, or of connecting files.

    d. Additional arms and equipment used by flame thrower assault parties may include: carbines, sub-machine guns, demolition charges, bangalore torpedoes, rocket launchers, smoke grenades (HC or WP), fragmentation grenades, rifle grenades, wire cutters, pyrotechnics and signal equipment.

6. <u>Principles of Tactical Employment of Flame Throwers</u>. a. Flame throwers should not be used unsupported by other weapons. A minimum of one flame thrower detail (par 5c(1)) will be employed in each flame thrower assault party. Additional flame thrower details or half details may be added as required.

    b. All elements using the weapon should know its capabilities and limitations so that its use may be fully exploited.

    c. Flame thrower assault parties should be used only when the location or construction of the enemy fortification precludes the effective use of other available weapons. The flame thrower is primarily an offensive weapon. Situations involving its use call for prior rehearsals. Certain limitations of the weapon require that maximum coordination be carried out. The flame thrower is <u>NOT</u> a weapon of opportunity.

    d. Thorough reconnaissance is necessary in order to determine the composition of the flame thrower assault party and whether one or more parties should be used, and so that before the assault, these parties may have all available information affecting the mission.

    e. Tactics should conform in general to basic infantry principles of fire and movement as applied to the particular situation. Smoke should be employed whenever it will aid the successful completion of the mission, either by screening or by deception as to intent.

    f. Single parties should only be used for the reduction of single bunkers. Several assault parties should be used for the reduction of enemy defensive area or perimeters. These parties should attack selected bunkers simultaneously.

"g. A holding force should, when practicable, neutralize fire of the objective bunker and its supporting bunkers during the approach of the flame thrower assault party, and neutralize enemy supporting fire during the assault.

h. Flank attacks are usually preferable. When frontal attacks must be made, it may be necessary to increase the size of the party or the number of parties, and in the absence of natural cover the need for smoke will be greater.

i. There are no fixed assault patterns. The security detail usually should establish defense to afford all-around protection to the flame thrower detail and to assist its effort by supporting fires. Type patterns for delivering effective flame thrower neutralization fires are:

(1) Both weapons filled with liquid fuel: Operator No. 1 fires across port from flank and remains there firing additional bursts as needed to protect operator No. 2. Operator No. 2 moves into position under cover of fire by operator No. 1 and fires into the port, first from the oblique and then from the front.

(2) Both weapons filled with thickened fuel: Operator No. 1 fires into bunker ports from oblique. Operator No. 2 moves into position under cover of fire by operator No. 1 and fires into the bunker from a frontal position. When using thickened fuel, it is necessary to direct the flame jet onto the target.

(3) One weapon filled with liquid fuel, the other with thickened fuel: Operator No. 1 from flank or an oblique position burns fire lane for operator No. 2. Operator No. 2 with thickened fuel, as soon as fire lane is cleared, fires from oblique or frontal position into bunker as in paragraph 6i(2) above.

(4) The above are types of assault patterns and many variations are possible. The type described in paragraph 6i(3) may require one or more complete flame thrower details equipped with one or more flame throwers filled with liquid fuel to clear lanes depending upon vegetation and terrain conditions. In the foregoing and other types of assault patterns in which the simultaneous employment of two flame throwers are planned, one weapon may fail to function. Therefore, each operator must be prepared to accomplish with his weapon the fires of both weapons, or to bring the plan of assault within the capabilities of one weapon. In this case, the decision must be made on the spot by the operator of the efficient weapon.

j. The flame thrower can be effectively used in mopping up operations to smoke and burn enemy personnel out of emplacements, dugouts, buildings, and other structures. The flame thrower, using liquid fuel, fires a flame which rolls and billows into all cracks and corners. No corner of a dugout, room, or emplacement will provide protection from it. It is superior to hand grenades in this respect. Also, it can be fired into open doors, windows, or ports without getting into the angle of fire from these openings because of its rolling effect. It is best to use liquid fuel for mopping up.

k. The flame thrower is not particularly well adapted to anti-mechanized defense because of the difficulty of having a limited number of flame throwers where they are needed. If flame throwers should happen to be where they are needed, they can be used to burn the rubber parts off of treads and wheels, they can be used to set engines on fire, they will blind a tank (liquid fuel leaves a smudge on glass-covered slits) and in some instances they will burn the men inside of the tank.

l. The flame thrower can be used as an incendiary against inflammable objects (airplanes, motors, ammunition), but it is not effective against objects with high kindling points.

m. Flame throwers used in large numbers in one locality are very demoralizing upon enemy troops both in the attack and in the defense.

n. For the purposes described in paragraphs 6k and m, the flame thrower may be valuable in the defense.

o. No attempt to refill the flame thrower in the midst of combat should be made. Reserve operators should be available when needed to use other filled flame throwers. They will be used to replace operators who have become casualties or who have exhausted the contents of their flame throwers. Under some circumstances operators may be ordered to abandon their weapons when these have become exhausted.

7. <u>Care and Maintenance</u>. The portable flame thrower has many parts that will not stand up under abusive treatment. Reasonable care must be taken in its use. Precautions must be taken to avoid getting dirt or any foreign substance into the fuel, the pressure, and the hydrogen systems. 1st and 2nd echelon maintenance must be constantly performed by using elements.

By command of Major General FULLER:"

APPENDIX 9

HEADQUARTERS
SIXTH ARMY
Office of the Commanding General
APO 442

22 June 1944

TRAINING MEMORANDUM)
:
NUMBER   18   )

1. SCOPE:

This training memorandum prescribes a program for the technical and tactical training of an assault party.

2. OBJECTIVE:

Development of well trained assault parties capable of attacking and destroying strongly organized enemy bunkers, pillboxes and similar defensive installations.

3. ORGANIZATION:

Each infantry battalion and cavalry squadron will form and maintain at least one assault party, permanently organized and equipped in accordance with the following table:

Personnel	Arms and Equipment
1 party leader	Carbine or M1 rifle, hand grenades
1 assistant leader	M1 rifle, hand grenades
2 flame thrower operators	2 flame throwers, 2 pistols
2 assistant flame thrower operators	2 M1 rifles, WP and hand grenades
2 rocket launcher men	2 rocket launchers, 2 pistols
2 demolition men	2 M1 rifles, demolition charges, wire cutters, WP grenades
1 BAR operator	BAR

Trng Memo #18, Hq Sixth Army, 22 Jun 44--Contd.

Personnel (Contd.)	Arms and Equipment
1 assistant BAR operator	M1 rifle
4 riflemen	4 M1 rifles, grenade discharger and rifle grenades, WP and hand grenades

4. TRAINING:

    a. Each individual member of the assault party will be selected from those men best qualified for the position to be held.

    b. The four riflemen in the assault party will receive familiarization training in the operation of the flame thrower to provide adequate replacements within the team for the flame thrower operators.

    c. Team tactical training will include:

        (1) Coordinated methods of approaching and reducing fortified enemy positions consisting of mutually supporting bunkers, pillboxes and dugouts, to include performance with fire support from infantry weapons.

        (2) Assist squads and platoons in mopping up of fortified positions.

        (3) Active participation with the battalion or squadron in field exercises.

    d. All team training will emphasize close coordination. Confidence in the other members of the team must be instilled in each individual.

5. EMPLOYMENT:

    a. Each rifle battalion or squadron commander, executive officer, S-3 and all rifle company commanders will familiarize themselves with the capabilities, limitations and tactical employment of an assault party.

    b. The assault party will be initially held in reserve during combat in order to be readily available when needed.

6. TESTS:

Division and separate unit commanders will determine by appropriate tests that satisfactory progress in the training of the

Trng Memo #18, Hq Sixth Army, 22 Jun 44--Contd.

above prescribed assault parties is being made and that the desired objective is being attained.

7. RESCINDED:

Training Memorandum No. 8, Headquarters Sixth Army, 1 October 1943, is rescinded effective this date.

By Command of Lieutenant General KRUEGER:

/s/ O. A. NICKERSON
Lt. Col., A.G.D.
Asst. Adj. Gen.

DISTRIBUTION:
"A" & "C"

APPENDIX 10

HEADQUARTERS
33D INFANTRY DIVISION
APO 33

15 July 1944

TRAINING MEMORANDUM)
                    :
NUMBER   15)

BATTALION ASSAULT TEAM

1. This training memorandum prescribes a program for the technical and tactical training of a permanently-organized assault party.

2. The objective of this training is the development of well-trained assault parties, as permanently-organized units, capable of attacking and destroying strongly-organized enemy bunkers, pillboxes, and similar defensive installations.

3. In accordance with directive contained in Training Memorandum No. 18, Sixth Army (22 June 1944), each infantry battalion will form and maintain at least one assault party permanently organized and equipped in accordance with the following table:

Personnel	Arms and Equipment
1 party leader	Carbine or M1 rifle; hand grenades
1 assistant leader	M-1 rifle; hand grenades
2 flame thrower operators	2 flame throwers; 2 pistols
2 assistant flame thrower operators	2 M-1 rifles; WP and hand grenades
2 rocket launcher men	2 rocket launchers, 2 pistols
2 demolition men	2 M-1 rifles; demolition charges, wire cutters; WP grenades
1 BAR operator	1 BAR
1 assistant BAR operator	1 M-1 rifle
4 riflemen	4 M-1 rifles; grenades; discharger and rifle grenades; WP and hand grenades

4. Training.

   a. Each individual member of the assault party will be selected from those men best qualified for the position to be held.

   b. The four riflemen in the assault party will receive familiarization training in the operation of the flame thrower to provide adequate replacements within the team for the flame thrower operators.

Trng Memo #15, Hq 33d Inf Div, 15 Jul 44--Contd.

    c. Team tactical training will include:

        (1) Coordinated methods of approaching and reducing fortified enemy positions consisting of mutually-supporting bunkers, pillboxes and dugouts, to include performance with fire support from infantry weapons.

        (2) Assist squads and platoons in mopping up of fortified positions.

        (3) Active participation with the battalion or squad in field exercises.

    d. All team training will emphasize close coordination. Confidence in the other members of the team must be instilled in each individual.

5. **Employment.**

    a. Each rifle battalion commander, executive officer, S-3, and all rifle company commanders will familiarize themselves with the capabilities, limitations, and tactical employment of an assault party.

    b. The assault party will be initially held in reserve during combat in order to be readily available when needed.

6. Division and separate unit commanders will determine by appropriate tests that satisfactory progress in the training of the above-prescribed assault parties is being made and that the desired objective is being attained.

7. a. The training prescribed herein will be given priority over that prescribed in Annex No. 2, Training Memorandum No. 4-E, this Headquarters (22 June 1944).

    b. The training directed in Annex No. 2, Training Memorandum No. 4-E, remains in effect. It is desirable that personnel in squads or platoons be capable of operating as assault teams for specific operations in order to augment this permanently-organized assault team where necessary.

8. Administration. Assault parties outlined above will be organized immediately and training initiated at once. They will be quartered and messed together until they have satisfactorily passed required tests.

                By command of Major General CLARKSON:

APPENDIX 11

HEADQUARTERS
EIGHTH ARMY

1 October 1944

Inclosure No. 7)
   to)
TRAINING DIRECTIVE NO. 1)

Operations Against Japanese Fortifications

1. Instruction in the use of the flamethrower will be completed prior to this training.

2. Each infantry battalion and cavalry squadron will form and maintain at least two assault parties to be known as Assault Party (Flame Thrower) and Assault Party (Demolitions). The organizations listed below are destined to fill minimum requirements, and may be augmented by commanders to meet special situations.

    a. Assault Party (Flame Thrower):

Personnel	Arms and Equipment
1 party leader	Carbine or M1 rifle, hand grenades
1 assistant leader	M1 rifle, hand grenades
2 flame thrower operators	2 flame throwers, 2 pistols
2 assistant flame thrower operators	2 M1 rifles, incendiary grenades
1 rocket launcher operator	1 rocket launcher, 1 pistol
1 assistant rocket launcher operator	1 carbine
2 demolition men	2 M1 rifles, demolition charges, wire cutters, WP grenades
2 BAR operators	2 BARS
2 assistant BAR operators	2 M1 rifles
4 riflemen (will receive familiarization training with flame thrower)	4 M1 rifles, grenade discharger and rifle grenades, WP and hand grenades

    b. Assault Party (Demolition):

Incl #7 to Trng Directive #1, Hq Eighth Army, 1 Oct 44--Contd.

Personnel	Arms and Equipment
1 party leader	Carbine or M1 rifle, hand grenades
1 assistant leader	M1 rifle, hand grenades
1 rocket launcher operator	1 rocket launcher, 1 pistol
1 assistant rocket launcher operator	1 carbine
6 demolition men	6 M1 rifles, demolition charges, wire cutters, WP grenades
2 BAR operators	2 BARS
2 assistant BAR operators	2 M1 rifles
4 riflemen	4 M1 rifles, grenade discharger, and rifle grenades, WP and hand grenades.

    c. The assault parties will consist of men temperamentally and physically suited for the job.

    d. Party tactical training will include:

        (1) Methods of approaching and reducing fortified enemy positions supported by fire from infantry weapons.

        (2) Assistance to squads and platoons in mopping up of fortified positions.

        (3) Participation in battalion or squadron field exercises.

3. Units which have completed training in operations against permanent land fortifications under Army Ground Forces directives will conduct refresher training paying special attention to the Japanese type emplacements.

4. Units which have not completed this training will receive a thorough course employing replicas and mock-ups of Japanese type emplacements.

5. Training will include the attack of a fortified Japanese type area by combat teams the size of a battalion and smaller. Where practicable air units and non-divisional combat units such as tank destroyer, antiaircraft, and chemical battalions will be included in these exercises when conducted by division or separate infantry regiments. Timely requests for such non-divisional units should be made to this headquarters.

Incl #7 to Trng Directive #1, Hq Eighth Army, 1 Oct 44--Contd.

    6. References for instruction in this subject follow:

        a. FM 5-25
        b. FM 7-20
        c. FM 31-50
        d. FM 100-5, Section I, Chapter 12
        e. 1943 WD Training Circular No. 20, Antitank Minefields and Roadblocks.

APPENDIX 12

HEADQUARTERS
SIXTH ARMY
Office of the Commanding General
APO 442

6 August 1945

TRAINING MEMORANDUM)
 :
NUMBER   30)

1. PURPOSE:

This training memorandum prescribes a program for the technical and tactical training involved in the employment of assault parties by infantry and dismounted cavalry.

2. OBJECTIVE:

To train selected rifle squads in the employment of special assault weapons for the purpose of developing competent assault parties capable of attacking and destroying strongly organized enemy bunkers, pillboxes, and similar defensive installations.

3. SCOPE:

Infantry battalions and cavalry squadrons will train at least:

    a. Three (3) squads in each rifle company or troop.

    b. Four (4) men in each selected squad as flamethrower operators.

    c. Two (2) men in each selected squad as rocket launcher gunners.

    d. Two (2) men in each selected squad as a demolition party.

4. TRAINING:

    a. Squad training will include:

        (1) Coordinated methods of approaching and reducing fortified enemy positions consisting of mutually supporting bunkers, pillboxes and dugouts, to include fire and smoke support from artillery and infantry weapons.

Trng Memo #30, Hq Sixth Army, 6 Aug 45--Contd.

        (2) Application of the principles contained in WDTC 2, dated 19 January 1944.

        (3) Active participation in battalion or squadron field exercises.

    b. All squad training will emphasize teamwork and close coordination of individual actions. Confidence in the other members of the squad must be instilled in each individual.

5. EMPLOYMENT:

    a. Squads trained in accordance with the provisions of this memorandum will function as normal organic rifle squads until assault action is required. During assault activities the squad will normally function under the command of the platoon leader and be supported by the remainder of the platoon.

    b. Specially trained demolition parties may be attached to the squad as required.

    c. Each battalion or squadron commander, company or troop commander, S-3, and executive officer will familiarize himself with the capabilities, limitations, and tactical employment of assault parties.

    d. The regimental gas officer will be designated as the regimental flamethrower officer and will be the regimental commander's adviser on the technical aspects of the flamethrower.

    e. The ammunition and pioneer platoon leader (battalion gas officer) will be designated as the battalion or squadron flamethrower officer and will be responsible for the maintenance and servicing of the flamethrowers in the battalion or squadron.

    f. The battalion or squadron gas NCO will be trained as a flamethrower technician.

6. TESTS:

    Division and separate unit commanders will determine by appropriate tests that satisfactory progress in the training of prescribed units and individuals is being made and that the desired objective is being attained.

7. RESCINDED:

Trng Memo #30, Hq Sixth Army, 6 Aug 45--Contd.

    Training Memorandum No. 18, Headquarters Sixth Army, 23 June 1944, is rescinded effective this date.

    BY COMMAND OF GENERAL KRUEGER:

                                                          /s/ Andrew G. Beck
                                                              ANDREW G. BECK,
                                                              Major, A. G. D.,
                                                              Asst. Adj. Gen.

APPENDIX 13

HEADQUARTERS
FIFTH AMPHIBIOUS CORPS
c/o FLEET POST OFFICE, SAN FRANCISCO, CAL.

21 December 1943

CORPS TRAINING MEMORANDUM)
: Demolition and Flame Thrower Training
NUMBER..............13-43)

1. Experience gained in the recent occupation of the Gilbert Islands by United States Forces shows a deficiency in the number of assault troops trained in handling demolitions and flame throwers.

2. Due to insufficient personnel, the assault engineer troops with each combat team are unable to supply the infantry with the much needed crews for flame throwing and demolition, thereby making it necessary to train additional personnel in each infantry platoon.

3. It is believed that each infantry platoon should have a minimum of two (2) men trained in the use of the flame thrower and not less than four (4) men, preferably one (1) man per squad, trained in the use of demolitions to reduce barbed wire entanglements and minor emplacements.

4. Infantry demolition training should consist of both lectures and practical field work. The following subjects should be covered.

  a. Characteristics of military explosives.

  b. Safety precautions.

  c. Preparation of charges for non-electric firing.

  d. Charge-placing poles.

  e. Bangalore torpedoes.

  f. Practical training in the removal of barbed wire entanglements through the use of bangalore torpedoes and in assaulting minor obstacles with pole charges.

5. Infantry flame thrower training should cover the following subjects:

  a. Characteristics and mechanical functioning of the flame thrower.

Corps Trng Memo #13-43, Hq V Amphibious Corps, 21 Dec 43--Contd.

    b. Fuel mixtures.

    c. Care and cleaning of the flame thrower.

    d. range and windage estimation.

    e. Principles of practical firing.

    f. Effect of fire.

    g. Organization of the flame thrower party.

    h. Simple tactical problems involving the flame thrower party.

    i. Tactical employment of the flame thrower party with infantry units.

              ****

APPENDIX 14

HEADQUARTERS
V AMPHIBIOUS CORPS
C/O FLEET POST OFFICE, SAN FRANCISCO, CALIFORNIA

21 December 1943

CORPS TRAINING ORDER)
                           : Flame Throwers.
NUMBER........17-43)

   1. The information contained herein is published for the information and guidance of those concerned.

      (a) <u>General</u>.

          Flame throwers are not general purpose weapons and must not be used as such. Due to the short range of this weapon, casualties among flame-throwing personnel may be expected to be high. The intensely destructive and demoralizing factors connected with flame throwers, tends to cause concentration of enemy fire at flame-thrower personnel. Therefore, application of proper tactics must result in the use of this weapon against appropriate objectives and not as a substitution for a rifle.

      (b) <u>Characteristics of the M1 and M1A1 portable flame throwers</u>:

        (1) Capacity - 5 gallons.

        (2) Range   - Effective with thickened gasoline, 40 to 50 yards.

        (3) Weight   - Complete apparatus empty, 32 pounds, Complete apparatus filled, 68 pounds.
                       Fuel unit complete, empty, 24 pounds.
                       Fuel unit complete, filled, 60 pounds.
                       Gun unit, complete, 8 pounds.

        (4) Pressures- Fuel tanks, 375 pounds 1 sq. inch.
                       Hydrogen cylinder, 1500-2100 pounds.
                       Pressure cylinder, 1800-2000 pounds.

        (5) Duration of fire - Continuous or intermittent, 10 seconds.

Corps Trng Order #17-43, Hq V Amph Corps, 21 Dec 43--Contd.

    (c) <u>Ratio of Expended Supplies</u>:

        For every one hundred (100) chargings of the flame thrower, the following supplies are expended:

- 10 Commercial pressure cylinders (nitrogen or compressed air)
- 2 Commercial hydrogen cylinders. (Three, however, are required on the manifold, but only two will be completely expended in charging one hundred cylinders).
- 500 Gallons of fuel (thickened or liquid).
- 265 Pounds of Napalm gasoline thickener, if thickened gasoline is used.

    (d) <u>Choice of Fuel</u>:

        Since thickened gasoline gives more than twice the range of liquid fuels, it is often preferred for use in the portable flame thrower. The increased range affords the operator greater protection against enemy detection. Liquid fuels give a smoke screen and a much more brilliant and demoralizing display. However, the fuel is largely consumed in flight. Thickened gasoline, on the other hand, retains more of its effectiveness when it hits the target. The flaming mixture sticks to the target and the clothing and skin of personnel because of its glue-like consistency, and has little or no tendency to roll off. It continues to burn for several minutes. Because of the decreased dispersion of the thickened fuel more skill is required to hit a small target such as an embrasure.

        The use of a liquid fuel gives large volumes of smoke and flame, thus affording protection for the assaulting detachment. The large brilliant flame exercises a powerful demoralizing effect on the enemy, blinds them and drives them away from their weapons with the heat. The flames and smoke roll and billow which, in effect, enables the flame thrower to "shoot around the corners" from the blind angle.

        Thickened fuel containing 4% Napalm has the advantage of increased effectiveness when fired outside of the field of fire of the bunker due to its rolling and billowing tendency. The 8% Napalm thickened fuel has the advantage of increased range and greater aiming accuracy. The 6% Napalm thickened fuel is considered most effective against bunkers.

        The final choice of a fuel depends upon the situation, such as range and angle at which the embrasure may be approached.

Corps Trng Order #17-43, Hq V Amph Corps, 21 Dec 43--Contd.

    (e) <u>Filling Fuel Tanks</u>.

        Filling fuel tanks is not a front line operation. Reserve operators must be available where needed to use other filled flame throwers. A refueling dump must be established where tanks can be refilled. This dump must be located in areas cleared of aimed small arms fire.

    (f) <u>The Flame Thrower Party</u>.

        The flame thrower party must consist of an operator and an assistant. The assistant should be armed with a suitable weapon and supplied with hand and smoke grenades. He operates closely with the flame-thrower operator to support him in reaching a firing position and must be fully trained and qualified to replace the operator in case he becomes a casualty.

    (g) <u>Training of the Flame Thrower Party</u>:

        The training of the flame thrower party must include:

        (1) Effective range estimation for fuel being used.
        (2) Elevation and windage allowance required.
        (3) Firing procedure.
        (4) Firing from various positions and angles.
        (5) Mechanical functioning of the flame thrower.
        (6) Fuels and fuel mixing.
        (7) Filling procedure and precautions.
        (8) Care and cleaning of the flame thrower.
        (9) Effects produced by the flame thrower.

    (h) <u>Effects of the Flame Thrower</u>:

        (1) One portable flame thrower firing at each embrasure or pair of embrasures, using 4 - 8% Napalm thickened fuel will reduce Japanese bunkers by inflicting casualties on personnel by burning or suffocation.

        (2) At ranges of thirty (30) to fifty (50) yards one portable flame thrower for each embrasure or pair of embrasures will effectively block off the view of the occupants of the bunker.

        (3) The thickened fuel will cling to the logs around the embrasure and firing slits, and by smoke and flame, screen the opening to deny its use by personnel inside. This will serve in many cases to drive personnel away from the opening. Only if a considerable portion of the fuel is placed inside, can reduction of personnel be achieved.

Corps Trng Order #17-43, Hq V Amph Corps, 21 Dec 43--Contd.

(4) In the case of an average size bunker, five (5) gallons of gasoline burning inside the bunker will usually secure destruction of all occupants by suffocation. Due to its slower burning qualities, greater quantities of thickened gasoline are required for dependable results.

(i) Check List for Flame Thrower Personnel:

(1) Be sure the pressure gas is turned on before starting the last movement to a firing position.

(2) Be sure the ignition system works prior to operation.

(3) Be sure the pressure cylinder has proper pressure.

(4) Be sure that the fuel tanks are filled.

(j) Flame Thrower Missions:

The primary flame thrower mission is assault upon fortifications to reduce such fortifications and to produce casualty effect upon occupants. Secondary missions may include:

(1) Incendiary effect upon buildings, supply dumps and other inflammable structures.

(2) Screening effect of smoke produced by liquid fuel.

(3) Demoralizing effect upon enemy personnel.

(4) Defense against tanks and in tank hunting.

(5) Mopping up and forcing of entry.

(k) Technique of Flame Thrower Operation:

(1) Flame throwers must not be used unless supported by other arms. Sufficient flame throwers must be assigned to an operation to allow for casualties and for possible malfunctioning of the weapon. The flame thrower is primarily for offensive use.

In executing flame thrower missions, prior rehearsals are desirable where situations permit. Detailed reconnaissance should be undertaken in any case to locate the position of the fortification with reference to other fortifications in order to determine their mutual supporting capabilities. Embrasures of the fortification to be attacked must be accurately located in order that assault plans may be formulated and that approach may be planned from blind positions.

Corps Trng Order #17-43, Hq V Amph Corps, 21 Dec 43--Contd.

The limited time of the weapon requires that coordination be carried out to the split second. This factor also prevents this weapon from being used as a weapon of opportunity.

(2) Flame-thrower personnel may be divided into two (2) categories, the first being engineer personnel equipped with organic flame throwers and trained in the use of this weapon in conjunction with engineer assault tactics. The second category includes those infantry or other arms personnel that may be equipped with the flame throwers for a specific operation.

In the case of Infantry personnel so equipped, it is currently recommended that these personnel, together with their assistants, be withdrawn from their basic unit and be organized into a flame-thrower squad or section to operate under the control of the landing team commander. This recommendation is based on the following premises:

  a. The weight of the flame thrower would retard progress in keeping up with infantry riflemen.

  b. The tactical limitation of the weapon with respect to targets.

  c. The problem of refueling.

  d. The hazard to surrounding personnel in the case of a hit by a tracer or incendiary bullet into the fuel tanks.

In the case of an amphibious operation, flame-thrower personnel may be utilized in the leading waves. Departure from standard procedure will, in this case, result, since no preliminary reconnaissance will be available and the weapons will, in most cases, be required to be used as a weapon of opportunity to force the beach. Commanding officers must caution the operators, as to the limited time available for fire and stress the importance of overcoming commensurate resistance. In placing flame-thrower personnel in the leading wave, commanding officers must consider the hazard to the entire boat should the flame thrower fuel tank be hit.

An assembly area should be designated for flame thrower personnel where they will reassemble should no opposition be encountered on the beach.

(1) <u>The Attack of a Fortified Position</u>:

The attack of a fortified position can best be accomplished by engineer assault tactics. Here, the flamethrower has its

Corps Trng Order #17-43, Hq V Amph Corps, 21 Dec 43--Contd.

principle tactical use, particularly in the reduction of permanent or semi-permanent emplacements.

The assault team employing flame-throwers to neutralize bunkers should include a minimum of two (2) flamethrower parties. In action against multi-embrasured bunkers, the number of flame-thrower parties should be increased. When possible the two parties should approach the objective with sufficient dispersion in their routes as to reduce the possibility that both parties will become casualties before reaching their objective. Another advantage is that fire coming from different directions should increase the degree of neutralization achieved. If the assault squad includes flame throwers to mop up a neutralized bunker, it should have attached at least one more flame thrower party for neutralization missions only.

Frequently an operator must approach a bunker without information as to its size, shape, and direction of embrasure openings. The possibility that it contains thin firing slits in addition to or in lieu of automatic weapons embrasures must not be ignored. Once the operator has made the best possible estimate of his target and the exact area of the target that must be covered, he should deliver his fire in one long burst. He must have sufficient training and experience to make an accurate estimate of the amount of fuel that will be required. Upon firing his burst (which may require emptying his complete fuel load in many cases) he should immediately move to whatever cover is available.

The operator must be instructed as to whether he is to achieve neutralization of embrasures only or whether he should attempt to empty his flame thrower into the bunker in an effort to secure complete reduction. Frequently, occasions will arise whereby complete reduction can only be accomplished by the final breeching of the emplacement with explosives. In this case, the flame thrower will be used to provide neutralization sufficient to cover the advance of the demolition party.

(m) Mopping up:

Secondary flame thrower missions can be readily accomplished by infantry personnel trained in flame throwing operations. For those operations the high degree of coordination required for assault tactics is not necessary.

Liquid fuel is best used for mopping-up tactics. To mop up a bunker the operator should approach as closely as practicable. Although satisfactory results may be obtained with gasoline up to four (4) yards, the most effective method is to actually place the flame gun into an opening. Once the stream of fuel is directed so

Corps Trng Order #17-43, Hq V Amph Corps, 21 Dec 43--Contd.

that the fuel is entering the bunker, the operator should discharge the contents of the flame thrower in one continuous burst. When possible, ignition of the fuel should be delayed until most of the fuel is discharged. If gasoline is used, the operator must protect himself in the event an explosion occurs.

*****

APPENDIX 15

HEADQUARTERS U. S. MARINE CORPS

THIS PAMPHLET IS APPROVED FOR USE AT TRAINING CENTERS AND
FOR DISTRIBUTION TO OTHER UNITS AS INFORMATION ONLY

NAVMC 1019-DPP

BASIC TACTICS FOR THE PORTABLE FLAME THROWER

APRIL, 1944

Prepared by

CHEMICAL WARFARE SCHOOL
TRAINING CENTER, CAMP ELLIOTT
SAN DIEGO, 44, CALIFORNIA

TABLE OF CONTENTS

I.	INTRODUCTION	1
II.	TYPES OF TARGETS AND METHODS OF ASSAULT	2

    A. Assaulting the Bunker or Pill Box 2
    B. Position in Brush or Undergrowth. 3
    C. Tanks and Other Armored Vehicles. 3
    D. Grouped Enemy Personnel 4
    E. Use as an Incendiary. 4

III. FUEL MIXTURES 4

    A. Pill Box or Tank Mixture. 4
    B. Brush Penetration Mixture 5
    C. Alternate Pill Box Mixture. 6
    D. An Incendiary Mixture 6

IV. PRESSURE CYLINDER AND HYDROGEN CYLINDER 6

    A. Pressure Cylinder 6
    B. Hydrogen Cylinder 7

V. SUPPLY AND SERVICING IN THE FIELD 7

VI. CONCLUSION 7

Pamphlet, Hq U.S. Mar Corps, Apr 44--

1. INTRODUCTION

   A. The flame thrower has become an important weapon in warfare. As an important weapon, it should be used to obtain the greatest effectiveness. To be effective in all missions prescribed for this weapon, basic tactics must be outlined and carried out. In general, these tactics should conform to basic infantry principles of fire and movement, as applied to the particular situation.

   B. The flame thrower is primarily an assault weapon. It is designed to knock out targets that are adequately protected from fire of other basic weapons. Therefore, the flame thrower should be used only on targets of this sort, and not on ones that can be put out of action by other weapons.

   C. Due to the comparatively short range of this weapon, it is necessary for the operator to get close to the target. He should have at least two riflemen or automatic riflemen supporting him directly on his approach to the target and his withdrawal after engaging the target. In addition, there should be a holding force with automatic rifles or light machine guns who will neutralize enemy supporting weapons where possible and pin down occupants of the target during the advance of the flame thrower team. The best use of natural cover should be taken, and when necessary smoke should be used to supply concealment for the advance and withdrawal.

   D. Since the time for firing one filling of fuel is limited to eight to twelve seconds it is imperative that the operator know the range and other firing characteristics of the fuel he is using. This will insure hitting the target with the first burst. The flame and smoke from a flame thrower indicate readily the location of the operator, and will undoubtedly draw heavy fire. It is, therefore, very important for the operator to hit the target with the first burst, and to rapidly change his position to avoid concentration of enemy fire.

   E. There are a number of types of targets that may be engaged effectively with the flame thrower. There is the pill box or bunker, or any well-protected fortification. There is the tank or any other armored vehicle. There is the concealed or camouflaged position in brush or undergrowth. Whatever the target may be, before attacking it reconnaissance should be carried out to determine enemy strength and location of

Pamphlet, Hq U.S. Mar Corps, Apr 44--Contd.

supporting positions. This may, of necessity, be very rapid, but in no case should it be neglected. From this reconnaissance, the flame thrower team may determine the number of flame throwers and strength of support necessary to accomplish the mission, and also the best routes of approach to the target. Methods of engaging the different types of targets are discussed below.

II. TYPES OF TARGETS AND METHODS OF ASSAULT

A. Assaulting the Bunker or Pill Box

1. In the assault on an enemy position, it must always be considered that this position is well fortified. The enemy will have pill boxes and bunkers which support each other by fire from the flanks and above, as well as from the front. There will probably be barbed wire, mine fields, anti-tank obstacles, and anti-tank guns. Bunkers and pill boxes invulnerable to small arms and most shell fire will be situated in positions to protect these defensive installations. However, these bunkers and pill boxes are vulnerable to flame thrower fire. It is the job of flame thrower operators to get into positions from which they can knock out these bunkers. In getting into position the supporting riflemen (or automatic riflemen) will be on either flank of the operator and protect him from snipers and other exposed enemy personnel. From another position the flame thrower operator should be supported by fire from automatic rifles or a light machine gun which will lay down a constant intermittent fire on firing apertures of the bunker until the operator is in position to use his flame thrower. Prior to the assault, shell fire and bombing will have made craters which will give the flame thrower operator some protection to his approach to a firing position. If cover and concealment is insufficient, WP smoke grenades carried by the supporting riflemen (or automatic riflemen) will be used to supply a smoke screen. These men should be trained in the proper use of these grenades, taking into consideration wind direction and velocity. If possible, the bunker should be approached from the rear, the flanks, or from a blind side. Reconnaissance will have determined the best approach. Care should be taken to protect against supporting fire from other bunkers and emplacements, as well as the one being attacked. If the bunker is fairly large, with several firing apertures, do not hesitate to use more than one flame thrower or to increase the support. It is usually wise to employ two or more flame throwers simultaneously from different positions. If one weapon does not function properly, the other or others will be able to accomplish the mission.

Pamphlet, Hq U.S. Mar Corps, Apr 44--Contd.

    2. When the flame thrower operator is in a position where he is certain to hit the bunker with the first burst he should spray the walls with fuel and follow with flame. This will cause fire and flame on the bunker obscuring the vision of the occupants, and allow the operator to fire more readily into the larger apertures. Since his first burst will expose him, he should immediately change his position if possible. To complete the annihilation of the occupants, the operator should put the nozzle of the gun directly into a firing aperture for one burst, so that all the fuel and flame will go within. <u>Do not waste fuel, when one burst will do the job, use only one burst. Save fuel for other targets that may appear.</u>

    3. If the bunker is not neutralized before the fuel of the flame thrower is exhausted, the operator should remain under cover, and withdraw at the first opportunity with the flame thrower. <u>The weapon should not be discarded when empty.</u> The supporting troops should cover the withdrawal of the operator. The operator will immediately report to a service station for refilling.

    4. When two or more flame throwers are being employed on one target, the operators may fire bursts according to a pre-arranged plan.

    5. If there is a defense perimeter with a number of pill boxes and bunkers, as many of these as possible should be attacked at the same time with flame thrower teams. This will prevent to a degree enemy efforts to support one fortified position by another.

B. <u>Positions in Brush or Undergrowth</u>

    1. In jungle warfare, the enemy is very likely to have concealed positions in brush or undergrowth. The flame thrower is a good weapon to burn out this brush, thus de-camouflaging and exposing to view concealed positions. The approach and support should be similar to that outlined above.

C. <u>Tanks and Other Armored Vehicles</u>

    1. A tank, or other armored vehicle, is one target that will be encountered on the defensive rather than in the attack as long as the operator is not mounted. An enemy, attack or counter attack in which he throws in tanks, may readily

Pamphlet, Hq U.S. Mar Corps, Apr 44--Contd.

be dealt with by use of flame throwers at close quarters to knock out the tanks. The operator should have his riflemen support as he did in assaulting the bunker. He should hit the tank with a burst of fuel followed by flame. This will cause burning fuel on the tank, heating and smoking up the tank interior and causing the occupants to abandon the tank. The supporting riflemen should pick off the occupants as they leave the tank. It is advisable to fire from a deep foxhole or other emplacement which provides protection from tanks. The first tank may be effectively knocked out, but the flame and smoke make a good target for other tanks to over run.

D. <u>Grouped Enemy Personnel</u>

1. Another possible target for the flame thrower is enemy personnel who are bunched up in a group especially during night attacks. It is a characteristic Japanese tactic to mass during an assault. Machine guns and other small arms fire are very effective against such an attack, but a few bursts from a flame thrower along with the other firing should have a definitely demoralizing effect on the enemy as well as causing actual casualties. If the flame thrower is used for this type of target, the operator must be careful not to open fire until sufficient number of the enemy are within range of his weapon. <u>It must be understood that the flame thrower is not a weapon to replace small arms fire</u> even at short ranges. Its primary mission is to penetrate targets that are not vulnerable to small arms fire.

E. Use as an <u>Incendiary</u>.

1. When an incendiary is needed to destroy material or buildings, the flame thrower has proved itself to be extremely rapid and effective. A burst of fuel on the target, followed by flame, will do the trick, setting practically any combustible material afire. Additional fuel may be fired on the target to hasten its destruction. However, if there is no great time factor involved, a bit of gasoline or kerosene and a match will do the same job and should be used. <u>Always remember to conserve fuel. Do not fire at just any target.</u> Then, when a target appears that demands the use of the flame thrower, there will be flame throwers available for the mission.

Pamphlet, Hq U.S. Mar Corps, Apr 44--Contd.

III. FUEL MIXTURES

    A. <u>Pill Box or Tank Mixture</u>

        1. This mixture has been found to be most effective for assaulting the pill box type of fortification and also the tank or other armored vehicle. It produces an extremely hot flame with a range of thirty-five to fifty yards. The fuel has a tendency to stick to the target, and will burn there for some time.

        2. Process of Mixing:

           a. Mix in forty gallon batches.

           b. Pump twenty gallons of gasoline into an open-end 50-55 gallon drum.

           c. Add ten gallons of diesel oil.

           d. Pump ten gallons of gasoline into a 10-gallon pail and add ten and one half pounds of Napalm Thickener. Stir this until an applesauce effect results.

           e. Immediately pour the above thickened gasoline into the open-end 50-55 gallon drum and stir the forty gallon mixture until a partial gel takes place. Be sure that the Napalm does not have a tendency to settle.

           f. When there is no longer a tendency to settle, transfer the mixture to a storage drum (closed 50-55 gallon drum) and allow it to age for at least twenty-four hours. The longer it ages, the more effective the mixture.

    B. <u>Brush Penetration Mixture</u>

        1. This mixture has been found effective for burning and clearing away brush which might be concealing an enemy position. It has a broader flame than the pill box mixture and a range of thirty to forty yards.

Pamphlet, Hq U.S. Mar Corps, Apr 44--Contd.

2. Process of mixing:

   a. Mix in forty-gallon batches.

   b. Pump ten gallons of gasoline and twenty gallons of diesel oil into an open-end 50-55 gallon drum.

   c. Fill a 10-gallon pail with gasoline and add ten and one half pounds of Napalm Thickener.

   d. Stir this mixture until an applesauce effect results.

   e. Pour this mixture into the open-end 50-55 gallon drum and stir until a partial gel results. Be sure that the Napalm shows no tendency to settle.

   f. Pour this mixture into a storage drum and allow it to age for at least twenty-four hours.

C. <u>Alternate Pill Box Mixture</u>

1. If there is no diesel oil available, this mixture is quite effective against pill boxes. The stream of fuel is quite narrow requiring more accurate marksmanship when fired. It sticks and burns on the target for some time, and has a range of thirty-five to fifty yards.

2. Process of Mixing:

   a. The process is similar to the above mixture. Mix ten and one half pounds of Napalm Thickener in twenty gallons of gasoline. Then add twenty more gallons of gasoline and stir until a partial gel takes place. Store for at least twenty-four hours.

D. <u>An Incendiary Mixture</u>

1. Any of the above mixtures may be used for incendiary purposes. However, if the flame thrower is to be used expressly for incendiary missions, a liquid fuel is better for the purpose than any of the thickened mixtures. The range is shorter with a pure liquid mixture, but the spray is broad and covers a larger target at once.

Pamphlet, Hq U.S. Mar Corps, Apr 44--Contd.

    2. This mixture is made up of not more than three fifths of strained crankcase draining, the remainder being diesel or light motor oil. If too large a part is crankcase drainings, a difficulty in igniting the fuel will result. The fuel upon being mixed is ready for use. No aging is necessary.

    3. In the absence of NaPalm Thickener, this mixture may be used for other missions. A mixture of four fifths strained crankcase drainings and one fifth gasoline will produce the same results. Range of both mixtures is fifteen to twenty yards.

IV. PRESSURE CYLINDER AND HYDROGEN CYLINDER

  A. Pressure Cylinder

    1. There will be used <u>only nitrogen</u> gas or <u>compressed air</u> in the <u>pressure cylinder</u>. Always use nitrogen when it is available. The use of other gases has resulted in explosions disastrous to the operators. Be careful not to put hydrogen in the pressure cylinder.

  B. <u>Hydrogen Cylinder</u>

    1. <u>Only hydrogen</u> will be used in the <u>hydrogen cylinder</u>. Other inflammable gases may cause an explosion or ruin the gas burner.

V. SUPPLY AND SERVICING IN THE FIELD

  A. The present allocation of flame throwers is based on one per rifle squad. This calls for nine to a rifle company or twenty-seven to an infantry battalion. The amount of equipment necessary to service twenty-seven flame throwers is heavy and bulky. The amount of equipment to service nine flame throwers is practically the same. It is therefore more practical to have a servicing unit in the battalion rather than in each company, even though it will take slightly more time for operators to refill at the battalion than in the company.

  B. The most effective fuel mixtures are thickened liquids which have high viscosity, and which do not pour readily. Fuel of this type must be pumped into the flame thrower,

Pamphlet, Hq U.S. Mar Corps, Apr 44--Contd.

and cannot be poured. However, straight liquid fuel mixtures may be poured from cans directly into the flame thrower. This type of fuel may be carried in five gallon cans directly with the units for refilling the flame throwers. The charged pressure and hydrogen cylinders are detachable and may also be carried by the units. Using a pure liquid fuel, it may be practical for units to carry it with them, doing away with the necessity of reporting to a battalion service station. However, it must be remembered that the thickened fuels are by far the most effective for all purposes except as an incendiary, and should be used when available.

VI. CONCLUSION

   A. The tactics outlined here are very basic. Units that make use of the flame thrower in battle will be confronted with innumerable targets under varying circumstances. Unit commanders will have to deal with them accordingly. These tactics may vary somewhat with experience evolving from wider use, and with the development of flame throwers mounted on tanks and other vehicles.

   B. The tactics herein outlined deal only with the portable flame thrower without consideration of any type of mounted flame thrower.

   C. Important Points to Remember:

      1. An effective flame thrower team is made up of the following:

         a. At least two flame thrower operators, armed with flame throwers.

         b. At least two riflemen or automatic riflemen (should be at least one automatic rifleman) per flame thrower for direct support. These men should be qualified flame thrower operators so that one of them can take the weapon in case the operator becomes a casualty. These men should carry WP smoke grenades.

      2. A flame thrower team should be supported by automatic rifles, light machine guns, or other weapons as the situation demands.

Pamphlet, Hq U.S. Mar Corps, Apr 44--Contd.

    3. Reconnaissance should be carried out prior to assaulting a target.

    4. It may be necessary for a wire cutting detail to precede the flame thrower team if wire obstacles have not been cleared by other means.

    5. A rocket detail may accompany the flame thrower team to assist in knocking out the target.

    6. It is advisable for a demolitions detail to follow the flame thrower team, in order that the target can be blown up to prevent reoccupation by the enemy.

D. Areas comprising a series of mutually supporting bunkers, and pill boxes arranged in accordance with usual Japanese practice for organized tactical localities should be constructed and training in demolitions and flame thrower operations should be intensified to the end that a minimum of delay will be entailed in assault and mop up operations against targets of this nature.

APPENDIX 16

HEADQUARTERS
3D MARINE DIVISION
FLEET MARINE FORCE
IN THE FIELD

16 December 1944

TRAINING ORDER)
       : Organization for Employment of Flame Throwers, Rocket
NUMBER...45-44) Launchers, and Demolition in the Infantry Battalion.

  1. <u>Pioneer and Ammunition Platoon</u>.

    a. In order to provide flexibility in the employment of flame throwers, rocket launchers, and Dmls in Inf Bns, a Pion and Am Plat will be organized in each Inf Bn and included in the Bn Hq Co. This will be effected immediately.

    b. The Plat will consist of twenty (20) men who will be drawn from the "Other duty" privates in R Cos and Bn Hq Co as follows:

      Six (6) per R Co.
      Two (2) per Bn Hq Co.

    c. All members of this Plat will be trained in the technique and Opn of flame throwers, rocket launchers, and Dmls, and their Tac employment. They will also be trained in the Maint and servicing of flame throwers.

    d. In addition, a Min of one (1) man per R Sqd will be trained in the Opn, Maint, and servicing of the flame thrower in order to provide a Repl for the regular Opr should he become a casualty.

    e. Personnel of the Pion and Am Plat will be armed with the Cbn. Twenty pistols, caliber .45, will be issued to the Plat, for further issue to individuals when they are actually carrying the flame thrower or rocket launcher.

  2. <u>Employment of Flame Throwers</u>.

    a. The Tac assignment of the flame throwers will be at the discretion of the Inf Bn Comdr, and will depend on the Tac situation. They are placed under his Contl so that he may at any time attach all or a portion of the flame throwers to either of his assault Cos.

Trng Order #45-44, Hq 3d Marine Div, Flt Mar Force, 16 Dec 44--Contd.

    b. Normally in a landing six (6) flame throwers will be assigned to each assault Co, to be used at the discretion of the Co Comdr. As soon as the situation indicates the lack of necessity for flame throwers they will be returned to Bn Contl.

    c. When maximum Spt by flame throwers is desired, the Inf Bn Comdr may have nine (9) flame throwers in Opn; nine (9) standing by to replace those in need of servicing and nine (9) being serviced at the Bn service unit. In the plan as outlined above, Oprs will be with the flame throwers actually in Opn and the flame throwers standing by. The Oprs returning to the Bn service unit with flame throwers to be serviced will pick up a serviced flame thrower and then move forward to the stand-by position.

    d. The flame throwers and servicing equipment will be transported under Bn Contl. Servicing of flame throwers will be accomplished by the Pion and Am Plat. Flame throwers and servicing equipment will be transported as far forward as the Tac-situation and the terrain permit. Forward of this they must be manhandled.

   3. <u>Employment of Rocket Launchers</u>.

    a. The AT Rocket Launchers will be carried in the Pion and Am Plat. This method is adopted in order to place under the direct Contl of the Bn Comdr a Wpn for the AT defense of the Bn. AT defense of the Cos is provided by the AT grenade and launcher which is carried in each fire Gp of the R Sqd.

    b. In a normal situation, and when not in use, the rocket launchers will be transported with the flame throwers under Bn Contl. This will facilitate the Mvmt and Am Sup for this Wpn.

    c. Disposition of rocket launchers will be at the discretion of the Bn Comdr. He may attach all or a portion of them to the Cos, or he may keep them under his Contl in order to best dispose them to meet hostile Tk Atks directed against the Bn. In a landing it will be normal to make attachments to assault Cos.

    d. A Min of two (2) men per R Plat will be trained in the Tech and Tac employment of the rocket launcher in addition to the Pion and Am Plat.

   4. <u>Employment of Demolitions</u>.

    a. One (1) Dml kit will be assigned to each R Plat to be carried by the Plat Dml Corp.

Trng Order #45-44, Hq 3d Mar Div, Flt MarForce, 16 Dec 44--Contd.

    b. One (1) additional kit per R Co will be carried by the Co. Dml Sgt.

    c. The fifteen (15) remaining Dml kits of the Bn will be transported in the Pion and Am Plat, and Repl kits furnished each Co as required.

    d. The Pion and Am Plat will prepare and Trans thirty (30) pole charges, ten (10) per R Co, to be issued as required.

    e. Nine (9) lengths of Bangalore Torpedo, three (3) per R Co, will be transported by the Pion and Am Plat. to be issued as required.

    f. In an assault landing each R Sqd may carry one (1) pole charge. If these charges are not used they will, on order of the Bn Comdr, be collected by the Pion and Am Plat and retained for future use.

    g. A Min of one (1) man per R Sqd will be trained in Dmls in addition to the Pion and Am Plat.

    5. It is emphasized that the organization of the Pion and Am Plat and the normal retention under Bn Contl of the flame thrower, AT Rocket Launcher, and the bulk of the Dml equipment is designed to provide maximum flexibility in the employment of these Wpn. It is the responsibility of the Bn Comdr to provide units of his Bn with the necessary means to carry out the missions he assigns them. If the Bn Comdr's Info indicates that the right assault Co will encounter numerous hostile bunkers or pill-boxes in a projected Atk, while the left assault Co will be opposed by few, if any, he should attach the bulk of the flame throwers, AT Rocket Launchers, and Dmls to the right assault Co. In addition to flexibility in employment, retention under Bn Contl favors servicing and Maint of flame throwers and Maint of AT Rocket Launchers. It also reduces wear and tear on the flame thrower Opr by transporting the flame thrower when not needed in Opns.

    BY COMMAND OF MAJOR GENERAL ERSKINE:

    R. E. HOGABOOM,
    Colonel, U. S. Marine Corps,
    Chief of Staff.

DISTRIBUTION:
C plus CG	G-3
ADC	G-4
C of S	Ordnance Officer
G-1	Adjutant
G-2	Rec Sec

OFFICIAL:

A. H. BUTLER,
Colonel, USMC
ACofS, G-3.

APPENDIX 17

HEADQUARTERS
3D MARINE DIVISION
FLEET MARINE FORCE
IN THE FIELD

19 December 1944

TRAINING ORDER)
) : Tactical Employment of Flame Throwers.
NUMBER...50-44)

1. GENERAL.

    a. The following Tac doctrine will be adopted and followed by all Inf units of this Div.

    b. The tactics outlined here are very Bsc. Units that make use of the flame thrower in battle will be confronted with innumerable targets under varying circumstances, and unit Comdrs will have to deal with them accordingly. These tactics may vary somewhat with experience derived from wider use, but should conform to the Bsc Inf principles of fire and Mvmt.

2. CHARACTERISTICS.

    a. The flame thrower is primarily an assault Wpn. It is designed to destroy targets that are adequately protected from the fire of other Bsc Wpn. Therefore, the flame thrower should be used only on targets which cannot be put out of action with other Wpn.

    b. Due to the comparatively short Rg of this Wpn, it is necessary for the Opr to get close to the target. He should have at least one BAR team in direct Spt during his approach and withdrawal. In addition, there should be a holding force with Auto rifles or LMGs to neutralize enemy supporting Wpn where possible, by pinning down occupants of the position during the Adv of the Flame thrower Opr. The maximum use of natural cover should be made, and when necessary, smoke should be used to provide concealment for the Adv and withdrawal.

    c. The time for firing one filling of fuel is limited to a period of eight to twelve seconds, therefore, it is imperative that the Opr know the Rg and other firing characteristics of the fuel he is using to insure hitting the target with the first burst. The flame and smoke from a flame thrower readily indicates the location of the Opr, and will undoubtedly draw Hv fire. Thus it is necessary to hit

Trng Order #50-44, Hq 3d Mar Div, Flt Mar Foe, 19 Dec 44--Contd.

the target with the first burst, and rapidly change position to avoid Conc of enemy fire.

3. TYPES OF TARGETS.

    a. Targets that may be effectively engaged by flame throwers are as follows:

        (1) Emplacements.

        (2) Tks, or other Armed vehicles.

        (3) Positions in brush or undergrowth.

4. RECONNAISSANCE.

    a. Before attacking any target a Rcn must be made to determine the enemy strength, and the location of supporting positions. This may, of necessity, be very rapid, but in no case should it be neglected. From this Rcn the unit Ldr will determine the No of flame throwers, and the strength of the Spt necessary to accomplish the mission, and the best routes of approach to the target.

5. METHODS OF ASSAULT.

    a. <u>Assault of the Emplacement.</u>

        (1) In the assault of an enemy position, it must always be considered that this position is well fortified. The enemy will have Empls mutually supporting, and will, in addition, have snipers in trees covering defiladed routes to the position.

        (2) The flame thrower Opr, in covering the Adv of the Dml man, sprays the walls of the Empl with fuel and then with flame. This will set fire to the fortifications thereby obscuring the vision of the occupants, and allow the Opr to fire more readily into the larger apertures. Since his first burst will expose him, he should immediately change his position. When the Dml man is not available, the Opr will place the nozzle of the gun directly into a firing aperture for one burst, so that all the fuel and flame will be forced inside, annihilating the occupants.

        (3) To accomplish the mission stated above, the flame thrower Opr will be supported by the assault and fire Spt team in accordance with Training Order 51-44. (Assault and Reduction of Empls).

Trng Order #50-44, Hq 3d Mar Div, Flt Mar Fce, 19 Dec 44--Contd.

(4) Prior to the assault, shell fire and bombing will have made craters which will give the flame thrower Opr some protection on his approach to a firing position. If cover and concealment is insufficient, WP smoke grenades carried by the assault team will be used to provide a smoke screen. If possible, the Empl should be approached from the rear, the flanks, or from the blind side. Rcn will have determined the best approach.

(5) If the Empl is fairly large, with a No of firing apertures, several flame throwers should be used. It is usually best to employ two or more flame throwers simultaneously from different positions. If one weapon does not function properly, the other, or others, will be able to accomplish the mission. Oprs may alternate firing according to a prearranged plan.

(6) If the Empl is not neutralized before the fuel of the flame thrower is exhausted, the Opr should remain under cover and withdraw at the first opportunity with the flame thrower, and another Opr with flame thrower should replace him and continue the assault. The assault and fire Spt teams cover the withdrawal of the Opr, and the Opr will upon disengagement immediately report to the Bn service unit and exchange the empty flame thrower for a serviced one.

(7) Where an enemy defensive position consists of a number of mutually supporting Empls, as many of these as possible, should be simultaneously attacked with flame throwers. This will prevent, to some degree, enemy efforts to Spt one Empl from another.

b. <u>Assault of Position in Brush or Undergrowth</u>.

(1) In jungle warfare, the enemy is very likely to have concealed positions in brush or undergrowth. The flame thrower is a good Wpn to burn out this brush, thus exposing to view concealed positions. The approach and Spt should be similar to that outlined above.

c. <u>Assault of Tks and Other Armd Vehicles</u>.

(1) A Tk, or other Armd vehicle, is one target that will be encountered in the defense rather than in the Atk, as long as the flame thrower Opr is not mounted. An enemy Atk, or counterattack, in which Tks are employed, may readily be dealt with by use of flame throwers at close Rg to destroy the Tks.

(2) The Opr should be supported in the same manner as in the assault of an Empl. He should spray the Tk with a burst of fuel followed by flame. This will cause burning fuel on the Tk, heating

Trng Order #50-44, Hq 3d Mar Div, Flt Mar Fce, 19 Dec 44--Contd.

and smoking the Tk interior, and force the occupants to abandon the Tk. The supporting riflemen should pick off the occupants as they leave the Tk.

(3) The Opr should fire from a deep foxhole, or other Empl which provides protection from Tks, since, although the first TK may be effectively destroyed, others will bring fire to bear on the Opr.

6. MISCELLANEOUS USES

  a. Against Enemy Personnel.

(1) Another possible target for the flame thrower is enemy personnel who are bunched, especially during night Atks. It is characteristic of the Japanese to mass during an assault. Mg and other SA fire is very effective against such an Atk, and a few bursts from a flame thrower, in addition, will have a definite demoralizing effect on the enemy as well as causing him actual casualties. If the flame thrower is used for this type of target, the Opr must be careful not to open fire until a sufficient No of the enemy are within Rg of his Wpn. It must be understood that the flame thrower is not a Wpn to replace SA fire even at short Rg. Its primary mission is to destroy targets that are not vulnerable to SA fire.

  b. As an incendiary.

(1) When an incendiary is needed to destroy material or buildings, the flame thrower may be used. A burst of fuel on the target, followed by flame, will set practically any combustible material afire. Additional fuel may be fired on the target to hasten its destruction. However, if time is not a factor, some gasoline or kerosene and a match will accomplish the same mission and should be used. Always remember to conserve fuel. Do not fire at just any target.

7. SUPPLY AND SERVICING IN THE FIELD.

  a. The present allocation of flame throwers is based on twenty-seven (27) to an Inf Bn. The servicing equipment will be transported by the Pion and Am Plat of the Bn Hq Co. Reservicing of all flame throwers will be accomplished by the Pion and Am Plat.

  b. The most effective fuel mixtures are thickened liquids which have high viscosity, and which do not pour readily. Fuel of this type must be pumped into the flame thrower, and cannot be poured. However, straight liquid fuel mixtures may be poured from cans directly

Trng Order #50-44, Hq 3d Mar Div, Flt Mar Fce, 19 Dec 44--Contd.

into the flame thrower. This type of fuel may be carried in five gallon cans directly with the unit for refilling the flame throwers. However, it must be remembered that the thickened fuels are by far the most effective for all purposes except as an incendiary, and should be used when available.

8. SUMMARY.

    a. Important Points to Remember:

        (1) An effective flame thrower team is made up of the following:

            (a) At least two flame thrower Oprs armed with flame throwers.

            (b) At least one BAR team for direct Spt.

            (c) At least one man of the assault team should be a qualified flame thrower Opr so that in case the flame thrower Opr becomes a casualty, a Repl is immediately available.

        (2) Rcn should be carried out prior to assaulting a target.

        (3) The flame thrower must cover the approach of the Dml man to the Empl.

        (4) Maximum use of natural cover must be made by the flame thrower Oprs.

    b. Training in the Tac Employment of the Flame Thrower.

        A fortified position should be constructed by all units, and training in the Tac employment of flame throwers should be intensified so that in combat a Min of delay will be entailed in the assault and mopping-up Opns against defenses of this nature.

                      BY COMMAND OF MAJOR GENERAL ERSKINE:

                            R. E. HOGABOOM,
                        Colonel, U. S. Marine Corps,
                            Chief of Staff.

DISTRIBUTION: B, F and D partial (CG   G-2)
              A. H. BUTLER   (ADC G-3)
              Colonel, USMC,   (CofS G-4)
OFFICIAL: AC of S, G-3.   (G-1 adj)

APPENDIX 18

HEADQUARTERS FIFTH ARMY
A. P. O. #464, U. S. Army

5 April 1944

TRAINING MEMORANDUM)
                   :
NUMBER   8)

TECHNIQUE AND TACTICAL USE OF FLAMETHROWERS

    1. <u>Portable Flamethrowers</u>. Flamethrower, portable, M1A1 is the present standard. This model is described completely as to mechanical construction and operation in TM 3-375, dated May 1943. The portable flamethrower M1 is obsolete and any weapons of this model on hand should be turned in to the nearest CWS depot. An improved portable flamethrower (the E-3) will shortly be available as CWS Class IV supply for special operations when required. This model ignites the oil stream by means of a slow burning flare cartridge in the nozzle instead of a stream of burning hydrogen. Consequently, the E-3 eliminates filling and supply of hydrogen cylinders and electric batteries, but requires an ignition cylinder for each ten shots. A descriptive pamphlet comes in each chest. The M1A1 and the E-3 models each will discharge nearly four (4) gallons of fuel in ten seconds total operating time.

    2. <u>Tank Mounted Flamethrower E-4 and E-5</u>. The E-4 has a capacity of 16 gallons of fuel. This model is designed for mounting on a light tank. The flame gun displaces the machine gun in this mount. The E-5 flamethrower is designed for mounting in Medium tanks. It is somewhat larger than the E-4. These flamethrowers will be available in the near future as Class IV Army CWS supplies for special operations.

    3. <u>Pressure, Fuel and Range</u>. The range depends upon size and construction of the nozzle, the gas pressure used, and the type and amount of thickening used in the fuel. Ordinary truck (80 octane) gasoline thickened by adding two (2) packages (10 lbs.) of NaPalm thickener to 50 gallons of gasoline should be used except in very hot weather when three (3) packages should be used. This gives fuel the appearance and feel of "applesauce". More thickener will give greater range but less vigor of burning. An operating pressure of about 350 pounds per square inch in the fuel

Trng Memo #8, Hq Fifth Army, 5 Apr 44--Contd.

tanks is needed for best results. A pressure of about 1500 pounds is carried in the pressure cylinder. The reducing valve regulates the operating pressure in the fuel tanks. Against the wind ranges are reduced. With the wind the range is increased. With a clean nozzle and 350 pounds pressure the following ranges and flame characteristics can be obtained in still air.

Fuel	Flame Characteristics	Effective range in Yards
Mixed gasoline & fuel oil	Big bright flame. Much black smoke.	15
"Applesauce" gasoline. (2 pkgs NaPalm per 50 gallons of gasoline)	Bright narrow flame in air. Fuel mostly on target. Little smoke.	40
Hard jelly-like gasoline (5 pkgs Napalm in 50 gallons of gasoline)	Like a burning rod in air. Slow burning on the target.	50 - 60

4. <u>Technique</u>. a. Always fire the flamethrower in short bursts of about two seconds each and allow a second between shots for the pressure to build up in the fuel cylinder. This gives uniform range and effective flame.

b. The flame-man should be within easy range of the target before opening fire. He should give the target one or two shots of oil without fire. This gets the target wetted down with gasoline and is called "basting". Then a third shot should be delivered with flame whereupon the gasoline already on the target takes fire and, aided by the heat of the flame from the weapon, envelopes the target in an intensely hot swirling flame. This technique is known as "Basting before baking".

5. <u>Suitable Targets</u>. The flamethrower is a short ranged weapon. It's principal value is to "shoot through cracks and around the corner" when other and lighter weapons can not accomplish the job. <u>The flamethrower is a special operation weapon</u>. Suitable uses are as follows:

Trng Memo #8, Hq Fifth Army, 5 Apr 44--Contd.

    a. For clearing out rooms and barricades in street fighting.

    b. For close attacks on bunkers and pill boxes.

    c. For defense against tanks from slit trenches.

    d. For use when mounted on tanks in clearing personnel out of trenches and buildings.

    e. For morale effect on green or inexperienced troops.

6. <u>Tactical Use</u>. a. The flame-man must be protected until he reaches his target and hits it with flame. <u>Alone he is helpless.</u> He is weighted down with a load of fifty pounds. He must get within grenade range of the enemy in order to be effective. Therefore the flame-man, whether armed with a portable model on his back or an E-4 model mounted in a M-IV tank, must be protected during his advance to the target; during his action; and afterward. Two flame-men should always work together and these two men must be part of a trained team. Eight men are recommended as a standard team. This team should be made up of one NCO and 1 rifle grenadier, four (4) riflemen and two (2) flame-men.

    b. The following sketch illustrates three steps in a type attack on Japanese bunkers and pill boxes in Guadalcanal area that proved successful:

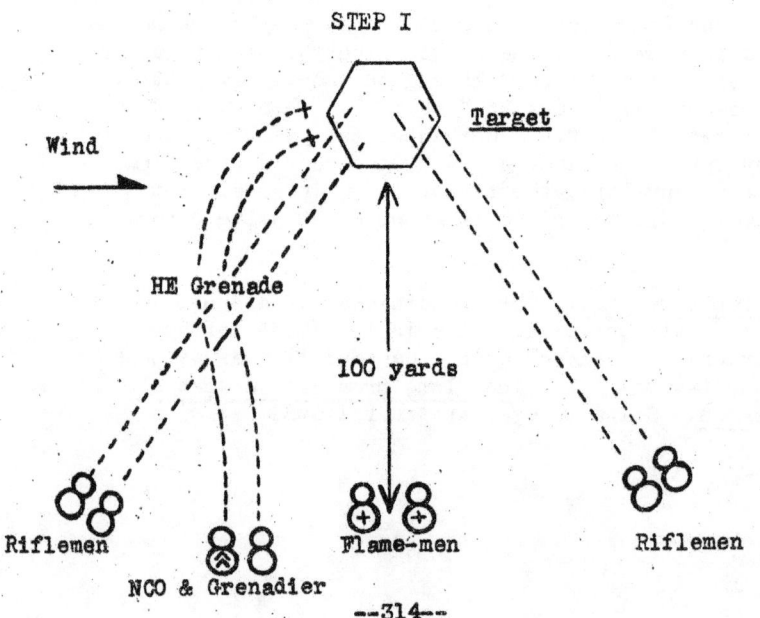

Trng Memo #8, Hq Fifth Army, 5 Apr 44--Contd.

STEP II

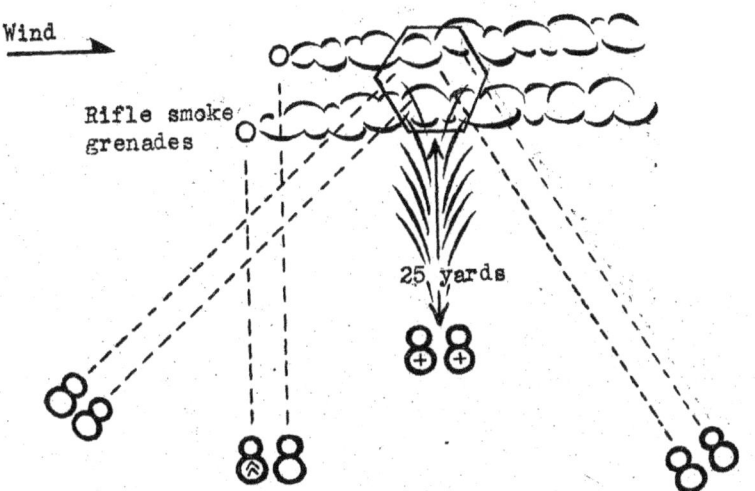

Note: Rifle fire switched to the flanks as soon as the pill box is enveloped in flame.

STEP III

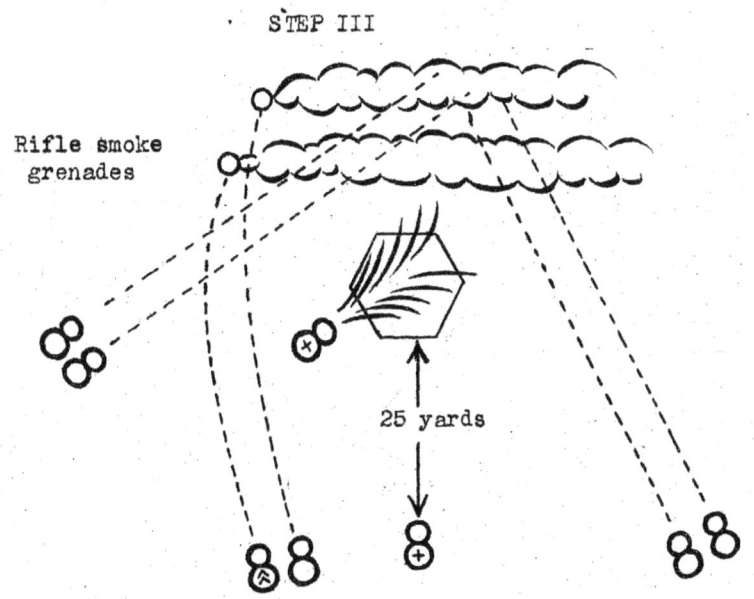

NOTE: (see next page)

Trng Memo #8, Hq Fifth Army, 5 Apr 44--Contd.

    NOTE: In this way your team advances the last flame-man to a point where he can kill all the members of the defending force who are left in the pill box by inserting the nozzle of the flamethrower in an opening and burning out the interior. You can then use this fort for your own purpose since it is not destroyed.

    7. <u>Tank Mounted Flamethrowers</u>. a. The following description from a report by VI Corps indicates the standard German tactics of attacking a ground position with flame-throwing tanks as part of the attack team. Note that in this case the flamethrowing tanks are "just members of the team".

    b. "The 3 Mark IV tanks moved forward, shelled and machine-gunned the position at 50 yards range. The enemy infantry platoon was equipped with machine pistols during this action and moved forward together with the armored vehicles. When our troops attempted to withdraw from the sector the flamethrowing tanks joined the action. They were used intermittently over a thirty (30) minute period and were said to have a range of approximately 30 yards."

    By command of Lieutenant General CLARK:

                                           A. M. GRUENTHER,
                                         Major General, G.S.C.,
                                             Chief of Staff.

OFFICIAL:

    /S/ D. W. Brann

        D. W. BRANN,
        Brig. Gen., GSC,
        AC of S, G-3.

DISTRIBUTION:
    "D"
American and French Troops only
Plus G-3 (10)
     CWS (20)

APPENDIX 19

Hq ETOUSA

Training Memo 33 6 Oct 1943

SECTION I. Aircraft Recognition Training (Ground Troops).
SECTION II. Portable Flame Thrower.

******

II--PORTABLE FLAME THROWER

1. PURPOSE. The purpose of this memo is to assist the unit commander in the training of his personnel in the tactical employment and technical operation of the portable flame thrower. This memorandum contains material which has recently become available and which supplements the WD publications listed in Par 6.

2. TACTICAL USE. a. General. Many new tactics and techniques for the use of the flame thrower have been developed since it was first introduced by the Germans in 1915. However, the flame thrower is still a short range weapon primarily useful for close combat. While it has some application on the defense it is essentially an offensive weapon. The greatest advantages of the flame thrower, however, over other weapons are its demoralizing effect on enemy morale and its ability to "shoot round corners". For example, when neutralizing a pill box, flame and burning fuel can be directed into embrasures from positions in the dead area of the pill box.

b. Against Enemy Troops. The horrifying effect of flame throwers on the morale of the enemy cannot be overlooked, but it must be recognized that this effect will be greatly reduced against properly trained or battle experienced troops. In the open, casualties are caused only when the burning fuel actually reaches the enemy personnel; in closed emplacements casualties through burns and suffocation may be caused without direct contact with the fuel. Flame throwers are not especially effective against tanks although at close range it is sometimes possible to blind the driver and set fire to the engine and rubber parts, especially those on the wheels and tracks. Combustible enemy shelters of all sorts can be set on fire and the metal parts of the enemy's weapons can be made too hot to handle.

c. Against Enemy Fortifications. The most important single use of the flame thrower is the neutralization of pill boxes and other fortifications. The flame and fuel when directed into the ports and embrasures is temporarily effective in putting the emplacement out of action by forcing the defenders to close the ports or evacuate the pill box. In some cases it will make casualties of all

Trng Memo #33, ETOUSA, 6 Oct 1943, contd.

occupants. The flame throwers must have the protection of frontal fire and/or smoke from their assault team during their advance to engage the pillbox. The flame thrower in turn gives protection to the demolition party which places pole or "satchel" charges in the embrasures when the defenders are forced from their weapons.

d. Other uses. Flame throwers are especially useful in mopping up operations where they facilitate cleaning out slit trenches and other prepared positions. In street fighting they can be used to supplement hand grenades in eliminating snipers from cellars and buildings.

3. TECHNIQUE. a. Team. A 3-man team is normally used with each flame thrower. The operator and assistant usually advance together to the objective. The refill carrier follows the assault team by bounds using available cover. This procedure provides an immediate replacement should the operator become a casualty, and provides a second replacement--the refill carrier--should both the operator and assistant become casualties. In assault landings, space restrictions may make a 2-man team necessary.

b. Surprise. Surprise is essential. A forewarned enemy is a prepared enemy and much of the effectiveness of the flamethrower is lost. German soldiers have been instructed that the best defense against flame throwers is to shoot the operators. Because the operator with the bulky and easily recognizable pack is an obvious and valuable target to the enemy, he must conceal his advance. Full use must be made of cover, craters and other natural means of concealment. Camouflage suits should be worn if possible and hands and faces colored with paint or mud. In defense surprise is equally important. Because of the short range, ambush and concealment are necessary to the successful employment of the flame thrower.

c. Fire Cover. The technique of covering the flame thrower party by an effective fire and/or smoke cover is one that cannot be avoided if the operation is to be a success. One recently developed technique involves the use of the rocket launcher which continues to fire at the embrasures after direct fire has been lifted. Once the flame thrower gets his first burst on the target he is master of the situation and is able to provide the necessary cover for the demolition party in their advance. It must be remembered, however, that his charge will be used up in a very short time and that the demolition party will have to work very quickly. The men of the demolition party must take over the operation of the flame thrower if all of its members become casualties. Signals between flame thrower operator

Trng Memo #33, ETOUSA, 6 Oct 1943, Contd.

and demolition men must be arranged so that the demolition men are ready to place their charges immediately after the flame thrower has been discharged.

4. TRAINING METHODS. a. Scope. A minimum of two 3-men teams for each authorized flame thrower should be trained in all phases of the repair, maintenance, operation and employment of the equipment. Thorough training is essential to the success of battle use of the flame thrower. Certain aspects of maintenance and operation not covered in WD publications listed in Par 6 are discussed in the following sub-paragraphs.

b. Early Training. Initial stages of training should be conducted using water and 5% cutting oil (or light lubricating oil) in the fuel tanks. The hydrogen cylinder and battery are not used. The use of water permits personnel to become acquainted with the mechanisms and "feel" of the equipment with greater safety and economy. The gun should not be pointed at individuals. The water is ejected under considerable pressure and may cause serious injury at distances as great as 10 yards. After use with water the entire Flame Thrower assembly must be carefully cleaned and dried. Flushing with gasoline will assist in the drying.

c. Accuracy. Accuracy with the equipment is a prime essential and emphasis must be placed on training operators to estimate distances and ranges of their flame throwers accurately. Targets consisting of slit trenches (real or painted on the ground) and enemy "emplacements" made of earth, corrugated iron or other material may be set up to lend reality to advance training. The "emplacements" must have real or represented gun slits and embrasures if they are to be satisfactory. In this connection the paramount importance of conserving fuel and maintaining the fuel supplies must be installed. A complete charge will fire for only 12 to 15 seconds; every burst must count and fuel must not be wasted. Short bursts of one to two seconds are most effective. The effect of wind must be considered. Best results are obtained with or against the wind; cross winds break up and disperse the rod of the fuel. As the contents are discharged the gun should be raised to maintain the range.

d. Wearing Equipment. Training is required to enable each man of the team to remove the equipment from a fallen operator and do it quickly for action. Personnel should be trained to wear the pack straps tight. If the pack is loose serious head injuries will result when the operator assumes a prone position.

e. Combined Training. The flame thrower party must be trained how to make the most use of the fire from the cover party without exposing

Trng Memo #33, ETOUSA, 6 Oct 1943, Contd.

itself to this friendly fire. The demolition team must be ready to place their charges when the flame thrower has been discharged at the embrasure. The flame throwing and demolition parties must be trained in each other's jobs in the event that either party becomes casualties before the mission is completed. Coordination of these three parties can be achieved only thru thorough, realistic combined training.

f. <u>Care of Equipment</u>. Equipment which is dirty or otherwise improperly maintained will fail when most needed. A flame thrower is valueless if it does not function at the exact instant it is wanted; there is seldom opportunity for a second try. Men must be taught the importance of constant care of their equipment.

g. <u>Safety Precautions</u>. Because of the danger attending training with the flame thrower, discipline must be strictly observed. The rule that a gun, loaded or unloaded, should never be pointed at anyone but the enemy applies particularly to the flame thrower. The fuel, of a highly inflammable nature, must be handled with caution and respect. Equipment which fails to function properly or appears defective should be referred to chemical warfare officers immediately.

5. TECHNICAL DATA. a. <u>Fuel</u>. As a result of numerous trials with thickened flame thrower fuels, fuel K M1A1 (British "FRAS") has been adopted as the thickened fuel for use in this theater. It is not contemplated that other fuels such as Diesel oil, fuel oil or blends with their reduced range will be used. Fuel K is ready for use as received; it is poured directly from the shipping container into the flame thrower. However, no moisture must be allowed in the fuel or the flame thrower. The Kit, Fuel Mixing, M1A1, is no longer necessary as no special mixing equipment is required with this fuel.

b. <u>Pressure Adjustment</u>. In order to obtain the maximum performance from fuel K it has been found necessary to readjust the pressure regulating valve on the M1A1 flame thrower from approximately 375 lbs per square inch to 275-300 lbs per square inch. The M1A1 service kit and fuel pressure cylinders (nitrogen cylinders---2000 lbs per square inch) are required in making the readjustment. The procedure is as follows:

(1) The flame thrower is first assembled as if for use but without fuel. The pressure gauge (from the service kit) is substituted for the normal fuel tank cover. The brass cover plate held in place by two pins is then carefully removed with the aid of a small screw driver or knife blade from the pressure regulating screw of the reduction valve. The hexagonal socket wrench is used to adjust the pressure regulating screw; lowering the screw (turning it clockwise) increases

Trng Memo #33, ETOUSA, 6 Oct 1943, Contd.

the pressure setting and raising it (turning it counter clockwise) reduces the pressure.

(2) The cylinder valve is then opened so that there is pressure in the fuel tank. By operating the gun valve and observing the pressure gauge it will be possible to obtain the desired pressure by adjusting the pressure regulating screw. When the gun valve is opened the gauge pressure will drop somewhat but should return from 275 to 300 lbs per square inch when the valve is closed. After adjustment, pressure setting should be checked in actual operation but with the pressure gauge attached to see that the pressure returns to the proper level after each of a number of bursts. Short bursts are best although a burst of about 3 seconds when the tank is filled will indicate whether or not the reducing valve is functioning properly.

(3) After final readjustment the brass cover plate is replaced. It may be necessary to drill out the old pins and replace them with new ones or with small machine screws. The flame thrower should then be marked "Regulating Valve Reset 300 lbs" and a record made of its serial number.

c. Cleaning. Each time the flame thrower is refilled, it is advisable to clean out the 20 hydrogen orifices in the burner, using a wire, stiff straw, or thin nail. These small holes tend to clog when the flame thrower is "blown down" after all fuel has been fired.

d. Hydrogen. In combat the hydrogen cylinder should be changed every time the flame thrower is refilled. For training purposes, however, it is quite possible to obtain satisfactory ignition for two fillings of the flame thrower with one hydrogen cylinder, and this economy is desirable wherever possible.

e. Pack Carrier Refill. A portable pack carrier which contains everything required for one complete refill has been developed. It has been standardized and will be available for issue soon. It consist of a pack board, 5-gallon "Jerrican" for Fuel K, hydrogen cylinder, nitrogen cylinder, pouch and necessary wrenches. The Hydrogen and Nitrogen Cylinders are obtained from the refill Kit M1A1 (see App 1). A pack weighs approximately the same as the filled flame thrower and permits re-charging of the equipment by two men in three to five minutes. Thus, in fact, the fire power of each flame thrower is nearly doubled.

6. REFERENCES. a. Current Publications. The following WD publications contain material describing the flame thrower and its operations:
        TM 3-375 "Portable Flame Throwers, M1-M1A1."
        TC No. 33 "Attack on a Fortified Position,"
                Mar 1943.

Trng Memo #33, ETOUSA, 6 Oct 1943, Contd.

b. **Proposed Publications.** Advance information received from the WD indicates that a new FM 5-16 "Attack of a Fortified Position" is being prepared. FM 100-5 "Operations" is being revised and will contain information of the employment of flame throwers. (AG 470 PubGC)

                    By command of Lieutenant General DEVERS:

                                    I. H. EDWARDS,
                            Major General, GSC, Chief of Staff.

OFFICIAL:
      s/ RALPH PULSIFER (B.T.S.)
      t/ RALPH PULSIFER,
Colonel, AGD, Adjutant General.   DISTRIBUTION: "B"
REPRODUCED HQ SOS 9 Oct 1943   DISTRIBUTION: "C" less
                                                            Non-SOS

M.H.E. /I/ M.H.E.

APPENDIX 20

HEADQUARTERS
EUROPEAN THEATER OF OPERATION
UNITED STATES ARMY

5 April 1944

TRAINING MEMORANDUM:

NUMBER   10:

I - PORTABLE FLAME THROWER

1. RESCISSION. Sec II, Training Memo 33, 6 Oct 1943, is rescinded.

2. TACTICAL USE. a. General. Many new tactics and techniques for the use of the flame thrower have been developed since it was first introduced by the Germans in 1915. However, the flame thrower is still a short range weapon primarily useful for close combat. While it has some application on the defense it is essentially an offensive weapon. The greatest advantages of the flame thrower, however, over other weapons are its demoralizing effect on the enemy and its ability to "shoot round corners." For example, when neutralizing a pill box, flame and burning fuel can be directed into embrasures from positions in the dead area of the pill box.

   b. Against Enemy Troops. The depressive effect of flame throwers on the morale of the enemy cannot be overlooked, but it must be recognized that this effect is greatly reduced when the weapon is used against properly trained or battle experienced troops. In the open, casualties are caused only when the burning fuel actually reaches the enemy personnel; in closed emplacements casualties through burns and suffocation may be caused without direct contact with the fuel. Flame throwers are not especially effective against tanks, although at close range it is sometimes possible to blind the driver and set fire to the engine and rubber parts, especially those on the wheels and tracks. Combustible enemy shelters of all sorts can be set on fire and the metal parts of the enemy's weapons can be made too hot to handle.

   c. Against Enemy Fortifications. The most important single use of the flame thrower is the neutralization of pill boxes and other fortifications. The flame and fuel, when directed into the ports and embrasures, is temporarily effective in putting the emplacement out of action by forcing the defenders to close the ports or evacuate the pill box. In some cases it will make casualties of all the occupants. The flame throwers must have the protection of frontal fire and/or smoke from their assault team during their advance to engage the pillbox.

Trng Memo #10, Hq ETO, USA, 5 Apr 1944--Contd.

The flame thrower in turn gives protection to the demolition party which places pole or "satchel" charges in the embrasures when the defenders are forced from their weapons.

    d. <u>Other uses</u>. Flame throwers are especially useful in mopping up operations where they facilitate cleaning out slit trenches and other prepared positions. In street fighting they can be used to supplement hand grenades in eliminating snipers from cellars and building.

3. <u>TECHNIQUE</u>. a. <u>Team</u>. A 3-man team is normally used with each flame thrower. The operator and assistant usually advance together to the objective. The refill carrier follows the assault team by bounds, using available cover. This procedure provides an immediate replacement should the operator become a casualty, and provides a second replacement (the refill carrier) should both the operator and the assistant become casualties. In assault landings, space restrictions may make a 2-man team necessary.

    b. <u>Surprise</u>. Surprise is essential. A forwarned enemy is a prepared enemy and much of the effectiveness of the flame thrower is lost. German soldiers have been instructed that the best defense against flame throwers is to shoot the operators. Because the operator with the bulky and easily recognizable pack is an obvious and valuable target to the enemy, he must conceal his advance. Full use must be made of cover, craters and other natural means of concealment. Camouflage suits should be worn, if possible, and hands and faces colored with paint or mud. In defense surprise is equally important. Because of the short range, ambush and concealment are necessary to the successful employment of the flame thrower.

    c. <u>Fire Cover</u>. The technique of covering the flame thrower party by an effective fire and/or smoke cover is one that cannot be avoided if the operation is to be a success. One recently developed technique involves the use of the rocket launcher which continues to fire at the embrasures after direct fire has been lifted. Once the flame thrower gets his first burst on the target he is master of the situation and is able to provide the necessary cover for the demolition party in its advance. It must be remembered, however, that his charge will be used up in a very short time and that the demolition party will have to work very quickly. Rifle smoke grenades can be employed under the control of the assault team commander in order to provide a smoke cover for the advance of the flame thrower operator (or operators and demolition party) so that the flame thrower operator can employ his weapon against the embrasures or weapon slits and the demolition party can be ready to place their charges. The men of the demolition party must take over the operation

Trng Memo #10, Hq ETO, USA, 5 Apr 1944--Contd.

of the flame thrower, if all of its members become casualties. Signals between the flame thrower operator and the demolition must be arranged so that the latter are ready to place their charges immediately after the flame thrower has been discharged.

4. TRAINING METHODS. a. Scope. A minimum of two 3-men teams for each authorized flame thrower should be trained in all phases of its repair, maintenance, operation and employment. Thorough training is essential to the success of battle use of the flame thrower. Certain aspects of maintenance and operation not covered in War Departments publications listed in Par. 6, below, are discussed in the following subparagraphs.

b. Early Training. The initial stages of training should be conducted using water and 5% cutting oil (or light lubricating oil) in the fuel tanks. The hydrogen cylinder and battery are not used. The use of water permits personnel to become acquainted with the mechanisms and "feel" of the equipment with greater safety and economy. The gun should not be pointed at individuals. The water is ejected under considerable pressure and may cause serious injury at distances as great as 100 yards. After use with water the entire flame thrower assembly must be carefully cleaned and dried. Flushing with gasoline will assist in the drying.

c. Accuracy. Accuracy with the equipment is a prime essential and emphasis must be placed on training operators to estimate distances and the ranges of their flame throwers accurately. Targets consisting of slit trenches (real or painted on the ground) and enemy "emplacements", may be set up to lend reality to advanced training. The "emplacements", made of earth, corrugated iron or other material, must have real or represented gun slits and embrasures if they are to be satisfactory. In this connection the paramount importance of conserving fuel and maintaining the fuel supplies must be installed. A complete charge will fire for only 12 to 15 seconds; every burst must count and fuel must not be wasted. Short bursts of one to two seconds are most effective. The effect of wind must be considered. Best results are obtained with or against the wind; cross winds break up and disperse the rod of the fuel. As the contents are discharged the gun should be raised to maintain the range.

d. Wearing Equipment. Training is required to enable each man of the team to remove the equipment from a fallen operator and don it quickly for action. Personnel should be trained to wear the pack straps tight. If the pack is loose serious head injuries will result when the operator assumes a prone position.

Trng Memo #10, Hq ETO, USA, 5 Apr 1944--Contd.

 e. <u>Combined Training</u>. The flame thrower party must be trained how to make the most use of the fire from the cover party without exposing itself to this friendly fire. The demolition team must be ready to place their charges when the flame thrower has been discharged at the embrasure. The flame throwing and demolition parties must be trained in each other's jobs in the event that members of either party become casualties before the mission is completed. Coordination of these three parties can be achieved only through thorough, realistic, combined training.

 f. <u>Care of Equipment</u>. Equipment which is dirty or otherwise improperly maintained will fail when most needed. A flame thrower is valueless if it does not function at the exact instant it is wanted; there is seldom opportunity for a second try. Men must be taught the importance of constant care of their equipment.

 g. <u>Safety Precautions</u>. Because of the danger attending training with the flame thrower, discipline must be strictly observed. The rule that a gun, loaded or unloaded, should never be pointed at anyone but the enemy applies particularly to the flame thrower. The fuel, of a highly inflammable nature, must be handled with caution and respect. Equipment which fails to function properly or appears defective should be referred to chemical warfare officers immediately.

5. <u>TECHNICAL DATA</u>. a. <u>Fuel</u>. As a result of numerous trials with thickened flame thrower fuels, fuel K M1A1 (British "FRAS") has been adopted as the thickened fuel for use in this theater. It is not contemplated that other fuels such as Diesel oil, fuel oil or blends, with their reduced range, will be used. Fuel K is ready for use as received; it is poured directly from the shipping container into the flame thrower. However, no moisture must be allowed in the fuel or the flame thrower. The Kit, Fuel Mixing, M1A1, is no longer necessary as no special mixing equipment is required with this fuel.

 (1) Fuel K has been redesignated FTF, Heavy No. 1 (FTF being the abbreviation for Flame Thrower Fuel).

 (2) In the event FTF, Heavy No. 1, is not available in sufficient quantities for training Napalm may be used to thicken petrol as follows: Mix 5.2 pounds of Napalm with 20 US gallons of motor petrol, either leaded or unleaded. The temperature of the petrol at the time of mixing must be above 50^0 F. The petrol must be moisture-free and due care exercised to prevent any water coming in contact with the moisture. (Moisture causes the gel to break down.) The petrol may be warmed by dropping previously heated stones or bricks into it, or

Trng Memo #10, Hq ETO, USA, 5 Apr 1944--Contd.

by setting the petrol containers in hot water baths. Further instructions for the preparation of thickened fuel are contained in TM 3-375. Petrol for this purpose can be procured under the provisions of Sec. XXVII, pamphlet, Hq ETOUSA, 24 Jan 1944, file AG 451/2 PubGC, subject: "Maintenance and Operations of Motor Vehicles". Requisitions will indicate the basis on which the petrol is drawn. Quantities of petrol will be equal to the allowance of thickened fuel on an equal gallonage basis. Napalm can be requisitioned from the Chemical Warfare Service.

    b. <u>Pressure Adjustment</u>. In order to obtain the maximum performance from fuel K it has been found necessary to readjust the pressure regulating valve on the M1A1 flame thrower from approximately 375 lbs per square inch to 275-300 lbs per square inch. The M1A1 service kit and fuel pressure cylinders (nitrogen cylinders -- 2000 lbs per square inch) are required in making the readjustment. The procedure is:

        (1) The flame thrower is first assembled as if for use, but without fuel. The pressure gauge (from the service kit) is substituted for the normal fuel tank cover. The brass cover plate held in place by two pins is then carefully removed with the aid of a small screw driver or knife blade from the pressure regulating screw of the reduction valve. The hexagonal socket wrench is used to adjust the pressure regulating screw; lowering the screw (turning it clockwise) increases the pressure setting and raising it (turning it counter clockwise) reduces the pressure.

        (2) The cylinder valve is then opened so that there is pressure in the fuel tank. By operating the gun valve and observing the pressure gauge it will be possible to obtain the desired pressure by adjusting the pressure regulating screw. When the gun valve is opened the gauge pressure will drop somewhat but should be returned to 275-300 lbs per square inch when the valve is closed. After adjustment, pressure setting should be checked in actual operation but with the pressure gauge attached to see that the pressure returns to the proper level after each of a number of bursts. Short bursts are best although a burst of about three seconds when the tank is filled will indicate whether or not the reducing valve is functioning properly.

        (3) After final readjustment the brass cover plate is replaced. It may be necessary to drill out the old pins and replace them with new ones or with small machine screws. The flame thrower should then be marked "Regulating Valve Reset 300 lbs" and a record made of its serial number.

    c. <u>Cleaning</u>. Each time the flame thrower is refilled, it is advisable to clean out the 20 hydrogen orifices in the burner, using

Trng Memo #10, Hq ETO, USA, 5 Apr 1944--Contd.

a wire, still straw or thin nail. These small holes tend to clog when the flame thrower is "blown down" after all fuel has been fired.

    d. <u>Hydrogen</u>. In combat the hydrogen cylinder should be changed every time the flame thrower is refilled. For training purposes, however, it is quite possible to obtain satisfactory ignition for two fillings of the flame thrower with one hydrogen cylinder, and this economy is desirable whenever possible.

    e. <u>Pack Carrier Refill</u>. A portable pack carrier which contains everything required for one complete refill has been developed. It has been standardized and will soon be available for issue. It consists of a pack board, 5-gallon "Jerrican" for Fuel K, hydrogen cylinder, nitrogen cylinder, pouch and necessary wrenches. The hydrogen and nitrogen cylinders are obtained from the refill Kit, M1A1 *****. A pack weighs approximately the same as the filled flame thrower and permits re-charging of the equipment by two men in from three to five minutes. Thus, in fact, the fire power of each flame thrower is nearly doubled.

    f. <u>Supply of Compressed Gases</u>. Hydrogen and nitrogen may be supplied in either British or US type cylinders. In order to connect the British type cylinders to the filling lines special adapters are required. These adapters will be requisitioned for each M1A1 Service Kit by all units, through normal supply channels, on the basis of four (4) nitrogen filling line adapter couplings and three (3) hydrogen filling line adapter couplings, per service kit.

    (1) In using these couplings care will be exercised not to cross threads. Left hand threads are indicated by a notch cut in the nuts.

    (2) A special key is required to open and close the valves on the British cylinders, and one of these keys will also be requisitioned, through normal supply channels for each service kit.

    (3) Adapters and keys will hereafter be included as part of the service kit.

    By command of General EISENHOWER:

    R. B. LORD,
    Brigadier General, GSC, Deputy Chief of Staff.

OFFICIAL:

    R. B. LOVETT,
Brigadier General, USA, Adjutant General   DISTRIBUTION: F"

APPENDIX 21

HEADQUARTERS
EUROPEAN THEATER OF OPERATIONS
UNITED STATES ARMY

3 Feb 1945

TRAINING MEMO 4

TRAINING IN USE OF FLAME THROWERS

This Training Memo is supplementary to Sec I, Training Memo 10, 5 Apr 1944. The material contained herein is adapted from a training directive issued in the Pacific area and furnished to this headquarters, as information, by Headquarters, Army Ground Forces.

---

1. <u>Technique of Fire</u>. a. <u>Position of Fuel Tanks</u>: During the firing, the top of the fuel tank should be higher than the bottom. The reason for this is that the flame thrower is designed to discharge completely at an angle of 45 degrees with the ground. The flame thrower will leave one-third of the fuel in the tanks if laid flat on the ground.

b. <u>Time Length of Burst</u>: It should be impressed upon the students that the gun is more effective when fired in short bursts at intervals of five or more seconds. Long bursts make the heat too great for the operator, reduce the range, and produce excessive heat, causing vertical rise of the flames. Short bursts can be aimed more accurately.

c. <u>Balling the Flame</u>: Balling the flame is the technique of firing the flame thrower in such a manner that the flame travels just along the top of the ground, and, as it reaches its destination, gathers and forms a large rolling mass of flame that resembles a huge ball of fire. When the operator learns to ball the flame these advantages are gained:

(1) <u>More Range</u>: This is accomplished because the low-traveling flame allows no hot air to form under it and force it vertically into the air.

(2) <u>More Heat</u>: This is accomplished because the maximum amount of the flame reaches the target.

(3) <u>More Accuracy</u>: Balling the flame permits more accuracy because the rolling flame can be better controlled and will strike low-placed ports.
To accomplish the desired effect of balling, the flame gun must be held parallel with the ground and about six inches above it, pointed at the target and fired in short burst of two or three seconds.

Trng Memo #4, Hq ETO, USA, 3 Feb 1945--Contd.

2. <u>Tactical Employment with Assault Detachment</u>. a. <u>General</u>: The flame thrower must not be used without the support of other weapons. Its principal tactical use is in the attack of fortified positions by assault detachments. At least two flame throwers should be included in each assault detachment, an operator and an assistant operator with each gun. The operator should not be encumbered with arms, though the assistants should be armed with weapons such as grenades and carbines.

b. <u>Reconnaissance</u>: The flame thrower operator must be taken on the actual reconnaissance of the objective. It is essential that the operator and the assistant operator know exactly where the fortified position is located.

c. <u>Approach</u>: (1) Before entering within the range of small arms fire, the flame thrower operator and assistant operator must test for leaks, proper gas combustion, and readiness to fire.

(2) Because of the silhouette presented by the flame thrower in position on the operator's back it will often be necessary to drag it along the ground during the final infiltration into firing position. The assistant operator assists in this.

(3) When natural cover is not available for the approach to effective range (25 yards), smoke should be used, preferably from WP grenades or other small smoke munitions, impacting upwind of the area to be screened. Smoke placed directly on the target will blow away and leave the detachment uncovered at the critical moment, unless a dead calm exists. Advantage should be taken of the T-2 chemical grenade adapter for use with rifle grenade launchers in projecting smoke grenades on targets that are beyond throwing distance.

(4) The assistant flame thrower operator must have incendiary grenades (WP or Thermite) available for use in the event of ignition failure. If the first burst of the flame thrower fails to ignite, a grenade should be immediately thrown by the assistant operator to a point as near the target as possible but between the flame thrower and the target.

d. <u>Reduction of an Emplacement</u>: (1) At least two flame throwers must work together in the attack on a bunker.

(2) When a covered approach is available on the flank, one team may be employed to deliver fire across the front of the emplacement. If properly applied this will drive the occupants from their weapons and enable the second team to fire directly into the ports from a frontal position. Great success has been obtained with such team work in combat.

Trng Memo #4, Hq ETO, USA, 3 Feb 1945--Contd.

(3) Liquid fuel only must be used from the flanking position, as it is the side heat that penetrates the ports and drives the occupants from their weapons. Success has been achieved in combat by the operator firing a burst obliquely on the target then rapidly shifting position and delivering the balance of his load from the front.

(4) Thickened fuel should be used where approach to within 25 yards of the target is not practicable.

(5) If flank and frontal fire are not sufficient to reduce the emplacement, or if complete destruction is desired, the demolition party may approach from the flank, under cover of frontal fire from the flame thrower, and place demolitions.

(6) Once a position has been taken, the assault detachment should not move on in search of another position, but should consolidate its position and organize attacks on other positions in the same systematic manner.

(7) To avoid cross-fire from mutually supporting emplacements in the open, detailed reconnaissance, careful planning, exact timing and the effective use of smoke in the approach with flame throwers is necessary. (AG 470.6 EdGC)

By command of General EISENHOWER:

R. B. LORD,
Major General, GSC, Deputy Chief of Staff.

OFFICIAL:

/S/ R. B. Lovett
R. B. LOVETT,
Brigadier General, USA, Adjutant General.   DISTRIBUTION: F

BIBLIOGRAPHIC NOTE

This study is based on a wide variety of sources, including the extensive personal experience of the author in the Pacific theaters of operation during World War II. The principal types of U.S., Allied and Enemy documents used, and which are cited in the footnotes, are:

I. Correspondence:

1. Official correspondence between the various elements of the Military Establishment in the Zone of Interior dealing with requirements, research, development and procurement of flame throwers, tactical doctrine and troop training in the employment of the weapon.

2. Official correspondence between all echelons of Army, Marine and Allied forces in theaters of operation as they pertain to flame warfare.

3. Official correspondence between theaters of operation and the War Department, including the Office of the Chief, Chemical Warfare Service.

4. Personal or direct correspondence between chemical warfare officers in theaters of operation and the Chief of the Chemical Warfare Service.

5. Radios and TWX's.

II. Reports:

1. From chemical warfare staff officers on all phases of flame thrower activities, including tactical doctrine, training, employment, development, maintenance, and supply.

2. Of tactical organizations on the employment of flame throwers and tactical doctrine developed.

3. Of technical observers, demonstration teams, research, development and testing agencies.

4. Technical intelligence, including military attache reports.

5. Inspection reports.

6. Of AGF Board, Armored Force Board, theater boards, e.g., USAFFE Board.

7. Campaign reports by armies, corps, divisions, etc.

8. Organizational histories, historical monographs, etc.

9. Logistical data, such as supply plans and policies, combat expenditures, etc.

III. Publications:

1. War Department, Navy, Allied and Enemy publications, including FM's, TM's, circulars, TO&E's, TBA's, etc.

2. Training memoranda, chemical annexes to field orders, etc., published by tactical organizations in the field, including theaters of operation.

3. Tactical and Technical Trends and other periodic intelligence issues published by MID, G-2, WDGS.

4. CWS Intelligence Summaries and Intelligence Bulletins.

5. CWS Theater of Operation Letter, of which thirty-one were issued between 3 May 1943 and 21 January 1946.

6. Biennial Reports of the Chief of Staff, U.S. Army.

IV. Miscellaneous:

1. Reports of conferences of chemical warfare officers.

2. Interviews with officers having first-hand observation or other types of direct knowledge of flame thrower operations.

3. Daily journals of staff chemical warfare officers.

Since the U.S. Army entered World War II with the portable flame thrower in a relatively untried state, all aspects of flame warfare activities were a war time development. Research, experimentation, the establishment of requirements and the formulation of doctrine occurred almost simultaneously in theaters of operation and in the Zone of Interior. Consequently, the records on the various phases of flame warfare are widely dispersed and generally elusive.

The most valuable single body of records containing flame thrower data is the files of the Chemical Warfare Section of the Sixth Army. The records of the Sixth and Seventh Armies are the only ones in which any considerable amount of chemical section files were retained intact. Since the Sixth Army employed flame throwers on a larger scale and over a longer period of time than any other U.S. army, the chemical warfare records of this organization were extremely useful.

One of the most valuable sources is the five-volume History of the CWS in the Middle Pacific, which consists principally of basic chemical warfare documents, with a minimum of historical narrative. This account begins with 7 December 1941 and extends through VJ-Day, and is especially valuable for data on mechanized flame throwers, since virtually all mechanized flame throwers employed in the Pacific theaters were manufactured or improvised in Hawaii.

On tactical doctrine and training the most fruitful sources are the records of divisions (infantry and marine), corps and armies. In the absence of published War Department doctrine other than two training circulars, tactical units, on the basis of the experimentation, exercises, demonstrations and advice of staff chemical warfare officers, published their own training memoranda. These memoranda prescribed the tactics to be followed and constituted the directives governing the employment of flame throwers. The first War Department technical manual on portable flame throwers (TM 3-375) was published in May 1943.

For the record on actual employment of the weapon, the various types of action reports of battalions, regiments and higher echelon units (infantry, engineer and marine) are most fruitful. Of equal or greater value, are the special and periodic reports of staff chemical warfare officers who, in many cases, exercised strong initiative in collecting detailed data on flame thrower operations and submitting special or periodic reports through channels. Examples are: the Chemical Operations and Technical Periodic Reports of the Chemical Officer, I Corps; Chemical Activity Reports of XI Corps; Preliminary Technical Report -- Letter Reports (numbered) by the Chemical Officer, 41st Infantry Division; and the periodic CW Activities Reports by the staff chemical officers of nearly all divisions and corps.

www.ingramcontent.com/pod-product-compliance
Lightning Source LLC
Chambersburg PA
CBHW060229240426
43671CB00016B/2893